Opening the Floodgates

CRITICAL AMERICA

General Editors: Richard Delgado and Jean Stefancic

Recent titles in the Critical America series include:

Science for Segregation: Race, Law, and the
Case Against Brown v. Board of Education
John P. Jackson, Jr.

Discrimination by Default: Why Racism Isn't the Problem
Lu-in Wang

The First Amendment in Cross-Cultural Perspective:
A Comparative Legal Analysis of the Freedom of Speech
Ronald J. Krotoszynski, Jr.

Feminist Legal Theory: A Primer
Nancy Levit and Robert R. M. Verchick

The Emergence of Mexican America: Recovering Stories of
Mexican Peoplehood in U.S. Culture
John-Michael Rivera

Law and Class in America: Trends Since the Cold War
Edited by Paul D. Carrington and Trina Jones

The Sense of Justice: Empathy in Law and Punishment
Markus Dirk Dubber

No Seat at the Boardroom Table: How Corporate Governance and
Law Keep Women Out of the Boardroom
Douglas M. Branson

White by Law: The Legal Construction of Race, Revised Edition
Ian Haney López

Opening the Floodgates: Why America Needs to
Rethink Its Borders and Immigration Laws
Kevin R. Johnson

For a complete list of titles in the series, please
visit the New York University Press Web site
at www.nyupress.org.

Opening the Floodgates

Why America Needs to Rethink Its Borders and Immigration Laws

Kevin R. Johnson

NEW YORK UNIVERSITY PRESS

New York and London

NEW YORK UNIVERSITY PRESS
New York and London
www.nyupress.org

© 2007 by New York University

Library of Congress Cataloging-in-Publication Data
Johnson, Kevin R.
Opening the floodgates : why America needs to rethink its borders
and immigration laws / Kevin R. Johnson.
p.   cm.
Includes bibliographical references and index.
ISBN-13: 978-0-8147-4286-0 (cloth : alk. paper)
ISBN-10: 0-8147-4286-6 (cloth : alk. paper)
1. Emigration and immigration law—United States. 2. United
States—Emigration and immigration—Government policy. 3. United
States—Boundaries. 4. Illegal aliens—Government policy—United
States.   I. Title.
KF4819.J645 2007
342.7308'2—dc22   2007016966

New York University Press books are printed on acid-free paper,
and their binding materials are chosen for strength and durability.

Manufactured in the United States of America
10 9 8 7 6 5 4 3 2

Contents

Preface and Acknowledgments   vii

1   A Call for Truly Comprehensive
Immigration Reform   1

2   A Brief History of U.S. Immigration Law
and Enforcement   45

3   Bordering on the Immoral: The Moral
Consequences of the Current System
of Immigration Regulation   87

4   The Economic Benefits of Liberal Migration
of Labor Across Borders   131

5   Why Open Borders Are Good for All Americans   168

6   The Inevitability of Permeable Borders   200

Notes   213
Index   275
About the Author   289

122946

Preface and Acknowledgments

My book The *"Huddled Masses" Myth: Immigration and Civil Rights* (2004) analyzed the civil rights impacts of the U.S. immigration laws throughout U.S. history and how that history often compares unfavorably with the myth that the United States welcomes to its shores the "huddled masses" from the world over. That book critically examines how immigration touches on sensitive issues of race and civil rights, which helps explain the vociferousness of the public debates that the topic consistently generates.

In the past decade, it has become readily apparent to almost all informed observers that the problems with U.S. immigration law and its enforcement have worsened. Thousands of migrants have died on the U.S./Mexico border, as enforcement measures in the major border hubs, such as San Diego, California, and El Paso, Texas, funneled migrants into isolated deserts and mountains where the risks of the journey were much greater—in fact, deadly—than had been the case for all of U.S. history. Moreover, the U.S. government's "war on terror" after the tragic events of September 11, 2001, focused almost exclusively on immigrants. Many blatantly discriminatory and arbitrary immigration measures were adopted in the name of making the country safer.

Despite aggressive steps to enforce the border, immigration law has failed to achieve its goals. Undocumented immigration continues unabated as migrants pursue the American Dream. The nation, by most accounts, appears no more secure than it ever has been. In 2005–2006, immigration reform again dominated the national consciousness. The U.S. House of Representatives passed a harsh enforcement-oriented proposal that provoked marches of tens of thousands of immigrants and their supporters in cities across the United States.

This book steps back to scrutinize the foundational premises of U.S. immigration law. It offers an intellectual starting point for the comprehensive reform necessary to remedy the chronic enforcement, civil rights, and other problems that have plagued past and current U.S. immigration laws. By questioning the concept of the border as a barrier to entry rather than simply a regulatory checkpoint monitoring entry into and exit from the United States, this book offers a fresh approach to immigration law and enforcement for the twenty-first century.

A roundtable discussion of open borders at the Immigration Law Teachers Workshop in May 2002 at Loyola–New Orleans School of Law sparked my initial interest in writing about open borders. Although personal circumstances prevented me from attending the workshop, my thinking benefited from the written submissions of the roundtable participants (David Abraham, Daniel Kanstroom, David A. Martin, and Leti Volpp).

The book began in earnest as an article prepared for the *UCLA Law Review*'s Symposium on "Law and the Border: Examining the Frontier Between the United States and Mexico," in January 2003. The article presented at the symposium was published as "Open Borders?" in 51 *UCLA Law Review* 193 (2003). Parts of that article have been adapted in various chapters of this book. Richard Delgado, Steve Legomsky, Thomas Wuil Joo, Miroslava Chavez-Garcia, Joel C. Dobris, Victor C. Romero, Rob Correales, Jack Ayer, Rachel F. Moran, Peter Margulies, Holly Doremus, Diane Amann, and Michael Scaperlanda offered helpful comments on a draft of the article. The comments of Alex Aleinikoff, Christopher David Ruiz Cameron, George Martínez, Rachel F. Moran, and Mary Romero at the symposium at UCLA School of Law where I initially presented the article helped my thinking on the issues.

Comments on the introductory chapter of this book on a panel at the 2005 Law & Society annual conference sharpened my thinking. Thanks to Rubén García for organizing that panel, which included Rubén, Bill Hing, and Margaret Stock. I also presented a draft of the first chapter of the book at the Mid-Atlantic People of Color Legal Scholarship Conference at American University, Washington College of Law, in Washington, D.C., in January 2006. Thanks to Dorothy Brown for inviting me to participate. I also presented a draft of the first chapter at the 2006 Immigration Law Teachers Workshop at the University of Nevada Las Vegas and benefited from the comments. Thanks to Raquel Aldana, David Abraham, Evelyn Cruz, Jennifer Gordon, Jim Hathaway, Ernesto Hernández-López, Aarti Kohli, Cristina Rodriguez, Jonathan Weinberg, and Michael Wishnie for their challenging thoughts and comments. I also benefited from the comments of the BYU faculty members who allowed me to present this project in October 2006. Thanks to Kif Augustine Adams for arranging this workshop.

In October 2006, I presented the book concept at an immigration conference at California State University, Sacramento. Christina Bellon organized the conference. Sharon Barrios offered perceptive comments on my project.

Richard Delgado first suggested that I write a book on this topic. Richard and Jean Stefancic, coeditors of NYU Press's Critical America series, have been supportive of this book, as well as all of my scholarly work. I thank them for their continued support. I also am indebted to Jack Ayer, who suggested the topic of open borders to me years ago and, since then, has forwarded me relevant information on the topic, and Joel C. Dobris, who for years has sent me copies of immigration articles from a plethora of eclectic sources and encouraged me to write on borders and their meaning. Conversations with George Martínez over a number of years helped my thinking on immigration, race, and civil rights. Michael A. Olivas has provided intellectual and personal support to me throughout my academic career for which I am forever indebted. Friends, including Bill Hing, Jennifer Chacón, Amagda Pérez, Angela Onwuachi-Willig, and many colleagues at UC Davis School of Law, too numerous to name, have offered me encouragement for my scholarship at every juncture. NYU Press Senior Editor Deborah Gershenowitz was tremendously supportive of this project. Last but not least, thanks to Dean Rex Perschbacher for his enduring support of my scholarship and other endeavors.

UC Davis law students Cerissa Salazar Parreñas, Stella Schmidel, Laura Urias, Wynter O-Blanquet, and Jessica Gill provided valuable research and editorial assistance. Jessica Gill's careful editing greatly improved the manuscript. All of my research assistants' commitment to the humane treatment of immigrants is inspiring. As always, Brigid Jimenez provided outstanding editorial and other support above and beyond the call of duty. Glenda McGlashan and Cynthia Coble offered important editorial assistance, as well.

Parts of chapter 2 are adapted from "National Identity in a Multicultural Nation: The Challenge of Immigration Law and Immigrants," 103 *Michigan Law Review* 1347 (2005), which I coauthored with my colleague Bill Ong Hing. Thanks to Bill for working with me on that project and for allowing me to adapt a portion of that essay in this book. David Yun, a law student at UC Davis, provided valuable research assistance on that essay.

The immigration law professors blog, http://lawprofessors.typepad .com/immigration/, which I manage with my colleagues Jennifer Chacón and Bill Hing, allowed for an outlet for ruminations on immigration. My participation in that project helped keep me apprised of matters that made my research easier.

UC Davis School of Law, UC MEXUS, and the Mabie-Apallas Chair provided generous funding to assist in the research for this book.

Peg Durkin, Susan Llano, Erin Murphy, Aaron Dailey, and Elisabeth McKechnie, all UC Davis law librarians, provided invaluable research assistance. They responded to my many requests in an efficient manner with good cheer. I appreciate their efforts.

My family, Virginia Salazar, Teresa, Tómas, and Elena, provide the moral foundation for this book, as well as for all my other work. Their love, patience, and support make what I do meaningful.

1

A Call for Truly Comprehensive Immigration Reform

By every measure but one, the Gonzalez family of Jefferson City, Mo., are model citizens. Marvin was a courier for then-Missouri Gov. Bob Holden, delivering messages and screening the governor's mail. Marina taught Spanish and was the after-school care director at her parish grade school. Their daughter Marie was a star pupil at Helias High, on the track and tennis teams, with dreams of becoming a lawyer. . . . There was just one thing wrong with this picture: The Gonzalezes aren't citizens at all. They came to Jefferson City in 1991, on a six-month visitor's visa from their native Costa Rica. . . . And for their troubles, the federal government has formulated its response: Next Tuesday it will deport the Gonzalezes back to Costa Rica.   —*Washington Post,* June 2005[1]

[The Minutemen] are coming to [Arizona] to help the Border Patrol spot illegal immigrants entering our country. TIME magazine says more than 3 million illegal immigrants slipped past the undermanned Border Patrol last year. . . . Most citizens see it as an outrageous breach of national security. Millions are perplexed and angered by the president's willful blindness to the dangers posed by open borders. . . . Our open borders are a national catastrophe. . . . The Border Patrol is understandably concerned about the potential for violence if the Minutemen run into gun-toting drug smugglers. . . . If violence breaks out during this protest, the ultimate responsibility rests squarely on the federal government for failure to secure our borders.
      —Tom Tancredo, U.S. House of Representatives, April 2005[2]

These two contrasting perspectives on immigration find deep roots in the national psyche. The United States often characterizes itself as open to the "huddled masses," as the inscription on the Statue of

Liberty proudly proclaims. Consistent with this ideal, the United States has historically allowed large numbers of immigrants to come to this land of freedom. America stands out in the Western world for its generosity in the admission of immigrants.

At the same time, however, the United States has an immigration dark side. A mean-spirited, anti-immigrant impulse has sporadically gripped the nation, particularly during times of social stress. During these times, the U.S. immigration laws have been harsh, discriminatory, and aggressively enforced. Consequently, U.S. law has barred many innocent groups of people from its shores for the very worst of reasons. The near-complete prohibition of immigration from China, which lasted from the late nineteenth century until 1965, is perhaps the most famous example. The measures taken by the federal government against Arab and Muslim noncitizens—and generally against all noncitizens—after the tragic events of September 11, 2001, are the most recent.

Snapshots from the headlines illustrate that immigration and immigrants draw widely divergent reactions from the American public. As the debate over immigration reform in 2006 exemplified, the mere mention of immigration often triggers an outburst of emotion from the public, activists, pundits, and politicians. The wide divergence of opinion on the subject renders any attempt to fundamentally address immigration law and policy treacherous at best. For politicians, it is ordinarily far easier to duck the issue than to attempt to intervene in the morass in any meaningful way. Nonetheless, immigration remains one of the most pressing, controversial, and difficult public policy matters facing this generation.

At its most basic level, immigration is a pressing public concern because many people desire to migrate to the United States.[3] A liberal democracy, the nation enjoys many robust political freedoms not common in countries around the world. Economically, the United States offers incredible opportunities not available in many nations. This political and economic freedom magnetically attracts citizens of foreign nations willing to try to stake a claim in America. Geographically, the country has two lengthy land borders that make migration easier than if the country were an island, for example. Simple geography makes strict border enforcement in the face of high demand for immigration exceedingly difficult.

Gripping human stories of immigrants tug at the heartstrings, reminding many Americans of their ancestors' difficult journeys to this country, the conditions they left, the adversities they overcame, and the dreams they pursued. Today, refugees fleeing political persecution risk life and limb to come to this land of hope and freedom. Boat people flee Haiti in ramshackle boats and make the dangerous journey to America. Impoverished migrants from Mexico, China, and many other countries desperately seek better lives for their families in the United States. Intellectually, the proverbial "nation of immigrants" cannot easily turn its back on these dreamers. In practice, however, it often does.

In the past few decades, border control measures in the United States have greatly increased the risks for persons seeking to surreptitiously enter the country. The unprecedented enforcement buildup along the U.S.-Mexico border, designed to reduce undocumented immigration, appears to have had minimal impacts on decreasing the flow of people. Nonetheless, the growing human toll is nothing less than tragic. Thousands of people have died. A week rarely goes by without a newspaper story about some poor migrant from Mexico dying of exposure in the desert, in the back of a truck, or in the trunk of a car. Sadly enough, death on the border has become a fact of daily life in the U.S.-Mexico border region.

It does not have to be this way. Although it may be politically popular to build a figurative moat around the United States, nobody ordered the U.S. government to transform the borders into a death trap. Nonetheless, the drums continue to beat about the need to fortify and reinforce the border. Immigration reform proposals, such as the ones that percolated in Congress in 2005 and 2006, almost inevitably include calls for increased border enforcement and ever-harsher penalties on undocumented immigrants. In fact, the House of Representatives passed a bill in late 2005 that would have made the mere status of being undocumented a felony.

Despite the rising death toll, there is no sense of urgency among the public and policymakers to put an end to the human tragedy. Rather, the death beat goes on. Complacency in the United States over the deadly state of border affairs suggests a blindness or indifference to the true human suffering that directly results from border enforcement. Enforcing the border has proven to be extremely difficult. Rather than formulate policies that work, it is far easier to dehumanize the migrant as the "other" and to consider the deaths of "illegal aliens" as simply collateral damage as the nation seeks to defend against a "foreign invasion."

In response to immigration reform proposals, an immigrant civil rights movement emerged in the United States. Protesting the punitive measures under consideration in the U.S. Congress, marchers demanded that immigrants be fairly and humanely treated. In March 2006, more than 100,000 people marched in the streets of Chicago to protest proposed reform legislation, and, soon after, more than half a million people marched in Los Angeles. Cities across the United States saw similar protests.[4]

Despite this emerging movement, the public as a whole remains deeply divided about immigration. Many Americans register vocal opposition to immigration and immigrants. In an April 2005 Fox News poll, 91 percent of the persons surveyed believed that undocumented immigration was a "very serious" or "somewhat serious" problem, primarily because of the feared impact of immigrants on jobs, the economy, and national security. At the same time, however, more than 60 percent of those polled favored giving undocumented immigrants temporary worker status, and only 43 percent favored eliminating all forms of public assistance, including education and health benefits, to the undocumented.[5] This poll, consistent with many before and after, exemplifies the nation's profound ambivalence about undocumented immigrants.

Ambivalence among the U.S. public, however, can quickly turn into fear and loathing. The public expresses outrage at any hint of "criminal aliens" preying on citizens or immigrants abusing the social welfare system. In 1994, California voters supported an initiative known as Proposition 187 by a 2–1 margin. Absent judicial intervention, the law would have denied benefits, including a public education, to undocumented immigrants and cracked down on "criminal aliens."[6] The strong political support for Proposition 187 convinced then-President Clinton to greatly increase federal border enforcement and rapidly militarize the U.S.-Mexico border.[7] Although the federal budget as a whole shrank over the 1990s, the budget of the now-defunct Immigration and Naturalization Service skyrocketed as border enforcement became a national priority.

At the dawn of the new millennium, action-movie star Arnold Schwarzenegger became the governor of California, in no small part because of an anti-immigrant backlash. Former governor Gray Davis had signed into law a bill making undocumented immigrants eligible to obtain what may only loosely be characterized as a "public benefit"—a license to drive an automobile. The new governor quickly orchestrated repeal of that law on the dubious claim that it endangered national security. Approaching this as a civil rights issue, immigrant advocates contended that denial of driver's licenses negatively affected undocumented immigrants' ability to live and work.[8] Their arguments, however, proved unavailing. In 2005, Congress passed the REAL ID Act, which mandated tougher federal standards for state-issued driver's licenses.[9]

Although regulation of immigration is a federal power, immigration has deep political, economic, and social impacts at the state and local levels. In summer 2005, the governors of Arizona and New Mexico declared states of emergency along their borders with Mexico, claiming that the federal government had not done enough to combat drug smuggling and criminal activity associated with illegal immigration.[10] Nor was immigration an issue just in the U.S.-Mexico border region. One city in New Hampshire made national news when it took the extraordinary step of trying to use its criminal trespass laws to prosecute undocumented immigrants.[11] In cities across the country, the local impacts of immigration have led to discussions on increasing state and local enforcement of the U.S. immigration laws, with some cities passing ordinances that, for example, bar landlords from renting to undocumented immigrants.[12]

Some of the debate has focused on the Southwest region of the United States. For many years, the troubled desert that straddles the U.S.-Mexico border has been the site of skirmishes involving ranchers, militia, immigrant rights activists, and immigrants. In 2005, a small yet vocal group of self-proclaimed Minutemen—whom President Bush aptly called "vigilantes"—massed on the Arizona border with Mexico, threatening to take the immigration laws into their own hands.[13] Claiming to assist the Border Patrol, this group sought to identify, chase, and report border crossers to the authorities. Minutemen on patrols, who loudly disparaged "illegal aliens" from Mexico, often were armed, if not dangerous. Decrying the Minuteman Project, counterprotesters defended the civil rights of immigrants.

Sadly, the Minutemen cannot be dismissed as kooks. At various times, they have enjoyed the support of some elected politicians, including Arnold Schwarzenegger, Patrick Buchanan, and Congressman Tom Tancredo. In 2005, the founder of the Minuteman Project ran for Congress in southern California as a member of the American Independent Party, which emerged in 1968 with the arch-segregationist George Wallace as its presidential candidate, and received more votes than the leading Democratic candidate.[14] At times, hate dominated the immigration debate. Presumably because they are visible Mexican-American political leaders, Antonio Villaraigosa, the mayor of Los Angeles, and Lieutenant Governor Cruz Bustamante, received death threats in the midst of the national turmoil over immigration.[15]

Despite the human costs of border enforcement and the political agitation to close the border, meaningful immigration reform has eluded Congress time and time again.[16] The deep gulf in public opinion makes a thoughtful approach to immigration reform extremely difficult. Repeatedly during the twentieth century, political considerations and compromise resulted in immigration reforms that failed to effectively address the immigration needs of the modern United States. Instead, law- and policymakers delay adopting truly comprehensive solutions to our immigration problems. Every few years, a perceived crisis triggers the passage of ill-considered legislation that adversely impacts immigrants but offers no long-term solution to making the nation's immigration laws more enforceable.

This book hopes to offer a truly comprehensive approach to immigration reform, not simply one more incremental reform that, if implemented, will fail to offer enduring solutions to the immigration challenges facing the nation.

The Assumptions Underlying U.S. Immigration Law

In order to understand the current state of immigration law and its future viability, we must examine its foundational premises. The debate over immigration law and policy in the United States generally rests on several important assumptions. The fundamental assumption driving immigration law is that entry into this country is a precious commodity that must be limited. Although they differ on how to allocate the scarce resource, both advocates for immigrants and restrictionists generally agree that we simply cannot liberally admit immigrants, much less open the borders.

Rather than focus on keeping people out of the country, the U.S. government should facilitate the entry of migrants, while at the same time striving to deny entry to true dangers to society. As the following chapters in this book demonstrate, open borders are better for the United States morally, economically, politically, and socially. They also are more humane to immigrants who for the most part want nothing more than access to the American Dream. Easy entry into the United States is more in keeping than the current restrictive admissions system with the nation's devotion to the freedom, liberty, and equality endorsed in the U.S. Constitution.

Before any move toward open borders, however, the United States as a nation would need to adjust psychologically to the idea of permeable borders and accept and accommodate, rather than resist and object to, the changes to U.S. society that come from migration. In this book I hope to change our thinking about immigration and to lay the foundation for a new system of immigration regulation in the United States for the twenty-first century and beyond.

This book addresses head on the need for closed borders. It questions the necessity for the substantial restrictions currently found in U.S. immigration law on the number of immigrants admitted into the country and the perception that strict limits must be enforced or the nation will be overrun with the hordes of the developing world. In so doing, I challenge the foundational premises upon which immigration restrictions in U.S. law are based.

Borders and Their Meaning

Before addressing the rules governing the crossing of borders, we must reconsider the conception of borders and their creation. Law experiences extreme difficulty in attempting to demarcate and enforce clear boundaries between legal categories or, put colloquially, in drawing lines. Border theorists maintain that such uncertainty demonstrates the inherent inability to establish hard and fast boundaries between socially constructed categories.[17] All borders are less than definite, permeable, and subject to shifts and changes. Although perplexing, the concept of the "border" is central to an understanding of immigration law.

Throughout world history, international borders have been subject to interpretation, debate, and transformation for reasons as varied as love and war, feast and famine. Borders can be redrawn, and their meaning may change depending on, among other things, the government in power. Defined by law, borders between nations unquestionably are legal and social constructs, reflecting all the ingenuity yet frailty of the human mind.

At bottom, borders are what we as a country say they are; they mean what we say they mean. "Borders are not inherently significant, they are significant because we attach meaning to them. We can change the significance of borders without changing their location by changing what they signify—what comes along with them."[18] The same is true for many sorts of political boundaries within the United States, such as those defining states, municipalities, and congressional districts, which are all subject to change.[19]

Although the reliance on geography makes the task of constructing borders between nations easier in certain respects, the *meaning* attached to borders is socially defined and, consequently, continuously in flux and under stress. The globalization of the world economy, rapid technological change, and changing conceptions of nation-states have all contributed to a decline in the practical importance of physical borders between nations. Information, culture, goods, and services regularly flow across the borders between nations. Although globalization indeed has its critics,[20] many observers consider the decline in the significance of borders to be a positive development.

In certain respects, the United States has begun in small ways to change its immigration and nationality laws in response to the pressures of globalization. For example, since a change in U.S. policy in the early 1990s, many more U.S. citizens now hold dual nationality and citizenship and are thus members of two national communities. The fear that people might have allegiances to two or more nations in times of war succumbed to recognition of the inevitability in these times of a growing number of people possessing ties to more than one nation.[21] The change in U.S. law and policy responded to global changes as movement between nations became increasingly more common.[22]

Borders are the building blocks of immigration law. International borders must necessarily be defined in order to determine what imaginary line must be crossed to constitute immigration into a country. In addition, because a nation's laws often extend only to its borders and not beyond, borders effectively define the outer limits of U.S. law.[23] Most nations firmly believe that they enjoy the power to define the border and the rights that attach to those who cross it, as they see fit. Nations thus can be as generous—or not—as they want to be. Within the loose restrictions of current constitutional law, the United States embraces this philosophy in limiting the bundle of rights held by noncitizens who live within its borders.

U.S. immigration law is constructed on the bedrock idea that it is permissible, desirable, and necessary to restrict immigration into the United

States and to have the border operate as a barrier to entry rather than as simply a port of entry. Based on the presumption that migrants are inadmissible, U.S. law restricts immigration in many ways and guarantees limited rights to noncitizens. Disputes frequently arise in the United States about the meaning attached to the fact that one is a noncitizen.

Neither aspect of this approach to immigration and immigrants is mandated or preordained. One could imagine a system, for example, in which there were limits on entry into the United States combined with equal rights, including the right to vote, to enjoy public benefits, and to serve on juries, for all persons, immigrants and citizens alike, who are physically present in the country. Residency, not citizenship, would be the critical determinant of full membership in the community. To a certain extent, this tends to be the model followed in modern Europe, which with the rise of the European Union has seen greatly increased social, political, and economic integration over the past thirty years.

Alternatively, one could also imagine easy entry and full membership rights for all residents. This would look like a true liberal democracy with full respect for the right of free movement and equality among all people who live in a community. Both of these scenarios are more consistent with the devotion to individual rights, equality, and democracy in the United States than the current system. However, they require that we reimagine the meaning and significance of the international border.

This book articulates the case for eliminating the border as a legal construct that serves as an impediment to the movement of people into this country. In making a case for permeable borders, this proposal calls for nothing less than a fundamental reevaluation and rejection of the foundational tenets of current U.S. immigration law.

The call for liberal admissions obviously runs counter to the wave of border fortification and fear of foreigners that swept the United States in the 1990s, increased dramatically to a crescendo pitch with the antiterrorism measures taken in the wake of the tragic events of September 11, 2001, and frequently finds strong support with politicians and the general public. Since September 11, the federal government has aggressively employed immigration law to arrest, detain, and remove Arabs and Muslims having the most attenuated, if any, links with terrorism.[24] Security, however, can be improved with more open borders and better tracking of all people present in the United States.

Liberalizing admission of immigrants would obviously frighten the restrictionist wing of the Republican Party. But it might also strike fear into liberals who fear being overwhelmed by immigrants, with a concomitant loss of control, and changes to culture and national identity. Often fearing the impact of immigrants on the wage scale, Democrats have historically sided with labor unions in supporting immigration restrictions. Conservative employers and big business might be expected to support freer migration, which would increase the size of the labor force and bring more skilled and unskilled workers to the United States and, not coincidentally, tend to place downward pressures on wages.

As this suggests, immigration is not a liberal/conservative, Red State/Blue State, Democratic/Republican issue. *Both* popular political parties have restrictionist and expansionist immigration wings. *Both* parties have contributed significantly to the immigration regime in which we live. *Both* parties have consistently failed to offer true comprehensive immigration reform proposals.

The Taboo of Open Borders

Any serious mention of "open borders" has long been the political kiss of death for a serious immigration reformer.[25] Whatever their true position, immigrant rights activists are often smeared and dismissed as advocates of open borders. Even though few observers in fact advocate open borders, the concerted effort to discredit the defenders of immigrants, to a certain extent, prevails with the public.

Generally speaking, the tilt in the immigration debate is strongly against open borders, which in the minds of some implies lawlessness and anarchy. Political, cultural, and social upheavals in American social life have often sparked anti-immigrant impulses among the general public. Economic hardship doomed Chinese immigrants in the late 1800s, who were barred from entering the country, and persons of Mexican ancestry during the Great Depression, who were deported en masse. The Red Scare after World War I and the Cold War resulted in witch hunts for communists. Mass deportations of immigrants suspected of having dissident political views followed.

Presumably because of the public's seemingly natural predisposition toward restrictionist measures, particularly in times of social stress, politicians do not consider open borders to be a viable policy option. For politicians, it ordinarily pays election-day dividends to take a "tough on immigrants" position. Noncitizens barred from entry obviously cannot vote. Unnaturalized immigrants cannot vote and lack the political clout of U.S. citizens. Consequently, a vocal minority of citizens embracing a restrictionist agenda is able at times to greatly influence immigration law and policy.[26]

Immigration law scholars ordinarily avoid discussing open borders without much of an explanation. To the extent that the idea of open borders is even mentioned in public discussions, it is immediately brushed off as hopelessly impractical and not worthy of in-depth analysis and consideration as a possible policy option.

Consider a few examples of the shunning of open borders by serious scholars. In a recent history of U.S. immigration law, one commentator stated that "arguments on behalf of 'open borders' appear perennially as the playful musings of free-market ideologues."[27] In criticizing the doctrine that the courts could not interfere with the political branches' "plenary power" over immigration, Louis Henkin hastened to add that "*[d]oubtless,* . . . our society [is] not necessarily open to all comers at all times."[28] Although advocating legal protection of the rights of immigrants in the United States, Owen Fiss emphasized that he does not "question[ ] the validity of laws regulating the admission of immigrants to this country. . . . *My point is not to subvert the admission process or otherwise open the borders.* . . ."[29] Frederick Whelan observed that the idea of open borders "is contrary to common opinion, and startling in its radicalness. Nearly everyone rejects it, preferring instead to stand on the established principles of state sovereignty. . . ."[30] While endorsing judicial review of the constitutionality of the immigration laws, Frank Wu unequivocally condemned open borders:

> [I]t *would be naive verging on utopian to argue for open borders and against the existence of nations.* In a world with severe socioeconomic differences among nations, and for a country that has an extensive welfare system, it would be impossible to adopt a policy of allowing entry to every potential immigrant. . . . *National sovereignty must be accepted.*[31]

Many assumptions are built into the rejection of open borders. The conventional wisdom, for example, is that open borders undercut national sovereignty. However, that need not be the case. A nation, in exercising its sovereign powers, for political, social, economic, and moral reasons could decide to adopt liberal admissions policies. Historically, many nations have allowed for easy entry of immigrants. Not until it sought to join the European Union in the 1980s, for example, did Spain have a comprehensive law restricting immigration.[32] For its first century of existence, when the nation was preoccupied with settling the Western frontier and attracting the people necessary to develop and assume control of the continent, the United States did not have a national immigration law.[33] Except perhaps in major urban centers, overcrowding, floods of immigrants, and similar concerns were not at the forefront of the popular consciousness.

Even today, migration between the various states of the Union is unfettered and generally not viewed as a social problem. Mass migrations do not regularly occur in the United States except as a temporary response to natural disasters, such as Hurricane Katrina in 2005. Political upheavals, such as the violence in Haiti and civil wars that raged in Central America in the 1980s, may temporarily bring large refugee flows to this country. But these are exceptions, not the rule.

Advocates of more closed borders often claim that public benefits serve as a "magnet" attracting unworthy immigrants to the United States. However, the idea that immigrants come to this country for social benefits, including an extensive welfare system, lacks support in the academic literature. It is especially difficult to see how public benefits can be a "magnet" when the U.S. welfare system is meager compared to those of other Western democracies. Indeed, in light of welfare reform in 1996, immigrants are eligible for few federal benefit programs and undocumented immigrants for even fewer. Undocumented immigrants using fraudulent documents contribute billions of dollars to the U.S. Social Security system, with no hope of ever securing benefits.[34] These immigrants fund a benefit system from which they in all likelihood will never receive benefits and in fact subsidize the growing numbers of retirees in the United States.

Nor are open borders somehow hopelessly "utopian," a label that, if it sticks, immediately dooms a proposal. Rather, this book contends that permeable borders for labor, comparable to those that exist for goods and services, are a practical necessity in the modern, deeply interconnected, and interdependent global economy.

Of course, migration has never been, and will never be, painfree. Tensions will result as populations relocate and communities change. Racial, class, religious, cultural, social, and other conflicts emerge with migration. At various times in United States history, social fissures have resulted from immigration. The hard question, however, is how to address the conflicts that come with the changes brought by immigration, not to engage in doomed efforts to foreclose change.

Needless to say, the proposed opening of the borders to migrants would face vociferous resistance. Legitimate fears of the possible adverse social, economic, and political impacts on U.S. society would be invoked. Nativism and racism, a strong undercurrent to this country's immigration history, would likely infect the debate, as well. The specter of hordes of people of color descending on the United States necessarily would influence—and possibly even end—any consideration of the liberalization of immigration restrictions.

Besides feared political, economic, and social impacts of immigration, restrictionists fear how immigration is changing what we are as a nation. Worries about a changing national identity, with racial, religious, cultural, linguistic, and other components, are often at the core of the immigration debate.[35] Immigration law historically has been seen as a way of regulating and enforcing a particular national identity. Many people unquestionably would resist the thought of surrendering this tool of social control.

Throughout U.S. history, fears over perceived change in the national identity have generated unsavory attacks on the largest and most visible immigrant group of the day, whether it was Irish, German, Chinese, Japanese, southern and eastern European, Mexican, Vietnamese, or Arab and Muslim. Such concerns are difficult to discuss in popular discourse when U.S. *citizens* are at the center of discussion. It is difficult—although not unheard of—to claim, for example, that African Americans are undermining the national identity. Although some complain of separate ethnic enclaves created by minority communities,[36] limits exist on what can be said in polite company, as well as on what can be done under color of law to U.S. citizens. Consequently, the nation finds it easier to debate concerns with national identity in connection with immigration and immigrants than to consider them as they apply to citizens and to embrace law and policy that punish immigrants for their difference.

Not surprisingly, race and racism find themselves deeply intertwined in U.S. immigration history and, importantly, in the modern debate over immigration. The United States has a checkered history with respect to the civil rights of racial minorities. Similarly, discriminatory immigration laws often have punished people of color, with racial hatred often transferred from citizens in the United States to immigrants who share similar ancestries.[37] The adoption of harsh policies directed at Mexican immigrants, for example, often has translated into discrimination against Mexican-American citizens. Immigration enforcement, in turn, has had negative impacts on Mexican-American citizens, who are often presumed to be foreigners because of their physical appearance, surnames, and ancestry.

Today, because so many immigrants are people of color, discrimination against immigrants often translates directly into discrimination against people of color.[38] In modern times, there is often a distinctively anti-Mexican, and at times anti-Asian, tinge to the debate over immigration. Since September 11, there also has been a much more visible anti-Arab, anti-Muslim component, cloaked in the alleged necessity for harsh measures against Arabs and Muslims to protect national security. Concern with the race of immigrants quickly bubbles to the surface in any serious discussion of immigration and the treatment of immigrants in the United States. It also can contribute to hate crimes, like those directed at Arabs, Muslims, and others since September 11.[39]

As the discussion suggests, civil rights consequences often flow directly from the efforts to regulate the quality and quantity of the immigrants coming to the United States. For example, racial profiling in immigration enforcement results in the questioning of Mexican-American citizens and lawful Mexican immigrants about their citizenship and, more fundamentally, their membership in U.S. society. By allowing immigration authorities to consider "Mexican appearance" as one factor in an immigration stop, the Supreme Court has facilitated racial profiling.[40] Detention of immigrants, which has increased dramatically since Congress enacted immigration reforms in 1996,[41] and the deaths resulting from border enforcement raise serious civil and human rights issues.

Minority activist groups understand the racial animus that underlies the immigration debate. Such groups often become involved in immigration advocacy even though certain segments of minority communities may not be directly affected by immigration law and its enforcement and, in fact, may support restrictions on immigration. For example, some established Mexican-American citizens often want to restrict and control the migration of immigrants from Mexico.[42] Latina/o and Asian-American advocacy organizations lobby on behalf of immigrants and see the communities they represent as including immigrants or ancestors of immigrants who are treated as perpetual "foreigners" to the United States.

Closed borders allow us to respond to our deepest and darkest fears. They also have damaging impacts on the nation, as well as on immigrants. Still, it has proven to be extraordinarily difficult to dislodge the view that strict immigration restrictions are essential to the well-being of the United States.

The nation's response has generally been to attempt to reduce the number of immigrants coming to the country—or, alternatively, to change the nations from which they came—in order to keep inferior "races" of people out of the country. Time and time again, legal reforms have created but another regrettable chapter in U.S. immigration history. History shows that such efforts have done little other than to make the lives of immigrants more difficult.

Nevertheless, policymakers readily accept without serious question the idea that the United States can restrict immigration and must aggressively enforce the border. Assuming that immigration restrictions are the unfettered right of every nation-state and that greater enforcement of the immigration laws is essential, politicians often reflexively and expediently support immigration controls without considering whether the enforcement of the immigration restrictions is in fact possible.

Prospective immigrants have come up with ingenious ways to circumvent harsh enforcement measures. Efforts to exclude future Chinese immigrants, for example, led to the rise of "paper sons" who claimed that their Chinese fathers had immigrated lawfully to the United States and that they therefore fell within an exception to Chinese exclusion.[43] Today, millions of undocumented immigrants, a majority of them from Mexico, live in this country despite the biggest border enforcement buildup in U.S. history. If nothing else, history has proven that harsh restrictionist measures almost inevitably fail.

For their part, immigration scholars, generally speaking, fail to ask the hard questions, including whether (1) restrictions on immigration, as well as permitting deportations of certain groups of immigrants, are socially desirable, and (2) increased border enforcement can in fact effectively reduce undocumented immigration. Rather, academics generally assume that these two questions are correctly answered in the affirmative. Consequently, these unproven assumptions serve as the starting point of analysis for any system of immigration law and policy. The reforms that follow from these assumptions do little more than tinker at the margins and fail to address the economic and other realities of immigration.

Examples abound of incremental reform that fails to offer long-term immigration solutions. The guest worker program initially proposed by President Bush in 2004, tightened asylum rules in the REAL ID Act of 2005, the earned legalization for long-term undocumented immigrants proposed in 2005 and 2006, and the authorization to extend the fence along the U.S. border with Mexico are examples. These reforms are more fire than light. Although deflecting political heat from the issue for the immediate moment, incremental reform only delays for another day the need for true responses to the real immigration issues.

This book confronts the hard questions. The answer, I argue, is not doomed attempts to close the borders. First, the modern United States is better off economically, socially, politically, and morally, and places itself on the moral high ground, with liberal immigration admissions and open, welcoming borders. Despite the many fears related to open borders, the benefits are many, the costs few. Second, under modern circumstances, overbroad exclusions buttressed by strong border controls simply cannot halt immigration. Incredibly strong economic, social, and political forces spur a continuous flow of migrants from Latin America and Asia into the United States. And employers and many Americans benefit handsomely.

We as a nation should take great pride in the fact that the United States is viewed as a land of economic, political, and social opportunity. People in countries across the globe want to be part of America. At the same time, we should be ashamed that many immigrants, especially the undocumented, are exploited by employers and condemned to the underclass as a caste of laborers and that they must live in the darkest shadows of our great nation. It is time to change our immigration laws and demonstrate that the United States is in fact committed to welcoming the "huddled masses" of the world.[44]

The Plenary Power Doctrine's Limits on Immigration as the Antithesis of Open Borders

U.S. immigration law and policy often have been harsh, with the political branches often acting punitively toward immigrants. The persons most directly affected by U.S. immigration law and enforcement lack formal input into the political process and have limited informal means, such as political protests, lobbying, and other political action, at their disposal. Immigrant and ethnic advocacy groups, of course, play a role in the immigration law and policymaking process. These groups, however, lack the clout possessed by other groups. To make matters worse, when the political process has punished immigrants, the courts have been reluctant to intervene to protect their rights.

Immigration law provides a ready ally to immigration controls adopted by the political branches of government. The Supreme Court has immunized from judicial review Congress's judgments about which noncitizens to admit and which to exclude from the United States.[45] The so-called plenary power doctrine, the vitality of which has been under debate for generations,[46] has been a longtime fixture of immigration law. Congress, the Court has proclaimed, has "plenary power" over the admission of immigrants into the United States.[47] Under a strict plenary power regime, the U.S. government may act as if it is in a state of nature without legal constraints in a modern "survival of the fittest" world.[48] Justice Felix Frankfurter articulated the plenary power doctrine in terms that should make those committed to justice and equality under the law to shudder: "[W]hether immigration laws have been crude and cruel, whether they may have reflected xenophobia in general or anti-Semitism or anti-Catholicism, the responsibility belongs to Congress."[49]

The plenary power doctrine means that Congress has virtually unfettered discretion to exclude immigrants; the doctrine allows for a natural defense for closed borders. However, the plenary power doctrine, like other assertions of unfettered national sovereignty, is seriously out of step with world events, the onset of globalization, and the ascendance of international law. Indeed, premised on the notion that the sovereign has unfettered power over immigration, the doctrine is wholly inconsistent with evolving notions of international law. Modern international law, which bars racial discrimination in immigration laws, generally requires a rational reason for immigration restrictions. In certain circumstances, nations owe duties to citizens of other nations.

Moreover, a plenary power regime is dramatically out of synch with the century of rights-based constitutional jurisprudence in the United States. This constitutional order emerged years after the U.S. Supreme Court created the plenary power doctrine at the end of the nineteenth century. Despite the changing legal landscape, the plenary power doctrine remains firmly intact as the law of the land.

The era of unabashed sovereign national rights is ancient history. Human rights commissions, world trade tribunals, international criminal courts, and a plethora of international institutions have dramatically altered the nation-state and its powers. Such change is likely to continue, with cooperation and interdependence between nations essential in an era of rapid globalization.

Scholarly criticisms of the plenary power doctrine are legion.[50] Not long before September 11, immigration law scholars seriously suggested that the doctrine was on life support because it was so out of step with modern constitutional doctrine. They predicted that it would soon be relegated to the dustbins of history. The expansive powers assumed by the U.S. government after the tragic events of September 11, however, made clear that the Executive Branch continues to exercise plenary power over the treatment of immigrants. The Bush administration, for example, relied heavily on its plenary power over immigration to justify the extraordinary steps taken against immigrants, including arrest, detention, and denial of basic constitutional rights, in the "war on terror."

Although often criticized, the plenary power remains the topic of academic discussion. In stark contrast, few scholars seek to justify the deregulation of the borders. Indeed, plenary power critics as a general matter fervently deny the claim that they advocate opening the country's borders.[51] Rather, they generally argue only in favor of extending basic constitutional principles to immigration admission criteria—an entirely sensible conclusion assuming the continued existence of migration controls.

The Thesis of This Book

Much legal scholarship treats closed borders as the natural state of immigration law, with the law facilitating the efficient, fair, and rational administration of a comprehensive system of immigration controls. Reformers generally offer ideas on incremental improvements to the current system, rather than questioning its foundational premises.[52] More open migration policies have often generally been dismissed without serious consideration or analysis. Such policies, however, deserve fuller consideration.

As observed by voices from the left and the right, the current immigration scheme is broken and must be fixed. In considering how to best remedy the United States's immigration woes, we must reject the claim that the "sky would fall" with liberal immigration admissions. Such a claim is deeply flawed, severely overstated, and just plain wrong.

Much has been written about the deficiencies of the U.S. immigration laws and their civil and human rights consequences. Nor is it only immigrants' rights advocates who are critical of the status quo. Employers frequently complain of difficulties in attracting workers for certain jobs in agriculture, the meat and poultry industry, hotels and restaurants, and the high-tech industry. Criticism is also directed at the onerous paperwork required of those who wish to participate in the small guest worker programs or to secure employment-based visas, which exist under current U.S. law. Restrictionists claim—and rightly so—that the laws barring the employment of undocumented immigrants are not enforced. They do not readily admit, however, that the borders cannot be closed and that it is unrealistic to expect the enforcement of the current immigration laws to put an end to undocumented immigration.

Given the failures of the current immigration system, it is time to consider new solutions. Hoping to extend the discussion of liberal migration controls more deeply into the public debate in the United States, this book attempts to marshal the strongest possible arguments for open borders. Even if unsuccessful in convincing the United States to welcome immigrants rather than seek to build more barriers to their entry, I hope to create the intellectual space for a more open and honest conversation about immigration controls. Such a dialogue, I hope, will, at a minimum, encourage lawmakers and policymakers to attempt to offer explanations for the need for, and the practicality of, strict border enforcement.

Serious discussion of open borders, the antithesis of the current U.S. emphasis on immigration restriction and tough immigration enforcement, is long overdue. With increasing frequency, observers outside the law have voiced support for the liberal admission of immigrants and a regime with fewer immigration restrictions than are found in the United States.[53] On the basis of a study of the moral, economic, and policy justifications for open borders, this book outlines the possible move toward open labor migration or, as an alternative, regional integration akin to that which has evolved in the European Union as a possible precursor to broader change.

To place the liberal admissions regime into perspective, Chapter 2 offers a capsule summary of the history of the U.S. immigration laws and ties it into the modern controversy over immigration and immigrants from Mexico. Premised on the need for exclusion of immigrants, immigration laws have historically reflected the biases of our times—biases that, except in hindsight, we as a society often fail to appreciate.

Most Americans, for example, today look with shame at the exclusion of Chinese immigrants in the late 1800s and of southern and eastern Europeans, including many Jews, in the early twentieth century. Mass deportations of Mexican immigrants throughout the twentieth century, such as "Operation Wetback" in 1954, are blemishes on this nation's proud history. Racial minorities, the poor, gays and lesbians, political dissidents, women, and other "undesirables" have suffered a long history of discrimination under the U.S. immigration laws. The exclusion of these groups is difficult to square with the lofty ideals that the nation regularly touts to the world, as well as the nation's stated commitment to equal justice under law.

The immigration laws and their enforcement have had serious civil rights consequences.[54] They have had crushing impacts on immigrants, as well as their family, friends, and communities, and have often done little more than make the lives of immigrants tougher than they already are. The United States should refashion modern immigration law and policy to avoid such lamentable consequences. We must learn from our immigration history or we are bound to repeat its mistakes.

Chapter 3 considers the philosophical arguments for liberalizing the admission of immigrants into the United States. Political theorists have found it extremely difficult to justify intellectually efforts to close national borders, especially in light of the emphasis on individual rights in liberal theory. The United States, of course, holds itself out as the champion of individual freedoms, and the U.S. Constitution strives to protect the rights of the individual against the state. But by allowing national power to severely restrict the free movement of people, U.S. immigration law is inconsistent with modern notions of freedom and liberty.

Closed borders also implicate serious moral concerns regarding the human impacts of border enforcement, such as the resulting violence and deaths, racial discrimination, the trafficking in human beings, and the creation of an exploitable racial caste in the U.S. labor market. All of these intolerable consequences flow directly from the current system of immigration restrictions and enforcement in the modern United States. Nonetheless, "[w]hile many people dispute either the wisdom or the justice of particular provisions of the immigration laws, relatively few have questioned the underlying premise that a nation-state has the moral power to enact restrictions."[55] Chapter 3 seriously engages this fundamental question.

Importantly, at the most basic level, the U.S. government's efforts to seal the borders have resulted in downright immoral consequences. Overzealous and publicly condemned enforcement measures, such as the nation's shunning of Jewish refugees fleeing the Holocaust during World War II, often are taken in the name of immigration enforcement and dutiful compliance with the immigration laws.[56] Today, the human impacts of border enforcement implicate serious moral concerns. One can fairly ask how the horrible enforcement consequences, including death and labor exploitation, are consistent with the goals and ideals of a liberal democracy, much less one that claims to embrace the "huddled masses." The nation likely will look back with sadness and regret at the latest border enforcement measures, with their deadly human consequences, and the entire "war on terror," with its harsh impacts on Arab, Muslim, and other citizens and noncitizens, almost all of whom have nothing whatsoever to do with terrorism.

The suppression of the rights of *noncitizens* can also lead to harsh policies directed toward certain groups of U.S. *citizens,* as demonstrated by the internment of persons of Japanese ancestry, citizens and noncitizens alike, during World War II.[57] More recently, harsh measures in the war on terror, initially directed at noncitizens, were later followed by deprivations of the rights of U.S. citizens. The U.S. government held the U.S. citizens Jose Padilla and Yaser Hamdi without criminal charges or access to an attorney for several years after the horrible events of September 11, 2001.[58] With little discussion or debate, Congress passed the USA PATRIOT Act, a law with many provisions that punished immigrants. Moreover, by expanding law enforcement officers' authority to engage in electronic surveillance in the United States, the act directly affected the civil rights of U.S. citizens.[59]

History has proven that it is extremely difficult to cabin harsh treatment of minorities under the law to only noncitizens. Indeed, punitive government action may well encourage discrimination against certain groups of immigrants as well as U.S. citizens who share common characteristics. Specifically, anti-immigrant sentiment in modern times often translates into anti-Mexican sentiment. In this way, immigration law and its enforcement affect U.S. citizens of Mexican ancestry as well as noncitizens. Such immoral consequences of U.S. immigration law deserve redress.

Moving from the moral to the utilitarian, Chapter 4 considers the economic arguments for more liberal admission of immigrants. Utilitarian considerations militate in favor of free migration between nations. In an era of globalization, why not facilitate labor's ability to cross national borders, given that capital, goods, and services are permitted and encouraged to do so? International trade principles suggest that labor migration is a net benefit to the national economic welfare of the United States. Studies demonstrate that added labor from immigration spurs economic growth, moderates inflation, and increases national wealth.

The nations that make up the European Union (EU) came to the conclusion that economic benefits would come from allowing labor migration between and among the member nations. Free labor movement has flourished in the EU, without much of a hitch. The North American Free Trade Agreement (NAFTA), however, stopped short of this step, permitting free trade of *goods and services* but not allowing for the migration of *people* among the United States, Canada, and Mexico.[60]

NAFTA failed to address migration within the trading bloc for the same reason that labor migration was not initially a part of the compact between the EU members. A deep fear that racially and culturally different migrants would flood the developed world, wreaking havoc on society and causing change and tension, removed migration from the talks that culminated in NAFTA and, at least initially, the EU. Europe, to a certain extent, eventually overcame that initial apprehension and eventually allowed migration between member nations and then, after some controversy, expanded the partnership to include much of eastern Europe and other nations, such as Bulgaria and Romania.

Freer migration in North America, emulating the labor migration permitted within the EU, would do much to cure the ills of the current immigration scheme. Of course, the EU is not without its problems, especially with respect to its efforts to bar entry of those, especially North Africans and Muslims, from outside Europe. Nevertheless, a North American Union that allowed free labor migration between member states might be a start toward more liberal admission of immigrants and would recognize the special relationship that U.S. society has historically had with immigrants from Mexico. A long history of migration from Mexico to the United States, with employers and the U.S. government often encouraging labor to come north, facilitates current immigration flows. A North American Union might well demonstrate that mass migrations need not follow a liberalized migration regime. Consequently, a successful labor migration pact in North American might facilitate movement toward a more generally open migration system.

However, there are real economic concerns with immigration that must be considered in any alternative allowing for more liberal immigrant admissions. Immigration may have wealth distribution consequences, with employers benefiting at the expense of workers. Many employers support liberal immigration as a way to ensure the ready availability of low-wage labor. Unskilled citizens, in turn, may experience downward pressures on wages as a result of the influx of immigrants.[61] Such bread-and-butter concerns, which contribute to the populist appeal of the restrictionist movement in the United States, cannot be ignored by advocates of immigrants and liberal admissions.

Economic concerns of poor and working-class citizens help explain why the anti-immigrant sentiment has held general populist appeal throughout U.S. history. Historically, the nativist impulse has often been triggered by economic fears. Labor unionists on the West Coast, for example, viciously attacked Chinese immigrants during the hard economic times of the 1880s. The Chinese exclusion laws resulted from anti-immigrant agitation directly linked to popular economic fears and inflamed by racism.

In addition, the rank-and-file of restrictionist movements have often tended to be composed of vulnerable U.S. citizens who felt economically, and otherwise, threatened by immigration and immigrants. Indeed, African Americans, often at the forefront of the struggle for civil rights, have at times supported restrictionist positions and nativist stances because of the perceived impact on Blacks of the influx into the United States of low-wage immigrant labor.[62]

It is important to remember that negative economic consequences for domestic workers flow from the current system. Millions of undocumented immigrants are exploited in the workplace and compete with domestic workers for low-skill jobs. As a result, wages for those with the least are suppressed. Union organizing is more difficult with a ready and available low-wage labor force.

A better system for addressing these economic concerns would be to abandon ineffective efforts to bar the entry to immigrants and instead attempt to better regulate the flow of migrants, while enforcing labor protections for *all* workers in the United States. Understanding this reality, the AFL-CIO, which in the past advocated restrictions on immigration, has redirected its efforts in recent years to organizing all workers in the United States. With new noncitizen unionists joining the struggle for increased wages and better conditions, labor hopes that future organizing will build on recent successes.[63]

In addition, wealth redistribution schemes might alleviate skews in the flow of economic benefits from a system of more open migration. Of course, as the history of welfare in the United States demonstrates, the creation of transfer programs is far easier said than done. There would be resistance from those—primarily corporate and business—interests threatened with the loss of any of the increased wealth that results from immigrant labor. However, implementation of such a policy option is simpler, more manageable, and more effective than attempting to close the borders in a way that the United States has failed to do with its monumental border enforcement efforts.

There also are environmental concerns raised about immigration. Some restrictionists express fears about overpopulation of the United States. They contend that the nation already is overpopulated and therefore should not accept any more immigrants. Segments of the environmental movement have had distinctly anti-immigrant, nativist strands.[64] These concerns resound with the "not in my backyard" mentality that is prevalent in zoning and siting decisions regarding hazardous activities in communities across the United States. With its environmental protections and a commitment to conservation not often found in the developing world, the United States in many ways offers a more environmentally conscious alternative to a migrant's homeland. Environmental arguments thus militate for, not against, open borders.

True, change will come with open borders. The population of the United States might increase. We as a nation will face environmental challenges with an increased population. However, the population changes may occur even if the law fails to authorize more liberal admissions of immigrants. Absent legal avenues for migration, undocumented immigrants still will come, but without the imprimatur of the law. The United States must learn to manage migration flows in sensible ways, rather than attempt to deny their existence or engage in the impossible task of completely cutting them off.

Chapter 5 offers reasons why liberalized immigration is simply good policy for the United States. An open-borders regime would recognize the almost irresistible economic, social, and political pressures that fuel international migration in the modern world. Border controls cannot end unlawful migration in the modern world with international interchange in all aspects of social life. Indeed, it is futile to pursue policies that seek to do so.

As with the United States's failed prohibition of the alcohol trade in the early twentieth century, it has proven to be virtually impossible to enforce the immigration laws and put a halt to undocumented immigration. Otherwise law-abiding people surreptitiously enter the United States or overstay their temporary visas. Otherwise law-abiding citizens, even nominees for high positions in the federal government with significant immigration enforcement responsibilities such as the Attorney General, the Secretary of Labor, and the Secretary of Homeland Security, have employed undocumented immigrants. U.S. society at large simply does not generally consider either the employers or the undocumented immigrants to be criminals, even though they have violated the law. Employers are engaged in conduct that is widespread and, with little more than a wink and a nod, accepted by all parties. To make matters worse, as discussed in Chapter 5, modern border enforcement, like Prohibition, promotes criminal activity, leads to abusive law enforcement practices, contributes to a caseload crisis in the immigration bureaucracy and the courts, and undermines the very legitimacy and moral force of the law.

Open borders would help address these problems and offer other policy benefits. They would reduce racial discrimination and reduce the federal/state and international tensions growing out of disputes over border enforcement. Importantly, liberalized immigration admissions would improve national security by allowing immigration authorities to focus on true dangers to public safety and national security, rather than spread themselves thin as they seek to check in detail the many nuances of the story of every noncitizen seeking to enter the United States.

Chapter 6 contends that, in important respects, open borders are inevitable. Nobody can deny that it is far easier to migrate in the modern world than in days past. Transportation makes movement much easier than it was for all of human history, with international flights available today that were inconceivable just a few decades ago. Trade in goods and services require people to travel around the world. Technology makes the exchange of information fast and easy. Knowledge about opportunities in different places helps to fuel migration.

Global transportation and information networks make immigration much easier than in the past. Moreover, economic and political opportunity in the United States attracts people to this country from the world over. Ultimately, the pressures for global migration will not go away—at least not in the foreseeable future. In a world of stark economic disparities, easy transportation, free flows of information, and less uncertainty about what one might encounter in a new land, migration of people will undoubtedly occur at higher rates than in the past. Indeed, one might logically conjecture that migration of people to countries might increase dramatically as the new millennium advances, with transportation and technological innovation and increased economic trade and other connections between people across borders resulting from globalization. Such developments, in turn, suggest, at a minimum, that migration issues will remain in play throughout the world for the foreseeable future.

The issue is not whether we can close our borders but how we might best manage the flow of migrants into the country and integrate those who live here. We as a nation must ensure that our immigration laws comport with modern political, economic, and social reality. If not, they will prove to be untenable, just as they are today.

The Fears of Permeable Borders

At the outset, it seems prudent to address head-on two major concerns about liberalizing the borders. Both significantly influence the public debate over immigration and the treatment of immigrants residing in the United States. However, both sets of fears should not derail a proposal for more liberal immigration admissions.

"Opening the Floodgates"

Fears abound that the minimization of border controls will open the "floodgates," allowing millions of immigrants from around the world to overwhelm, if not destroy, the United States as we know it.[65] The floodgates concern betrays an attitude of U.S. superiority and the assumption that, if the opportunity existed, people the world over could not resist coming to the best of all nations. As we have learned in recent years, however, not all people cherish life in the United States. Most of the world does not try to immigrate, or even consider immigrating, to this country. Most Mexicans, for example, stay in Mexico. The same is true for most of the people in Europe, Africa, Asia, and North and Latin America. As one commentator observed:

> Most people have no inclination to leave their native soil, no matter how onerous conditions become. Would-be emigrants must fight off the ties of family, the comfort of familiar surroundings, the rootedness in one's culture, the security of being among "one's own," and the power of plain inertia. Conversely, being uprooted carries daunting prospects: adjusting to alien ways, learning a new language, the absence of kith and kin, the sheer uncertainty of it all.[66]

The glue of the familiar—family, friends, culture, language, geography, and other characteristics of any physical location—anchor many people to where they were born. Free movement *within* the United States generally has not led to mass migrations, even though economic, political, and social disparities exist between the various states.[67] For example, many, if not most, Mississippians remain in Mississippi despite the superior economic opportunities in many other states. Migration between states occurs, but, for most of U.S. history, open borders between the states have generally not resulted in large population readjustments.

Despite human inertia and the general affinity for family and homeland, the deep-seated fear persists that, absent strict migration controls, the United States risks being overwhelmed by hordes of immigrants of different races, cultures, and creeds who will "take over" the country. This fear is perhaps the major impediment to any proposal to ease migration controls and open the borders. Thus, any debate about immigration—from relatively minor efforts to more aggressive ones—must invariably confront the floodgates concern.

There is one significant empirical blind spot to the call for open borders. Uncertainty exists about the size of the possible flows of immigrants into the United States if the nation were to adopt an open-borders regime. One influential supporter of the reduction of immigration controls declined to advocate open borders because of, among other reasons, the lack of data that would allow for an accurate estimate on the resulting flow of immigrants to the United States.[68] However, while better empirical estimates undoubtedly might help, they are unlikely to be definitive. Few empirical studies in the realm of immigration have proven to be. Debate rages, for example, about the costs and benefits of immigration. Consequently, we do not know precisely how many migrants would pursue a life in the United States if the opportunity were more freely available. That lack of information makes it harder to engage in a reliable cost/benefit analysis of an open-borders system. Regardless, the bottom line is that there is no hard evidence that the "floodgates" would burst if migration controls were eased. At a minimum, however, the system of migration would be more orderly, humane, and fair than the current one.

The concern that immigrants will overrun the nation is not unique to the United States. Great trepidation initially greeted the European Union's experiment with labor migration within the borders of the common market, which today is viewed as a success. Specifically,

> Concerns of massive inflows of cheap labor [were] raised before the accession of Greece, Spain and Portugal to the [European Union (EU)]. . . . [I]t was predicted that between 1.5 million and 1.6 million people from Spain and Portugal would emigrate to the rest of the EU. . . . However, fears of massive migration flows did not materialize. [69]

In Europe, concerns with large population shifts across national borders led to some transitional arrangements for free movement of workers, with some nations requiring work permits or imposing transitional ceilings while others immediately opened their borders. In the end, nothing approaching a mass migration followed the elimination of border controls. One comprehensive study concluded that "fears of massive inflows of workers and devastating impacts on receiving labor markets were unfounded, since inflows of foreign workers have generally supplemented rather than replaced domestic labor and helped sustain solid economic growth, while at the same time keeping local wages stable."[70]

The relatively painless experience with expanded labor markets in Europe led to the addition of new member nations and an expansion of the EU. As Table 1.1 shows, the economic disparities among Greece, Spain, and Portugal and the rest of the EU member nations at least currently are not as great as those with some of the nations in Eastern Europe that later joined. For example, the two newest members, Bulgaria and Romania, have a lower per capita Gross Domestic Product (GDP) than Mexico. Two candidates for EU membership, Turkey and Macedonia, have per capita GDPs significantly lower than Mexico's.

Closer to home, the economic disparities between the island of Puerto Rico, a U.S. territory populated by U.S. citizens with the right to travel

TABLE I.I
Per Capita Gross Domestic Product in
European Union Member Nations

Country	2005 GDP Per Capita in U.S. Dollars
Luxembourg	$65,900
Ireland	41,100
Denmark	34,800
Austria	32,500
Belgium	31,100
Finland	31,000
Netherlands	30,300
Germany	30,100
United Kingdom	30,100
Sweden	29,800
France	29,600
Italy	28,700
Spain	24,600
Greece	22,300
Cyprus	21,600
Slovenia	21,500
Czech Republic	20,000
Malta	19,700
Portugal	19,000
Estonia	17,500
Hungary	16,300
Slovakia	16,300
Latvia	13,700
Lithuania	13,700
Poland	13,100
Croatia (Candidate)	12,400
Bulgaria (Joined Jan. 1, 2007)	9,600
Turkey (Candidate)	8,400
Romania (Joined Jan. 1, 2007)	8,100
Macedonia (Candidate)	7,800

SOURCE: World Factbook, United States Central Intelligence
Agency (CIA) (June 29, 2006), available at https://www.cia.gov/
cia/publications/factbook/rankorder/2004rank.html, last visited
November 27, 2006.

to the mainland, and the mainland United States has not led to a mass
exodus from Puerto Rico. As Table 1.2 shows, the per capita GDP of the
United States is twice that of Puerto Rico. Although there is a steady
stream of migration from Puerto Rico to the mainland, there has not
been a flood of migration from that island, and its population is relatively stable. Cultural and national affinities for Puerto Rico among its
inhabitants contribute to limited migration from the island. Even though
superior economic opportunities and public benefits are to be found on
the mainland, most Puerto Ricans do not leave.

TABLE I.2
*Per Capita Gross Domestic Product among
North America Nations*

Country	2005 GDP Per Capita in U.S. Dollars
United States	$41,600
Canada	33,900
Puerto Rico	18,700
Mexico	10,700

SOURCE: World Factbook, United States Central Intelligence Agency (CIA) (June 29, 2006), available at https://www.cia.gov/cia/publications/factbook/rankorder/2004rank.html, last visited November 27, 2006.

Both the European experience and that of the United States fail to offer support for the fears that mass migration will follow open borders. In short, there is little evidence that the United States would truly be "opening the floodgates" to the masses of the world if it greatly eased immigration restrictions and relaxed its border controls.

It is true that liberal migration policies might well result in initial population readjustments between nations. Any such readjustments, however, can be managed. One way of avoiding a massive influx of immigrants into the United States would be to have a phased implementation of an open-borders system, with numerical limits that might remain in place for several years before they sunset. A phased approach would tend to ameliorate fears that the proverbial flood of immigrants would overwhelm us and help to make adoption of a liberal admissions scheme more politically palatable. Even if the annual limits were not reached, their existence at the outset might calm national concerns about a more liberal and generous immigration scheme.

A corollary of the floodgates fear is the social cohesion argument. The argument is that, with large numbers of immigrants of different races and cultures coming to the United States, racism, cultural conflict, and social tensions generally would increase. One in a long line of Eastern intellectuals who have decried the impacts of immigration on the nation, Samuel Huntington, whose restrictionist views are analyzed critically in Chapter 2, contends that current levels of immigration from Mexico are in effect destroying America by undermining its national cultural identity.[71]

The social cohesion concern assumes that, in an open-borders regime, large numbers of migrants will come to the United States who are not already migrating, an assumption that is not necessarily true. Rather than attempt to restrict immigration through increased border enforcement, we might do better to direct our efforts at attempting to integrate immigrants into American social life and building better social cohesion in our increasingly diverse, multicultural society. Integration policies, such as increased English-as-a-second-language classes and naturalization workshops, are much more likely to succeed than efforts to close the border.

Taken literally, the social cohesion argument would more generally place into question the enforcement of the antidiscrimination laws and the Equal Protection Clause of the Fourteenth Amendment. In the 1950s and 1960s, the efforts to ban racial discrimination initially spawned great resistance. Fortunately, the Supreme Court, and the nation as a whole, refused to capitulate as the U.S. government moved to desegregate the Jim Crow South. At times, troops were necessary to enforce the law, but the nation proceeded nonetheless.[72]

Although race cannot be ignored in the analysis, the race of immigrants should not lead the United States to embrace, as it has in the past, a restrictive—and unenforceable—immigration system. Open borders are more consistent with the national commitment to multiculturalism, inclusiveness, and the respect for all races, cultures, creeds, and peoples. If, as Nathan Glazer says, "we are all multiculturalists now,"[73] we should make our immigration laws consistent with that view. If not, we should say so.

Still, the nation should direct efforts to promote social cohesion and to facilitate the integration of immigrants into American social life. Along these lines, increased English-as-a-second-language programs and streamlined naturalization procedures that make it easier for immigrants to gain citizenship would seem most appropriate. Such efforts are significantly more likely to smooth the conflicts that arise due to immigration than doomed efforts to close the borders and keep people of different backgrounds and heritages out of the country.

The "War on Terror"

In an important respect, this book is not calling for wholesale elimination of border controls and the immigration laws. The proposal instead is for minimal controls that would be much more focused and narrow in scope than those found in the current U.S. immigration laws.

Efforts would be made to bar hardened criminals and those reasonably suspected of terrorist activities from entering the United States. Persons who pose true threats to national security and public safety could be denied entry into the country. Unlike the current law, the run-of-the-mill dreamer searching for economic opportunity would be embraced, not spurned.

The U.S. government's understandable preoccupation with terrorism since September 11, 2001, makes this an inopportune historical moment to raise the possibility of minimizing immigration controls and easing the entry of migrants into the United States. The horrific events of September 11 understandably raised legitimate national-security and public-safety concerns. Terrorism has affected the entire world and led to military conflicts in Afghanistan and Iraq and the deaths of thousands of civilians and combatants. In the name of national security, the highest levels of the U.S. government have engaged in a concerted effort to close, not open, the borders.[74] The public generally has strongly supported these efforts and, for the most part, has been more restrictionist in mood since the World Trade Center crumbled to the ground.[75]

In no small part because the law allows the government great leeway in its policies toward immigration and immigrants, immigration law has been ground zero of the U.S. government's so-called war on terror. Put differently, immigration served as a handy antiterrorism tool after September 11 for the administration of President George W. Bush. The law affords great flexibility to the government in the realm of immigration. In addition, immigrants have a much smaller bundle of legal rights that the government must respect than U.S. citizens.[76] In the wake of September 11, arrests, interrogation, detention, and removal of Arab and Muslim noncitizens occurred by the thousands. The U.S. government went so far as to implement a special registration system for noncitizens from a select group of nations. These measures have resulted in many arrests, detentions, and deportations, but few, if any, based on charges of terrorism.

Unfortunately, the "war on terror" has been used to rationalize a wide variety of aggressive policies that have had little to do with national security and public safety. For example, in the name of fighting terrorism, the Department of Justice announced that it would begin enforcing a rule allowing for the deportation of immigrants who fail to report their change of address within ten days.[77] Then-Attorney

General John Ashcroft claimed that he would deport Muslim "terrorists" for any infraction, including "spitting on the sidewalk." One court invoked concerns with terrorism to justify a run-of-the-mill border check that escalated into ripping open a spare tire in the search for drugs.[78]

Security checks and removal campaigns resulted in record levels of deportations, even though almost all of the noncitizens had nothing whatsoever to do with terrorism. Many were not Arab or Muslim. Importantly, the vast majority of the record numbers of immigrants deported since September 11 have been from Mexico and Central America, not known to be havens for terrorists.[79] Although it has been claimed that increased border enforcement along the U.S. southern border with Mexico will improve national security, one study found that "[n]ot one terrorist has entered the United States from Mexico."[80]

While the war on terror has dominated the national and international consciousness, constructive immigration reform efforts have fallen by the wayside. Serious discussions of a bilateral agreement that would have regularized migration between the United States and Mexico ended abruptly on September 11. Efforts to remove the harsh edges of 1996 immigration reform laws—thought by some observers at the time to be as draconian as any in U.S. history—disappeared as the political climate made any less restrictionist changes in the immigration laws next to impossible. Over the past few years, President Bush's efforts to recommence discussion of immigration reform, especially a guest worker program, have faced stiff resistance.[81]

Contrary to intuition, open borders are entirely consistent with efforts to prevent terrorism. More liberal migration policies with fewer time-consuming bureaucratic paperwork requirements would allow the U.S. government to pay full attention to, and focus its enforcement efforts on, the true dangers to public safety and national security. Rather than routine checks on mundane matters, U.S. immigration authorities could focus on terrorists, dangerous criminals, drugs and other contraband, and public-health risks. There no longer would be a need to engage in the endless search to come up with a reason to keep every noncitizen out of the country. Enforcement efforts could move beyond the morass of visa requirements, exclusion grounds, per-country caps, and the many complexities of the Immigration and Nationality Act that have made its enforcement unwieldy, ineffective, and unfair.[82]

Complex inquiries into migrants' family histories, incomes, and purpose for entering the country, however, would be for the most part irrelevant to the U.S. government. Such inquiries are the bread-and-butter of current border enforcement officers and the bane of visa applications, consular officer interviews, immigration stops, and document checks. Time and effort would be saved in the vast majority of immigrant admissions. Time and expenditures could be reallocated to the relatively few cases that involve serious criminal and terrorist activities—the very cases that deserve careful attention by a government seeking to protect the safety of its citizens in these troubled times.

Narrower exclusion grounds in the U.S. immigration laws would be more realistic. With fewer time-consuming bureaucratic requirements, the nation could devote scarce enforcement resources to efforts to ferret out the true dangers to public safety and national security. More liberal migration would allow the U.S. government to pay full attention to, and focus its enforcement on, terrorists, dangerous criminals, those who smuggle drugs and other contraband, and those who pose public-health risks. Such a true public-safety and security focus would make the nation much safer than the current diffuse, unfocused enforcement emphasis that has dominated U.S. border controls throughout its history.

Most important, open borders would allow for the better tracking of all entrants into the United States. The nation would be better positioned to keep records, including names and addresses, of all immigrants in the country. Currently, millions of undocumented immigrants live in the shadows of American social life. We know precious little about who they are, where they live, and what they are doing in this country. The nation does not have the names and addresses of undocumented immigrants and has no idea why they are in the United States. It is difficult to see how such a situation could be in the national interest, especially in a time when national-security concerns are at their zenith. Nor, as we shall see, is there any evidence that the U.S. government as a practical matter could end undocumented immigration and remove all of the undocumented immigrants from the country.

Historically, U.S. immigration laws have been dramatically overbroad in attacking the perceived evil of the day, whether it be racial minorities, the poor, political dissidents, or others.[83] To be effective, the war on terror should attempt to exclude from admission the true dangers to national security and public safety, rather than simply try to seal the borders, which has proven to be virtually impossible. Currently, U.S. law has failed to seal the borders, and a population of people lives under the radar, subject to exploitation, and effectively unprotected by law.

As has been seen in other areas of law enforcement, more focused immigration law enforcement has a greater likelihood of rooting out dangerous and potentially unlawful conduct than scattershot efforts that infringe on the civil rights of many people. Consider that racial profiling by police has done little to make our streets safer and has alienated and angered communities whose cooperation is needed to effectively fight crime. Similarly, carefully crafted immigration enforcement is less likely to frighten immigrant communities—the very communities whose assistance is essential if the United States truly seeks to successfully fight terrorism.

Demand for evasion of the law by millions of undocumented immigrants has created highly organized networks that pose true risks to the national security. The trafficking of human beings, with its devastating impacts, is a direct result of heightened immigration enforcement and harkens back to the days of slavery in the United States. A booming business, trafficking has been a growth industry, with its tentacles reaching across the entire United States. International criminal syndicates, which dominate the trafficking market, profit handsomely. Death and human misery often result. Immigrants are enslaved to pay off smuggling fees, and thousands of immigrant women forced into the sex industry and other exploitative work relationships.

With time, the United States's jitters generated by the horror of September 11 will fade. Indeed, tempers and emotions have already calmed to a certain extent. As a nation, we returned to serious consideration of immigration reform in 2005–06. None of the reform proposals seriously considered by Congress, however, would have regularized the migration between the United States and Mexico. They instead offer short-term solutions and purported quick fixes that will necessitate further reform efforts in only a few years. The migration flow from the south into the United States has been continuous for generations. Given the economic, political, and social realities of the situation, the demand for migration to this country does not appear to have any immediate end in sight. When the appropriate time comes, this country will, it is hoped, study the important issues implicated by opening the borders and regularizing the flow of labor from Mexico into the United States. Only real comprehensive reform will minimize the tragic human costs that result from immigration restrictions in the U.S. immigration laws.

The Real Challenge to Open Borders

This book lays out the arguments for the liberal admission of immigrants to the United States. It is hoped that the arguments are convincing. But, even if they are, "there is an important difference between appreciating the feasibility and moral logic of a legal rule of free entry, and being psychologically 'ready' to collectively implement such a rule in practice."[84] In the United States, and perhaps much of the Western world, the psychological barrier may be the most formidable one to open borders.

Today, limited admission of immigrants is viewed as the natural and necessary order of things. Times change, however, and the American public may come to see the inevitability of liberal admissions and a truly open society. Many Americans naturally believe that, absent immigration restrictions, the nation will be overrun by hordes of migrants and that the United States will never be the same.

The nation has changed—and is changing—due to legal and illegal immigration. Reversal of those changes is simply impossible. Even after the monumental efforts to secure the borders after September 11, 2001, immigrants—legal and undocumented—continue to come to this land of opportunity. Massive border enforcement measures have failed to reduce the undocumented immigrant population in the United States. Indeed, more undocumented immigrants live in the United States today than did before that fateful day.

The choices for the United States are painfully simple. The nation can keep its head in the sand and continue to implement incremental reforms that have little impact on undocumented immigration and make the lives of immigrants more difficult. Or, the nation can move boldly to reconceive and radically change the laws of immigration to better comport with political, economic, and social forces and to truly protect national security. The United States has the opportunity to make its immigration laws more realistic, more just, and more moral.

The Proposal in Brief

By design, this book outlines a general proposal with, as one might say, the devil remaining in the details. The coming chapters expand on and defend the proposal as essential under the political, economic, and social circumstances fueling migration to the United States in the twenty-first century. Importantly, open borders are more consistent with the nation's moral and constitutional traditions than the current immigration system and will avoid many of the immoral consequences of modern border enforcement. A safe and sane open-borders system is practical and can be accommodated easily through reliance on existing systems, with important modifications described in the pages that follow.

An Open-Admissions System

Under my open-borders proposal, the borders of the United States would be open, with no numerical limits on the number of immigrants who can enter the country in any given year. The current family and employment preferences and diversity visa system, as well as the per-country caps that limit immigration annually from any one nation, would be abolished in their entirety. The nation would eliminate the current hypercomplex system of immigration controls, which have proven difficult to enforce and relatively easy to circumvent. An open-admissions system would be far simpler, fairer, efficient, and realistic.

The proposal does not envision, however, complete dismantling of border controls. Rather, immigrants generally would need to secure a visa from the U.S. government in order to gain lawful admission through a port of entry. The strong legal presumption at all stages of the visa application process would be that the noncitizen applicant is entitled to admission into the United States, the precise opposite of the current legal presumption. The visa application process would, as it currently does, require a background check and scrutiny of each noncitizen's criminal record and health history. The government would strive to ensure that various federal and international law enforcement agencies share all available information about possible criminal or terrorist ties of visa applicants. Noncitizens seeking long-term admission into the country would apply for a visa that would afford them with the status equivalent to that of a current lawful permanent resident.

Much government time and effort would be saved by streamlining the entire visa system and eliminating the many quotas, ceilings, complex immigrant visa requirements, and myriad exclusion grounds that exist under current U.S. law. Moreover, the system would be far fairer than current law to noncitizens. Many would-be migrants who currently have no avenue for entry under the current system for immigrating to the United States would have one. This new system would eliminate the per-country ceilings of less than 26,000 persons per year, which result in long waits for immigrants seeking entry under certain family and employment preferences from high-immigration nations, such as China, India, Mexico, and the Philippines. While these prospective migrants may have to wait decades for lawful admission under current law, similarly situated immigrants from the rest of the world have much shorter waits. The disproportionately long lines create strong pressures to circumvent the law and enter the country unlawfully or to secure a temporary visa and overstay its terms.

The Sole Limit to Open Borders: Real Dangers to National Security and Public Safety

The only bar to entry in the open-borders system proposed here would be a narrowly drawn exclusion based on a showing by a preponderance of the evidence that a particular noncitizen posed a clear and present danger to the national security or public safety of the United States. Only noncitizens persons guilty of crimes demonstrating that they pose a danger to public safety, proven terrorists, and persons with communicable diseases that constitute a substantial public-health risk would be denied entry into the United States. Such a change in the law would represent a radical departure from the many requirements and long laundry lists of overbroad exclusion grounds that exist under the current U.S. immigration laws and result in the denial of lawful admission to tens of thousands of potential entrants each year.

Any prospective entrant denied admission would be entitled to a hearing in the current immigration courts or their equivalents, subject to the constraints of the Due Process Clause of the Fifth Amendment of the U.S. Constitution. In this hearing, the burden would be on the U.S. government to demonstrate by a preponderance of the evidence that the noncitizen is a clear and present danger to the national security or public safety. Unless the government sustained its burden of proof, the noncitizen would be admissible into the United States. A court could review the initial ruling on the immigration visa application.

My open-borders proposal requires that the national-security and public-safety exclusion be narrowly construed, with limited agency discretion to deny entry to any noncitizen. Otherwise, the system might evolve into a closed-border regime not that different from that which currently exists in the United States.

The Rights of Entrants

Persons who entered the United States as lawful permanent residents (LPRs) would have the same rights, with their limitations, and responsibilities as current LPRs possess in the United States under existing law. The obligations owed by state and local governments to noncitizens who enter the United States in the proposed open-admissions system would also be similar to those owed to lawful permanent residents under current law. LPRs would continue to enjoy the protections of the laws and be eligible for certain public benefits.

Importantly, the current naturalization process, with its various requirements, which include a period of five years of residency in this country before one ordinarily can become a citizen, would fit comfortably into an open-borders system. Of course, minor changes to the naturalization rules could be made with or without an open-borders regime. However, to be true to the ideal of creating a truly open society, the relatively easy naturalization requirements should remain intact, if not be eased, as some commentators have advocated.[85]

Removal of Noncitizens

An open-borders regime does not necessarily preclude legal provisions that allow for the removal of certain noncitizens. Deportation of noncitizens who lawfully entered the United States could be subject to the same general rules that currently apply under existing law. However, I, along with some other commentators, might prefer a narrower set of grounds for removing long-term resident noncitizens from the United States to those in place today.

Narrower deportation grounds than are currently in place are more consistent with open borders and notions of fundamental fairness to the noncitizen. Specifically, removal grounds based on a showing that the noncitizen is a danger to the national security or public safety would be most consistent with the open-borders system advocated in this book. In addition, such removal grounds might justify exclusion of a previously removed noncitizen if he or she later seeks to re-enter the United States.

Of course, this general removal ground is much narrower than the lengthy list of grounds for deportation that exist under current law, grounds that Congress has expanded substantially in recent years.

Borders and Territorial Sovereignty

Under the system that I have outlined, the United States would still have territorial borders and sovereign control over them. The system of rules and regulations governing the entry of noncitizens into the country would approximate those that exist for goods, services, and capital that enter the United States from many nations. Borders would exist but would recede in significance for the vast majority of potential migrants. It would be a sovereign decision to facilitate the entry of migrants for the national good. The United States would not cede any power to an international tribunal or foreign power, as has occurred under various international accords in the last few years. U.S. immigration law, however, would be significantly scaled back in scope and be much less intrusive to the individual than current law.

In effect, I am advocating the deregulation of immigration law. The heavy legal presumption would favor admission of each and every noncitizen seeking entry into the United States. The public-safety and national-security exclusion would be quite narrow, with the burden on the U.S. government to justify denial of admission.

The Benefits of Open Borders to the United States

Many benefits would accrue to the people of the United States from an open-borders system. Lawful immigration would be much easier and more available than under the current system. Open borders would eliminate the many complications, excessive cost and inefficiencies, and frustration of the current failed system. Time-consuming labor certification requirements for certain employment visas and the efforts to test family relationships would be abolished. Crafty efforts to game the legal immigration system, such as creative efforts to secure employment visas (by showing, for example, that a noncitizen seeking admission is a gourmet chef of exceptional abilities rather than a simple fry cook) would be unnecessary, as would efforts by the federal government to uncover and police such charades. Noncitizens, U.S. employers, and consumers would benefit from the enhanced mobility of labor.

Legal immigration would be a realistic possibility for most noncitizens seeking entry into the United States. Because legal immigration would be relatively easy for most noncitizens, undocumented immigration would dry up. It would presumably be limited to those who are excludable under the law because they pose a true risk to U.S. society. Unlike the current system, aggressive enforcement of the law against the small population of people who would be barred from entry could be justified to protect the national security and public safety.

Importantly, open borders hold the promise of bringing order to the sheer chaos of the current immigration scheme that exists under U.S. law, marred by large-scale entry without inspection, widespread violation of the law, and vigilantes like the Minutemen hunting down undocumented immigrants. The blanket denial of entry to working and poor noncitizens who are classified as likely "public charges"—the majority of the substantive grounds for the denial of visas today—would end. In an open-borders regime, the immigration laws would more closely approximate market demand for immigration, with limited negative externalities and wasteful costs. As a symbolic matter, the United States would more closely match its stated ideal of embracing the "huddled masses" of the world.

Border enforcement could focus on the true dangers to U.S. society, rather than the exclusion of hardworking people simply seeking to better their lives in pursuit of the American Dream. The immigration laws would thus stand to better protect national security and public safety than the current ones do. The current system is woefully inadequate at basic tracking of the noncitizen population. The United States, by ensuring the legal entry of most noncitizens, would have a much better record than it currently does of who in fact is entering the country and where they live once here, furthering the important goal of protecting public safety and national security. Millions of noncitizens would not be living in the shadows of American society, outside the purview of law enforcement and the protections of the law, as they are today.

With immigrants' fear of removal reduced significantly, exploitation of undocumented immigrants in the workplace might well decline on its own accord. Employers would not hold the strong lever of undocumented status over these immigrants, which often allows employers to dictate the terms of the employment relationship to workers. However, better enforcement of basic labor and employment law would presumably still be necessary. Governmental resources could be redirected from wasteful border enforcement efforts to enforcing basic workplace protections for all workers. Removing the stigma of "illegal" immigration status thus would benefit all workers. In no small part, this would happen because the current dual labor market—one regulated by law and the other that is not—that exists today would be dismantled, thus creating the opportunity for regulation of the workplace of all workers.

Legal avenues for immigrating to the United States would replace illegal means of entry. Open borders thus hold the promise of drastically reducing deaths on the border, an everyday occurrence in contemporary times. They would also reduce the current racial discrimination that plagues immigration enforcement in the United States and seeps into all aspects of American social life. Human trafficking would be reduced, as would the criminal element engaged in the deadly, exploitative, and downright horrifying trade in human beings.

In essence, open borders would go far to clean up the inequality and injustice that are perpetrated by the current U.S. immigration laws and their enforcement.

The Limits

An open-borders solution is, of course, not the silver bullet that would instantly cure all of the nation's woes. Far from it. Inequalities in the modern U.S. capitalist system will persist. The receding of the immigration laws will allow greater labor mobility and free the labor market to operate more efficiently in response to market forces than the current system of immigration controls does. Efficient markets, however, rarely operate without perpetuating or increasing economic inequality. Other tools would be needed to address the endemic problems of economic inequality in American social life.

Several proposals in this book, however, are designed to help ameliorate the problems of economic inequality exacerbated by open borders. Wealth redistribution policies that transfer benefits from those economic actors who gain from easy labor mobility to the poorest citizens of the United States constitute one possibility. Those, such as lower-skilled workers, who benefit little—or perhaps lose ground—because of the immigration of workers should receive transfer payments or tax reductions funded by taxes paid by the beneficiaries of free labor migration, primarily businesses and employers.

In addition, the federal government, which collects the lion's share of tax revenues paid by noncitizens, should provide adequate resources to state and local governments that today provide services, such as emergency services and a public education, to immigrants. To a limited extent, states have aggressively—at times successfully—pressed the federal government on an ad hoc basis for financial assistance to defray the costs of immigration and immigrants. To help cover those costs, resources could be redirected by the federal government to states with large immigrant populations. This would reduce the fiscal pressures at the state and local levels, which often fuel resentment and anti-immigration sentiment.

Last but not least, the federal government must do much more to ensure that wage and labor protections are enforced for all workers in the United States. Currently, the law completely fails to regulate the secondary labor market, in which immigrants are exploited and lack wage and labor protections. The existence of the unregulated secondary market undercuts the efforts of labor in the primary market, in which employers tend to comply with the law, to improve its treatment by employers.

On a related note, open borders as advocated in this book would do nothing to solve the dilemmas of democracy American style. That project, of course, deserves the nation's attention. As the presidential elections of 2000 and 2004 show, much work remains to be done in the United States to ensure that all U.S. citizens enjoy a truly democratic election process that does not disenfranchise a large percentage of the greater community. With millions of noncitizen residents barred from voting, the United States already has serious problems with ensuring true democracy for all residents. A similar problem continues to afflict many minority citizens. One possibility to improve the responsiveness of government to immigrants, which is beyond the scope of this book and would surely provoke controversy, might be to extend the franchise to noncitizen residents of the United States.[86]

A Second-Best Alternative

In the event that open borders prove to be nothing more than an academic pipedream, we still could look to the European Union (EU) as a model for immigration reform in the United States, a possibility foreshadowed earlier in this chapter. The EU began as a free-trade bloc that permitted the free flow of goods, services, and capital among the

Western European nations. It has become something much more, with internal migration generally permitted within the EU nations, including but not limited to France, Germany, Italy, Portugal, and Spain. With the success of this integration, more nations have sought to join. Consequently, the number of nations constituting the EU has expanded over time to now include many nations, including Bulgaria and Romania.

The North American Free Trade Agreement (NAFTA) entered into by the United States, Mexico, and Canada could follow a similar trajectory. The free flow of goods, services, and capital is now the rule for the three NAFTA nations. The free flow of *people* is a possible next step in the NAFTA relationship. Such an arrangement is not without its drawbacks, however, because the border of North America would not be permeable and border enforcement, with all its shortcomings, would remain at the outer perimeter of the regional bloc. As we shall see, this option still would be preferable to the status quo.

2

A Brief History of U.S. Immigration Law and Enforcement

U.S. immigration law is famous for its cyclical, turbulent, and ambivalent nature. At times, the nation has embraced some of the most liberal immigration admissions laws and policies in the world. The nation's immigration laws, in these times, have been truer to the ideal of offering open arms to the "huddled masses" than they are today. Despite the law's current restrictions on immigration, U.S. law remains more open in terms of admissions and access to citizenship than the laws of many developed nations.

At other times in U.S. history, however, the nation has capitulated to the nativist impulse and embraced immigration laws and policies that, in retrospect, make us cringe with shame and regret. Time and time again, fear and social stress have sparked fiery attacks on the nation's most vulnerable outsiders. Punitive immigration laws and tough enforcement, as well as harsh treatment of immigrants and minorities who shared similar characteristics in the United States, followed.

The cyclical nature of immigration politics—and thus immigration law and policy—often has been directly linked to the overall state of the U.S. economy and the perceived social evils of the day. A wide divergence in popular opinion about immigration and immigrants has contributed to the wild fluctuations in U.S. policy. War, political and economic turmoil, and other tensions affect the nation's collective attitude toward immigration. Social stresses, like terrorism in modern times, find a ready and unimpeded outlet in immigration law and its enforcement. Immigration law, unlike the vicissitudes of the economy or the whims of terrorists, can be controlled (even if enforcement might not work).

In a similar fashion, policies directed at *immigrants* in the United

States have varied dramatically over time. The noncitizen in U.S. society is vulnerable. The United States has consistently afforded fewer rights to immigrants than to U.S. citizens. Immigrants are denied the right to vote and access to public benefits (even those for which they contribute tax dollars) for which citizens ordinarily are eligible. At times, federal, state, and local governments have adopted harsh policies toward immigrants, including engaging in efforts at coerced assimilation, attempting to force people to speak English, and invidiously discriminating against noncitizens living in the United States. In these and other ways, noncitizens are denied full membership in U.S. society. To make matters worse, deportation from the country is always a possibility facing noncitizens.

Above all, the threat of deportation alone undermines an immigrant's feeling of belonging to the United States. The possibility of deportation is a critical difference both practically and symbolically in the social and legal status of U.S. citizens and noncitizens. Whatever their conduct, citizens can *never* be deported or banished from the United States. Noncitizens, in contrast, can be forcibly ejected from the country for a wide variety of transgressions, ranging from relatively minor technical violations of the immigration laws to the commission of violent crimes. Indeed, Congress has vastly expanded the criminal grounds for possible removal in recent years to include many relatively minor crimes, with the result being record numbers of deportations.

The fear of deportation haunts many immigrants. They know that they can be torn away from established lives, family, friends, and community in an instant for lacking the proper immigration papers or for even something as minor as failing to file a change of address form with the U.S. government within ten days of moving. The undocumented immigrant who drives a car without a license faces the possibility of deportation every time he turns the key. An immigrant's entire life in the United States is constantly at risk.

Immigrants become easy targets for harsh treatment because they have a distinctively negative image in popular culture. Although not officially found in the omnibus immigration law, the Immigration and Nationality Act of 1952, the emotion-laden phrase "illegal aliens" figures prominently in popular debate over immigration.[1] "Illegal aliens," as their moniker strongly implies, are law-breakers, abusers, and intruders, undesirables we want excluded from our society. The very use of the term "illegal aliens" ordinarily betrays a restrictionist bias in the speaker. By stripping real people of their humanity, the terminology helps rationalize the harsh treatment of undocumented immigrants under the immigration laws.

Immigrants, as noncitizens, have little direct input in the political process, a process that ultimately controls their destinies. Unlike other minority groups, they cannot vote. Although interest groups, such as Latina/o and Asian-American advocacy groups, advocate on behalf of immigrants along with citizen minorities, they have limited political clout in arguing for fair treatment of people who cannot vote. Politicians generally do not court the "immigrant vote." In the end, immigrants' interests can be ignored by law- and policymakers in ways that other citizen minorities' simply cannot be.[2]

At various times, the U.S. government has attempted to coerce immigrants and people of color to assimilate into the mainstream and adopt "American" ways. Coerced assimilation of noncitizens was particularly popular early in the early twentieth century. In a time when U.S. society openly suppressed domestic minorities and racial segregation was the norm, such measures were much easier to put into place. The national rise of a civil rights consciousness, and a public commitment to respect and tolerance for different cultures and peoples, changed everything. Today, it is much more difficult, although not impossible, to adopt coercive measures that mandate assimilation or to criticize as somehow inferior the culture of people of Mexican ancestry.

The forced assimilation of immigrants is inconsistent with the nation's modern sensibilities and commitment to multiculturalism. Nonetheless, demands for immigrant assimilation, and complaints about the failure of today's immigrants to assimilate, reappear in the public debate with remarkable consistency. Such demands, however, tend to be more refined than in the past. Relatively few claims are made—at least, in polite company—that the *racial* inferiority of today's immigrants makes assimilation next to impossible.

The claim that immigrants fail to assimilate has led to two consistent policy responses that often find much political support in the United States. The near-instinctive response has been to call for increased restrictions on immigration and to heighten border enforcement. A second response has been to demand policies that encourage, and at times coerce, immigrants to assimilate into the mainstream.

However, these responses to immigrants' so-called failure to assimilate are inconsistent with the United States's stated commitment to individual rights. As a nation, we take pride in being "the land of the free" and regularly condemn other nations that lack a similar commitment to individual rights. The depth of the commitment of the United States, however, has been placed in serious question throughout U.S. history by the nation's immigration policies and coercive efforts to mandate assimilation into the Anglo norm.

Immigration regulation has led to some of the most regrettable chapters in all of U.S. history. Intolerance, particularly in the form of racism and nativism, has deeply and indelibly influenced U.S. immigration law and policy. To make matters worse, the courts have rarely intervened to halt the raw excesses of the political process. Consequently, periodic waves of harsh exclusions and deportation campaigns dominate the history of immigration law and its enforcement. Restrictionist measures, such as the Chinese exclusion laws, the anti-Semitic national-origins quota system, and sporadic deportation campaigns that targeted Mexican nationals, are monuments to times when anti-immigrant sentiment dominated the political process and carried the day. These sordid chapters in U.S. immigration history are exceedingly difficult to square with the nation's commitment to equality under the law. Few modern defenders attempt to justify them.

Nor are these regrettable episodes simply ancient history. In modern times, the United States continues to use its immigration law and policy to respond to the perceived social problems of the day. Today, many people in the United States view Mexican migration as a serious social problem. Many Americans express the belief that the United States has "lost control" of its borders and that too many immigrants are coming to this country. In 1981, in words echoed often as the twentieth century drew to a close, Attorney General William French Smith told Congress that "[w]e have lost control of our borders. We have pursued unrealistic policies. We have failed to enforce our laws effectively."[3]

The perceived loss of control of the borders exacerbates popular fears about the impacts of immigration. American workers worry about the effects of immigrants on their jobs, wages, and conditions of employment. Fear of cultural and social change also contributes to the disfavor of immigration and immigrants. Fiscal concerns help generate frustration and unhappiness at the state and local levels, where governments provide an elementary and secondary school education to immigrant children, offer emergency services to immigrant communities, and enforce the criminal and other laws that protect all residents.

The 1990s saw nothing less than a momentous shift toward aggressive immigration enforcement in the United States. Border enforcement became one of the nation's highest priorities and received great increases in funding. Greater immigration enforcement was consistent with the tough stance on crime adopted by the Democratic president Bill Clinton, which included congressional passage of a comprehensive crime bill that, among other things, authorized the imposition under federal law of the death penalty for certain felonies.

In 1996, Congress enthusiastically joined the fray. Bent on curbing undocumented immigration, deporting criminal aliens, protecting the nation from terrorists, and guarding the public fisc, Congress passed a series of "get tough on immigrant" laws.[4] Detention of many aliens became mandatory, with the number of immigrants detained increasing dramatically in local jails, federal penitentiaries, and privately run detention facilities. "Criminal aliens," the vast majority from Mexico and Central America, have been detained and deported in record numbers since 1996.[5] The U.S. government vigorously enforced the 1996 reforms with little regard for the rights of immigrants.[6]

Congress also in 1996 greatly expanded the definition of "terrorist activity" that could subject a noncitizen to deportation and other immigration consequences. An apparatus, including a procedure for holding secret evidence hearings, was established to fight terrorism. It was fortified and expanded by the U.S. Congress in the form of the USA PATRIOT Act,[7] increased funding, and other laws and regulations affording the Executive Branch even greater authority to act in the name of national security. Many of the immigrants adversely affected in the "war on terror" were people of color, which historically has been the case with immigration responses to the perceived crisis of the day.

The antiterrorism policies after September 11, 2001, dramatically— and negatively—affected the civil rights of immigrants in the United States. Muslims and Arab communities in particular have been under siege. They have been targeted for arrest, detention, and interrogation. They face an entire array of onerous immigration requirements that target individuals on the basis of racial, national-origin, and religious profiles rather than any specific suspicion of wrongdoing by the individual. As government effectively labeled them terror suspects and, thus, enemies of the United States, hate crimes against Arabs, Muslims, and others followed in the wake of the government's frequently proclaimed "war on terror."[8]

Other immigrant groups have also suffered the ripple effects of the "war on terror." Immigrants generally were adversely affected. The deportation of Mexican and Central American immigrants, which had increased to record levels after the 1996 immigration reform measures kicked in, escalated dramatically in the days after September 11, 2001.[9] Nor were the harsh immigration policies something that emerged only after that fateful day.

The United States has historically excluded disfavored groups from its shores. In the early days of the Republic, political dissidents were punished with impunity through the Alien and Sedition Acts. During the Red Scare after World War I and the McCarthy era of the 1950s, any communist sympathy of the loosest variety could result in the deportation of a hapless noncitizen, even a long-term resident. In one such case, a long-term lawful permanent resident faced the prospect of indefinite detention on Ellis Island because of his allegedly communist sympathies. The flimsy evidence initially relied on by the U.S. government was not revealed to him; as it turned out, there was insufficient evidence to support the government's claim that the noncitizen was a danger to society.[10]

There is nothing more inconsistent with the nation's idyllic and oft-repeated commitment to the "huddled masses" of the world than to bar poor and working immigrants from coming to the United States. But poor and working-class immigrants have been excluded in large numbers from this country for much of U.S. history. The driving force behind their exclusion has been the idea that poor people likely would contribute little to the U.S. economy and might use precious public benefits. The nation therefore simply has no use for them.

The immigration laws have also sought to keep out immigrants who shared characteristics with groups unpopular in the United States. The historical exclusion of women, gay men and lesbians, the disabled, and many other groups have reflected biases in U.S. society generally. Indeed, until 1990, the immigration laws classified homosexuals as "psychopathic personalities" who could be lawfully barred from coming to the United States.

In restricting the admission of undesirable noncitizens, immigration law has been used to systematically maintain the racial demographics of the United States. For much of U.S. history, race has been expressly incorporated into the immigration laws and their enforcement. Laws like the Chinese exclusion laws, the national-origins quota system, which preferred immigrants from northern Europe, and the requirement that an immigrant be "white" to naturalize, which was the law of the land from 1790 until 1952,[11] exemplify this express racial bias. Before 1952, immigrants from Asia who were somehow able to enter the United States still were barred from citizenship, refused full membership in U.S. society, and denied the right to vote. National identity was a primary justification for those measures, as the nation attempted to preserve its predominantly white, Anglo-Saxon, Protestant roots.

At the same time that the nation strived to maintain its whiteness, U.S. society denied the long history of diversity in the United States. Native Americans and African Americans were two large groups of nonwhite residents that were denied acknowledgment, much less full membership in this land. Mexican, Asian, and other minority populations have been kept in the shadows, as well.

The civil rights movement of the 1950s and 1960s in the United States dramatically changed the law in ways completely at odds with the racial exclusions in place in the U.S. immigration laws. The triumph of that movement, and its embrace of the antidiscrimination principle and the accompanying demise of Jim Crow, led Congress to remove expressly race-based exclusions from the immigration laws. The Immigration Act of 1965[12] eliminated the discriminatory national-origins quota system and embraced colorblindness in immigrant admissions. For that reason, the year 1965 is a watershed in U.S. immigration history.

Since 1965, with the abolition of racial exclusions, many more immigrants from Asia have come to the United States than had previously.[13] This "mass migration" has worried restrictionists concerned about maintaining the American way of life—now generally coded in terms of national identity—as well as by those concerned about immigration's impact on labor markets and wages.[14]

Even though the law is colorblind on its face, the modern U.S. immigration laws continue to have discriminatory impacts. People of color from the developing world, especially those from nations that send relatively large numbers of immigrants to the United States, are the most disadvantaged of all groups, especially those of a select few high-immigration nations. They suffer disproportionately from tighter entry requirements and heightened immigration enforcement. For example, under certain visa categories, many noncitizens from India, the Philippines, and Mexico face much longer waits for entry into the United States than similarly situated noncitizens from other nations. Consequently, although there are no express racial limits on immigration to the United

States, disparate racial impacts remain. The disparate impacts of the immigration laws are no surprise to the people affected or to many of the restrictionists who press for immigration reform. In this important way, the tune has changed, but the song remains the same.

U.S. Immigration Law: A Growing List of Undesirables

Until the late 1800s, the United States did not have a comprehensive federal immigration law. From 1776 to 1885, various states attempted to regulate the migration of certain people, particularly criminals and the poor, into their territories.[15] Even so, there was nothing in place like the massive immigration bureaucracy, with its complex set of admission, exclusion, and deportation criteria, that exists in the United States today. The liberal admissions system worked fairly well. With the help of a steady stream of immigrants, settlement and the development of the United States progressed steadily over the course of the nineteenth century.

Near the tail end of the nineteenth century, however, a severe economic downturn triggered great concern about immigration from China to the West Coast. Chinese immigrants stood accused of taking jobs from U.S. citizens in the late 1800s, engaging in rampant crime, and generally debasing the "American" way of life. Fanned by economic uncertainty, racism led to passage of a series of laws known as the Chinese exclusion acts.

Since these first federal immigration laws, immigration has been the subject of exclusive and extensive federal regulation that has removed control of immigration from the states. The rationale for federal preemption of the field is that immigration has foreign relations, national security, and other distinctly national impacts that require uniform federal rather than piecemeal, state-by-state regulation. Nevertheless, the states, such as California, have at various times sought to regulate immigration, often through policies directed at immigrants living in their jurisdiction. In many instances, the courts have seen through such artifices and halted state efforts to regulate immigration.[16]

Since comprehensive federal immigration came into place in 1875, the United States has had an unbroken history of immigration laws that restrict immigration and attempt to ensure a certain quality standard among immigrants. The Chinese exclusion laws were a series of laws in which Congress sought to restrict admission into the United States. The Chinese, the poor, criminals, prostitutes, and the disabled were among the first would-be immigrants denied entry into the country under federal law. The law labeled these groups as undesirables who, in the eyes of Congress and much of the American public, would hurt the United States if allowed to continue immigrating to this country.

The grounds for exclusion have grown slowly but surely over time. Racial exclusions, such as the original ones that barred the Chinese, expanded quickly. Around the turn of the twentieth century, Congress added Japanese and other Asian immigrants to the list of noncitizens barred from the United States. But it did not stop with immigrants from Asia. In 1924, Congress imposed strict national-origin quotas on southern and eastern Europeans because of the belief, supported by reports produced by the Dillingham Commission (named after its chair, Senator Walter Dillingham)[17] that those immigrants were racially inferior. Through the quota system, Congress sought to restore the racial demographics of the United States as of 1890, a time before the large flow of southern and eastern European immigrants into the country. Anti-Semitism, along with other prejudices, unfortunately influenced Congress in the enactment of those discriminatory laws.

The judiciary has rolled over time and time again to the whims of Congress and has posed no obstacle to Congress's passing of discriminatory immigration laws. In 1889, the Supreme Court refused to disturb one of the first of the Chinese exclusion laws. In fact, the Court did precisely the opposite by making any legal challenge to the substantive admission criteria for immigrants next to impossible. It created out of whole cloth the "plenary power" doctrine, a form of which also shields from judicial scrutiny laws that affect Indian tribes and residents of U.S. territories (such as Puerto Rico), immunizing the substantive immigration laws from review by the courts. The *Chinese Exclusion Case,* which the Supreme Court has not overruled to this day, held that the political branches of the federal government have the unfettered discretion—denominated "plenary power"—to act in the field of immigration. The Court emphasized unconditionally that Congress's judgment is "conclusive on the judiciary."[18]

The lack of any judicial check on the excesses of Congress left the issue of immigration, and the fate of noncitizens, firmly in the hands of the political process, where immigrants were not represented and not infrequently were demonized and punished. Not surprisingly, political solutions to the racism in the U.S. immigration laws were slow in coming. Racial restrictions on immigration remained in place for decades and deeply affected the racial demographics of the United States. Similarly, the exclusion of political dissidents, the poor, homosexuals, and others also affected the characteristics of today's population in tangible ways. The composition of the United States today would be very different if discriminatory restrictions had not been in place for nearly a century.

The Immigration and Nationality Act (INA), which has been amended almost annually since its passage in 1952,[19] is the comprehensive federal law that currently regulates immigration into the United States. A product of the Cold War, a fervently anticommunist time in U.S. history, the law is not particularly generous to immigrants. Although parts have been improved over the past fifty years, the INA still reflects a deep suspicion of each and every immigrant seeking admission into the United States. The firm presumption under the INA is that noncitizens are not eligible to enter the United States unless they prove that they are admissible under the law.[20] Consequently, when seeking admission, prospective immigrants bear the burden of proving that they satisfy each of the requirements for an immigrant visa.[21]

A similar skepticism exists about noncitizens seeking to temporarily visit the United States for a vacation, business, or some other reason. The rebuttable presumption is that any noncitizen seeking a nonimmigrant (temporary) visa, such as a business, tourist, or student visa, is lying and is, in fact, an immigrant seeking permanent residence in this country. Unless the presumption is rebutted, such visitors must satisfy the more rigorous requirements for an immigrant visa.[22] All told, the immigration laws presume that, absent an affirmative showing to the contrary, a noncitizen is inadmissible and should be barred from entering the United States. The INA's presumption that a noncitizen is not legally entitled to enter the country is based on the assumptions that entry is a scarce and precious resource, that entry in fact can be substantially restricted and limited, and that, generally speaking, the fewer immigrants admitted into the country the better.

As later chapters demonstrate, the entry of migrants need not be substantially limited. Economic and other benefits may accrue to the nation from a system of liberal admission of noncitizens. Nor, as the U.S. experience with Mexican migration over the past fifty years demonstrates, may it even be possible in modern times, marked by the increased integration of the world economy, improved travel, and the Internet, to narrowly restrict admission in the way that the U.S. immigration laws attempt to do and that many restrictionists advocate.

Besides facing the barrier of the presumption against potential entrants, a prospective immigrant may fall into one of a lengthy list of exclusions that bar large categories of immigrants from coming into the United States. Racial minorities, the poor, criminals, political dissidents, homosexuals, and other undesirables, have been—and some continue to be—excluded under the immigration laws. Currently, the exclusions under which noncitizens can be denied entry into the country under the Immigration and Nationality Act fit into the following general categories:

1. Health risks
2. Criminal risks
3. Security risks
4. Likely "public charges" (and possible public-benefit recipients)
5. Those who lack labor certification for an employment visa
6. Those guilty of immigration violations
7. Those with document problems
8. Those ineligible for citizenship because, for example, of past political affiliations
9. Aliens previously removed from the country[23]

It makes sense to bar some of these categories of immigrants from entry into the United States. It is reasonable, for instance, to deny admission to those who pose threats to national security and public safety. However, Congress made many of the exclusion categories extraordinarily broad in scope. Consequently, many noncitizens who in fact pose little, if any, safety or other risk of harm if admitted into the United States are barred from entry.

The many exclusions in the immigration laws are difficult to defend in a country that proclaims that it is committed to individual rights and freedoms. Many of the exclusions discriminate against groups that could not be discriminated against if they lived in the United States. States, for example, cannot impede the poor from other states from moving into their jurisdiction. Laws that discriminate against poor and working people are generally disfavored. Consider, however, the "public-charge" exclusion, part of the original federal immigration laws. Today, this exclusion is the substantive ground most frequently invoked by U.S. immigration authorities to deny entry to noncitizens into the country.[24] This exclusion allows the U.S. government to deny admission to any alien who is otherwise eligible for admission (e.g., the relative of a citizen family member) who is "likely at any time to become a public charge."[25] As tightened by Congress in 1996,[26] the public-charge exclusion requires the government to consider the alien's age, health, family status, assets, resources, financial status, and education and skills in determining whether he or she may become a user of public benefits. The sponsor of an immigrant must provide an "affidavit of support" promising to, if necessary, financially support the noncitizen. The sponsor, among other requirements, must "demonstrate[] . . . the means to maintain an annual income equal to at least 125 percent of the Federal poverty line."[27] If the immigrant ultimately does access public benefits, the affidavit can be enforced in the courts and the sponsor required to reimburse the state.[28]

In practice, the public-charge exclusion can have harsh consequences. Several years ago, the elderly grandmother of one of my law students, whose parents had immigrated to the United States from China, sought to come here to visit her children and U.S.-citizen grandchildren in this country. Seeking entry on a temporary tourist visa, she was denied entry as a likely public charge. A State Department consular officer, known colloquially as a "munchkin" because of the position's relative status in the bureaucratic hierarchy, denied the visa application because he concluded that she was "likely . . . to become a public charge." This decision was not subject to review by any court of law.[29] The fear apparently was that the elderly grandmother would come to the United States, remain indefinitely, and seek to secure health and other public benefits, which some critics have claimed to be a problem among elderly Chinese immigrants.[30] As a result, the grandmother lost the last chance to visit her family in the United States before she died.

At its essence, the public-charge exclusion is invoked to bar the poor from immigrating to the United States. Unskilled, elderly, and disabled noncitizens find it most difficult to avoid the public-charge exclusion. As it is enforced, the public-charge exclusion results in thousands of people of color from developing nations being denied entry for no reason other than that they are of modest means or have no relatively wealthy sponsors. Today, immigrants from China, Mexico, the Philippines, and India, for example, face formidable barriers in seeking to obtain entry, given the mere fact that they are from developing countries that lack the income and wealth found in the developed world. Consequently, the persons barred from entry are predominantly people of color from Asia, Africa, and Latin America. The public-charge exclusion thus has racial impacts and tends to screen out more noncitizens of color than white noncitizens. This result, of course, fails to square with America's stated immigration ideal of embracing the "huddled masses."

The United States's focus on limiting immigration and enforcing its borders has carried over to the admission of refugees, many of whom are people of color from the developing world who are fleeing political violence. Individual adjudications of asylum claims have served to greatly limit the number of applications granted. Like the public-charge exclusion, the denial of asylum applications, including those of many noncitizens with plausible claims that they will be persecuted if returned to their homelands, tends to deny access to the United States to many noncitizens of color from the developing world. Race, for example, unquestionably influenced the nation's ungenerous treatment of Haitian refugees in the 1980s and 1990s.[31]

Like the exclusion grounds, the deportation of immigrants from the United States has also had disparate impacts on certain national-origin groups. During the Great Depression of the 1930s, mass deportations of persons of Mexican ancestry, including many U.S. citizens, occurred. In 1954, Operation "Wetback" resulted in the deportation of hundreds of thousands of Mexican workers and their family members. In modern times, the vast majority of persons removed from the country are noncitizens from Latin America. Even though there are many immigrants of other national origins who are just as deportable, those immigrants are not targeted for removal.

The modern debate about undocumented immigrants in the United States tends to focus myopically on Mexican immigrants, even though most estimates are that Mexicans constitute only about 60 percent of the undocumented population in the United States. Since the tragic events of September 11, 2001, Arab and Muslim noncitizens have also been removed from the United States in large numbers, although very few have been shown to have had any connection with terrorism. In fact, noncitizens in general have been deported in record numbers, the vast majority immigrants from Mexico and Central America.

Despite the many exclusion and deportation grounds in the U.S. immigration laws, some segments of the public demand even more restrictions and greater border enforcement. Anti-immigrant activists, buoyed by the stiff laws and policies in place, claim that the U.S. government has failed to enforce the law. By appealing to adherence to the law, they seek to take the moral high ground. The ripple effects can be seen in the hate crimes against Arabs and Muslims that were widespread in many cities throughout the United States after September 11 and in the vigilante groups that have terrorized Mexican migrants along the U.S.-Mexico border for the past decade.

As this suggests, the idea of blaming immigrants for society's stresses is alive and well in the United States. As has happened throughout U.S. history, the most vulnerable—legally and otherwise—group is singled out as the "problem." Attacking the group that has caused the identified problem is viewed as the solution. Few political barriers inhibit the enactment of excessive immigration laws and policies. And, as we have seen, the courts generally are reluctant to intervene.

Nor should this be in the least bit surprising. Time and time again, immigration has proven to be a volatile political issue in the United States. Although the nation often proclaims proudly to be "a nation of immigrants," sporadic outbursts of anti-immigrant sentiment mar its history.[32] As a nation, the United States seems either unable or unwilling to avoid the cyclical grip of nativist outbursts.

In sum, the United States has a long history of excluding and deporting certain categories of undesirable and disfavored immigrants. It also has a long history of restrictionist agitation that fuels calls in the political process to add to the groups excluded from our shores. In important respects, the current restrictionists are not that different from those of previous generations. We apparently have failed to learn the lessons of our immigration history.

The Restrictionist Tradition—Voices of the Left and Right

Throughout U.S. history, restrictionists have regularly made calls to drastically reduce immigration to the United States, claiming that, if the nation did not, it would suffer horrible consequences. Anti-immigrant positions grab the headlines, add sensational flare to Fox News and CNN (Lou Dobbs in particular), and sell tremendously well in bookstores. Often little more than anti-immigrant polemics, the restrictionist tracts tap into a populist concern with immigration and immigrants.

Alarmist books about the evils of immigration have a long, if not illustrious, history. Early in the twentieth century, Madison Grant, in *The Passing of the Great Race, or The Racial Basis of European History* (1916), and Lothrop Stoddard, in *The Rising Tide of Color Against White World-Supremacy* (1920), both titles that betray their appeal to claims of white racial superiority, helped define the national immigration debate.[33] The restrictionist, fervently anti-immigrant reasoning offered by Grant and Stoddard offered intellectual justification for the discriminatory national-origins quota system enacted by Congress in 1924.[34] These laws, which favored immigrants from northern Europe over all others, were unquestionably based on racially discriminatory views and the fervent belief that it was necessary and proper to curtail immigration to ensure white supremacy.

Concerns with the racial composition of the United States links the restrictionists of yesterday and those of today. The past decade has seen a proliferation of best-selling books advocating the need to drastically reduce the current levels of immigration to the United States. Recent bestsellers in the restrictionist genre include Victor Davis Hanson, *Mexifornia: A State of Becoming* (2003);[35] Patrick J. Buchanan, *State of Emergency: The Third World Invasion and Conquest of America* (2006);[36] Patrick J. Buchanan, *Death of the West: How Dying Populations and Immigrant Invasions Imperil Our Country and Civilization* (2002);[37] Michelle Malkin, *Invasion: How America Still Welcomes Terrorists, Criminals, and Other Foreign Menaces to Our Shores* (2002);[38] and Peter Brimelow, *Alien Nation: Common Sense About America's Immigration Disaster* (1995).[39] The titles alone suggest the depth of the antipathy for immigration and immigrants and the ominous "crisis" posed to the United States by those twin evils.

Restrictionist analysis reflects two fundamental errors. First, restrictionists fail to appreciate the lessons of history, specifically that, at any moment in time, racial and other biases often distort the nation's collective views of immigration and immigrants. History demonstrates that the nation is prone to serious and profound errors in judgment in its treatment of immigrants. Second, restrictionists assume, without explanation or much inquiry, that it is possible to close the gates and dramatically restrict immigration to the United States. Both misplaced views deserve critical examination. Samuel Huntington's best-selling 2004 book *Who Are We? The Challenges to America's National Identity*[40] is an appropriate place to begin such a study.

As we have seen, Huntington is far from the first to sound the immigration alarm. However, because he is a respected intellectual—and a Harvard professor—who many believe predicted the conflict between Islam and the Western world that has dominated global politics in the past decade,[41] *Who Are We?* garnered a great deal of public attention upon its release and helped commence a national dialog about immigration and immigration reform that lasted for several years.

Harvard's ivory tower, often thought of as a liberal bastion, has produced a number of epic calls for dramatic immigration reform. In *The Disuniting of America: Reflections on a Multicultural Society*,[42] Professor Huntington's colleague Arthur Schlesinger contends that the multicultural society brought about by immigration is literally tearing the nation apart. Similarly, the Harvard economist George Borjas, himself an immigrant from Cuba, has devoted his career to arguing that too many low-skilled immigrants are coming to the United States and that the immigration laws should be amended to increase the number of skilled immigrants and decrease the number of unskilled ones.[43]

Importantly, commentators of many different political persuasions advocate restrictionist positions. Indeed, at least until relatively recently in his career, Samuel Huntington, who questioned the war in Vietnam, had been viewed as something of a liberal. Some progressives embrace restrictionism in the name of protecting poor, minority, and working U.S. citizens. In this vein, Todd Gitlin, *The Twilight of Common Dreams: Why America Is Wracked by Culture Wars* (1995);[44] Michael Lind, *Next American Nation: The New Nationalism and the Fourth American Revolution* (1996);[45] and Roy Beck, *The Case Against Immigration: The Moral, Economic, Social, and Environmental Reasons for Reducing U.S. Immigration Back to Traditional Levels* (1996)[46] all contend that immigrants undercut the wage scale and that domestic racial minorities, and working people generally, would benefit from dramatic reductions in immigration.

Like past restrictionists, Samuel Huntington contends that timing makes his call for immigration restrictions different from those of the past. For Huntington, the United States today faces a national immigration crisis. Throughout the 1990s, many observers, including Huntington, expressed concern about the changes that had swept the nation due to immigration and the emergence of a truly multiracial, multicultural nation.[47] Such concerns are deeply intertwined with domestic unhappiness with the "excesses" of the civil rights movement, such as affirmative action, identity politics, and a growing racial consciousness among the nation's minorities.

With the events of September 11, 2001, public fears over immigration escalated dramatically. Immigration law is known for the remarkably vast powers delegated to the Executive Branch and to Congress. It became the focal point of the nation's domestic war on terror. In light of the fact that noncitizens were responsible for the horrible death and destruction of September 11, this, to a certain extent, is understandable. Many observers, however, believe that the federal government went overboard in its response, sacrificing the civil rights of many Arab and Muslim noncitizens, as well as many others, with minimal, if any, gains to national security.[48] Protests over the excessive surveillance powers given to the federal government by the USA PATRIOT Act, for example, resulted in changes before Congress agreed to reauthorize a narrower version of the law, in 2006.[49]

Relying on the types of arguments made by the modern restrictionists, anti-immigrant groups agitate for severe reductions in the current levels of immigration. Some promote hate as well as immigration restrictions, such as the so-called American Patrol, with its inflammatory Web site.[50] American Patrol seeks to dramatically reduce levels of immigration and viciously attacks immigrants, especially those from Mexico. The rhetoric used by such groups, including the Minuteman Project, which early in the twenty-first century emerged as the most publicly visible anti-immigrant group, often thinly veils deep racial antipathy toward Mexican immigrants, if not outright challenges to the rights of all Mexican-Americans.

Restrictionist calls are premised on the fundamental idea that it is permissible, desirable, and necessary to restrict immigration into the United States. They fail to recognize that powerful social, political, and economic forces bring immigrants to this country, a land of remarkable economic, social, and political opportunity. These forces have proven time and again to be difficult to thwart through immigration enforcement alone, especially enforcement that is at all consistent with American conceptions of individual rights. Indeed, even though the United States greatly fortified its border with Mexico during the 1990s and even though the events of September 11, 2001, led to further increased border fortifications and monitoring, we have seen an *increase* in the undocumented immigrant population in the United States, which currently is estimated to be around 12 million people.[51]

A Modern Nativist: Old Wine, New Bottles?

In his provocative book *Who Are We? The Challenges to America's National Identity*, Samuel Huntington expresses his fear that the increasingly multicultural United States could disintegrate into the type of ethnic strife that destroyed the former Yugoslavia in the 1990s or that, in less dramatic fashion, divided Quebec for much of the twentieth century. Forming a cohesive national identity with a heterogeneous population is a formidable task and critically important to the future of the United States. In the hopes of securing a cohesive national identity, however, Huntington advocates steps that would ensure a more racially and culturally homogeneous nation.

Huntington identifies and analyzes a perceived loss of national identity in the United States at the twentieth century, during roughly the same period that the civil rights revolution forever changed the nation. He sounds a familiar—if not tired—alarm that immigration and immigrant law and policy are out of control and must be reformed. Concerned about the impacts of immigrants—specifically Mexican immigrants—on the United States, its culture, and, most fundamentally, the "American" way of life, Huntington sees immigration and immigrants as transforming a white Anglo-Saxon cultural nation. He fears what he sees on the horizon for the United States, which he suggests is something apocryphal, raising the specter of the fall of Rome.[52] In expressing such fears, Huntington highlights the relationship between immigration and national identity. He sees the identity of the United States changing slowly but surely for the worse as new and different—culturally and otherwise—immigrants are coming in large numbers to the United States.

Huntington is undoubtedly correct that national identity is central to the discussion of immigration and immigrants and that the race and culture of immigrants are important to the effects of immigration on the nation. Immigration, as it has done throughout U.S. history, is changing the literal and figurative face of the nation. Moreover, immigration law and its enforcement deeply affect domestic minority communities and civil rights in the United States.[53] Because of the racial foundations of immigration enforcement, a crackdown on Mexican immigration, for example, likely will affect U.S. citizens of Mexican ancestry. The difficult question is what should be done to respond to the changes to U.S. society brought by immigration.

When analyzing *Who Are We?*, one sees that Huntington's prescription of immigrant assimilation and the end of any racial and ethnic consciousness is a more general critique of identity politics and, at its core, a head-on challenge to multiculturalism. He worries about the racial changes to U.S. society. He leaves little doubt that he deeply disagrees with the national embrace of multiculturalism and tolerance toward all cultures and peoples.

However, Huntington's prescriptions for closing the border and demanding immigrant assimilation are just not realistic. Immigration has contributed to the multiracial, multicultural nature of the United States and has thus transformed the nation and its civil rights agenda.[54] True, if we hope to avoid potential unrest from those who oppose the transformations taking place, we as a nation cannot ignore the impacts of immigration on national identity, race, and civil rights. Vigilante groups in Arizona threaten to use violence to enforce the immigration laws[55] even as immigrants resist efforts at forced assimilation, deportation, and other actions that adversely impact their communities. With the marches in spring 2006 protesting punitive immigration reform proposals, we see popular resistance to harsh immigration reform proposals at perhaps an all-time high.

The integration of immigrants into the political, social, and economic fabric of the United States undisputedly warrants the careful attention of academics and policymakers. Law and policy should strive to foster integration of immigrants into U.S. society, for example, by seeking to eliminate the immigrant caste structure in the labor market. Unfortunately, the law, in a variety of ways, has often contributed to the development of a secondary labor market that offers separate, dead-end jobs to undocumented immigrants and that operates absent almost any legal regulation.

Chapter 4 of this book outlines how immigration law helps to create a dual labor market, with one set of low-wage jobs with few rights reserved for undocumented immigrants and another set of jobs with better wages and conditions and more labor rights for U.S. citizens. To this end, the Supreme Court has held that undocumented immigrants cannot recover back pay for an employer's flagrant violation of federal labor law, including firing a worker for trying to organize a union.[56] Such distinctions between the legal rights of undocumented immigrants and those of citizens thwart, not facilitate, their assimilation into American social life. The law in this instance effectively encourages employers to hire undocumented workers and exploit them in the workplace.

One can acknowledge the changes brought by immigration, proclaim the need for the assimilation of immigrants, and, at the same time, offer more constructive approaches than the alarm, pessimism, and negativity evident in *Who Are We?*[57] Like most restrictionist tracts, it is a book of deep gloom and doom.[58] It offers a general critique of the immigration status quo and a sweeping endorsement of efforts to reduce immigration at almost any cost. To make matters worse, Samuel Huntington's book is surprisingly slim on concrete policy recommendations that have any chance of success.[59]

Another glaring weakness of *Who Are We?*, as well as of most other restrictionist works, is that it wholly overlooks the *positive* impacts of immigration and immigrants. Consequently, Huntington's study resembles a cost-benefit analysis that focuses exclusively on costs and accounts for none of the benefits. Such a one-sided analysis does little to move the analytical ball forward in the immigration debate.

Huntington fails to understand that immigration is a function of complex economic, social, and political pressures that are not wholly within any one nation's sovereign control. As later chapters in this book contend, closed borders are simply not a policy option in the United States today. Nor, in light of the modern civil rights consciousness, are blanket prohibitions on the immigration of certain races or national origins generally viable. Indeed, the various national-origin, religious, and other profiling measures utilized by the federal government in the "war on terror"—with national security perhaps the most compelling justification for such measures—provoked considerable controversy and remain deeply controversial.[60]

The Specific Fear: The Immigration of Mexicans

The most controversial part of Samuel Huntington's book is his treatment of immigration and immigrants from Mexico, the true focal point of the modern public debate over immigration. He unequivocally proclaims that immigration from Mexico is a threat to the national identity and national unity.[61] Huntington views Mexican immigration as particularly dangerous because of the unique relationship between Mexican immigrants and the United States. He further asserts that Mexican immigrants are different from other immigrant groups because of the proximity of Mexico to the United States, the number of immigrants, legal and undocumented, from Mexico, the regional concentration of Mexican immigrants in the Southwest, the persistence of high levels of immigration from Mexico, and the historical claim of persons from Mexico to U.S. territory.[62]

Huntington perhaps deserves credit for making explicit something that is ordinarily an unstated undercurrent to the modern debate over immigration. Public concern with immigration in the United States often translates into a concern with the immigration of people from Mexico. Anti-Mexican sentiment is seen more frequently—and clearly—in local political battles over immigration and immigrants than on the national political stage. There, of course, is also a concern with the migration of terrorists to the country, especially after September 11, 2001. However, a recurring fear about immigration to the United States has focused on the changing racial demographics of the nation resulting from the fact that today's immigrant stream is made up of many immigrants from Mexico. Indeed, the public often considers immigration, especially undocumented immigration, to be an exclusively Mexican phenomenon, which is far from the case.

Samuel Huntington views Mexican immigrants as nothing less than a dire threat to the security of the United States. Their residence in this country directly places our national identity into question. The claim is that there are simply too many Mexicans immigrating to the United States; they are ruining the nation and, consequently, their immigration must be curtailed. When Huntington previewed his rant on Mexican immigration in a magazine article before release of the book,[63] it provoked a firestorm of controversy.[64] But it is an all-too-common gambit, adopted expressly in recent years by Victor David Hanson in *Mexifornia* and Peter Brimelow in *Alien Nation*.[65]

Unlike past restrictionists, however, many of whom focused on the *race* of the immigrants of the day, Huntington ostensibly grounds his concerns in the changes caused by Mexican immigrants to the nation's *culture*. He places particular emphasis on language (Spanish rather than English) and religion (Catholic rather than Protestant). In certain circumstances, however, language and religion serve as convenient proxies for race and national origin. Thus, even if Huntington says that his positions on immigration are not racist, his cultural arguments can be relied on by those with racist sympathies and those motivated to act on the basis of more subtle racial fears. Moreover, restrictionist laws and policies that pursue his cultural ends can be expected to have disparate racial impacts.

Chapter 9 of *Who Are We?* is titled "Mexican Immigration and His-panization." It begins with the conclusion that "[i]n the late twentieth century, developments occurred that, if continued, could change America into a culturally bifurcated Anglo-Hispanic society with two national languages."[66] Huntington invokes fears of the possible "reconquista" (reconquest) of the Southwest and the territory ceded by Mexico to the United States at the end of the U.S.-Mexican War in 1848.[67] This separatist nightmare, an all-too-common trope in the restrictionist literature, is little more than a red herring. Still, because it is invoked time and time again by restrictionists attempting to strike fear into the hearts of the masses, the claim that Mexican immigrants seek to reconquer the Southwest is worth discussing.

The truth of the matter is that virtually nobody believes that a separate Mexican nation will emerge from the Southwest. Years ago, Chicana/o Studies activists envisioned the *symbolic* Aztlán as part of the reemergence of Chicana/os from the shadows of American social life. However, actual secession from the United States is not the true goal of Chicana/o leaders or of most Chicana/os in the United States. Most Mexican-Americans and Mexican immigrants have not even heard of Aztlán. Most Mexican-Americans enthusiastically embrace the United States and are truly American. Many immigrants left Mexico because of their unhappiness there and, as they say, voted with their feet. In any event, a new independent Chicana/o nation in the Southwest of the United States is just not in the cards. Ironically enough, the alleged "reconquista" is much more likely to be discussed today among restrictionists rather than among Chicana/o activists.

Samuel Huntington also fears the development of a strong group identity among Latina/os. He worries about the ethnic enclaves that flourish in certain parts of the country, such as Miami and parts of the Southwest, in which Spanish is the dominant language. Over the past fifty years, there has been a linguistic, cultural, and demographic transformation of parts of the United States. Huntington presents some data that suggest that Mexican immigrants lag in English language acquisition, educational attainment, occupation and income, and naturalization rates.[68] However, he presents few of the existing data to the contrary.

Moreover, Huntington fails to recognize the emerging literature on segmented assimilation, that is, the slow assimilation facilitated by initial settlement by immigrants in welcoming and supportive immigrant communities as they ease their way into U.S. social life.[69] This means that, even if migrants and their families initially settle in communities where their native language predominates, they will increasingly learn English over time.

Contrary to the claim that a separatist Mexican nation is emerging in this country, *all* immigrants do in fact assimilate to a certain degree into U.S. social life. The available empirical evidence shows that, in the aggregate, immigrants from all nations, including Mexico, overwhelmingly participate in the labor market, learn English, are firmly committed to family, and participate in community life in ways comparable to those of other Americans. This is not surprising, given that most immigrants come to the United States because they embrace American political values and economic freedoms, especially the fundamental rights that many U.S. citizens take for granted.

Huntington accuses Latina/o immigrants in the United States of refusing to learn English as if it were a crime.[70] Yet, about 93 percent of all Mexican immigrants agree that residents of the United States should learn English.[71] Knowledge of English remains an economic necessity in this country, especially for the ambitious person seeking economic opportunity and upward mobility. Spanish-speaking immigrants usually read English fluently within ten years.[72] Those immigrants who have been in the country for fifteen years regularly speak English.[73]

None of this should be taken as suggesting that stresses and tensions do not result from immigration and the presence of newcomers, Mexican and otherwise, in the community. The times in which we live suggest otherwise. Immigrants do not integrate into the mainstream instantly. The integration process is not without individual and social stresses. Nevertheless, the integration of immigrants into U.S. society has generally prevailed over the generations.

Consequently, any suggestion that aggressive efforts must be made to curtail Mexican immigration and that mandatory assimilation programs are necessary to destroy Mexican culture and cabin Catholicism and to force Mexican immigrants to embrace Protestant values is misplaced. Change brought by immigration, as well as cultural change generally, is normal and something that simply cannot be halted in its tracks by severely reducing immigration or mandating "being American."

To further complicate matters, it is left unsaid what Huntington would have immigrants assimilate to, what exactly "being American" means. Despite Huntington's endorsement of Anglo culture, there is no cookie-cutter American. The American in Baton Rouge, Louisiana, is very different, culturally and otherwise, from the American in Cambridge, Massachusetts.

Ultimately, Huntington's account fails to appreciate some fundamental lessons of U.S. history. Assimilation of immigrants has persistently been viewed as reflecting a problem with the immigrants of any particular period. Early in this nation's history, for example, the claim was that German and Irish immigrants were racially inferior and refused to assimilate into mainstream U.S. society. Complaints about German and Irish immigrants were later replaced by similar complaints about Chinese, Japanese, and southern and eastern European immigrants: They were deemed to be racially inferior and accused of steadfastly refusing to assimilate into mainstream U.S. society. These claims were buttressed by the assertion that the current cohort of immigrants differed from the previous group for a variety of reasons. In hindsight, many of these groups have successfully integrated into American social life. Most informed observers understand past efforts to limit the immigration of "unassimilable" persons as unfortunate mistakes that mar this nation's proud history.

In many respects, today's immigrants are not all that different from those of past generations. Indeed, given the dissemination of U.S. culture throughout the world, immigrants in the twenty-first century may be better equipped to assimilate than past immigrants in our history. Ease of travel and the technology of the information age make it more likely that individuals will immigrate with previous experience with American society (possibly even a visit or visits to the United States) and a better understanding of this country and its people, culture, and traditions.[74]

Nonetheless, the fact that many immigrants to the United States are people of color—and much more racially diverse than those of the past—complicates matters considerably. That difference arguably makes true integration into American social life more difficult than it was for most groups of white immigrants. In addition, although not all immigrants from Mexico are poor and unskilled, many are.[75] This makes their economic integration into U.S. society somewhat more difficult.

In evaluating the meaning of Latina/o identity for the future of the United States, Samuel Huntington appears firmly wedded to the past and the unified national identity that he believes once existed in the United States. He worries about the splintered national identity and longs for the cohesive, English-speaking, predominantly Protestant nation that existed before the monumental civil rights changes of the twentieth century. Part of that healthy Anglo identity rested on beliefs in racial superiority and the suppression of minority groups. Huntington is not calmed by the post–September 11 reaction of the people of the United States and the wave of patriotism that swept the country.

Alternatively, if there is a concern with ethnic separatism, the question is what can be done to fully integrate immigrants into society. This task desperately needs the nation's attention. Integration requires affirmative laws and policies that facilitate immigrant assimilation, not laws that seek to halt increased racial diversity by stopping immigration in its tracks. While ignoring the former, Samuel Huntington seems to endorse the latter.

Huntington's claim that Mexicans "fail to assimilate" lacks an appreciation for the complexities of measuring integration into society. Consider one example. In arguing that Mexican immigrants fail to assimilate, Huntington cites dated statistical data about the low naturalization rates of Mexican immigrants.[76] He does not squarely address the increase in naturalization rates in the 1990s, when Mexican immigrants suffered consistent attacks as anti-immigrant laws were enacted and undocumented immigration and immigrants became a heated and divisive political issue in the United States.[77] A careful analysis, for example, might consider whether the uptick in naturalization rates is a sign of increasing integration of Mexican migrants into American social life.[78] Increased naturalization will likely continue for all immigrant groups because the strict measures taken in response to September 11 have struck fear in the hearts of many immigrant communities, not just among Arabs and Muslims.

In a part of the book that does not focus on Mexican immigrants, Huntington refers to increasing naturalization rates and reasonably asks whether it is really advisable for immigrants to naturalize to avoid removal from the country, to ensure access to public benefits, and to be able to vote, rather than out of heartfelt allegiance to the United States.[79] Some might contend that, on the basis of the evidence, the spike in naturalization rates in the 1990s reflected naturalization out of fear in response to the harsh 1996 immigration reforms, rather than out of any affinity for this country. This is an important issue well worth thorough analysis. It is one, however, that Huntington fails to fully investigate.

There is a need to reconsider and revitalize the modern conception of citizenship in an era of globalization. Academics have written on the need to promote a modern form of civic nationalism.[80] However, no one has yet determined a practical way of revitalizing feelings of belonging through citizenship and integrating immigrants into civil society. This endeavor warrants careful consideration, as the integration of immigrants into U.S. society is a problem that is likely to remain with us for the indefinite future. It is integration, not closing the borders, that warrants inquiry.

Ultimately, Samuel Huntington suggests that the problems with immigration and immigrant assimilation would miraculously end with a dramatic reduction of immigration from Mexico. Presumably, debates over contentious issues such as undocumented immigration, bilingual education, and assimilation would simmer down and eventually disappear. But all of this depends on Huntington's implicit assumption that this "silver bullet" of closing the borders is a realistic possibility. To the contrary, however, from all appearances, migration appears to be a fact of life in the modern world.

Specifically, migration from Mexico to the United States has deep and enduring social, political, and economic roots in both nations. There is a long history of migration from Mexico to the United States. The two nations share an expansive land border of thousands of miles in length. Migration across that border has occurred for centuries, at times with the help and encouragement of the U.S. government. Indeed, much of the American Southwest, including large parts of Arizona, New Mexico, California, Utah, and Colorado, were once part of Mexico but changed hands after the U.S. military victory over Mexico in 1848. The long history of migration has created deep and enduring economic and social networks that span national boundaries. Given those networks, the possibility of sealing the U.S.-Mexico border is more a pipedream than a realistic policy outcome. Huntington fails to examine whether stemming the flow of immigration is in fact possible. This omission constitutes a fatal flaw in his only real prescription for reform.

This, of course, raises a more global question. Is immigration, including immigration from Mexico, bad for the United States? Huntington, like restrictionists generally, answers in the affirmative by focusing on its allegedly negative impact on the formation of a national identity and its undermining of the "American" way of life. That argument, as summarized here, is debatable. But, among other things, Huntington, with his exclusive focus on national identity and culture, wholly ignores the economic arguments for freer immigration.[81] As outlined in Chapter 4, many observers credit immigrant labor for contributing to the substantial economic boom in the United States in the 1990s.[82] The benefits of immigration to the U.S. economy warrant further consideration and analysis.

Nor does Huntington fret over the moral consequences of closed borders, the topic of Chapter 3. Indeed, he wholly fails to address the human costs of immigration enforcement directed at Mexican immigrants, who have been subject to extreme immigration policies for decades. Border operations have had nothing less than deadly impacts. Thousands of immigrants—most of them Mexican nationals—have died in the past decade while attempting to journey to the United States across deserts and mountains.[83] This ongoing tragedy continues, with the personal accounts of the death and despair of the migrants nothing less than heartwrenching.[84]

Like most restrictionists, Samuel Huntington suggests the need for a dramatic reduction in the level of immigration because the nation faces, in his view, an unprecedented period of "persistent high levels of immigration."[85] At the same time, however, he admits that the nation has historically adapted to comparable immigration levels.[86] Even if one were to conclude that today's immigrants from Latin America were not assimilating, the real answer would be to fashion law and policy that truly fosters their integration into American social life, not to attempt to close the border. Formulating policies that facilitate the integration of immigrants into U.S. society is where time and effort must be spent. It is an area, however, that restrictionists almost wholly ignore except to criticize as inappropriate because it effectively encourages immigration.

The Need for Assimilation

The United States has historically demanded that immigrants assimilate into the mainstream Anglo-Saxon norm. As we have seen, restrictionists long have claimed that immigrants somehow "fail to assimilate." The same claim has been leveled time and time again against the dominant group of immigrants of the day, whether it be the Irish, the Chinese, the Germans, the Japanese, or the Mexicans.[87]

To Samuel Huntington, the ties that bind the American people are "Anglo Protestant culture,"[88] the "American Creed" (the commitment to a set of political values),[89] and the Christian religion.[90] Assimilation to this core American culture and its values is vitally important to the very survival of the United States. Apparently finding that the proverbial "melting pot" failed to adequately capture what he has in mind, Huntington adds another colorful metaphor that he sees as illustrating the need for immigrant assimilation: "[I]mmigration adds celery, croutons, spices, parsley, and other ingredients that enrich and diversify the taste, but which are absorbed into what remains fundamentally tomato soup."[91] One obviously could take this image in many different directions. However, it is far from certain what it is actually supposed to mean.

In analyzing national identity, Huntington discusses the assimilation of immigrants (or the lack thereof) extensively. He asserts that the United States must reduce immigration to promote and facilitate assimilation, as the nation did in the past. Dual nationality and citizenship, which Huntington believes has discouraged the formation of an American identity among immigrants, should be strongly disfavored.[92]

At a fundamental level, Samuel Huntington seems to praise the immigration laws that have limited racial diversity in the United States, such as the national-origins quota system added in 1924, and embraces them as a model for positive policy today.[93] If replicated today, such measures, he thinks, would help rebuild a cohesive national identity. This unfortunately represents a profound misunderstanding of U.S. immigration history and amounts to nothing more than an endorsement of racial— although he might claim it to be cultural—discrimination toward immigrants. It also implicitly damns citizen minorities in the United States that share similar characteristics as disfavored immigrants.

The Jim Crow–like immigration laws that remained in place until 1965 have few, if any, modern defenders. Such blatant national-origin discrimination is, of course, totally inconsistent with modern notions of civil rights and equality that prevail in the modern United States. Although Samuel Huntington fails to offer any real defense of such discrimination, he intimates, as have past restrictionists, that extreme measures are necessary to save the nation from nothing less than its ruin.

In so doing, Huntington fails to appreciate the practical realities of modern immigration to the United States. One of the conundrums facing proponents of immigrant assimilation is how to deal with the estimated 11 to 12 million undocumented immigrants who live in this country.[94] Undocumented immigrants live and work in this society but exist in a sort of legal never-never land. They are denied basic rights of membership, such as the right to vote, labor protections, and access to the public benefit safety net.[95] This subordinate status helps to generate a virtually never-ending array of hotly debated public policy disputes, such as whether undocumented children should receive a public education, whether undocumented immigrants should be eligible for driver's licenses, and whether undocumented students should be eligible for in-state resident fees at public universities.

The question whether and, if so, how to integrate undocumented immigrants into U.S. society deeply confounds policymakers. In 1986, an amnesty program offered legal resident status to millions of undocumented immigrants.[96] By regularizing their immigration status, the program helped facilitate the legal integration of undocumented immigrants into the mainstream. In order to thwart the growth of a new population of undocumented immigrants, a program was created to sanction employers who employed undocumented workers. The sanctions succeeded in making employers fearful of hiring workers of certain national-origin groups, resulting in discrimination against citizens and lawful immigrants on the basis of national origin. However, they were almost wholly ineffective at stemming the growth of a new population of undocumented immigrants. Consequently, proposals have been on the table for years since the 1986 amnesty to regularize the status of a new, and growing, undocumented immigrant population.[97]

The problem of undocumented immigrants proves especially difficult because the nation must decide how to treat those who are not supposed to be in the country but who unquestionably reside here. An important step in the integration of the current undocumented immigrant population into American social life arguably is the regularization of their immigration status. But, to this point, every effort to regularize the immigration status of undocumented immigrants through amnesty programs has been accompanied by the subsequent growth of a new undocumented immigrant population.

Rather than squarely confront the complexities of the issue of integrating immigrants into American social life, Samuel Huntington chooses to rail against undocumented immigration: "Illegal immigration is . . . a threat to America's societal security. The economic and political forces generating this threat are immense and unrelenting. Nothing comparable has occurred previously in the American experience."[98] He, however, fails to offer much in the way of policy reform. This is a most serious omission. Because one cannot close the borders, the question is how to promote the integration of, and the formation of a cohesive national identity among, millions of undocumented immigrants. This is no small task and requires considerable creativity, ambition, and energy.

Current laws have unquestionably failed to do the trick. The Supreme Court has vacillated on how to treat the undocumented. At times, the Court affords them rights, thus treating them as members of the national community. For example, in *Plyler v. Doe* (1982),[99] the Court invalidated a Texas law that barred undocumented children from attending public schools. The Court ruled that the children could not be denied an elementary and secondary education despite being in this country unlawfully. At other times, however, the Supreme Court has denied undocumented immigrants fundamental labor law protections. In *Hoffman Plastic Compounds, Inc. v. NLRB* (2002),[100] the Court held that undocumented immigrants could not recover back pay despite the employer's undisputed violation of federal labor law. By denying an important labor law remedy to undocumented workers, this decision increased their vulnerability in the workplace. The contrasting cases nicely represent the U.S. Supreme Court's deep legal ambivalence about undocumented immigrants.

Importantly, *Who Are We?* presents immigrant assimilation as all positive. Huntington approaches the process in an antiseptic fashion, with little, if any, sensitivity to the feelings of, or empathy for, the flesh-and-blood people affected by the assimilation process.[101] Little attention, for instance, is paid to the human costs to immigrants who struggle to adapt to a new and foreign society. One is left with the firm impression that Huntington does not really understand or appreciate the immigrant experience. Because of this, he falls into the trap of considering "Americanizing" the immigrant through rose-colored glasses. This, of course, is a problem with the ivory-tower approach to most problems.

Assimilation unquestionably has human costs. It is difficult for immigrants to adjust to a new land, society, culture, and language. They experience differences in nearly every aspect of life in the United States. With massive adjustments in one's way of life come stress and strain. Such turmoil requires support and assistance through law and policy, rather than blanket demands to assimilate. Huntington's failure to account for the integration difficulties faced by immigrants is another serious omission from his analysis but is consistent with his general view that the ends of protecting national identity justify the means, whatever the human costs.

As is true of many restrictionists, Huntington offers an analysis of immigration that is about much more than immigration and immigrants. It touches on the civil rights of all racial minorities and changes to U.S. society. To Huntington, a cohesive national identity has been replaced in the United States by the unrepentant evil of multiculturalism. It is multiculturalism that he fervently believes is destroying the nation he loves: "The deconstructionists promoted programs to enhance the status and influence of subnational racial, ethnic, and cultural groups."[102] Because multiculturalism challenges the nation's core Anglo-Saxon Protestant culture, it is, in his estimation, a danger to the very existence of the United States.

Huntington's analysis demonstrates the serious tensions between assimilation and multiculturalism. In fact, "[a]ssimilationism can be thought of as the mirror image of multiculturalism."[103] Endorsing assimilation in its classic form, Huntington would require adoption of the dominant culture—and he makes it clear that he considers "American" culture to be superior to all others, rejecting race or ethnic consciousness and repudiating the idea of the equal value of cultures. Assimilation is an obligation that must be imposed on all immigrants, with the demand that they assimilate as white European immigrants did in the past. Huntington fails to acknowledge that this is not as easily realized by people of color, who today account for more than 80 percent of the immigrants to the United States.[104] He also fails to acknowledge that his tough-love brand of assimilation has been discredited by scholars for decades.

In the end, Huntington's concern about national identity is not limited to immigration. For example, he is worried about the assimilation of all people of color—citizens and noncitizens alike—into the mainstream. Huntington's concerns with affirmative action, multiculturalism, and language betray much more than a simple concern with immigration and immigrants. This concern, which recurs in the restrictionist literature and rhetoric, is revealing. It suggests that immigration is a convenient scapegoat for the general discomfort with social fissures, such as those related to race and civil rights. At the same time, debates over immigration avoid the hard edge of race. Little is more common in the modern immigration debate than the denial of racism by the proponents of firmly anti-immigrant positions. They can emphasize that noncitizens, aliens, and foreigners, rather than people of color, are the people directly affected. Immigrants, not people of color, are their concern. Because immigration law directly affects racial minorities, its operation affects what we are as a nation and, at bottom, our national identity, with race at its very core.[105]

In an era of Jim Crow and unforgiving assimilationist measures, the United States unquestionably had a more coherent national identity. Huntington longs for the "good old days," while paying little attention to the harsh subordination of minority communities that created the outward appearance of national unity. He completely fails to admit the close relationship between the cohesive national identity and the subordination of racial minorities that the nation embraced for much of its first two centuries of existence.

Samuel Huntington, however, is not entirely ahistorical in his analysis. He acknowledges, in passing, the atrocities committed throughout U.S. history against African Americans, Latina/os, Asians, and other groups.[106] In remembering the halcyon days when the nation enjoyed a cohesive national identity, he mistakenly assumes away the existence of the groups that were denied basic membership in U.S. society and whose group identity was suppressed, at times violently. There is cursory mention of the harsh treatment of African Americans, Latina/os, Native Americans, and Asian Americans in the time of this vibrant and unified national identity. But that national identity, and community among citizens, was based in part on racism, as the community festivities surrounding the lynching of African Americans in early-twentieth-century America grotesquely demonstrate.[107]

However, as revealed by the 1954 U.S. Supreme Court decision in *Brown v. Board of Education*,[108] the nation has undergone a profound change in its racial sensibilities. The end of racially restrictive immigration and nationality laws has contributed to growing diversity and larger communities of people of color in the United States. Modern civil rights sensibilities embrace that diversity and condemn the restrictionist and coercive assimilationist measures of the past. These developments require new approaches to address the important changes and tensions that arise. Put differently, immigration and immigrant law must catch up with modern conceptions of civil rights and equality in the modern United States.

Building a sense of community in a multicultural nation like the United States is a serious and formidable challenge. It is much easier to ensure a unified national identity when a society is not multiracial and multicultural or when minorities are suppressed and subordinated. But suppression has its consequences. As the world sadly watched, the former Yugoslavia exploded in tribal violence and unspeakable bloodshed in the 1990s after its failure to address and manage cleavages caused by ethnic and religious difference and the death of a unifying leader.

Unfortunately, Samuel Huntington does not provide any true insights or answers as to how a national identity can successfully be forged in a multiracial, multicultural United States. Rather, he seems to advocate a return to an idyllic racially and culturally homogeneous nation with a cohesive national identity. This is the classic response—immigration is a problem, we must tighten the borders; immigrants are the problem, make them assimilate. Unfortunately, it fails to appreciate the lessons of history and offers us little in terms of viable policy options. The immigration debate deserves better.

The "Costs" of the Failure to Assimilate and Today's Immigrants

Racial justifications for restricted immigration have a long history. Unfortunately, that history is far from over. In his best-selling restrictionist book, *Alien Nation,* Peter Brimelow contended that immigration undermines the nation's "need for homogeneity"[109] and that "the American nation has always had a specific ethnic core. And that core has been white."[110] Samuel Huntington is more subtle than Brimelow. He hints at the racial foundations of his concerns with immigration but requires the reader to connect the dots.

Huntington notes that "Americans [feel] passionate about race and ethnicity."[111] Many restrictionist works attempt to inflame those passions to help convince the reader to embrace the anti-immigrant agenda. Huntington mentions that anti-immigrant, antiminority movements are a possible response to the changing racial demographics of the nation: "White nativist movements are likely to include people with differing priorities concerning racial balance, 'white' culture, immigration, racial preferences, language, and other issues."[112] Calls for immigration reform regularly have come strongly from, among others, hate groups that have antiminority as well as anti-immigrant sympathies.

However, the possible reaction of whites is not directed just at the growth in the number of immigrants in the United States. Huntington expresses concern not only with immigration but, as we have seen, with identity politics generally. Unless we reform, he warns that whites may react to much more far-reaching changes to American social life. "If blacks and Hispanics organize and lobby for special government-sponsored privileges, why not whites? If the National Association for the Advancement of Colored People and La Raza are legitimate organizations, why not a national organization to promote white interests?"[113]

By raising the specter of racial violence and fanning the flames of racial conflict, Huntington apparently hopes to prod the nation to act. This stance tacitly encourages restrictionists like the vigilantes now patrolling the nation's southern border with Mexico, as well as their sympathizers. The immigration debate deserves greater care and sensitivity.

It is not clear what Huntington hopes to do in raising the specter of a strong, perhaps violent, nativist response to immigrants, except to inflame passions about race and ethnicity. The growth of nativist movements throughout the United States has been well documented.[114] Immigrants, however, are not at fault for this negative reaction. Why should immigrants be punished and criticized for the nativist reaction to their very existence and presence in the United States? Such a result would raise serious concerns about the morality and legitimacy of the law. Giving in to the nativists would allow the xenophobes to dictate policy and abandon immigration law- and policymaking to the extremists. The approach would effectively abandon the rights of immigrants and disavow any national commitment to the "huddled masses."

Alternatively, one could reject the white supremacist attack on immigration and immigrants and view the increasing diversity brought by immigrants as a positive. A diverse work force economically benefits the United States in ways discussed in Chapter 4. As the racial demographics of the country evolve, business managers make innovations in response to the needs of the changing population. Indeed, responding to demographic changes can help increase corporate profits. Commercials with slogans like "se habla español" and advertisements in the Asian Yellow Pages to attract new business must be coupled with the cultivation of a staff that can readily develop a rapport with the new customers. This all means new markets and more business.

More generally, immigrants represent a potential resource for adding and improving American culture. Although the United States continues to be a leader in business, political, scientific, and social innovation, it is not the sole source of innovation in the world. To remain competitive in the world market, we should be open to new ideas from people of different cultures, who may have new and improved ways of approaching business operations, environmental protection, health, stress, interpersonal relations, and education.

In the end, Huntington fails to offer a convincing argument to the cohesive national identity of the past. Cultures slowly but surely change over time. The presence of immigrants influences the ongoing evolution of American culture. As a result, the definition of what an American is changes and expands to embrace differences. Samuel Huntington's stingy definition of national identity tied to white Anglo-Saxon Protestant culture fails to comport with the realities of life in the modern United States. Demographic changes have already occurred and cannot realistically be reversed. The proper question is not how to erase the changes but how we constructively address the conception of national identity in light of those changes.

The Ignorance of the History of Immigration Restrictions and Coerced Assimilation of Mexican Immigrants

Any thoughtful discussion of assimilation must account for the excesses of the assimilationist mandate in U.S. history. A long list of immigrant groups, such as the Irish, the Germans, the Chinese, the Japanese, and the Mexicans, has suffered in similar ways as the nation sought to coerce assimilation. As Samuel Huntington does in his book, the use of the English language often has been viewed as a bellwether for assimilation. At a time of high German immigration to the United States, for example, state and local governments sought to regulate German-language schools out of existence.[115] The Supreme Court struck down Nebraska's World War I–era law that criminalized the teaching of German in the public schools.[116]

The painful history of the efforts to forcibly assimilate Mexican immigrants through most of the twentieth century reveals the risks of the prescriptions of the modern restrictionists. Historically, immigrants from Mexico have faced a series of restrictionist immigration measures designed to limit their numbers in the United States. Unlike the outright exclusion of immigrants from Asia, however, constraints on immigration from Mexico were not imposed through racial bars. Instead, a variety of exclusion grounds historically has served to limit Mexican migration to the United States.

In the twentieth century, concern with immigration from Mexico ebbed and flowed. Immigration from Mexico and the perceived refusal of Mexican immigrants to assimilate often contributed to a negative public reaction to immigration. In the early part of the twentieth century, immigration from Mexico during and after the Mexican revolution sparked concerns. Increased border enforcement culminated in the creation of the Border Patrol, which replaced the Texas Rangers, the group charged with enforcing the nation's southern border with Mexico.[117] In addition, aggressive efforts were made to assimilate immigrants. In the 1920s, for example, full-fledged assimilation campaigns were directed at persons of Mexican ancestry.[118] These campaigns focused on teaching American ways to Mexican women, who were believed to run the households. Mexican women received instruction on such things as why rice and beans were *not* part of a healthy American diet.

The assimilation campaigns, however, were far from effective at truly integrating Mexican immigrants into U.S. society. The Great Depression saw an upswing in public concern with Mexican-Americans and Mexican immigrants because of their alleged use of public benefits and their taking of "American" jobs. Local officials, with the encouragement and assistance of the federal government, sought to remove Mexican immigrants from the country. An estimated 1 million persons of Mexican ancestry, roughly two-thirds of whom were U.S. citizens by birth, were "repatriated" to Mexico.[119] Although it would be a clear violation of international law today, this ethnic cleansing of the Great Depression failed to generate much of a public response in the 1930s.

Episodes of anti-Mexican hysteria continued to be common throughout the twentieth century in the United States. Racial tensions increased during World War II, when many persons of Mexican ancestry, including many immigrants, and African Americans moved to urban areas in pursuit of jobs to aid in the war effort. As the established and new populations interacted, tempers at times flared. The "Zoot Suit" riots in Los Angeles were in fact race riots between Anglo servicemen and Mexican-Americans, triggered when young men of color adopted a cultural stance in opposition to that of the mainstream.[120]

Beginning in World War II and lasting until the 1960s, the Bracero Program brought Mexican guest workers to the United States to work in U.S. agriculture. Once here, these workers were exploited in violation of the law.[121] Even though the braceros were invited "guests," fears of a brown "invasion" grew with their presence. In 1954, the federal government implemented "Operation Wetback," which resulted in the removal of tens of thousands of persons of Mexican ancestry from the United States.[122]

Public concern with undocumented immigration escalated again in the 1970s and 1980s, reaching a fever pitch in the mid-1990s.[123] In the early 1990s, Mexican immigrants were accused of, among other things, overconsuming public benefits, taking jobs from Americans, committing crimes, speaking Spanish, and living in separate ethnic enclaves.[124] Against a backdrop of racial antipathy, voters in 1994 overwhelmingly passed California's infamous Proposition 187. This measure was designed to reduce immigration from Mexico by, among other things, denying undocumented children access to a public school education, making undocumented immigrants ineligible for public benefits, and otherwise punishing the undocumented.[125] About a decade later, after a heated campaign similar to the one that prevailed in California, Arizona voters passed a similar law.[126]

There is one critical difference between the old days and today that make pro-assimilation policies more difficult to implement. The policies pursued to compel the assimilation of persons of Mexican ancestry— U.S. citizens as well as immigrants—were much easier to develop and implement in a time when the sense of racial and cultural identity among minority groups was much more diluted than it is today. Forced assimilation, which pressured many persons of Mexican ancestry to adopt a Spanish—and unquestionably white—identity, was far easier in a time when racial and ethnic pride were nonexistent.[127] The positive Chicana/o identity that emerged in the 1960s, and that flourishes today,[128] makes stringent efforts to coerce assimilation more likely to encounter resistance in modern times.

In any event, efforts to assimilate persons of Mexican ancestry failed to fully incorporate them into U.S. society. Indeed, the assimilationist policies of the past had a sort of boomerang effect that helped forge a community among Latina/o immigrants. Indeed, coerced assimilation, combined with widespread discrimination, helped create a Latina/o identity. The modern debate over immigration possesses many of the same qualities.[129] Language regulation, for example, is an issue of Latina/o concern even though most Latina/os in the United States speak English. The language wars represent a venue for Latina/os to fight for status with Anglos in the United States.[130] Hot-button issues such as immigration often reveal deeper conflicts between Anglos and Mexicans over social status in the modern United States.

The United States must accept and learn from the history of immigration restrictions and counterproductive coerced-assimilation policies. Samuel Huntington has not. The time could not be more ideal for a new response to the perceived problems with the assimilation of immigrants. As a nation, we must not continue swimming against the currents bringing immigrants to the United States and must instead formulate laws that in fact regulate and permit immigration consistent with the practical realities.

The Response to the New Nativists

In his book *Who Are We?*, Samuel Huntington argues for immigration restrictions to reduce migration from Mexico. However, the civil rights revolution has shaped Huntington's arguments, rendering his position significantly different from that of many past restrictionists. Explicit racism has for the most part been driven underground. Huntington expressly denies reliance on *race* and focuses on the *culture* of today's immigrants. This is a distinctive change from the approach of pre-1960s restrictionists. Although this represents an improvement of sorts in the public debate over immigration, it may well be more dangerous. Neutral laws carry the mantle of legitimacy that renders them less vulnerable to a legal challenge. This allows racism to silently but surely influence the entire immigration debate.

Part of the solution suggested by the modern restrictionists is to exclude from the country immigrants believed to be responsible for contributing to greater national disunity. Like the public in general and policymakers, restrictionists assume that immigration restrictions and greater border enforcement can put an end to the flow of immigrants. There is little evidence that this is the case, however. A topic of later chapters, the ineffective nature of U.S. border enforcement, even after the tragedy of September 11, 2001, suggests that social, economic, and political pressures have much more impact on the immigration flow than border enforcement.

Suppose one acted on the view that Mexican immigrants constituted a special problem, that their entry into the United States should be limited, and that assimilation should be demanded of any and all immigrants in the United States. Such policies are destined to fail. Indeed, this country has a long tradition of failing to accomplish such goals. As we have seen, the U.S. government invoked the public-charge exclusion to bar the entry of many Mexican immigrants in a time when racial exclusions did not apply to immigrants from Mexico.[131] More recently, the federal government massively ramped up the border enforcement along the southern border with Mexico. Despite these measures, the Mexican immigrant population in the United States has grown consistently and substantially.

Moreover, exclusionary measures have significant collateral consequences. Besides unfairly discriminating against certain groups of immigrants, the exclusions stigmatize and harm domestic groups that share the same characteristics as the persons excluded.[132] With the alleged goal of reducing social tensions, efforts have been made over the course of U.S. history to exclude immigrants from certain nations, including Chinese, Japanese, and Mexican immigrants.[133] Because of fears of their negative impacts on the nation, the poor, criminals, political dissidents, women, and gays and lesbians also have been denied access to the United States.[134] By sending the messages that these groups are undesirable, the exclusions help to further marginalize these disfavored groups in American social life.

In a post-civil-rights-era world, it is far from self-evident that we can recapture the American national identity of the 1950s, assuming that we would want to do so. Racial minorities are no longer willing to be ignored, have their cultures denigrated, or accept mandatory assimilation. It would also be difficult to convince the nation as a whole that such policies were consistent with modern civil rights sensibilities. Consequently, given the nation's embrace of a civil rights consciousness and multiculturalism, a return to the racially—even if labeled as culturally—restrictive immigration laws of the past would create nothing less than a national uproar. The same is true of other restrictions, such as ideological litmus tests for admission and the blanket ban on the admission of homosexuals.

Restrictionists are undoubtedly correct about the need for immigration reform.[135] However, as we strive to formulate realistic reform proposals, the economic and social pressures that fuel immigration cannot be ignored. The truth of the matter is that closing the borders is simply not realistic in twenty-first-century America. Nor should the nation respond to the calls of restrictionists like Samuel Huntington. Fortunately, the United States is not ready or willing to adopt the types of policies used at the border of the former East Germany to keep migrants from entering. Machine guns and the killing of border crossers simply cannot be the solution. The true challenge, which is a formidable one, is to come up with a rational system that allows for the effective management of the flow of migrants into the United States and is consistent with the nation's constitutional values.

A broad-based solution to immigration between the United States and Mexico seems in order—or at least worth discussing, analyzing, and criticizing. Immediately before September 11, a possible migration accord between the two nations was on the table. However, as the events of that day shifted the nation's focus from immigration liberalization to border security, the accord evaporated.[136] Given that migration from Mexico continues, renewed talks about cooperation between the United States and Mexican governments are necessary.

Economic development of Mexico is another way to decrease migration pressures. A better economy, with more economic opportunities for Mexican citizens, would tend to reduce the impetus for much labor migration. The Mexican economy is growing, and migration pressures may decrease as time goes by. Economic development, however, of course, is a notoriously slow process that will likely take generations.[137] For now, other options must be investigated.

Long-term reform measures, such as a migration accord between the United States and Mexico, do not negate the need for possible short-term policy reforms. Strategies that promote assimilation and integration are necessary today. Policies consistent with modern civil rights sensibilities would probably prove to be relatively uncontroversial.

For example, one option is to increase access to English-as-a-second-language (ESL) classes for noncitizens. ESL classes in many urban centers are greatly oversubscribed and cannot accommodate all the persons who want and need to take them. The high demand for English-language instruction among immigrants militates in favor of devoting greater resources to ESL courses. More generally, a commitment to better education for immigrants might improve the integration of new immigrants and their children. The need for, and the advantages of, such measures hardly seems debatable.

Policies that encourage naturalization are another way to promote immigrant assimilation. Citizenship allows full political participation and full legal membership in U.S. social life. To avoid naturalization out of fear, steps could be taken to encourage naturalization and allegiance to the United States. President Clinton's administration attempted to do this in the 1990s, only to be accused by Republicans of pursuing partisan political ends.[138] Many restrictionists, however, in criticizing dual citizenship and nationality, seem to want to make naturalization more, not less, difficult. This is contrary to a growing body of scholarship, which hopes to promote immigrant assimilation into U.S. society.[139]

One way to ensure economic integration is to increase workplace protections. Exploitation of immigrants is a serious problem in the United States. Immigrant labor markets often exist separate and apart from the labor market for citizens.[140] This is particularly the case for undocumented workers, the most exploited of all immigrants,[141] a topic analyzed in Chapter 4. History teaches that true assimilation occurs through economic integration.

Some policymakers fully understand the need to bring immigrants into the mainstream. In 2005, Governor Rod Blagojevich, of Illinois, issued an Executive Order requiring the state to develop a "New Americans Immigration Policy" that would facilitate immigrant assimilation.[142] Such initiatives are vital to promote immigrant assimilation in American social life. Integration policy initiatives deserve much more attention than futile efforts to close the borders.

Conclusion

The United States finds itself at a historical crossroads. Immigration is on the front pages of newspapers across the country. Restrictionist messages fill talk show radio and the national news. Immigration deserves the nation's attention. But it warrants sober analysis, not sound bites designed to rile base instincts and insult and alienate members of the national community. A real effort must be made to address the most fundamental problem with U.S. immigration law: that our laws are dramatically out of synch with the social, economic, and political reality of immigration in the modern world.

Samuel Huntington articulates what many people feel is the problem with immigration in the United States. Immigrants are changing the country in ways that trouble many people and cause a scramble for solutions. Although they make changes at the margins to make their ideas more palatable to modern civil rights sensibilities, the modern restrictionists have cobbled together the tired arguments of the restrictionists of the past. Unfortunately, the policies endorsed by the modern restrictionists fail to appreciate the lessons of history, as well as the economic, political, and social realities of immigration to the modern United States. However, it is important that, in forging the immigration policy of the future, we learn the lessons of the past and try to avoid our previous mistakes. Restrictionists, old and new, pay no heed to that history but instead claim that "things are different" today, which is just not true.

Time and time again, the nation has embraced restrictionist policies that, from the outset, are doomed. It has also adopted policies that do little more than punish innocent people pursuing the American Dream. It has enforced laws that are unfair, immoral, and shameful.

In the end, massive border enforcement efforts have done little to stem the tide of immigrants to this land of great social, economic, and political opportunity. The only discernible impact is that immigrants' lives have been made more difficult. Hundreds of border crossers have died horrible deaths in the U.S.-Mexico borderlands. Human traffickers prey on undocumented immigrants. Absent truly comprehensive immigration reform, eliminating the undocumented population in the United States simply is not possible.

Moreover, history teaches that we cannot compel assimilation of immigrants into some sort of American national identity, as envisioned by Samuel Huntington. We can, however, adopt policies that seek to encourage and facilitate the integration of all immigrants in U.S. social life.

The United States has much to be proud, and ashamed, of in its immigration history. Unfortunately, U.S. immigration history is not consistent with the nation's self-concept as the land of freedom, liberty, and equality. Closed borders are extremely difficult to reconcile with the nation's stated devotion to the rights of the individual. This becomes clearer when we look at the moral foundations of the United States's commitment to individual rights.

The rest of this book builds on the true possibilities for comprehensive reform of U.S. immigration laws and the humane treatment of immigrants, who are nothing less than people who are part of the communities in which we live. It is important for immigration law to be in keeping with modern sensibilities about who we are as nation.

3

Bordering on the Immoral
The Moral Consequences of the Current System of Immigration Regulation

As a nation, the United States is philosophically committed to individual freedom and equality. The U.S. Constitution codifies and symbolizes this deep and enduring commitment. The discriminatory provisions in the U.S. immigration laws are extremely difficult to reconcile with those lofty ideals. Indeed, it is nothing less than a clear contradiction for the nation to endorse freedom *within* the country while strictly limiting travel *into* the United States. Moreover, immigration restrictions effectively relegate many noncitizens to the lower rungs of a caste-like labor system in the United States. They also perpetuate a worldwide one. Dramatic change is necessary to bring the immigration laws into line with the nation's moral compass.

Liberal admissions, combined with equal treatment of citizens and noncitizens residing in the United States, would be much more consistent with the nation's stated ideal of admitting and embracing the "huddled masses" than is the current immigration system. This chapter considers the philosophical arguments for open borders and outlines how a liberal immigration scheme is more in keeping with the nation's dominant moral and constitutional values. It further highlights the immoral consequences of the current U.S. immigration laws and their enforcement and outlines how we can ameliorate such impacts by bringing those laws into line with the national commitment to individual rights. The aim is to encourage a sophisticated consideration of the moral arguments for an immigration system that more liberally admits immigrants into the United States than does the current one.

The world's commitment to fundamental individual rights, which has a lengthy historical pedigree, grew substantially after World War II.[1] The rights of refugees, for example, expanded substantially under international law. Despite these changes, U.S. immigration law failed to adapt in any meaningful way. Immigration restrictions, although refined and improved in important respects, still strictly circumscribe the right to travel into this country. Like those of many Western nations, the U.S. immigration laws remain restrictive and, in many respects, largely indifferent to the rights of individuals seeking entry into the United States.

A growing body of literature questions the strict border restrictions enforced by most Western nations.[2] One clear lesson emerges from this scholarship. Liberal theory, with its commitment to the protection of individual rights, has not satisfactorily reconciled closed borders with liberal freedoms and the basic respect for fundamental individual rights.

Most liberal theorists hold similar views about immigration restrictions. "[I]n a truly liberal polity, it would be difficult to justify a restrictive immigration law or perhaps any immigration law at all."[3] Mark Tushnet, an influential U.S. constitutional law scholar, has proclaimed that, "[a]s a matter of principle, liberals ought to be committed to relatively unrestricted immigration policies."[4] He states unequivocally that "what's best about the United States would be preserved by a policy of open borders and naturalization available to anyone who agreed with the fundamental principles that animate our polity."[5]

Embracing rights-based views similar to those advocated by liberal theorists, church and religious leaders periodically criticize the morality of modern immigration policies and call for more humane treatment of immigrants.[6] Many religious leaders have urged the United States to adopt a more generous approach to immigration law and policy. Religious arguments about immigration ordinarily are based on the moral imperative that immigrants should be treated in a humanitarian way.[7] Diverse religions, from the Catholic Church to the Mormon Church, endorse laws that protect, rather than punish and ostracize, immigrants.

At times, religious leaders have gone so far as to risk criminal prosecution to provide assistance to immigrants in need. In the 1980s, movements blossomed in many parts of the United States that offered sanctuary to refugees from the violent civil wars that ravaged Central America.[8] In assisting desperate refugees fleeing political violence, sanctuary workers violated federal law. To those sanctuary workers, the threat of criminal prosecution was outweighed by the moral imperative of providing aid to asylum seekers. Remnants of the sanctuary movement have remained vibrant long after the end of the civil wars, with some former sanctuary workers today helping Mexican migrants survive the arduous journey to the United States.

Sadly, the passage of time has not alleviated the calls for more moral U.S. immigration policy. Today, religious groups, among others, provide water and emergency assistance to migrants seeking to navigate the treacherous desert en route from Mexico to the United States. In February 2006, Cardinal Roger Mahony of Los Angeles condemned the " 'hysterical' anti-immigrant sentiment sweeping California and the nation" and promised to instruct his priests to defy any law passed by Congress that would require churches to ask for immigration documentation before providing humanitarian assistance to people in need.[9] Cities such as San Francisco have declared themselves sanctuaries and refuse to allow municipal employees to assist in the enforcement of federal immigration laws.

Despite the nation's stated commitment to liberal ideals and the willingness of some people to violate the law on moral grounds, the U.S. government has consistently failed to craft immigration laws and policies that satisfy these basic moral imperatives. To fully appreciate the conundrum that immigration controls pose to liberal theory, consider some of the groups of noncitizens currently excluded under the U.S. immigration laws. U.S. immigration law has permitted discrimination against the poor, political minorities, racial minorities, the disabled, and other marginalized groups.[10]

The most frequently invoked substantive ground for excluding noncitizens is that they are "likely at any time to become public charges."[11] The public-charge exclusion squarely conflicts with the anticaste foundations of U.S. law.[12] One of the promises of America is the potential for upward economic mobility. No person's station in life is dictated by class or caste. To that end, the framers of the U.S. Constitution prohibited titles of nobility. Nonetheless, the public-charge exclusion cements economic disparities in place for those denied entry into the United States. Through this barrier, the United States slams the door on poor and working people and thus denies access to the American Dream to those most in pursuit of it.

Immigration law allows the United States to do at its borders what it cannot do within them. Because the Constitution guarantees free movement between the United States, individual states cannot erect borders to limit entry. Therefore, efforts by individual states to prevent the poor living in other states from migrating into their jurisdictions have been found to be unconstitutional infringements on the right to travel. In its 1999 ruling in *Saenz v. Roe,* the Supreme Court invalidated a California law requiring that a resident live in the state for twelve months before becoming eligible to receive the maximum amount in welfare benefits. In so doing, the Court emphasized that the right to travel

> protects the right of a citizen of one State to enter and to leave another State, the right to be treated as a welcome visitor rather than an unfriendly alien when temporarily present in the second State, and, for those travelers who elect to become permanent residents, the right to be treated like other citizens of that State.[13]

Despite recognizing the right to interstate travel, the United States flatly refuses to acknowledge any right of migrants to cross national boundaries. Under the U.S. Constitution, the Supreme Court has drawn a bright line between citizens, who possess the right to travel within the United States, and noncitizens outside the country, who lack any rights of entry.

The poor are not the only group that, although enjoying the protection of the laws within the country, is denied that protection at the border. Joining the poor as inadmissible "aliens" who are barred from entry into the country are disabled persons. In the United States, they are protected by the Americans with Disabilities Act.[14] At the border, however, the disabled can be denied admission into the country simply on account of the fact that they are disabled.[15] Congress also has acted to exclude persons with the Human Immunodeficiency Virus (HIV), even though the U.S. Public Health Service concluded that HIV-positive noncitizens do not pose a significant health risk to the general population.[16]

Despite technically complying with the colorblindness demanded by the U.S. Supreme Court,[17] modern immigration laws also have racially disparate impacts. People of color are disproportionately barred from entering the country. Such a result is in tension with the nation's stated commitment to equality under the law.[18]

Although discrimination against the poor, the disabled, HIV-positive persons, or racial minorities would be patently unlawful if directed against citizens in the United States, it is nothing less than routine under the U.S. immigration laws. One is left to wonder what the moral justifications could be for keeping these groups out of the United States. The elaborate system of controls that inflicts disparate impacts on people of color raises similar questions. All of these excluded groups seem to fall squarely within the category of the "huddled masses" for whom the nation has long—and loudly—declared itself open. There is, however, a simple answer. Most of the exclusionary categories in U.S. immigration law are not based on fairness, equality, or any respect for individual rights. Instead, the restrictions and exclusions are based on crude and arbitrary utilitarian calculations of the relative costs and benefits offered by different groups of immigrants to U.S. society. Of course, such considerations are the antithesis of a liberal devotion to individual rights.

Liberalism struggles mightily to accommodate individual rights in a society deeply committed to strict limits on immigration.[19] A strong conception of national sovereignty,[20] which has historically served as the justification for border restrictions, exacerbates the conflict between immigration exclusions and liberal theory:

> [The] conflict between the concepts of national sovereignty and the inalienable human right of free movement is rarely noticed, testifying in part to the unquestioned status of national sovereignty. *Also contributing to the absence of controversy is that, unlike the police measures that would be required to deport large numbers of illegal aliens already within U.S. territory, legislation barring aliens outside its boundaries from legal entrance inconveniences few U.S. citizens. Such exclusion is thus carried out with little debate and relative political impunity.*[21]

Because immigration enforcement has conventionally been viewed as the sovereign power of a nation, little attention has been paid to the deep impacts that immigration law and enforcement have had on immigrants. In the world of immigration, the rights of the nation-state have historically trumped any interests of the individual. Thus, despite its commitment to individual rights, the United States has expressly denied noncitizens any general rights to travel into this country.

One can envision few personal choices that can have greater life-altering impacts than the decision about which country one chooses to live and work in. The ability to move can obviously have profound impacts on a person's—and his or her family's—entire life. Accordingly, free movement of people can be seen as the ultimate freedom and the fundamental right of all human beings.[22] The right to migrate between nations could—and should—be viewed as a basic civil right of the individual. Such a view would be more consistent with liberal theory than a claim that state sovereignty trumps any and all limits on immigration restrictions.[23]

In looking at U.S. policy, it has been argued that immigration law should try to protect rights, rather than treat immigrants as a law enforcement problem.[24] The U.S. government, after all, has criticized other nations for their unfair treatment of immigrants. The United States, for example, enthusiastically condemned the old Soviet bloc's practice of refusing to allow political dissidents, members of minority religious groups, and other disfavored people to emigrate out of the country. However, whenever other nations question its immigration policies, the U.S. government has been quick to invoke its sovereign powers, with little regard for the rights of noncitizens.

A corollary issue raised by a rights-based approach to immigration is whether noncitizens residing in a country should enjoy rights approximating those of citizens.[25] The basic question is whether immigrants should be treated as full members of civil society or as something less. Under U.S. law, the answer is clearly something less. Besides severely restricting the right of noncitizens to migrate into the country, U.S. law narrowly circumscribes the rights of noncitizens within the United States. Lawful immigrants have fewer rights than citizens and undocumented immigrants even fewer. The denial of even more rights to undocumented immigrants relegates them to exploitation in the secondary labor market, with low wages and few legal protections. This operates to create a sort of racial caste system that cannot be reconciled with modern conceptions of liberty and equality.

However, safety valves to the immigrant caste structure do exist. Lawful immigrants can naturalize and become citizens. Undocumented immigrants in the United States can give birth to U.S.-citizen children.[26] Some undocumented immigrants are eligible to regularize their status under the law and become lawful permanent residents and ultimately citizens. But before immigrants can enjoy any status within the country, they must be able to enter it.

Liberal and Communitarian Theory on Immigration Restrictions

In an influential article entitled "Aliens and Citizens: The Case for Open Borders," the political theorist Joseph Carens outlines the case for free migration.[27] He demonstrates how radically different contemporary approaches to political theory generally militate in favor of open borders. Carens begins his analysis by questioning the U.S. government's use of force in the 1980s to prevent Haitian boat people and Salvadoran and Guatemalan asylum seekers from entering the United States:

> What justifies the use of force against such people? Perhaps borders and guards can be justified as a way of keeping out criminals, subversives, and armed invaders. But most of those trying to get in are not like that. They are ordinary, peaceful people, seeking only the opportunity to build decent, secure lives for themselves and their families. On what moral grounds can these sorts of people be kept out? What gives anyone the right to point guns at *them?*[28]

In answering this question, Carens demonstrates that liberal theory militates generally in favor of a system of open entry. Liberal theory requires a strong presumption favoring the admission of noncitizens into the country. Any restrictions would center exclusively on imminent threats to public safety.

Carens recognizes that restrictions are needed to protect against a clear "threat to the public order."[29] Mass migration that would threaten chaos and effectively end liberal democratic society would be barred. He cautions, however, that "[a] need for *some* restrictions [on migration] would not justify *any* level of restrictions."[30] Thus, in order to take the rights of noncitizens seriously, a public-order exclusion would need to be narrowly tailored to achieve the desired end.[31] This approach finds a ready analog in American constitutional law. Under the First Amendment, speech may be regulated in certain narrow instances through the least restrictive means available to satisfy legitimate governmental purposes.[32] To be true to the liberal ideal, only narrow restrictions on the admission of immigrants, such as those modeled after a test like that required to regulate speech under the First Amendment, are appropriate.

In sharp contrast, Michael Walzer forcefully contends that the community should be able to adopt criteria to limit the admission of outsiders in order both to preserve community self-definition and to allow the community to make decisions that reflect shared community values.[33] "The heart of Walzer's argument is that admissions decisions are the legitimate and essential prerogative of the current members of any particular national community."[34] Political theorists often invoke Walzer's theory to justify immigration restrictions in a liberal world. A nation's absolute power to determine national identity is one endorsed in principle by much of the public, as well as by restrictionists like Samuel Huntington.

In making his case for open borders, Joseph Carens addresses the communitarian rationale for border controls. Ultimately, Carens finds Walzer's justification for broader admissions restrictions to be unpersuasive. As he observes, because such restrictions are inconsistent with individual rights to free movement, we do not allow local communities to limit entry into their jurisdiction to better control community self-determination and self-definition. This is true even though we generally value local self-determination.[35]

Some forms of self-determination are simply intolerable. Invidious discrimination cannot, at least morally, be a tool of self-determination. Racial segregation, for instance, could be viewed as a form of community self-definition. Walzer's argument therefore would seem to offer a defense to housing segregation or to immigration restrictions based on race as a means of preserving community identity.[36]

Consider the logical implications of Walzer's argument. Could a community decide to exclude the poor, the disabled, short people, or brunettes in the name of community self-definition? The possibility that a nation might desire to engage in such discrimination is not as unlikely as it might seem at first glance. Some nations identify their population in no small part by physical appearance. The citizens of some nations may be identified as white and blond. Nations in Scandinavia immediately come to mind. Could these nations, in the name of community self-definition, limit immigration on the basis of physical appearance? Although such arbitrary classifications are generally permissible in personal decisions in the private sphere, they are not ordinarily the type of distinctions that the U.S. Constitution allows law to make. To permit such distinctions would allow community values—arbitrary and capricious as they might be—to trump individual rights. This is the opposite of how individual rights generally operate under the U.S. Constitution.

To be fair, Walzer has suggested that moral limits exist on the admissions criteria adopted by a community. Racial restrictions are invidious and impermissible and thus cannot serve as the basis of immigration restrictions.[37] However, once the concession is made that *some* limits on the potential excesses of communitarian theory are necessary, the question becomes where the permissible restrictions end and the rights of the individual begin. In Walzer's defense of limits on immigration controls, one senses a hint of liberal rights theory influencing communitarian sensibilities.

Although there is some convergence between liberal and communitarian theories with respect to immigration restrictions, the two remain separate and distinct. Liberal theory militates in favor of more open borders with few restrictions on entry. Communitarian theory, on the other hand, allows the state to impose limits on migration but, at least as reasonably interpreted, imposes few restrictions on the types of permissible limits allowed. In contrast to Carens's liberal theory, Walzer's communitarian perspective leaves open the possibility that many restrictions could be justified by community self-definition.

To avoid taking communitarian theory to its logical extreme, Michael Walzer and other like-minded theorists must rely on certain liberal principles to demarcate the limits on a community's self-definition through immigration restrictions. Absent such limits, communitarian theory could support unacceptable racial restrictions for admission into a nation and other invidious limitations on entry. Ultimately, the logic of the communitarian rationale would allow closing the borders without any meaningful limits and on the basis of arbitrary classifications that would trouble anyone committed to equality and justice for all.

Importantly, Walzer's communitarian theory is ill suited to justify modern U.S. immigration law and policy. U.S. immigration laws tend to focus on utilitarian exclusions, such as generalized threats to the economy and the public safety and the public fisc, rather than on community self-definition. The laws are generally designed to exclude people who might be a net economic cost to U.S. society. Walzer thus defends exclusions not found for the most part in the U.S. immigration laws.

Liberal Theory versus the Plenary Power Doctrine

Liberal theory is devoted to the rights of the individual over the state. It serves as the basis for the U.S. constitutional order. However, a legal sleight of hand in the realm of immigration law has seriously undermined and nullified liberal theory's commitment to individual rights for noncitizens. Relying on the sovereign's power to exclude noncitizens from entry without legal constraint, the Supreme Court has justified the virtually unfettered "plenary power" of the federal government over immigration.[38]

In *The Chinese Exclusion Case*,[39] the Supreme Court upheld an infamous nineteenth-century law prohibiting virtually all immigration from China. In so doing, the Court emphasized that "[t]he power of exclusion of foreigners [is] an incident of sovereignty belonging to the government of the United States, as part of [its] sovereign powers delegated by the Constitution." Notions of sovereignty continue to serve to justify the many exclusions in the U.S. immigration laws.

In the United States, plenary power to regulate immigration has generally meant the fervent rejection of *any* limits on the sovereign's power to impose substantive immigration restrictions. For more than a century, the doctrine has served as a bulwark against liberal theory and liberal admissions, or even admissions subject to any constitutional scrutiny. The plenary power doctrine allows the government to, as a practical matter, limit immigration to the United States with little, if any, oversight from the courts.

Volumes of scholarship contend that ordinary constitutional constraints should apply to the U.S. government's immigration admissions criteria.[40] There is much to commend such an approach. Nonetheless, the current system has long allowed immigration regulation to operate with few legal constraints. Even though there has been glacial, jagged movement in the law over time, the political branches of government continue to enjoy vast amounts of discretion in the realm of immigration, much more so than in most other bodies of American public law.

The claim has long been made that international law affords the nation-state complete power over entry into its territory. Indeed, the Supreme Court adopted this view in *The Chinese Exclusion Case* as the primary justification for the plenary power doctrine. The reliance on state sovereignty as the justification for closed borders has led some observers to contend that a more liberal system of immigration admissions would deprive the state of some of its sovereign powers. However, that need not be the case.

Even when advocating liberal immigration admissions, one need not reject the sovereign power of the nation-state to regulate immigration. Although contending that no moral basis justifies closed borders and that the nation would benefit from open borders, R. George Wright, for example, studiously avoided challenging the power of the sovereign to restrict immigration. Importantly, a nation-state can exercise its sovereign power by affirmatively choosing open borders.[41] A nation could decide, for example, that a free labor market among and between nations would benefit the sovereign and its people. The U.S. government could decide as a matter of national policy that a more liberal admissions system was preferable to the restrictive approach it currently takes. Rather than amount to a surrender of sovereignty, such a decision would amount to an exercise of the nation's sovereign power over immigration.

Even assuming that international law affords nations complete authority over their immigration laws, each nation can decide which restrictions make sense for it in light of that nation's needs and commitment to justice and equality. This is how the world has behaved for much of its history. Historically, many nations have had relaxed, or virtually nonexistent, immigration laws.

Legal constraints in fact exist on the sovereign power of nation to regulate immigration. As a historical matter, however, international law has tended to focus on limits imposed by states on *emigration,* that is, restrictions placed by governments on people who want to leave the country, rather than immigration.[42] This was no doubt a response to the longstanding practice of nations in the former Communist bloc of strictly controlling the emigration of political dissidents, religious and other minorities, and other disfavored groups. Because of a preoccupation with emigration restrictions, international law tends to impose stringent obligations on nations to permit emigration of citizens who seek to leave a country and far fewer on states to permit immigration into their jurisdictions.[43]

With the demise of the Soviet Union, however, the issue of ensuring the right to emigrate is much less pressing as a matter of Western foreign policy than it once was. In modern times, few nations, with Cuba and China being two important exceptions, strictly limit the emigration of its citizens. Consequently, attention has turned to migration. Even if not as protective of the rights of migrants as it is with respect to emigration, international law simply does not afford any nation the complete power to deny entry to migrants.

To the extent that international law ever gave carte blanche to nations to regulate immigration, that unquestionably is not the case today. Modern international law seriously limits the ability of nation-states to restrict immigration.[44] James Nafziger brilliantly documented how international law had been completely misread to justify unfettered sovereign authority of nations-states to regulate immigration.[45] For example, well-established international law requires nations to provide safe haven to political refugees and to those who have been tortured in their native lands.[46] Various international instruments limit states' ability to deny entry into their country, especially on the grounds of racially discriminatory principles. Generally speaking, nations traditionally have felt required to offer some reason based on safety or self-preservation for the exclusion of certain categories of immigrants.

Regardless of movements in international law, the United States continues to assert unfettered national sovereignty through its enthusiastic adherence to the plenary power doctrine. Endorsement of the plenary power doctrine allows the government to enforce virtually any restriction on immigration, broad or narrow, with Congress determining which are appropriate without judicial interference. Under U.S. immigration laws, the political branches of the nation-state possess complete power.

In contrast, absent a strong showing that restrictions are necessary to protect national security or public safety, liberal theory favors free immigration. The stark differences between the positions of plenary power enthusiasts and liberal theorists reflect dramatically different commitments to, and conceptions of, individual rights. Liberal theorists recognize rights in noncitizens as well as citizens, while plenary power advocates see the sovereign as having near-complete authority to define the rights of noncitizens.

On the issue of immigration regulation, liberal theory is much more consistent with U.S. constitutional traditions than any kind of plenary power regime. It also is more consistent with the trajectory of international law, which has afforded increasing rights to migrants. Despite growing international challenges to the idea of sovereign power to restrict immigration, the U.S. government has proceeded in a direction consistent with the view that it possesses near-complete sovereign power over immigration controls.

Even with the growing protections afforded migrants by international law, U.S. border controls expanded steadily in the 1990s. Increasing restrictions on entry and new grounds for removal hit a new high in 1996 with congressional passage of two harsh immigration reform laws[47] and welfare reform that eliminated immigrant eligibility for most federal benefit programs.[48] Professor Peter Schuck describes the 1996 immigration reforms as "the most radical reform of immigration law in decades —or perhaps ever."[49] To top it off, shortly after the tragic events of September 11, 2001, Congress passed the USA PATRIOT Act, which again expanded the grounds upon which noncitizens could be removed from the country.[50]

Immediately before September 11, some informed observers had forcefully opined that the plenary power doctrine was a dead letter. However, President George W. Bush's administration has often relied on the doctrine in adopting harsh measures in the "war on terror." Indeed, the plenary power doctrine has been a powerful tool invoked as a legal justification for the U.S. government's entire "war on terror."[51]

Many of the security measures embarked upon by the U.S. government after September 11, 2001, have targeted immigrants. The measures are premised on the idea that the sovereign power of the government trumps individual rights and that the law only loosely constrains any measures taken in the name of national security. To that end, the government has taken many aggressive steps that show little respect for the rights of the persons affected. The U.S. government implemented special registration of Arab and Muslim noncitizens, indefinitely held "enemy combatants," and engaged in selective deportation campaigns based on national origin. The U.S. government claimed that the Geneva Convention did not protect prisoners it held in Guantánamo Bay, Cuba. The Bush administration went so far as to label a few U.S. citizens "enemy combatants," denied them basic constitutional rights, and placed them in indefinite detention.

Despite the recent popularity of plenary power, a move beyond complete sovereign power over immigration controls appears to be in order. Developments in international law suggest that there has been a general decline in the concept of complete national sovereignty. Nation-states have become increasingly interdependent over the twentieth century. Globalization has integrated the economies of many nations in ways that were unheard of in the era of unfettered national sovereignty. Political integration has followed under certain international and regional arrangements, with the European Union being a prominent example. In an era of increasing interdependence between nation-states, cooperation with regard to immigration policy makes perfect sense.[52]

Contrary to the conventional wisdom, international law simply fails to afford the unfettered power to states to restrict immigration. International law therefore simply cannot serve as a moral or policy justification for closed borders. However, a state can exercise its sovereign power to liberally admit immigrants. A government can decide that liberal admission makes the most sense for it as a nation.

The Moral Case for Open Borders

Liberal theory, with its devotion to individual rights, fails to provide a satisfactory rationale for closed borders, especially of the type enforced with great rigor by the United States. Substantive exclusions that go beyond those necessary to protect national security and public safety find little support in a constitutional order firmly committed to individual rights and equal protection under law. Liberal theory, which animates U.S. constitutional law and international law, unquestionably justifies more open borders than currently exist in the United States.

Free migration into the United States would not be without precedent. The comprehensive federal immigration scheme, with myriad bars to entry, that prevails in the United States today simply did not exist during the nation's first century. Open borders and easy admission of immigrants were generally the rule, and the general presumption favored their admission. Border controls were extremely limited and in no way resembled the elaborate array of barriers that face potential entrants to the modern United States.

The nineteenth century was a period of sustained territorial expansion in this country. For much of these 100 years, immigration was viewed not as a serious social problem but as necessary for the survival of the United States. Although tempers at times flared over the real and imagined impacts of immigrants on U.S. society, immigration was viewed as a desirable method for bringing labor and people needed to settle the continent. In the late 1800s, the United States quickly moved from open to closed borders, with increasing barriers to entry slowly but surely added to the immigration laws over the course of the twentieth century.

Immigration into the early United States was not completely unfettered. Gerald Neuman has carefully documented the regulation of immigration by the states during the nation's first century of existence and placed in question the conventional wisdom that the United States embraced wholly open borders during this time.[53] Many of the states attempted to regulate migration, especially of the poor and criminals, into their jurisdiction. Nevertheless, the United States was generally open to immigrants during its first century as a nation.

It is entirely possible for the United States to return to a system of more open borders. Although not perfectly analogous, the massive deregulation of various industries near the end of the twentieth century demonstrates the potential for moving from a highly regulated body of public law to a much less regulated system.[54] Although the deregulation of immigration would generate knee-jerk resistance, this model makes perfect sense for the United States. The micromanagement of migration against the tide of market, political, and social forces, as U.S. immigration laws currently attempt to do, is doomed to fail. We need look no further than the current immigration mess in which we find ourselves today to see that.

Even with the deregulation of immigration, the concept of self-defense and the need to protect the public order could justify certain types of narrow restrictions on migration that are consistent with liberal theory. The use of criminal background checks and evidence of past criminal activity such as reports from reliable intelligence agencies could allow the U.S. government to attempt to ensure that the nation did not admit migrants who endanger the public safety. Databases that provide reliable intelligence about noncitizens who represent colorable threats to the national security could assist in helping to screen for public-safety risks. Focused background checks looking for true dangers to national security and public safety could improve the accuracy of security checks and could ensure that safety and security were the true focus of screening of persons seeking to enter the United States. The safety-related focus of individual inquiries, however, would be much narrower than is the case under current law.

The law should presume that all immigrants are admissible to the United States unless a strong justification for exclusion based on a narrowly tailored set of criteria designed to protect national security and public safety is established. Narrow exclusions would prevent overbroad enforcement, which is arguably one of the deepest flaws in the modern U.S. immigration laws. Exclusions based on safety risks posed by individual immigrants, rather than blanket exclusions based on group membership and alleged group propensities, make the most policy sense and are the most consistent with liberal theory and the nation's commitment to individual rights.

Moral Justifications for Open Borders

Political theorists have long debated the propriety of border controls. It has proved difficult to reconcile individual rights and the nation's commitment to liberalism with the many blanket exclusions in U.S. immigration laws. This, however, only tends to show that restrictions are difficult to justify morally. The inherent deficiency in moral justification, however, does not necessarily point to any affirmative obligation to allow for the easy admission of immigrants into the United States. The rest of this chapter attempts to set forth affirmative moral justifications for open borders. The argument is relatively straightforward. Liberal admissions would eliminate the immoral consequences that flow directly from the modern enforcement of the U.S. immigration laws.

Although arbitrary constructs that are nothing more than legal fictions, borders contribute to human suffering and economic inequality. The accident of place of birth may effectively create a life of relative opportunity or deprivation. Today, however, it is far easier than ever before to rectify that accident.

Migration between nations is more common in the twenty-first century than it ever has been. Goods, services, and people regularly flow across borders. Elaborate transportation networks exist to move people and goods quickly and inexpensively all over the world. A fundamental question for any body of immigration law and policy therefore is whether it should facilitate migration and increased access to economic opportunity and social mobility or whether it simply should reinforce the inequalities attributable to the luck of the draw.

At a fundamental level, "[a]n open entry policy is a broad attack on the problem of morally arbitrary suffering and inequality."[55] Open entry is more egalitarian than closed borders, allows for the possibility of a more just world, and recognizes that people should not be trapped for life by the random occurrence of place of their birth. Consequently, an anticaste justification for open borders, which has also been an important basis for much of U.S. constitutional law, warrants the most serious consideration.

Other moral justifications exist as well, many of them stemming from the immoral consequences of current U.S. immigration law. Open borders can help eliminate the immoral consequences that directly result from the nation's efforts to close the borders, including racial discrimination, exploitation in the labor market, human trafficking and slavery, and deaths resulting from border enforcement.

Reducing Racial Discrimination

Racial discrimination and segregation are serious problems the world over.[56] Consistent with the almost universally accepted moral prohibition, international law prohibits racial discrimination.[57] Over the past few decades, the international community has increased efforts to enforce the antidiscrimination norm. The end of racial apartheid in South Africa, for example, came after years of domestic and international pressures.

Generally speaking, states cannot consistent with international law discriminate on the basis of race or enforce facially neutral laws in a discriminatory manner.[58] In 2001, the United Nations convened the World Conference Against Racism, Racial Discrimination, Xenophobia, and Related Intolerance, in Durban, South Africa.[59] This event brought much attention to the pressing worldwide problem of racial discrimination.

U.S. law generally has moved in a manner consistent with international norms. Foreign policy considerations helped shape the civil rights orientation of domestic law.[60] The antidiscrimination principle animates much of modern America and has grown significantly in influence over recent decades. In the modern United States, the antidiscrimination principle has a deep and powerful hold on the national consciousness.

The efforts to eradicate racial discrimination in domestic U.S. law are exemplified by the watershed Supreme Court decision in *Brown v. Board of Education*.[61] This 1954 case marked the beginning of the civil rights revolution in the United States. A decade later, Congress took steps to remove overt discrimination from the immigration laws by enacting the Immigration Act of 1965. Despite the elimination of the discriminatory national-origins quota system in 1965, stark racial disparities unfortunately persist in the enforcement of immigration laws.

As summarized in Chapter 2, the U.S. immigration laws have historically discriminated against persons from developing countries populated predominantly by people of color. Modern immigration laws continue to have racially disparate impacts because high demand for immigration to the United States consistently exists in the developing world. Most immigrants, and putative immigrants, are people of color from developing nations. Each year, citizens of nations in Asia and Latin America make up the vast majority of all entrants.[62] Consequently, punitive immigration laws necessarily, and adversely, affect large numbers of noncitizens of color.

Under current conditions, immigration controls also contribute to racism and discrimination within the United States. Undocumented workers, many of whom are people of color from developing nations, are vulnerable to exploitation. Working for low wages in poor conditions, these migrants form part of what is effectively a racial caste system of cheap labor. Of course, not all immigrants are nonwhite, and white immigrants are not immune from labor exploitation. Immigrants of color, however, dominate the ranks of day laborers, restaurant and hotel workers, farm workers, and domestic-service workers. Ultimately, this amounts to a loose racial caste system created and enforced by the U.S. immigration laws.

Although at some level undocumented immigrants "choose" to migrate and work under those conditions, the U.S. government, through its policies, has greatly magnified the potential harms of undocumented migration. The law and its enforcement have helped to create a system of exploitable labor in the United States that is particularly vulnerable because of its immigration status and because it is composed predominantly of people of color. The result is a racially segregated job market. This system has Jim Crow–like qualities that in some ways make it resemble the job market that existed for African Americans in the heyday of racial segregation in the United States.

Another way of evaluating immigration restrictions proves instructive in evaluating their racial impacts. Border controls have been characterized as a form of employment discrimination against noncitizens because they effectively bar many foreigners from accessing the U.S. labor markets.[63] Under the existing border controls, the persons barred from seeking domestic jobs are predominantly people of color from the developing world. Border controls thus serve to racially segregate international labor markets.

The discriminatory impacts of immigration regulation can be seen starkly in the post–September 11 heightened scrutiny of noncitizens. Almost all of the legal measures taken in the war on terror have been directed at the immigrant community, resulting in racially disparate consequences. The recent governmental targeting of Arabs and Muslims demonstrates how immigration law conveniently can be employed to focus upon disfavored minority groups. This targeting was accompanied by a precipitous rise in private racial discrimination and hate crimes directed against Arabs and Muslims in the United States.[64]

Importantly, the civil rights harms resulting from the enforcement of the U.S. immigration laws are not limited to noncitizens at the border. They in fact extend to legal immigrants and U.S. citizens of certain national origin ancestries in the interior of the country. Stigmatizing impacts similar to those attributable to the notorious national origins quota system, which barred immigration of "inferior" races from southern and eastern Europe and served as the bedrock of the U.S. immigration laws from 1924 to 1965, flow from border enforcement efforts aimed at particular groups of immigrants.[65] As plain-talking President Harry Truman put it when he unsuccessfully vetoed the Immigration and Nationality Act of 1952, the quota system was premised on the view

> that Americans with English or Irish names were better people and better citizens than Americans with Italian or Greek or Polish names. It was thought that people of West European origin made better citizens than Rumanians or Yugoslavs or Ukrainians or Hungarians or Balts or Austrians. Such a concept . . . violates the great political doctrine of the Declaration of Independence that "all men are created equal."[66]

The congressional repeal of the national-origins quota system, in 1965, allowed immigration to become more open, fairer, and less discriminatory than in the past. The removal of express racial discrimination from the U.S. immigration laws is in no small part a result of the civil rights revolution in the United States, which thoroughly discredited, on moral and other grounds, legally sanctioned racial discrimination in American social life.

After 1965, immigration from Asia increased dramatically,[67] and more immigrants of African ancestry now come to the United States.[68] A more open, multicultural society unleashed the forces that created a new, even more racially and culturally diverse America. Thus, the recognition of, and greater respect for, our diversity and the liberalization of the immigration laws led to even greater diversity.

The removal of express racial discrimination from the immigration laws, however, ended neither the use of the immigration laws to exclude undesirables nor their deleterious effects on citizens and lawful immigrants. The monumental efforts to prevent certain groups of outsiders from entering the country stigmatize those in the United States who share common ancestry with those excluded.[69] Specifically, the U.S. government's zealous efforts to seal the southern border in order to keep Mexican migrants out of the country effectively tell Mexican-American citizens living in the United States that they are disfavored and less than full members in U.S. society.[70] Efforts to stop the poor from coming into the United States provide many lessons about how the poor in this country are viewed by society at large. The same is true for the disabled, those who are HIV-positive, and other excluded groups. The "war on terror" has sent deeply disturbing messages to Arabs and Muslims about how society views their communities in the United States and just how shaky their legal status is in this country.

Of course, the utilitarian nature of the immigration laws may lead some to claim that the racial impacts are merely incidental and signify little as to the public view of undesirable groups. But this would be misguided. Unfortunately, the intricate code of immigration law is often used to obfuscate antiforeigner, racist views of immigrants in popular discourse. Such sentiments are bolstered by the heavy emphasis on the need to enforce the borders against the immigrant hordes. The hullabaloo over the activities of the Minuteman Project is simply a recent example of such dynamics at work. These vigilantes claim to seek only to enforce the law and to keep "illegal aliens"—Mexican migrants—from unlawfully entering the country. Sadly enough, deep racial antipathies underlay the activism of many restrictionist groups.

Racial discrimination in border enforcement injures noncitizens, of course, and citizens presumed to be immigrants because of the color of their skin. Border enforcement promotes animosity toward certain national-origin minority groups and makes them second-class citizens.[71] Such impacts run contrary to the general thrust of U.S. and international law to remedy racial discrimination. They contradict the anticaste foundations of U.S. law and the nation's commitment to multiculturalism and respect for all cultures and peoples.

Racial discrimination in immigration law and enforcement are also problems in other nations. This should not be surprising, given that racism is a deep and enduring social problem the world over. The claim has been made, for example, that the United Kingdom's immigration laws have discriminatory impacts.[72] The same is true for the European Union generally. In fact, immigration law and its enforcement are far from perfect in most Western nations in which immigration is in high demand. The public is often deeply resistant to "floods" of foreigners immigrating to their cities and believes that restrictions are necessary to prevent a flood of migrants coming to the West. The resulting policies have failed to solve the perceived immigration problem.

An open-borders system would be consistent with the prevailing anti-discrimination norm. Such a system would avoid some of the adverse consequences of border enforcement in the United States and remove a contributor to racial discrimination in modern American social life. Open borders would reduce the social costs of closed borders, including, but not limited to, the promotion of discrimination against a racially stratified labor force.

Embracing open borders would send an expressionist message that all people, including people of color from the developing world, have equal dignity.[73] Rather than be classified as undesirable and dehumanized "aliens" subject to exclusion and, at times, brutal border enforcement,[74] citizens of other nations would be welcomed as persons worthy of full membership in America. People of color would be valued as equals under the law in U.S. society. Unlike current immigration law and its enforcement, such important messages would tend to dampen— rather than exacerbate—the nativism and racism that often have infected public discourse on immigration and shaped the treatment of immigrants and certain groups of citizens in the United States.

Ending the Discriminatory Enforcement of Border Controls

Historically, border controls in the United States have often tended to be race and class based. The Chinese exclusion laws are a painful and jarring example.[75] Coming on the heels of the migration of Chinese laborers that helped build the transcontinental railroad, in the 1800s, these laws effectively prohibited immigration of most Chinese workers to the United States. In addition, they resulted in the mass detention, on Angel Island, in San Francisco Bay, of Chinese nationals seeking entry into the United States. Because Chinese women could not immigrate and because Chinese men in many states were legally prohibited from marrying white women, these laws maintained for generations in the United States a large, isolated Chinese male population unable to marry.[76]

To make matters worse, under the racial restrictions on naturalization that remained fully intact in U.S. law until 1952,[77] the courts classified Asian immigrants as not "white" and thus not eligible to become U.S. citizens.[78] Because of this, a permanent noncitizen caste of color was created that was barred from participation in the electoral process and ostracized from American social life. The whiteness prerequisite for citizenship racial made full integration into U.S. society simply impossible for Asian immigrants.

Fortunately, express discriminatory racial restrictions have for the most part been removed from the U.S. immigration laws. However, the laws continue to have racial impacts, although they are often hidden and obscured by the opaque technicalities of the letter of the law. These impacts stand in tension with modern notions of justice and equality. Racial profiling in immigration enforcement, for example, harms the dignity of persons stopped by immigration officers and stigmatizes U.S. citizens, especially Mexican-Americans, who are subject to immigration stops because they fit the "undocumented immigrant profile."[79] Profiling has been a problem for generations, and the law has done precious little to discourage—and done much to encourage—the practice.

Other facially neutral provisions of the immigration laws also have plainly racial impacts. The immigration law's annual limits on immigrants from any one country force some categories of immigrants from certain high-immigration nations, such as China, Mexico, India, and the Philippines—all developing nations populated by people of color—to wait years longer to come to the United States than prospective immigrants from other nations. The law thus treats similarly situated applicants differently solely because of their national origin.[80] For example, a Filipino brother or sister of a U.S. citizen may have to wait many years longer—perhaps twice as long, even, at times, decades—to lawfully enter the United States than the German brother or sister of a U.S. citizen.

Similarly, the so-called diversity visa system under the U.S. immigration laws favors white immigrants from the developed world by preferring noncitizens from "low-immigrant countries." In its early years, the diversity visa program set aside a certain percentage of the available visas for Irish immigrants. The elaborate formula now used to allocate diversity visas to various countries is designed to provide more visas for citizens of nations that send few immigrants to the United States. In many respects, these visas are designed to redirect immigration away from the developing world, from which levels of immigration are high. In one recent year, just as many diversity visas went to Europeans as to

Africans and Asians combined, even though the immigration demand from Asia and Africa greatly exceeds that from Europe.[81]

In operation, the diversity visa programs makes the immigration stream whiter than it would be were the system not in place. Professor Steve Legomsky has aptly remarked that the diversity visa "program is in truth an '*anti-diversity*' program: it causes the resulting population mix to be *less* diverse than it would otherwise be."[82] This program is designed to respond to the concern that too many people of color are immigrating to the United States and therefore attempts to maintain the current racial balance. However, it has not been entirely effective because of the high demand for immigration in countries, such as those in Africa, that historically have sent few migrants to the United States.

Persons of Mexican ancestry bear the brunt of immigration enforcement in the modern United States. Although immigration enforcement priorities have changed to a certain extent since September 11, 2001, U.S. border enforcement for much of the twentieth century centered on undocumented migration from Mexico. The immigration responses to the events of September 11 have had adverse impacts on the Mexican immigrant community in the United States, as well as on all other immigrants.[83] In the 1990s, the U.S. government's border fortification was aimed almost exclusively at the nation's southern border. The militarization of the southern border is often contrasted with the relative lack of enforcement along its northern border with Canada. This often is pointed to as evidence of racial discrimination in immigration enforcement.

The tough immigration reforms enacted by Congress in 1996 fall disproportionately on the Mexican immigrant community. Following these reforms, record levels of "criminal aliens" have been deported. By far, the largest number have been from Mexico. Removals increased fourfold, from about 42,500 in fiscal year 1993 (with about 64 percent from Mexico)[84] to more than 170,000 in fiscal year 1998, more than 80 percent of whom were immigrants from Mexico.[85] In fiscal year 1999, nearly 80 percent of the immigrants formally removed on criminal grounds were natives of Mexico,[86] which was about the same as in fiscal year 1998.[87] In 2003, there were more than 186,000 removals, more than 75 percent of them immigrants from Mexico. In total, only nine countries (Mexico, Honduras, Guatemala, El Salvador, Brazil, the Dominican Republic, Colombia, Jamaica, and Haiti) accounted for almost

92 percent of all removals.[88] In 2004, the number of removals increased to more than 200,000.[89]

Many of the immigrants removed are long-term residents of the United States. Some of the deportations are based on convictions for relatively minor crimes, such as, in certain circumstances, driving under the influence.

To make matters worse, the statistics fail to account for the hundreds of thousands of Mexican citizens who depart voluntarily each year. Many, many more immigrants avoid a formal hearing and deportation order by agreeing to depart than are formally removed from the country. If voluntary removals did not occur at these rates, the immigration system in the United States would become overburdened and soon shut down. Thus, removal statistics represent only the tip of the iceberg when it comes to Mexican citizens adversely affected by the U.S. immigration laws.

In addition to their effects on noncitizens, border enforcement operations often have impacts on minority citizens. For example, in July 1997, local police in Chandler, Arizona, engaged in a "roundup" of suspected undocumented immigrants. The operation was part of a community redevelopment campaign designed to remove undocumented immigrants seeking work on the streets of Chandler. Police questioned people who "looked" Mexican, spoke Spanish, or dressed in work clothes. As might be expected in a city with a large Latino population in which police used crude profiles, many Mexican-American *citizens* were stopped, interrogated, and detained. Activists protested the raid. Numerous civil rights lawsuits later settled for substantial sums of money.[90]

Unfortunately, the roundups are not uncommon. They occur with regularity throughout the United States and are notorious in Mexican-American communities. In many communities, law enforcement of this type is simply seen as a fact of daily life. It is uncommon, however, for such events to receive the publicity that the Chandler case did.

Efforts to limit undocumented migration within the borders, such as workplace enforcement to ensure that employers are not hiring undocumented workers, have been comparatively minimal.[91] In fact, workplace enforcement has declined significantly in recent years. This presumably is due to political pressures from business interests, which desire continued access to immigrant labor. Employers, as well as immigrant activists, oppose workplace enforcement. But, at the same time, the threat of enforcement has negatively impacted U.S. citizens and lawful immigrants of certain national origins. Some dutiful employers fear that certain groups of people of color might be undocumented immigrants and refuse to hire them.

Given that their effects are well known and entirely predictable, the disparate racial impacts under current immigration law enforcement undercut the ostensible bar on racial restrictions. Restrictionists, including those with racist sympathies, support such measures. This fact alone should be troubling to those who claim that race has absolutely nothing to do with the call for additional enforcement measures.

The damage caused by immigration controls would be difficult to justify morally even if the measures were in fact effective at reducing undocumented immigration. Since immigration controls are woefully unsuccessful, it is impossible to make any sense of the damage. By most accounts, enforcement has been a failure. The undocumented immigrant population has increased despite the unprecedented escalation in border enforcement over the past twenty years. Border enforcement measures have punished, stigmatized, and, at times, killed immigrants. But they have not significantly reduced undocumented immigration. Thus, they have been both ineffective and immoral.

Halting "Death at the Border"[92]

In the 1990s, the U.S. government heightened immigration enforcement by massing forces along its southern border with Mexico. These measures have resulted in a human toll that is nothing less than horrific. A week rarely goes by without press reports of undocumented Mexican immigrants who have died on the long, treacherous journey to the United States.[93] The title of one November 2002 *New York Times* article tells it all: "Skeletons Tell Tale of Gamble by Immigrants."[94] Unfortunately, many migrants die in the desert seeking nothing more than to make a better life for themselves and their families in the United States.[95] The vast majority of the border crossers in no way can be characterized as dangers to the national security or the public safety of the nation. They are simply seeking economic opportunity in this country.

Military-style operations on the southwest border have channeled immigrants into remote, desolate locations where thousands have died agonizing deaths from heat, cold, and dehydration.[96] At various times, to add to the danger, military forces have patrolled the border. In one infamous incident, Marines a few years ago mistakenly shot and killed a teenage goatherder (and U.S. citizen), Esequiel Hernandez, Jr.

As of March 2006, the California Rural Legal Assistance Foundation attributed more than 3,000 deaths to a single southern California border operation known as Operation Gatekeeper.[97] Numerous other operations have been put into place in the U.S.-Mexico border region. All have had similar deadly impacts. Despite the death toll, the U.S. government continues to pursue enforcement operations with great vigor. Indeed, Congress consistently enacts proposals designed to bolster border enforcement, with such proposals often representing the only items of political consensus when it comes to immigration reform.

Operation Gatekeeper demonstrates the U.S. government's callous indifference to the human suffering caused by its aggressive border enforcement policy. In the words of one informed commentator, "[t]he real tragedy of [Operation] Gatekeeper . . . is the direct link . . . to the staggering rise in the number of deaths among border crossers. [The U.S. government] has forced these crossers to attempt entry in areas plagued by extreme weather conditions and rugged terrain that *[the U.S. government] knows to present mortal danger.*"[98]

In planning Operation Gatekeeper, the U.S. government knew that its strategy would risk many lives but proceeded nonetheless. As another observer concludes, "Operation Gatekeeper, as an enforcement immigration policy financed and politically supported by the U.S. government, flagrantly violates international human rights *because this policy was deliberately formulated to maximize the physical risks of Mexican migrant workers, thereby ensuring that hundreds of them would die.*"[99] Apparently, the government rationalized the deaths of migrants as collateral damage in the "war" on illegal immigration.

Even before the 1990s, the Border Patrol had a reputation for committing human rights abuses against immigrants and U.S. citizens of Mexican ancestry.[100] Created to police the U.S.-Mexican border, the Border Patrol has historically been plagued by reports of brutality, shootings, beatings, and killings.[101] Amnesty International, American Friends Service Committee, and Human Rights Watch have all issued reports documenting recent human rights abuses by the Border Patrol.[102]

Migrants face other perils on their journey through the U.S.-Mexico border region. Criminals frequently prey upon unlawful entrants seeking to evade border inspection. Robberies, murders, and rapes of immigrants are commonplace. Lawlessness reigns along the U.S.-Mexican border. Absent serious reform efforts, nothing seems likely to change.

For years, many migrants have depended on smugglers for passage into the United States. However, since the new border operations went into effect, heightened immigration restrictions and bolstered immigration enforcement have caused a rapid increase in the fees charged by smugglers. Smuggling fees increased from a few hundred to a couple of thousand dollars. It now is much more expensive to come to the United States than before the new border operations went into effect in the 1990s.[103]

Some migrants lack the cash to travel. To pay for the trip, many are forced to become indebted to their smugglers. Smuggling debts have been paid through forced labor, thus taking the exploitation of undocumented workers to new and frightening levels. Failure to work off the debts may result in brutal consequences.

But a migrant's ability to pay is not the only problem with human trafficking. The passage itself is replete with hazards. Among the many risks faced by migrants is the possibility of being abandoned. In May 2003, nineteen migrants, including a five-year-old child, died of asphyxiation, heat exposure, and dehydration in the back of a smuggler's truck in South Texas. The smuggler had fled, leaving the migrants to die. One of the dead "had worked five years in the United States before he returned to Mexico to fetch his children, hoping to provide them comforts he could not give them in Mexico."[104]

Today, because of the money to be made in this black market, criminal syndicates thrive in the trafficking of human beings. A product of ill-considered law enforcement, these syndicates resemble the crime networks that emerged in response to the federal government's efforts during Prohibition's ban on the commerce in alcohol. Criminal elements grew and asserted control over a new lucrative industry.

But it gets worse. Some undocumented immigrants have been enslaved. Reports of slavery have increased dramatically in the past few years. One 2005 report concluded as follows:

> Our research identified 57 forced labor operations in almost a dozen cities in California between 1998 and 2003, involving more than 500 individuals from 18 countries. . . . Victims labored in several economic sectors including prostitution and sex services (47.4%), domestic service (33.3%), mail order brides (5.3%), sweatshops (5.3%), and agriculture

(1.8%). . . . Victims of forced labor often suffer severe hardships and deprivations. Their captors often subject them to beatings, threats, and other forms of physical and psychological abuse. They live in conditions of deprivation and despair. Their captors may threaten their families. Perpetrators exert near total control over victims, creating a situation of dependency. Victims come to believe they cannot leave. . . . They are terrified of their captors but also fear law enforcement, a fear often based on bad experiences with police and other government officials in their countries of origin.[105]

Today, in no small part because of the operation of the immigration laws, cases of involuntary servitude regularly make the news.[106]

The U.S.-Mexico border region is filled with other risks, as well. Vigilante groups now patrol the borders and threaten violence to undocumented immigrants.[107] Undoubtedly feeling encouraged by the tough immigration laws and border enforcement efforts, along with the harsh rhetoric of political leaders, vigilantes purport to assume the moral high ground and claim that they are simply doing what the federal government has failed to do—enforce the law.

In 2005, the Minuteman Project, with great fanfare, patrolled the U.S.-Mexico border in search of undocumented immigrants. Its members engaged in armed hunting expeditions, looking for migrants along the border. They received public support from a member of the U.S. Congress, Tom Tancredo, and a longtime anti-immigrant adherent, Pat Buchanan. The Minutemen frequently express thinly veiled antipathy for Mexican immigrants.

In spite of the high human costs, increased border enforcement has proven to be woefully ineffective. Its self-defeating nature is demonstrated by its counterintuitive consequence. Contrary to expectations, migrants who come to the United States under the current regime are more likely to remain permanently in the country than those who came in the past. Understandably, undocumented immigrants who have made it to the United States do not want to risk running the gauntlet of border controls and literally place their lives on the line a second time.[108] As a result, the undocumented immigrant population in the country has *increased* from an estimated 5 to 7 million when the various border operations were put into place in the 1990s to approximately 11 to 12 million today.

This bears repeating. The undocumented population has *increased* despite the monumental border enforcement initiatives adopted in the past decade, efforts that have cost millions of dollars and resulted in the deaths of thousands of people. The undocumented immigrant population has also risen in the face of the unprecedented focus on immigration enforcement after September 11.

Ultimately, the border buildup has failed as a matter of policy *and* has had serious moral costs. Years of bona fide reform efforts, such as increased training, creation of civilian oversight boards, and impact litigation, have failed to ameliorate the human costs of border enforcement. Proposals for incremental reform strategies, including those made by the blue-ribbon Select Commission on Immigration and Refugee Policy in the 1980s and the U.S. Commission on Immigration Reform in the 1990s,[109] have failed to change much. Despite prolonged efforts, neither immigration law nor its enforcement has improved in any meaningful way. In fact, both arguably have become less fair and effective in recent years. They unquestionably are more deadly.

Unfortunately, the fact that it is Mexican persons being killed has muted any public outcry over the thousands of deaths. Indeed, the ever-rising death count has failed to trigger much of a reaction from the American public. The general public is indifferent to or unaware of the rising death toll. These policies can perhaps be equated with other unsavory chapters in U.S. history, such as the Jim Crow era, the era of Chinese exclusion, the Japanese internment, and previous mass deportation campaigns directed at unpopular minorities.

History will look back on the harsh border enforcement measures of the twentieth century, as well as the post–September 11 "war on terror," with regret and shame. This is especially the case with the measures that have resulted in thousands of deaths but have failed to have any impact on reducing the undocumented immigrant population. The resulting deaths have had limited enforcement benefits. At most, they have decreased migration so that the undocumented population is not quite as high as it would have been absent the measures. The government may have removed the flow of undocumented immigrants from public view. The flow of people, however, has continued virtually unabated. To make matters worse, such aggressive actions have encouraged vigilantes to join in the hunt for undocumented immigrants at the border, thereby creating the risk of horrible, perhaps deadly, confrontations.

Open borders hold the potential to change the U.S.-Mexico borderlands from a lawless death trap. They would allow for orderly and safe entry into the United States by migrants looking to work in the United States. Whatever one thinks about more permeable borders, there can be no moral justification for the human tragedy that today occurs daily in the desert between the United States and Mexico. The deaths of thousands of people deserve our attention and immediate action, not ignorance and indifference.

The Immoral Treatment of Immigrants and Refugees

The comprehensive immigration restrictions in U.S. law obviously require enforcement, a daunting task easier said than done. Responding to political pressures over time, the now-defunct Immigration and Naturalization Service (INS) developed an enforcement mentality that contributed to a pattern of aggressive policy choices of dubious morality. Before its demise in the wake of disclosures regarding its inept performance related to the events of September 11, 2001, the INS had a reputation as a rogue agency that ran roughshod over the rights of immigrants.

The jury is out on whether the new Department of Homeland Security will move away from the ways of the INS. However, as the name of the agency (along with the reason for its creation) suggests, one could reasonably expect its focus to be on national security and counterterrorism, rather than on the fair treatment of noncitizens. In any event, the reorganization does not appear to have resulted in a fundamental overhaul in immigration priorities. Border enforcement continues to trump all other immigration functions.

Consider a few examples of the U.S. government's overzealous enforcement of the U.S. immigration laws. In implementing 1996 immigration reform legislation, the INS indefinitely detained noncitizens subject to deportation who could not be removed from the country because their homeland would not accept them, a policy that a conservative Supreme Court found unlawful.[110] Similarly, until the Court intervened, the INS enthusiastically read the provisions of the 1996 laws as barring *any* judicial review of many deportation decisions.[111] The agency vigorously—and retroactively—applied the new deportation grounds contained in the 1996 immigration reforms to criminal convictions entered before the passage of the law.[112] The INS emphasis was all on enforcement. Little effort was made to satisfy the agency's service obligations. In certain respects, the INS has sought to return the plenary power doctrine to the heights enjoyed during the Chinese-exclusion era.

The aggressive positions taken by the INS fell disproportionately on noncitizens of color and had significant impacts on many other noncitizens as well. Importantly, the Supreme Court, headed by the conservative chief justice William Rehnquist, rejected many of the government's most aggressive positions. The INS's zealous advocacy appears to have reflected the federal government's general attitude that it can take whatever actions it wants in deciding how to treat immigrants. This attitude flourished in the "war on terror," when immigration enforcement became ground zero for the U.S. government's purported efforts to protect national security.

An enforcement-over-all-else mentality has also adversely affected the implementation of immigration policies designed to be service oriented and humanitarian in nature. Providing benefits and service to immigrants never came easy. The government is notoriously slow to process naturalization petitions and has long had a reputation for rude and arbitrary treatment of immigrants. Because the old Immigration and Naturalization Service paid little heed to the "service" in its name, there had long been calls for separating immigration enforcement and service functions. This occurred to a certain extent when the immigration functions shifted to the Department of Homeland Security. But enforcement remains supreme.

Consider the impact of the enforcement mentality on the treatment of noncitizens seeking asylum in the United States. Political theorists generally agree that nations have a moral obligation to offer asylum to refugees fleeing persecution.[113] The "moral obligation to assist refugees and to provide them with refuge or safe haven has, over time and in certain contexts, developed into a legal obligation."[114] International law now imposes obligations on nation-states to afford temporary refuge to noncitizens who have fled political, religious, national-origin, racial, and related forms of persecution.

International law seeks to prevent conduct like the U.S. government's refusal to accept Jewish refugees during the Holocaust. The U.S. government, in no small part due to anti-Semitism, turned away thousands of Jewish refugees facing genocide and unspeakable horrors who sought nothing more than safety in America; the stated reason was that the quotas in the U.S. immigration laws had been filled for the year.[115] This episode in U.S. history rightly evokes condemnation as immoral and indefensible conduct. As was generally the case after World War II, the international community's focus on increasing the universal observance of human rights led to increased legal protections for refugees. Through the United Nations Convention Relating to the Status of Refugees,[116] international law embraced protections for refugees.

To implement international law, Congress passed the Refugee Act of 1980,[117] which extended protections to noncitizens who could establish past persecution or document a well-founded fear of future persecution on account of race, political opinion, religion, nationality, or membership in a particular social group. Unfortunately, the United States has failed to live up to the promise of the Refugee Act. Despite the requirement under international law of ideological neutrality in refugee admissions, asylum decisions are often subtly guided by U.S. foreign policy, rather than humanitarian concerns.[118]

The West often declares that migrants from nations experiencing severe political violence are economic migrants not entitled to relief under the law. This classification almost inevitably flows from the view that all immigrants are presumptive economic migrants who should be barred from entry absent affirmative proof that they should be admitted. Historically, many noncitizens, including Haitians and Central Americans, have been placed in this category by the United States. However, those who flee regimes on unfriendly terms with the U.S. government, such as Cuba and Iran, have not. The U.S. government has employed a clear double standard, willing to accept refugees from its enemies while denying relief to people fleeing its authoritarian allies. This demonstrates that, rather than make any effort to comply with its existing legal obligations to refugees, the United States prefers to use its immigration and refugee laws in a utilitarian manner.

Countries committed to strong, unyielding border controls, such as the United States and nations in Western Europe, find it difficult to satisfy the moral and legal obligations owed to refugees.[119] These repeated failures to respect the legal rights of refugees flow logically from the presumption that borders, as a general matter, remain closed to immigrants and that anyone seeking entry must fall within a narrow exception. These countries fear that floods of refugees will overwhelm them.

At virtually every juncture, the U.S. government has narrowly interpreted its obligations to noncitizens fleeing persecution. In the 1980s, the U.S. government arrested and detained tens of thousands of asylum seekers who were fleeing political violence in El Salvador and in Guatemala. It unlawfully pressured them to accept "voluntary" deportation without availing themselves of their legal rights, including the ability guaranteed by law to pursue a claim to asylum in this country.[120] Fears of mass migration led to the extreme measures.

More recently, the United States engaged in the interdiction and repatriation of desperate people who were fleeing the political turmoil and violence in Haiti. The U.S. government, as it has historically done in resisting refugee flows, maintained that the asylum seekers were "economic migrants," not "political refugees," and that they thus were not entitled to the protection of the law. With echoes of the plenary power doctrine, the Supreme Court upheld the harsh policy of interdicting all Haitians on the high seas before they could make it to the shores of the United States.[121] Again, fears of mass migration influenced, if not dictated, the harsh U.S. policy choice.

It is readily apparent that, as a practical matter, nation-states that devote resources to closed borders often find it difficult to shift gears and allow for the admission and humanitarian treatment of refugees. The U.S. government's emphasis on militarizing the border, for example, almost invariably contributes to the harsh treatment of refugees and to a failure to abide by the nation's moral and legal obligations to immigrants. One possible solution is more permeable borders, with migrants generally embraced and welcomed, rather than routinely spurned and turned away.

Preventing the Creation of an Exploitable Labor Force

Immigrant labor is unquestionably important to the national economy. A 2002 study found that, during the tremendous economic growth of the 1990s, immigrants accounted for more than half of the growth of the entire civilian labor force in the United States.[122] Millions of the new workers were undocumented. However, rather than reward the valued labor that handsomely benefits the economy, the U.S. government has enforced border restrictions that have contributed to the maintenance of a large and easily exploited undocumented immigrant workforce in the United States.

It is unquestionably the case that economic forces bring the majority of migrants to the United States. Many come to this country for economic opportunities far superior to those available to them in their homeland. Undocumented immigrants gain a wage that many of them could not have earned in their native countries. They, however, work for, at least by U.S. standards, low wages in this country.

A low-wage labor market composed of undocumented immigrants thrives in cities and towns across the United States. This labor force benefits both employers, who are able to keep down production costs, and consumers, who pay less for many goods and services. The immigration laws, which distinguish between legal and unlawful immigration status, facilitate the creation of this exploitable labor force. Precious few labor protections are afforded undocumented workers. This simple fact makes undocumented immigrants more attractive to employers in a number of industries but also helps to create a secondary labor market in which the workers are subject to exploitation.

The threat of deportation—and consequently the fear of loss of liberty and of separation from friends, family, job, and community[123]— bears heavily on the daily lives of undocumented workers. It tends to inhibit them from exercising whatever rights they have under the law.[124] With the fear of deportation shaping all social and economic interactions, many undocumented immigrants, not surprisingly, accept what employers offer, no questions asked, and work long hours for low wages and few benefits. Understanding that undocumented immigrants enjoy little in the way of actual legal protections and deeply fear deportation, many employers cannot resist the temptation to exploit them. The making of demands by undocumented immigrants on employers means loss of a job.

Laws other than the immigration laws also contribute to the exploitation of undocumented immigrants. In 2002, the Supreme Court ruled that the National Labor Relations Board could not order employers to provide back pay to undocumented workers who had been unlawfully discharged by their employer for union-organizing activities. According to the Court, to do so "would encourage the successful evasion of apprehension by immigration authorities, condone prior violations of the immigration laws, and encourage future violations."[125] Given this decision, undocumented workers now face much greater risks in seeking to unionize than do U.S. citizens and lawful immigrants. Many already find relations with employers difficult, given their vulnerable status in the United States, and no doubt generally fear losing their jobs if they seek to improve their wages and conditions. In addition, employers can now violate the rights of undocumented workers with little fear of meaningful punishment.

Some states have relied on the Supreme Court's reasoning to deny workers compensation and other benefits to undocumented workers.[126]

Employers often fail to provide worker's compensation insurance, pensions, unemployment insurance, or other benefits. Denial of benefits and protections to undocumented workers makes their labor less costly to employers. This creates even greater incentives for employers to hire them. Although employers benefit, undocumented workers lose out on the protections that U.S. law generally provides citizens and lawful immigrants.

Undocumented immigrants also lack other basic legal protections. The Supreme Court has held that Title VII of the Civil Rights Act of 1964, the major legal protection against employment discrimination in the United States, does not bar discrimination against employees that is based on immigration status.[127] In addition, although a provision of the immigration laws prohibits discrimination against noncitizens who are legally authorized to work,[128] enforcement of that prohibition has not been a high priority for the federal government. To make matters worse, the available evidence suggests that some employers discriminate against Latina/o and Asian-American citizens and lawful immigrants for fear of hiring undocumented immigrants.[129]

A significant uncertainty exists about whether Title VII of the Civil Rights Act offers any protections whatsoever to undocumented immigrants. Courts have not been consistent in determining whether the nation's major antidiscrimination law protects undocumented workers from racial, national-origin, or other forms of otherwise unlawful discrimination. Some courts have ruled that undocumented immigrants are *not* eligible for any relief under Title VII. Others courts have barred employers defending discrimination lawsuits from even inquiring into the immigration status of a Title VII plaintiff.[130] The Supreme Court has failed to intervene to clarify matters.

Discrimination against undocumented immigrants on the basis of race, national origin, and gender in the workplace constitutes a serious problem in this country. Because of their uncertain immigration status, they may fear pursuing any remedies to which they might be entitled under the law. In any event, whatever rights undocumented immigrants may have are far from clear.

Despite the fact that undocumented workers form a significant part of the U.S. force, they are not protected by the law in any meaningful way.[131] Rather, they inhabit a legal never-never land where their rights, obligations, and protections are never certain and constantly changing. Some laws, like minimum-wage and basic-working-condition laws, ostensibly protect undocumented workers in the workplace. However, government fails to enforce these laws in any meaningful way with respect to the undocumented workforce.

As a result, undocumented workers effectively form part of the secondary labor market and work outside legal and regulatory constraints.[132] A segmented labor market flourishes across the United States, despite the fact that its very existence is technically illegal. The immigration laws offer employers in the secondary labor market powerful leverage over undocumented workers. Undocumented workers often face a "take it or leave it" decision with respect to the terms and conditions of their employment. Today, in the United States, the rights of undocumented workers are effectively whatever employers say they are, nothing more, nothing less.

Not coincidentally, the disposable labor force that immigration law has helped to create in the United States is composed primarily of immigrants of color from the developing world.[133] In effect, we see the existence of a new racial caste system in the United States that has replaced the old system that existed in the days of Jim Crow. The current immigrant labor system is nothing less than a variant of the old sharecropping system in the South. Poorly paid, exploitative jobs are reserved for marginalized immigrants of color. Immigration law thus contributes to racial stratification in the U.S. labor market. In this way, labor exploitation overlaps with concerns about the racial discrimination embedded in the U.S. immigration laws and their enforcement.

Highly publicized cases abound of extreme instances of immigrant exploitation. These instances demonstrate another cost of an ineffective system of immigration and labor laws. In southern California, smugglers brought Thai immigrants to the United States and forced them to work for low wages in a garment factory surrounded by high walls, razor wire, and guards.[134] But immigrant exploitation is not limited to sweatshops. In another much-publicized case, human traffickers brought hearing-impaired and mute Mexican immigrants to this country and forced them to sell trinkets and beg on the streets of New York, only to be beaten if their earnings were deemed insufficient.[135]

However, highly publicized instances of unscrupulous persons holding noncitizens in horrible conditions represent only the tip of the exploitation iceberg.[136] As discussed earlier in this chapter, slavery has made a comeback in the United States.[137] Suburban sweatshops, with forms of labor exploitation less harsh than outright slavery, have arisen in locales across the country.[138]

With increased border enforcement, human trafficking has emerged as a major business, and international criminal networks have been spurred to enter this lucrative field. These elements now dominate the smuggling industry. The trafficking of human beings

> is the third largest international criminal enterprise, behind drugs and arms smuggling. This industry . . . generates a global income of $7 to $10 billion each year. . . . Human trafficking has grown to "epidemic proportions" within the last decade and continues to flourish. It is estimated that 600,000 to 800,000 people are trafficked transnationally each year. . . . *About seventy percent of all victims are women and girls, the majority of whom are forced to work in the commercial sex industry. Between 14,500 and 17,500 people . . . , are transported into the United States each year. Roughly half of U.S. victims are forced into the commercial sex industry while the other half are forced into sweatshops or domestic servitude.*[139]

Trafficking, slavery, and labor exploitation all have specific impacts on women immigrants, who often are the most exploited of all immigrants.[140] Forced prostitution of immigrant women is a serious, and growing, social problem.[141] Stories abound of women and children forced to sell their bodies.

The mistreatment of women, however, is not limited to the sex industry. It also exists as a more general labor market problem.[142] Unfortunately, undocumented women are regularly sexually harassed in the workplace.[143] Many day laborers—some of the most exploited laborers—are women.[144] Abuse runs rampant in the domestic-service industry, where women are heavily represented.[145] Many middle-class and professional families in the United States need domestic-service workers to assist in the home but compensate them poorly. Often, these workers labor long hours and live in the home of their employer. Impersonal, callous, and even harsh treatment of workers is all too common.[146]

Responding to the public outcry over the publicity generated by such abuses, the law has begun to address the problem. Congress passed the Trafficking Victims Protection Act of 2000 and the Trafficking Victims Protection Reauthorization Act of 2003.[147] Nonetheless, human trafficking continues to be a significant problem in the United States. According to the U.S. General Accountability Office, efforts to curb human smuggling need to be significantly improved.[148]

The morality of immigrant labor exploitation is even more questionable when contrasted with emerging international legal obligations to undocumented workers.[149] International law requires states to protect certain rights of migrants in their jurisdiction. For example, the Universal Declaration of Human Rights,[150] the International Convention for the Protection of Migrants,[151] and the International Covenant on Civil and Political Rights[152] all offer legal protections to immigrants.[153] Many prohibit the kinds of actions taken by, and the omissions of, the U.S. government. That immigrants suffer mistreatment in the United States in violation of international law suggests that the border controls that help facilitate that mistreatment are illegitimate. Such mistreatment further indicates a broken system in serious need of fixing.

Besides having few rights in the workplace, immigrants are eligible for few public benefits in the United States and lack the protections of the so-called safety net that citizens enjoy.[154] Free medical care, except for emergency services, is often not generally available to poor undocumented immigrants. For poor immigrants, there is no access to preventive medicine or to medical care to combat debilitating disease.

In addition, undocumented immigrants are often exploited in the housing market.[155] They often find themselves living in segregated neighborhoods that offer few public services and plenty of social problems. *Colonias,* unincorporated areas that lack the amenities of cities and towns, dot the border region. The lack of any legal protections for undocumented immigrants makes these poor conditions possible and enduring.[156]

Undocumented immigrants are more vulnerable than other groups and more at risk in all social and economic interactions. Immigration controls have helped to create a large undocumented labor force subject to economic exploitation.[157] Incremental reforms, such as the guest worker program proposed by President Bush, may subject workers to further exploitation.[158] This certainly was the case with the last large-scale temporary worker program, the Bracero Program, which was in place from World War II until the early 1960s. Temporary workers enjoyed few of the protections that the law guaranteed them, and employer abuses ran rampant.[159] Because of the potential for the exploitation of the guest workers, such programs are at most a second-best alternative to open borders.[160]

Liberal admissions would help to minimize the potential for the type of exploitative labor system that we see in the United States today. Removing the lever of uncertain legal status and engaging in meaningful workplace enforcement of wage, condition, and discrimination laws would do much to improve the working lives of many undocumented workers. No principled justification exists for employers' rampant failure to comply with the laws that protect the wages and working conditions of all workers. Nor can one morally justify the U.S. government's failure to intervene. Employers, however, have much to gain from the government's failure to enforce the laws protecting undocumented workers. They therefore can be expected to forcefully resist the extension of any legal protections to undocumented workers, just as they often resist any additional worker protections.

Special Moral Obligations to Mexican Immigrants

This chapter has argued that the United States owes moral obligations to noncitizens generally. However, in part because of the symbiotic relationship that has existed for many decades between the two nations, the United States and Mexico share a unique relationship.[161] Consequently, the nation arguably owes an even greater moral obligation to citizens of Mexico who seek to migrate to the United States.

The migration of Mexican labor to the United States has been long and sustained. The U.S. government has encouraged the migration through immigration law and its enforcement, and, at times, through lack of enforcement.[162] At least through the early twentieth century, migration from Mexico to the United States was relatively easy. The militarized border, so familiar to us today, was nonexistent. The Border Patrol, designed primarily to police against migration from Mexico, was not created until 1924.[163]

Until relatively recently, there had been no real effort to discourage migration from Mexico to the United States.[164] The U.S. government has historically enforced the immigration laws in ways that provide employers with a ready supply of low-wage labor.[165] At various times when low-skilled labor was in high demand, the U.S. government facilitated the entry of Mexican workers into the country in order to ensure that supply met demand.

Today, undocumented Mexican workers are critical to the economic viability of many businesses. Agriculture, hotels and restaurants, construction, and the domestic-service industry depend on these workers. Growers have relied upon generations of migrant labor to pick the nation's crops and keep produce prices down. Hotels and restaurants rely on immigrant labor to provide a ready and available labor force and to ensure profitability. With the number of two-wage-earner families having increased greatly in the past few decades, U.S. middle-class families demand domestic-service workers in abundance. That demand continues to increase because of the increasing participation of U.S. women citizens in the labor force.

Wage disparities contribute significantly to the continued flow of migrants from Mexico. Mexican workers migrate to earn higher wages than they ordinarily can earn in their homeland. U.S. employers look for cheaper labor than they ordinarily can obtain in this country. Because cheap labor lowers production costs, employers profit. Because lower costs of production mean lower prices for goods and services, U.S. consumers benefit, as well. But the workers whose labor allows such benefits generally go unrewarded.

The so-called Bracero Program institutionalized the labor arrangement for a time by bringing temporary workers to this country from Mexico from the 1940s to the 1960s.[166] Braceros established families and developed communities. As one might expect, they also later brought family members and friends to the United States. The program thus helped create the extensive family ties and social networks that helped fuel immigration and continue to promote Mexican migration today.[167]

At the same time, the U.S. government has not infrequently deported undocumented workers when their labor was no longer needed or the public simply grew concerned with Mexican immigrants in the greater community. Mass deportation campaigns like the "repatriation" campaign of the Great Depression and "Operation Wetback," in 1954, mar U.S. history.[168] This revolving door of disposable labor long has been central to the American economy. There, however, obviously can be no moral justification for race-based deportation campaigns.

The size of the flow of immigrants from Mexico and Mexico's proximity to the United States render Mexican migration unique. Mexico sends more immigrants to the United States than any other nation. From 1988 to 1998, for example, hundreds of thousands of lawful permanent residents from Mexico entered the United States annually.[169] Millions more entered outside legal channels. This large flow continues today.

A large undocumented Mexican population has lived and worked in this country for decades. That population has grown substantially in the past ten years. The federal government estimated that, in 1996, about 2.7 million undocumented immigrants from Mexico, accounting for about 54 percent of the total undocumented population, lived in the United States.[170] The federal government estimated that, as of January 2005, 10.6 million undocumented immigrants lived in the United States[171] and that the majority were from Mexico.

In 2005, the Pew Hispanic Center released a report estimating that 10.3 million unauthorized migrants lived in the United States. Approximately 57 percent of all undocumented immigrants were from Mexico.[172] More than two-thirds of the unauthorized immigrant population lived in eight states: California, Texas, Florida, New York, Arizona, Illinois, New Jersey, and North Carolina.[173] However, large immigrant populations, including large Mexican immigrant communities, have settled in states like Iowa, Missouri, Georgia, Arkansas, and North Carolina. Observers have characterized the phenomenon as the "Latinization" or "browning" of the United States.[174] By 2006, the Pew Hispanic Center estimated that 11.5 to 12 million undocumented immigrants were living in the United States and that roughly 56 percent were from Mexico.[175]

Surveys show that close to 60 percent of migrants plan to spend as long as they can, if not the rest of their lives, in the United States.[176] Some, however, do return to Mexico. The existence of return migration of Mexican citizens is often ignored and is generally not accounted for in studies of migration rates. Even so, the United States has a large Mexican immigrant population that is likely to remain, and is likely to grow, for the rest of the twenty-first century. Because of the social, economic, and political incentives for migration, it has not proven easy to stem the flow of migrants. Nor are there likely to be changes in the short term that would make it any easier to curtail Mexican immigration.

As a result of the long history of migration from Mexico to the United States, many Mexican immigrants in this country have deep community ties in, and allegiances to, both countries.[177] Their transnational identities have resulted in back-and-forth movement between the two nations and cultural and other bonds to both countries. With the recognition of dual nationality in the 1990s, these transnational identities have become formally recognized under both U.S. and Mexican law. Both governments now allow their citizens to assume dual nationality and to be citizens of both the United States and Mexico.[178] This legal recognition of migrants' ties to two nations represents a significant departure from the past, when most nations generally allowed their nationals to swear allegiance to only one sovereign.

Multinational ties have practical consequences. Recent years have seen the blossoming of hometown associations, in which migrants from certain cities in Mexico organize and collect funds to help pay for public improvements in their hometowns. These transfers from Mexican migrants to family members in Mexico, amounting to billions of dollars in remittances annually, have become critically important to the Mexican economy. Remittances fund municipal improvements, support families, and provide investment capital in Mexico.

Because this nation's policies have contributed to the great disparities in wealth between the two countries, the U.S. government arguably owes a special obligation to Mexican nationals. The economic disparities created by these conditions are the source of significant migration pressures.[179] Similar arguments could be made with respect to other developing nations where the United States is said to be responsible for poverty or other conditions, such as war and violence, that contribute to pressures for the emigration of people looking for safety and economic security. However, given that Mexico neighbors the United States and has an enduring and close economic relationship with this country, the moral obligations owed by the United States to Mexican migrants are especially great.

Despite the fact that this nation owes moral obligations to Mexican citizens, the U.S. government acts as if it had virtually no obligations to them, moral or otherwise. With its focus on restricting migration, the nation finds it easy to rationalize the claim that there are no limits on its sovereign right to deny entry to, or deport, noncitizens. The shield of national sovereignty works to protect the United States when critics challenge its restrictive immigration policies.

Over the past two decades, border enforcement efforts have centered almost myopically on keeping Mexican migrants out of the United States. The U.S. government has aggressively pursued strategies to deter and punish Mexican migrants. Deportations and criminal prosecutions for immigration crimes have increased greatly in recent years. Border enforcement policies have had deadly human consequences and have contributed to racial discrimination against Mexican migrants and Mexican-Americans in the U.S. society. Consequently, the United States would need to make a complete about-face in its immigration law and policy to recognize its moral obligations to Mexican immigrants.

Even if one wholly rejects open borders, U.S. obligations to Mexico and its citizens militate in favor of freer migration between the two countries. President Vicente Fox of Mexico has advocated open borders between the United States and Mexico.[180] Free migration within the North American trade bloc could resemble the system of labor migration that has evolved in the European Union. Time will tell, however, whether the U.S. government, and the American public, will be willing to institutionalize formal changes in the migration relationship between the United States and Mexico.

Conclusion

U.S. immigration law is wholly inconsistent with the nation's devotion to individual rights and to the moral underpinnings of the U.S. Constitution. National sovereignty has long served as the justification for strict border enforcement. International law, however, sets limits on a nation's powers to exclude and deport immigrants.

The current immigration law and enforcement system in place in the United States has immoral consequences, including racial discrimination, exploitation of undocumented workers, death, and human trafficking. It creates serious inequities due to race and national origin. Because avenues for legal immigration are limited, the laws facilitate undocumented immigration and result in the deaths of desperate migrants who, against all odds, risk their lives in search of jobs and family reunification in the United States. Innocent dreamers have died horrible deaths for no good reason.

To make matters worse, the law assists in the exploitation of immigrant workers by increasing their vulnerability once they enter the United States. Over the tail end of the twentieth century, a new, but often invisible, racial caste system slowly emerged in the United States. Immigration law in the United States allows for labor exploitation along racial lines. It is a new Jim Crow system.

Labor exploitation is a special problem with respect to immigrants from Mexico. Mexican citizens are the largest group of immigrants in the United States. The U.S. government's policies have, over time, encouraged their entry into this country, using them to supply an inexpensive, exploitable labor force beneficial to American employers and consumers. But the same government that encourages their migration has wholly failed to protect them from exploitation and abuse. It has persistently allowed these poor people to remain vulnerable to exploitation. Moral obligations grow out of such treatment but have yet to be recognized by the U.S. government.

In order to bring U.S. immigration law into line with the nation's moral compass, change is essential. The system, by almost all accounts, is broken. The fundamental question about which there is serious difference of opinion is the solution. The immigration issues that face the United States will not go away due to wishful thinking or tough talk. Such responses, unfortunately, dominate public discussion of immigration in the United States.

Border controls and their enforcement, and their immoral consequences, must be reexamined. This is the case even if the United States wants to maintain a closed-borders system. It is impossible to justify an ineffective *and* immoral immigration system.

More liberal immigration admissions would help ameliorate the rampant discrimination that the immigration laws aid and abet. The consequences of such a system need not generate fear. Open borders might ultimately have consequences similar to those brought by the increased migration of African Americans from the rural South to the urban North in the twentieth century. In the era of Jim Crow, interstate migration helped fuel economic growth and provided economic and other opportunities to subordinated African Americans. Similarly, freer movement of workers from the developing world would create economic opportunities and ensure orderly migration and the maintenance of a more fair and just set of immigration laws.

Open borders would result in a more moral immigration scheme in the United States. It would be more consistent with the national commitment to individual rights and the "huddled masses." It would help reduce the serious immoral consequences of current immigration law. It would make us a better nation.

4

The Economic Benefits of
Liberal Migration of
Labor Across Borders

It makes economic sense to open borders.
— *Financial Times,* June 2005[1]

[I]f Washington still wants to "do something" about immigration, we propose a five-word [constitutional] amendment: "There shall be open borders."   — *The Wall Street Journal,* July 1984[2]

In Chapter 3, I laid out the moral arguments based on liberal theory for more open immigrant admissions. This chapter offers a utilitarian justification for more open borders. It outlines the economic arguments for increasing the mobility of labor across national boundaries. Specifically, this chapter contends that liberal admissions, with orderly, efficient, and safe entry of immigrant labor, would significantly benefit the U.S. economy.

Free trade and free labor both enjoy a long intellectual pedigree. From an economic perspective, labor and capital are fungible factors of production in a market economy. Migration to the United States increases the labor supply in this country and thus directly impacts the economy.[3] This, of course, is elementary macroeconomic theory. Surprisingly enough, however, the United States often fails to give significant weight to economic considerations in the formulation of immigration law and policy.

What is necessary in the debate over immigration is a heavy dose of economic reality, pure and simple. This nation's economic future—and its continued existence as a world power—rests in no small part on how it addresses migration in the twenty-first century. The U.S. immigration laws must be fundamentally revised to make them and their enforcement more consistent with the economic needs of the nation.[4]

As the quotes from the *Financial Times* and *The Wall Street Journal* suggest, advocates for immigration come from the mainstream business community, as well as from immigrant rights activists. And it is not simply low-skilled labor that employers demand. Bill Gates, the billionaire founder of Microsoft, regularly complains that immigration restrictions hamper high-tech employers from securing skilled workers from other countries.[5] Many high-tech executives have registered similar complaints.

The arguments for facilitating the migration of highly skilled immigrant workers to the United States have become increasingly powerful in light of the globalization of the international economy. In the midst of globalizing markets in capital and goods, adherents of closed borders must justify the exclusion of labor from a system of increasingly permeable borders.

Economic arguments generally favor easy migration between nations and the ready mobility of labor to its most productive use. The labor market benefits of immigrant workers to the United States are undeniable. Nonetheless, as one policy analyst put it,

> U.S immigration policy is based on denial. Most lawmakers in the United States have largely embraced the process of economic "globalization," yet stubbornly refuse to acknowledge that increased migration, especially from developing nations, is an integral and inevitable part of this process. Instead, they continue in an impossible quest that began shortly after World War II: the creation of a transnational market in goods and services without a corresponding transnational market for the workers who make those goods and provide those services. *In defiance of economic logic, U.S. lawmakers formulate immigration policies to regulate the entry of foreign workers into the country that are largely unrelated to the economic policies they formulate to regulate international commerce.* Even in the case of Mexico . . . , the U.S. government tries to impose the same arbitrary limits on immigration as it does on a country as remote as Mongolia. Moreover, while the global trade of goods, services, and capital is regulated through multilateral institutions and agreements, U.S. policymakers persist in viewing immigration as primarily a matter of domestic law enforcement. . . . Lawmakers must devise a realistic solution to this dilemma. *Perpetuating the status quo*

by pouring ever larger amounts of money into the enforcement of immigration policies that are in conflict with economic reality will do nothing to address the underlying problem.[6]

In a similar vein, the Immigration Policy Center contends that "current U.S. immigration policies remain largely unresponsive to the labor needs of the U.S. economy by imposing arbitrary and static limits on employment-based immigration that have merely diverted labor migration to the undocumented channels or further clogged the family-based immigration system."[7]

Despite their inconsistency with economic reality, border enforcement efforts, like tough-on-crime measures, find ready and willing support among the public and politicians. At the same time, they offer precious little likelihood of success. Heightened border enforcement, like Prohibition and its similarly misplaced successor, the "war on drugs," offers a politically popular response to a perceived problem that fails to deliver the goods. This should not be surprising. Strict border enforcement runs squarely against economic currents that the law simply cannot overcome. To make matters worse, immigration controls ultimately damage the U.S. economy and seriously distort domestic labor markets in troubling ways.

As many economists have observed, in order to achieve steady economic growth with a minimum of inflation, an economy requires an expanding labor force. Over the past fifty years, the addition of immigrant labor to the economy has unquestionably had a dramatic effect on the domestic labor market. Economists have credited the influx of immigrant labor with helping to spark the economic boom times of the 1990s, one of the more sustained periods of economic growth in U.S. history.[8] Crediting the economic growth of the 1990s to immigrant labor, the much-revered former chair of the Federal Reserve Board, Alan Greenspan, further suggested that immigrants contributed more than their fair share to the economy.[9] Fundamentally, many immigrants take on low-wage jobs that are not particularly easy for employers to fill in many parts of the country.[10]

Many sectors of the global economy have become increasingly competitive. Some U.S. employers bank—figuratively and literally—on undocumented labor in order to compete in the global marketplace. Low-cost immigrant labor increases a business's capacity to compete by providing certain benefits to employers and the U.S. economy as a whole.

Consumers benefit from lower prices for many commodities, including fruits and vegetables, and meat and poultry, and for services such as domestic-service work, hotels and restaurants, and construction. In addition, the money spent by undocumented immigrants on goods and services spurs further economic activity and benefits every economic actor. These expenditures have ripple effects through all sectors of the U.S. economy.

Large employers in certain industries often rely heavily on undocumented immigrants. Recently, several high-profile companies have had their hiring practices exposed. The poultry giant Tyson Foods faced a criminal indictment, and was later acquitted, for participating in a scheme to traffic immigrant workers. Its employment of undocumented workers, however, could not seriously be disputed.[11] Wal-Mart repeatedly makes the news for its employment of undocumented immigrants.[12]

Entire industries, such as agriculture, meat and poultry processing, construction, and the hotel and restaurant sector, have come to rely heavily on undocumented labor to remain competitive. This dependence on undocumented labor has led to vigorous resistance to federal enforcement efforts. For example, when the federal government began an operation to enforce the laws barring the employment of undocumented immigrants in meat-packing plants in Nebraska in 1999, state and local politicians protested because of the impacts on the state economy.[13] An American Farm Bureau Federation study concluded that, *"if agriculture's access to migrant labor were cut off, as much as $5–9 billion in annual production of . . . commodities . . . would be lost in the short term. Over the longer term, this annual loss would increase to $6.5–12 billion as the shock worked its way through the sector."*[14]

Without undocumented workers, businesses in some industries would be forced to close. Such a collapse would drag down the U.S. economy. As the preeminent economist John Kenneth Galbraith stated,

> Were all the illegals in the United States suddenly to return home, the effect on the United States economy would . . . be little less than disastrous. . . . A large amount of useful, if often tedious, work . . . would go unperformed. Fruits and vegetables in Florida, Texas, and California would go unharvested. Food prices would rise spectacularly. Mexicans wish to come to the United States; they are wanted; they add visibly to our well-being. . . . Without them, the American economy would suffer.[15]

The popular 2004 film "A Day Without a Mexican" offered a tongue-in-cheek look at how the U.S. economy would dramatically stop in its tracks without Mexican workers. As with all humor, the movie offered a grain of truth. We know in our heart of hearts that at least part of the U.S. economy would grind to a sudden halt if immigrant workers were no longer available.

Despite the tangible economic benefits bestowed on the nation by immigrants, U.S. immigration law has been deeply ambivalent, if not downright schizophrenic, about immigration and immigrant workers. Overall, the law has done a poor job of balancing the economic interests at stake. The U.S. government often fails to even consider basic labor economics in formulating immigration law and policy. As a result, the nation has created a system in which undocumented workers are integral to the national economy but, at the very same time, find themselves exploited, marginalized, and abused. To make matters worse, because the labor pool depends on the vagaries of immigration enforcement, employers may face fluctuations in the supply of labor, which necessarily affects productivity and profits.

Billions of dollars are spent on enforcing immigration laws that are in effect unenforceable. The nation's massive border enforcement efforts resemble a never-ending war in Vietnam or, more recently, Afghanistan and Iraq. Like those wars, border enforcement results in the expenditure of billions of dollars and thousands of deaths with no tangible benefit. Nothing resembling victory, or even stabilization of the immigration flow, is currently in sight. Economically, nothing can justify this deadweight loss.

While the political clamor for immigration enforcement continues unabated, and Congress approves such misplaced measures as extending border fences, attention to the economic consequences of immigration has been minimal. Globalization of the world economy has been steadily proceeding over the post–World War II period. By the end of the twentieth century, economic integration of national economies had been achieved at a level never previously attained. For better or worse, multinational corporations have come to dominate the economies of many nations all over the world.

The dramatic escalation in the trade of goods and services between and among nations led one observer to opine that we live in a "borderless world."[16] Absent cataclysmic change, there is no way to reverse globalization at this juncture. But, despite globalization, and despite the increasingly interlinked economies between nations, borders, border guards, and border enforcement limit the movement of people into the United States.

Although the legal distinction between labor and capital is well established, the economic distinction is far from clear. From an economic standpoint, both are substitutable factors of production. Absent special justification, the law should treat the two as equivalents. A corollary of the anti-immigrant economic argument is that open borders in a welfare state will bankrupt the nation as immigrants overconsume public benefits. As explained later in the chapter, such fears for the most part are grossly exaggerated and lack empirical support.

Oddly enough, the United States continues to treat labor and goods and services differently. It embraces comprehensive immigration restrictions as it simultaneously opens its borders to trade and flows of capital, goods, and services. As Kitty Calavita has aptly observed, "the irony is that in this period of globalization marked by its free movement of capital and goods, the movement of labor is subject to greater restrictions than at the dawn of the Industrial Revolution."[17]

There is one critically important—and rather obvious—difference between goods and people: Workers are human beings. New people bring families, cultures, languages, and change to the nation. What they bring therefore is qualitatively different from what is brought by an influx of foreign capital or goods. As Max Frisch wrote in discussing guest workers in Germany, "[w]e wanted workers, but humans came."[18] This fact, as a political matter, seriously complicates the debate over immigration. People fear the cultural and other changes, including to the national identity, brought by new people. That fear animates the nativism that has arisen time and again in U.S. history. In certain instances, such fears have been allowed to trump economic imperatives.

It is true that immigrants transform the societies they join. But this transformation has occurred time and time again in world, and U.S., history. In many respects, change in societies is natural, expected, and essential to survival. Immigrants therefore should be viewed as the economic, social, and cultural lifeblood of U.S. society, rather than as a threat to be feared and punished.

Even though Congress passes immigration laws without considering the true economic impacts of immigration and immigrant labor, the U.S. government fully appreciates that immigration, including undocumented immigration, affects the national economy. The 2005 Economic Report of the President analyzes in detail the positive effects of immigration on the economy. The Report unequivocally concludes, in a passage that received virtually no public attention, that *"[a] comprehensive accounting of the benefits and costs of immigration shows that the benefits of immigration exceed the costs."*[19]

Freer migration makes economic sense for the United States. Only time will tell whether the nation will realize that liberal immigration admissions will handsomely benefit its economy and act accordingly.

Economic Justifications: A Utilitarian Rationale for Liberal Immigration Policies

Both micro- and macroeconomic arguments have long been made in support of liberal immigration policies.[20] At the macroeconomic level, a strong argument can be made that more open, less restrictive immigration laws and policies that promote labor mobility would confer economic substantial benefits on U.S. society. Conservative and liberal economists alike embrace free trade as beneficial to the United States. Virtually identical arguments can be marshaled in support of free migration.

Long an unabashed supporter of easy labor migration, *The Wall Street Journal* proclaimed in 1984 that "[i]f Washington still wants to 'do something' about immigration, we propose a five-word [constitutional] amendment: There shall be open borders."[21] This sentiment is far from a humanitarian gesture. Employers and business gain handsomely from the ready availability of relatively inexpensive labor, which is particularly advantageous in highly competitive industries. Put bluntly, employers generally support more open immigration policies because of the profits that they hope to reap through the employment of inexpensive immigrant labor.

At various times in U.S. history, business interests have vigorously supported less restrictive immigration laws.[22] Driven by the profit motive, employers may be expected to support policies, including guest worker programs and lax enforcement of employer sanctions, which allow them ready access to cheap immigrant labor. Employers resist and aggressively fight efforts at meaningful enforcement of the immigration laws. Even after congressional passage of the Immigration Reform and Control Act of 1986,[23] which for the first time made employers subject to sanctions for the employment of undocumented immigrants, many employers have continued to hire undocumented immigrants. In addition, business has strong economic incentives to advocate law and policies that ensure continued and expanded access to immigrant labor.

The employer interest in cheap labor helps explain the unique domestic politics that surround immigration law and policy. Conservative business interests generally favor more immigration and fewer immigration restrictions. As a result, "liberal-conservative," "red state-blue state" dichotomies do not nicely capture the complex nuances of immigration politics. Importantly, the major political parties have been deeply divided on immigration law and policy for decades.

Conservatives generally find themselves deeply split on the issue of immigration. Some staunch members of the Republican Party, including President George W. Bush, generally favor liberal admission policies, or at least more liberal policies than the ones currently in place. Economic conservatives see gains from immigration and inexpensive labor. In stark contrast, another wing of the Republican Party is deeply concerned with the alleged cultural impacts of immigration. This faction aggressively plays on populist fear about cultural changes blamed on immigrants and demands restrictionist policies and tougher border enforcement. Today, this arm of the Republican Party, represented most prominently by Congressman Tom Tancredo and the conservative icon Pat Buchanan, often exercises great influence over the direction of immigration law and policy by tapping into broad-based fears of economically and otherwise insecure U.S. citizens. Poor, working, and middle-income people worry about the changes wrought by immigration and are not likely to sympathize with the desire of big business for cheap labor.

On the other hand, Democrats also find themselves divided on immigration. Economically, they are concerned with immigration's downward pressure on the wage scale and its impact on a long-time base of Democratic support, labor unions. Although change has come in recent years, organized labor, often supportive of the basic Democratic agenda, has historically supported restrictionist immigration laws and policies. Many liberals, however, desire the humane treatment of immigrants and often push for pro-immigration and pro-immigrant laws and policies.

There, however, is some common ground. Many Democrats and Republicans often agree that increased border enforcement is necessary. Like tough-on-crime stances, this has proved time and time again to be a politically popular position. This is even true for those sympathetic to the plight of immigrants. In addition, influenced by public fears of being overrun by floods of immigrants, politicians of both parties often support limits on legal immigration and heavy border enforcement.

Of course, employers are not the only economic actors to benefit from immigrants. Upon migrating to the United States, immigrants often see tangible economic benefits in the form of increased wages. Indeed, economic opportunity is unquestionably one of the primary motivators behind many migrants' difficult decision to leave their homeland and come to this country. Not surprisingly, the immigrants most likely to migrate to the United States come from the developing world, where wages and economic opportunities are much less than those in this country.

Many, perhaps most, immigrants come to this country for jobs that pay more than those in their homeland. Earnings that are low by U.S. standards represent real improvements over what many migrants would be able to earn at home. Working conditions, while substandard by American lights, may well be worth the wage gains to the migrant worker from the developing world. Indeed, they may be comparable to, or perhaps better than, those available in the migrant's homeland.

But, there are other economic gains from undocumented immigrants. Undocumented immigrants living in this country are not just workers. They also are consumers who purchase goods and services. As the undocumented immigrant population has grown in this country, so has its purchasing power, and thus its importance to economic activity at the national, state, and local levels. Not surprisingly, businesses, seeing the future, have responded aggressively to this new, and growing, market.

In order to tap into new and lucrative markets, increasing numbers of banks (including Wells Fargo Bank), health insurers (Blue Shield of California and Blue Shield of Georgia, for example), savings and loans, and home mortgage companies have begun to accept foreign identification cards, rather than requiring official U.S. identification cards. For Mexican citizens, the acceptance of the *matricula consular* as recognized identification has opened the door to many economic opportunities and, for many businesses, new customers. For obvious reasons, businesses are eager to pursue new and expanding markets and are little concerned with the immigration status of paying customers.

Companies are now designing and marketing consumer products to undocumented immigrants—often Latina/o—in certain parts of the country.[24] Immigration and immigrants have triggered cultural changes in the market that have had economic ripple effects. Salsa, for example, has surpassed catsup as the most consumed condiment in the United States. Tacos are a staple in many American diets.

As economists know, a "multiplier effect" emanates from every dollar spent in the economy. Each added dollar is spent and respent many times, generating much more than one dollar of economic activity. Consequently, every expenditure in the economy stimulates the national economy. As a result, undocumented immigrants benefit the U.S. economy in at least two ways: (1) they provide relatively cheap labor, which reduces costs of many goods and services for consumers and fuels the overall domestic economy; and (2) they spend money in the economy, thereby stimulating further economic activity.

Not surprisingly, immigrants have helped to economically revitalize rundown urban centers. New York and Los Angeles are two well-known examples of cities that have seen urban decay transformed into renewal due to immigration. Immigrants come to these urban areas in search of economic opportunity. High-immigration areas often tend to be areas of high economic growth and great economic activity. That makes perfect economic sense. Migrants have no incentive to move to places where jobs and opportunities are not available. Bringing ambition, energy, and hope, migrants and their families have helped to turn around abandoned urban centers across the United States. They have added labor and new businesses.

In a closed-borders regime like that which exists in the United States today, undocumented immigration provides concrete economic benefits that encourage economic actors to violate the law. As one economist aptly put it:

> It is not easy to fashion a convincing economic argument against an open door toward temporary workers with employer sponsorship, and thus illegal immigration may be in large part the result of economically unsound U.S. policies. Furthermore, because illegal aliens participate only minimally in entitlement programs, do not vote, and usually pay taxes like other workers, it is by no means clear that their presence should be viewed as a "problem." Without an appropriate policy regarding the admission of temporary workers, illegal immigration may be a "second-best" response to the resulting economic inefficiencies.[25]

In the short run, the tension between free trade and closed borders can perhaps be explained by political exigencies. In the long run, however, the strong economic pressures in play will not be easy to forestall through border controls. Some day, borders as we know them today will be as antiquated as covered wagons, the use of leeches as a medical procedure, and mimeograph machines.

The Analogy to International Trade: Benefits to the National Economy

International trade analysis suggests that labor migration is a net benefit to the national welfare. The United States has much to gain economically from immigration. However, U.S. immigration law and policy continues to lag in considering the economic benefits of liberal immigrant admissions. To the extent that the nation considers labor market needs in formulating immigration law and policy, they usually are secondary to other concerns.

The economic arguments in favor of more open immigration policies resemble those employed by international trade advocates for the free trade of goods and services across national boundaries. The proliferation of trade agreements, including regional arrangements such as the European Union and the North American Free Trade Agreement, and global institutions, like the World Trade Organization, show the current worldwide popularity of free trade. Leaders of many nations have promoted the elimination of barriers to the exchange of capital, goods, and services. They have recognized that opening the borders benefits not only their own nation but the world community, as well.

Relying on international trade economics, Howard Chang has argued that liberalizing immigration policies would likely increase national and global economic welfare. In his estimation, freer migration policies would permit a more efficient use of the untapped source of relatively low-wage labor in countries across the world.[26] Some empirical evidence supports Chang's intuition. One influential econometric study found that, "[a]lthough highly speculative, the calculations reported here clearly suggest large potential worldwide efficiency gains from moving toward a worldwide labor market free of immigration controls."[27]

Moreover, immigration contributes to the greater global good. One of the most influential economists of the twentieth century, John Kenneth Galbraith, observed that "[m]igration . . . is the oldest action against poverty. It selects those who most want help. *It is good for the country to which they go; it helps to break the equilibrium of poverty in the country from which they come.*"[28]

The economic benefits of immigration, however, are not all easy to quantify, or to identify concretely. It is difficult, for example, to estimate precisely the impact of the ready availability of immigrant labor on consumer prices. The costs of immigration—such as the costs of providing a public education and emergency services by state and local governments—to the nation are far easier to quantify and are ably documented by advocates of immigration restrictions. For this and other reasons, the costs of immigration tend to dominate discussion of the economics of immigration. Because the benefits often are ignored, the economic impacts of immigration are frequently presented in a one-sided fashion.

Studies that have attempted to measure the overall economic impacts of immigration have not been entirely consistent. Some commentators conclude that the costs of immigration outweigh any benefits.[29] Other observers, including the U.S. government, contend that the alleged economic costs of immigration are overstated and are greatly outweighed by the benefits.[30] The most comprehensive empirical studies conclude that, in the larger scheme of things, any negative economic impacts of immigration on some segments of the labor market are relatively small and outweighed by the overall benefits to the economy.[31]

Even assuming that the costs of immigration on some segments of the U.S. economy do somewhat outweigh its benefits, opening the borders might still offer net welfare gains. In contrast to the current immigration laws' emphasis on family-based immigration,[32] greatly enhanced labor mobility might increase employment-based migration, especially among skilled immigrants. Many economists seeking to increase the economic benefits of immigration to the nation advocate this strategy.[33] In order to reap the greatest economic benefit from liberal admissions, the United States might even want to institutionalize systems that recruit the best and the brightest workers to come to work in this country. The economic upside of liberal admissions therefore could well be greater than it might appear at first glance.

Put simply, a more open U.S. immigration policy could benefit the national economy by encouraging the migration of skilled immigrants. Skilled workers would benefit certain employers and tend to stabilize, or possibly even push down, wages in those fields that, at various times, have seen shortages of skilled labor, such as the high-tech industry and nursing. The resulting "brain drain" from other nations would benefit the United States economically and offer opportunities to skilled immigrants the world over. By taking a nation's most skilled workers, it might, however, have negative effects on other nations, which in turn would implicate moral concerns.[34]

Because of the United States's position as a global economic leader, thousands of skilled workers migrate here annually. The desire to migrate already exists. However, there are many obstacles. The employment visa process "has been widely criticized as a broken system that is, at best grossly inefficient and, at worst, irrational."[35] Employers frequently complain about the labor certification process for legally bringing skilled workers into the United States because of the time and expense involved. Skilled workers must navigate a complex set of time-consuming and costly requirements that require the assistance of skilled —and often high-priced—attorneys. This unquestionably inhibits their migration. More open borders would eliminate many of the obstacles associated with the immigration of skilled workers and allow employers, and the nation, to more readily benefit from this labor source.

Because undocumented immigration currently occurs despite aggressive border enforcement efforts, it is entirely possible that a liberal admissions policy would not dramatically increase the number of immigrants entering the United States. It is hard to say but the possible benefits to the national economy justify taking that risk.

The Wealth Distribution Consequences of Open Borders and the Impact of Immigrant Labor on African Americans

According to some observers, globalization has led to increased economic inequality, with capital gaining at the expense of labor.[36] Adherents of this view vocally condemn the economic impacts of globalization. Perceived growing economic inequality resulting from globalization has generated controversy and, at times, protest.[37] Strong opposition to free trade, as exemplified by the sometimes violent protests in the 1990s against the World Trade Organization, has been voiced at various times in recent years.

Like global economic integration, any proposal to allow free migration can expect vociferous opposition. Immigration restrictionists often make forceful economic arguments for the maintenance of a limited-entry immigration system.[38] One major concern is that, although employers stand to benefit from an open-borders system, the concomitant costs would be imposed on poor and working people. Fears of greater economic inequality in the United States due to liberal immigration policies—with businesses getting wealthier while workers' wages decline with the influx of low-wage labor—often contribute to the populist, and often tumultuous, nature of anti-immigrant movements. Put differently, immigration often serves as ground zero in the modern class struggle.

Wage depression continues to be an issue in the modern immigration debate. The fear stems from the idea that immigrants will work for lower wages than U.S. citizens are willing to accept and that employers will consequently become unwilling to pay more than immigrants are willing to take. Employers and immigrant advocates, however, counter by claiming that immigrants are willing to perform labor that Americans simply will not do. Others argue that Americans would in fact take these jobs if they paid more. On the basis of this argument, some commentators have embraced immigration restrictions as a way of improving the wages and working conditions of unskilled workers in certain industries.[39]

Similarly, the claim that immigrant labor adversely affects *minority* citizens in low-wage jobs often finds its way into the immigration debate in the United States.[40] The argument knows no ideological limits and has been voiced by liberal as well as conservative commentators. For well over a century, immigration's impact on unskilled workers, especially African American workers, has been a frequently voiced concern. Some observers forcefully contend that, in recent years, immigration has adversely affected the economic fortunes of African Americans.[41]

Traditionally, workers in the United States have feared labor competition, and the downward pressure on wages, from immigrant labor. Labor unions have often been willing to support restrictionist immigration laws and policies. Organized labor's unequivocal support for the Chinese exclusion laws in the nineteenth century is a striking example. Labor's position on immigration, however, has changed significantly in recent years. As will be discussed shortly, organized labor today embraces the position that all workers in the United States should be organized. It focuses much less on advocating restrictionist positions than in the past. Nonetheless, U.S. citizens still fear losing jobs to immigrant labor and downward pressure on wages.

An inextricably related economic fear is that easy migration increases wealth inequality. This line of reasoning, which finds some support empirically, sees cheap labor allowing business to reap greater profits, accumulate more wealth, and gain at the expense of labor. As the old adage goes, the rich get richer, the poor get poorer. This, however, may well be an enduring characteristic of capitalism and a market economy, rather than the result of immigration and liberal admissions policies. Even if such fears were real, it may not be possible through border enforcement measures to halt highly motivated immigrants from entering the United States. Other policies are necessary to address wealth distribution concerns.

There is some evidence that low-wage immigrant workers in the United States, who immigrate to this country in substantial numbers, have palpable effects on the wage scale of the lowest-paid workers in the United States. Because these immigrants are willing to work for lower wages than are domestic workers, employers may offer to pay less. Unskilled U.S. citizens in urban, high-immigration areas are the most directly affected. One much-cited 2005 study by the Harvard economists George Borjas and Lawrence Katz attributed wage reductions for low-skilled workers to undocumented immigration from Mexico.[42] Other empirical studies, however, undermine this claim.[43] In fact, growing wage disparities may be attributable to factors other than undocumented immigration, such as globalization and decreasing unionization of workers in the United States.[44]

Even if the overall effects of immigration on unskilled citizens are relatively small, the impacts on discrete parts of the labor force are tangible and help generate tension between citizens and immigrants.[45] Unquestionably, immigration has transformed—and continues to transform—certain labor markets. Over the past few decades, jobs in the poultry and beef industries in the Midwest and the Southeast and the janitorial industry in Los Angeles have increasingly been filled by immigrants. In some circumstances, jobs that were held predominantly by African Americans have come to be taken for the most part by Latina/o immigrants.[46] These shifts have sparked tension and controversy.

Especially in major urban areas, immigrants—many of them Latina/o —may find themselves in direct competition with African American workers for low-wage jobs.[47] In addition, migration may not only affect the labor markets in high-immigration areas, where wages may be depressed, but also lead to migration of citizens outside those areas, which in turn has economic ripple effects throughout the United States.[48]

Despite these costs, economists have identified economic benefits from the migration of unskilled labor. Unskilled labor tends to increase demand for middle- and higher-skilled immigrants who are needed in order to efficiently utilize that unskilled labor. Complementarity of skills must be considered in evaluating the net benefit of immigrants on the labor market.[49] As one economist has noted,

> Foreign-born workers do not substitute perfectly for, and therefore do not compete with, most native-born workers. Rather the complementary nature of the skills, occupations, and abilities of foreign-born increases the productivity of natives, stimulates investment, and enhances the choices available to consumers. *As a result, immigration increases the average wages of all native-born workers, except those who do not have a high-school diploma.* Even for the small and shrinking number of native-born workers without a high school diploma, the decline in wages from immigration is much smaller than some have estimated.[50]

In fact, the relative decline in domestic wages due to immigration has been estimated at about 1 percent, quite small in the larger scheme of things.

In any event, even assuming that adverse distributional consequences result from liberal immigration policies, it is wealth redistribution policies, not immigration restrictions, that are in order.[51] If such policies were pursued, economic benefits from immigration could be reaped and the costs reimbursed to the economic losers from a portion of the net gains to the national economy. Transfer payments could be used to equalize the distribution of the benefits of easy labor migration. Workers adversely affected by immigration could receive direct or indirect transfer payments based on taxes charged to employers.

From an economic perspective, transfer policies that redistribute the economic benefits of immigration make much more sense than the dead-weight loss of ever-increasing expenditures on unsuccessful efforts to close the borders. Transfer policies, however, would obviously be strongly resisted. Politically, wealth transfer policies are difficult to enact into law because money is being taken from one group and given to another. Stigmatized as "welfare" or "taxes," such policies are often considered handouts to the undeserving poor or money grabs by big government.[52] Unlike the beneficiaries of immigration, the winners and losers in transfer schemes are clear for all to see.

For the most part, businesses and employers would be the losers in any wealth transfer scheme. They therefore have extremely strong incentives to resist such policies. They also have the resources available to mount strong political opposition to any such proposals. Thus, the biggest beneficiaries of open entry would no doubt resist redistribution proposals to reduce the wealth inequalities generated by open entry.

More permeable borders may exacerbate existing wealth disparities in the United States. Although such policies would be difficult politically, transfer programs make much more economic sense than the continuing fiscal drain of enforcing an elaborate system of immigration restrictions through border enforcement. Employers would have access to labor. Workers, as well as employers, would benefit.

Organized Labor and Immigrants

Any wage impacts due to immigration, according to economic studies, are relatively small.[53] Moreover, immigrants may contribute to overall gains to the economy, which ultimately translates into an overall increase in average wages for *all* workers.[54] The labor added by migrants may add to the overall economic growth of the nation. As the economy grows, benefits are realized by the entire nation. In the end, the benefits provided by immigrant workers appear to outweigh the costs associated with downward pressures on wages.

Despite the overall benefits of immigrants to the economy, organized labor historically has often taken restrictionist positions in the national debates on immigration. Traditionally, organized labor has greatly feared that downward pressures on the wage scale would result from an influx of immigrant workers. The impact of immigrants on the job market is a bread-and-butter concern that has contributed greatly to periodic xenophobic outbursts. These have, at times, dramatically affected the political process, culminating in patently restrictionist and punitive immigration laws. Historically, labor unions have supported restrictionist measures, including the infamous—and undisputedly racist—Chinese exclusion laws of the late nineteenth century.[55]

Anti-immigrant positions occasionally have even influenced the most progressive elements of the labor movement. The United Farm Workers (UFW), created by Mexican-American icon César Chávez, opposed the use of undocumented immigrants who served as strikebreakers as the UFW sought to organize the fields.[56] In fact, some UFW leaders may have been involved in violence directed at undocumented immigrant strikebreakers. For a time, the UFW even had a policy of reporting suspected "illegals" to the Immigration and Naturalization Service.

Times have changed. The UFW now tirelessly supports pro-immigrant measures. Instead of focusing its energies on keeping immigrant workers out of the United States, it directs the union's energies to the organization of all workers. Over time, the UFW's view of undocumented workers has shifted from pariahs to potential unionists. This ambivalence provides an example of how undocumented immigrants have confounded and perplexed the entire labor movement.

In recent years, organized labor more generally has moved away from its restrictionist past. Unions in the United States have dramatically shifted their position on immigration and are now exploring ways of organizing immigrant labor[57] and unionizing across national boundaries.[58] At the dawn of the new millennium, the AFL-CIO called for an end to employer sanctions and a new amnesty for undocumented workers.[59] Forced by reduced unionization rates to reconsider its position, the AFL-CIO announced its change after evidently coming to the realization that border controls and aggressive border enforcement have not prevented immigrant labor from entering the country and are unlikely to do so in the foreseeable future.[60]

Once one accepts the fact that the flow of immigrants into the United States is likely to continue, the most promising strategy for organized labor lies in unionizing *all* workers in this country, not just U.S. citizen workers. Levels of unionization are at an all-time low and could only benefit from expanding efforts to organize immigrant labor. With a broader base, unions would be in a much better position to fight for wage and condition improvements for all workers.

Given the realities of modern immigration, it is simply not realistic to support exclusionary measures in order to address the economic impacts of immigrants. Keeping immigrants out of the country does not appear to be possible, given the strong economic and family pull factors fueling modern immigration. Employers have too much to gain from cheaper immigrant labor. Immigrants from the developing world have too much to gain economically in terms of jobs and wage gains. Neither of these strong economic incentives is likely to change significantly in the foreseeable future.

Moreover, low-wage labor may be necessary to keep jobs and industries in the United States. Absent migration and an available low-wage labor force, businesses may relocate and move production facilities outside the United States in order to capitalize on lower labor costs in developing nations.[61] Over the past few decades, the migration of jobs and industries from the United States has occurred with increasing frequency. Absent a liberalization of the U.S. immigration laws, this movement is likely to continue to occur, and citizen workers may lose more jobs to developing nations.

As organized labor has realized, it is better to try to organize *all* workers—regardless of their immigration status—within the United States. The focus of labor advocates should be on enforcing wage and condition protections for workers and extending the law to apply to the undocumented labor force. Mass organization and activism among immigrant workers, including, for example, the Janitors for Justice movement and the Drywallers' strike in southern California in the 1990s, have occasionally been successful. However, as undocumented immigrant labor has little leverage in many industries and few protections under the law, much work will need to be done.

From organized labor's perspective, we currently have the worst of all worlds. Dual labor markets exist in the United States. One is regulated by law; the other is not. In the secondary market, undocumented and nonunionized workers are often paid less than the minimum wage and work in substandard conditions. Rather than try to remedy matters, the Supreme Court, with its 2002 decision in the *Hoffman Plastic* case, widened the gap between the rights available to undocumented workers and those of legal workers. The Court held that employers could not be ordered to reinstate undocumented immigrants who had been fired, in violation of the federal labor laws, for engaging in union organizing activities.[62] This ruling seriously undermines union efforts to organize undocumented workers and to challenge the existing dual-labor-market structure.

For employers, the allure of shifting jobs to the undocumented labor market is great because of the stark disparities between the rights and costs associated with the primary (legal) labor market and those associated with the secondary (illegal) labor market. Economically, it makes little sense for employers in some industries not to utilize undocumented workers for unskilled positions. Ultimately, the fact that undocumented immigrants lack fundamental legal protections makes it more difficult for U.S. citizen workers to effectively protect themselves. The more citizen workers demand, the more employers will feel pressured to shift jobs to the secondary labor market.

Immigrants and Public Benefits

Restrictionists historically have prevailed in convincing Congress to limit the immigration of poor and working noncitizens to the United States because of the widespread fear that they would empty the public coffers and fill the poor houses.[63] Based in no small part on popular stereotypes about immigrants of color from the developing world, the deep fear is that poor and working noncitizens who come to this country will consume public benefits, drain the economy of resources, and thus constitute a net drag on the national economy.[64] Few issues in the United States touch off the firestorm of controversy that is triggered by the perception that immigrants are consuming public benefits of which they are undeserving. Several important immigration milestones of the 1990s demonstrate the volatility of this issue.

California's Proposition 187, which voters passed by a 2–1 margin in 1994, exemplifies the heated public reaction to the grossly exaggerated belief that undocumented immigrants are excessively using public benefits.[65] This measure would have denied undocumented students access to the public schools and would have rendered them ineligible for virtually every public benefit. The campaign that culminated in the passage of Proposition 187 was inflamed by deeply anti-immigrant, and often anti-Mexican, rhetoric. More than a decade later, Arizona voters, after a similarly heated political campaign marred by a racially polarized vote, passed a similar law. Although a federal court barred Proposition 187 from going into effect because the state law intruded on the federal power to regulate immigration, its passage, and that of the Arizona measure, demonstrate how fears of that immigrants will receive public benefits may spark anti-immigrant laws.

Even though the available data suggest that immigrants benefit the U.S. economy more than they cost it,[66] the fear of immigrant welfare abusers deeply influences the public discussion of immigration. Stereotypes of fertile Mexican women sneaking into the United States to give birth to U.S. citizen children only adds fuel to the fire, just as images of the Black welfare "queen" deeply influence—"poison" might be a better word—the public policy debates over welfare. The public benefits issue arises sporadically and often influences virtually any controversy involving the rights of immigrants. For example, undocumented immigrant eligibility for a driver's license—an important public-safety issue—has been challenged by opponents who contend that undocumented immigrants are seeking some kind of public benefit to which they are not entitled.

The fear of immigrant benefit receipt is based on enduring stereotypes that are not supported by the data. One such stereotype is that immigrants—especially undocumented ones from Mexico—are wholly uneducated. But stereotypes are just that. Importantly, not all immigrants are poor and uneducated.

A 2002 study found that the education level of Latina/o immigrants, for example, has increased in recent years.[67] About one-half of all immigrants to the United States from Mexico reportedly have a high school diploma or college degree.[68] Educated Mexican citizens have much to gain economically from migrating, especially if they can secure jobs in the United States commensurate with their education. They are often willing to invest in their future and have the resources necessary to secure entry into the United States. Once in this country, they will likely work and are unlikely to access the available social benefits system.

Furthermore, few immigrants aim to consume public benefits. Many immigrants would never even consider attempting to access any public benefits program. They fear that receipt of any benefit could result in their deportation from the country. Provisions in the immigration laws give credence to this fear. The word is out in immigrant communities about the risk associated with receipt of public benefits.

In evaluating immigrant benefit consumption, it is important to note that immigrants are not even eligible for the most costly federal public benefits programs. In 1996, Congress enacted welfare reform that made both *lawful* and undocumented immigrants ineligible for Temporary Assistance to Needy Families and Food Stamps, two major federal public welfare programs.[69] Previously, lawful immigrants had been eligible for such benefits. Although many have criticized welfare reform, it nonetheless remains clear that immigrants who are ineligible for such benefits cannot bankrupt the public benefits system. Importantly, *undocumented* immigrants have *never* been eligible for the major—and most costly—public benefits programs.

The public is generally unaware that many undocumented immigrants pay federal, state, and local taxes, a fact militating in favor of their receiving certain public benefits. "[E]ach year undocumented immigrants add billions of dollars in sales, excise, property, income and payroll taxes, including Social Security, Medicare and unemployment taxes, to federal, state and local coffers. Hundreds of thousands of undocumented immigrants go out of their way to file annual federal and state income tax returns."[70] Undocumented immigrants are often counseled to pay taxes in order to improve their chances of regularizing their immigration status at a later date. Somewhere in the neighborhood of one-half of all undocumented immigrants pay federal taxes. Nonetheless, ineligible for major public benefit programs, undocumented immigrants see few direct benefits from their tax payments.

Despite not having a Social Security number, undocumented immigrants can and do pay federal taxes by securing a Taxpayer Identification Number. Hundreds of thousands of undocumented immigrants work under assumed names and false Social Security numbers. Undocumented immigrants thus help keep the financially strapped Social Security system afloat to the tune of billions of dollars. They contribute to the system without ever collecting benefits.[71] Thus, while many anti-immigrant activists howl at the unfairness of allowing immigrants, particularly the undocumented, to utilize public resources in the form of benefits, in actuality the current system, which denies immigrants access to many benefits, is patently unfair to noncitizens. The fact that undocumented immigrants pay taxes and contribute to the Social Security system militates in favor of granting them access to certain benefits. The fact that they are ineligible for most social benefit programs means that, under the current system, it is the government, and not the undocumented worker, which gains handsomely.

In any event, even if immigrants were to participate in the major public benefit programs, benefit consumption by noncitizens might still not cause formidable economic problems. Easy access to benefits by immigrants in Europe, for example, has not bankrupted the governments of those nations.[72] This is true even though most European nations offer a significantly more generous public benefits package than that provided by the United States.

One of the major sources of tension of immigrant public benefit receipt is the current allocation of the costs and benefits of immigration between the state and federal governments. Many of the economic benefits stemming from immigration accrue to the federal government and employers. State and local governments, on the other hand, see few of these economic benefits but are obliged to pay for some expensive public services, such as a public education and emergency health care and services, consumed by immigrants. This fiscal disconnect is often at the crux of the dispute over the costs of immigration.

Immigration has had especially significant fiscal impacts on states in which large numbers of immigrants live. The state and local governments in high-immigration states must bear substantial costs. Consumption of emergency health services alone can have substantial impacts on state and local governments.[73] The state of Arizona, for example, pays more than $90 million each year to provide emergency services to undocumented immigrants. The state is required to provides such services by federal law but receives only about $650,000 from the federal government to help cover the services, a fraction of its their costs.[74] A public education, which is generally paid for by state and local governments, is also costly, even if it turns out to be a good economic investment for the nation. The costs of providing law enforcement protections to immigrants also can be formidable.

Fiscal concerns with immigration help explain why states pay close attention to the economic impacts of immigration.[75] State and local taxes paid by undocumented immigrants provide some revenues for state and local coffers, but not enough to cover the costs of providing services to immigrants. Most tax revenues contributed by immigrants are collected by the federal government.[76]

For these reasons, the distribution of the fiscal costs and tax benefits of immigration causes tensions between state and federal governments. High-immigration states periodically press for federal financial support to help states cover their costs.[77] Given that the federal government (1) has exclusive authority to regulate immigration and enforce the immigration laws; and (2) requires the states to provide certain benefits, such as a public education, police and fire protection, and emergency services, to all residents, such support is entirely appropriate. Indeed, in some instances, the federal courts have barred states from attempting to deny certain benefits to immigrants.[78]

A few high-immigration states have aggressively pursued federal funds to help pay for the costs of immigration. Arizona, California, Florida, New Jersey, New York, and Texas all sued the U.S. government for compensation for the costs of immigration.[79] In 2005, Arizona and New Mexico experimented with a new ploy to offset the costs of immigration and declared immigration states of emergency, thus becoming eligible for federal emergency funding. All of these ad hoc strategies have yielded some positive results. In the 1990s, the federal government provided funds to several states experiencing high rates of immigration in order to help offset the associated costs.[80]

Rather than have fiscal issues addressed in a piecemeal fashion as is the case today, states may seek to regularize or institutionalize funding from the federal government. An open-admissions system would prove easier to implement politically, with greater potential for regularizing the sharing of resources between federal and state governments than exists under the current system. Even with the disparate fiscal impacts, it would be better from an economic perspective for states to raise these fiscal concerns with the federal government rather than continue political efforts to punish immigrants or promote immigration restrictions. Under the circumstances, revenue sharing by the federal government would appear to be the most appropriate way to help offset the out-of-pocket costs of the state and local governments.

Indeed, federal and state governments may need to devote more resources to immigration integration. The nation, for example, may not be capitalizing on the fiscal expenditures made by state and local governments in providing immigrants a public education. The U.S. government arguably fails to spend sufficient funds to ensure that immigrants have full access to American society.

In 1982, the Supreme Court held, in *Plyler v. Doe,* that undocumented children cannot constitutionally be barred from elementary and secondary education in the public schools. It reasoned that to deny undocumented children an education would "raise[] the specter of a permanent caste of undocumented resident aliens . . . denied the benefits that our society makes available to citizens and lawful residents."[81] As a result, state and local governments today spend millions of dollars annually providing such an education.

While states are required to provide an education through high school to undocumented children, an increasing number of states deny undocumented immigrants the lower fees paid by other state residents for public colleges and universities. This makes a public college education prohibitively expensive for many undocumented immigrants from poor and working-class families. To make matters worse, they are ineligible for federally insured student loan programs. The failure to treat undocumented residents whose families pay taxes as residents seems both unfair and economically shortsighted.

The controversial Development, Relief and Education for Alien Minors (DREAM) Act, which has languished for years in Congress, would authorize states to make undocumented immigrants eligible for in-state fees for college.[82] Economically, this makes perfect sense. It would improve access to college for ambitious and qualified undocumented immigrants. It would facilitate their education and enable them to learn valuable skills needed to be competitive in the U.S. labor force. This is precisely the reason for public subsidization of higher education. Without access to a college education, a high school–educated undocumented immigrant might well be forever relegated to the secondary, low-wage labor market—in effect, forever resigned to a "permanent caste of undocumented resident aliens," the very result that the Supreme Court sought to foreclose in its ruling in *Plyer v. Doe*. This would minimize, and even undermine, any benefit that a community might realize from its expenditures on providing a elementary and secondary education to undocumented immigrants.

Economic rationality and fundamental fairness, however, do not always carry the day in the world of immigration. In December 2005, nonresident students sued California colleges and universities, claiming that they were somehow discriminated against because they paid higher nonresident student fees while undocumented residents in the process of regularizing their immigration status paid lower resident fees. The lawsuit sparked a national furor. Many criticized the unjustified "public benefits" given to undocumented immigrants,[83] once again demonstrating the potential volatility of the perceived receipt of public benefits by immigrants.

Costs of Immigrant Crime

Like some U.S. citizens, some noncitizens in the United States commit crimes and are incarcerated. State and local governments prosecute many of these crimes and pay for the incarceration of many convicted criminals. Such costs may be substantial in high-immigration states. California, for example, pays millions of dollars annually for the incarceration of undocumented immigrants.[84] As a result of the "war on drugs" and the ever-increasing rates of incarceration of young men, costs have swelled over the past few decades.

Like the immigrant benefit recipient, the "criminal alien" generates great fear in the general public and often provokes political reaction. Criminals have few defenders in the political process. The same is true for immigrants. "Criminal aliens" have even fewer political allies. Because of this lack of political power, fears of criminal aliens have resulted in stringent provisions in the immigration laws, with the reforms of 1996 especially onerous.

However, despite popular stereotypes about the criminal alien, there is no evidence that the crime rate among immigrants in the United States is any higher than that among the general population. As Peter Schuck stated in a comprehensive review of the data a few years ago,

> *Although the systematic data on point are somewhat dated, legal immigrants do not appear to commit any more crime than demographically similar Americans; they may even commit less, and that crime may be less serious. Nor does today's immigrant crime appear to be worse than in earlier eras.* The immigrants who flooded American cities around the turn of the century (the ancestors of many of today's Americans) were also excoriated as congenitally vicious and usually crime-prone, not only by the public opinion of the day, but also by the Dillingham Commission, which Congress established to report on the need for immigration restrictions. The evidence suggests that those claims were false then, and similar claims appear to be false now.[85]

The evidence suggests that immigrants come to the United States to work, not to collect welfare or commit crime. A November 2005 study titled "Why Are Immigrants' Incarceration Rates So Low? Evidence of Selective Immigration, Deterrence, and Punishment" found that "[o]ver the 1990s, . . . immigrants who chose to come to the United States *were less likely to be involved in criminal activity than earlier immigrants and the native born.*"[86] One 2006 commentary published in *The Wall Street Journal* speculated that the recent drop in crime rates may be attributable to increased immigration.[87]

Nonetheless, concerns with criminal aliens remain politically popular, and the United States has focused much time and effort deporting them.[88] Increasingly, the federal government has coordinated with state and local governments to facilitate their removal.[89] It is likely to do more of the same in the future.[90]

The 1996 immigration reforms made deportation of criminal aliens a top priority and dramatically expanded the criminal removal grounds. More crimes subjected noncitizens to removals. A crime classified as an "aggravated felony" under the immigration laws was transformed to include crimes that now are not always particularly "aggravated" or a "felony" under the criminal law. The movie star Winona Ryder, convicted of shoplifting on Rodeo Drive in Beverly Hills, would be subject to detention and removal as an aggravated felon if she were a noncitizen.[91] The 1996 reforms also made detention of criminals awaiting deportation much more common, even mandatory in certain cases. Following the passage of the reforms, the federal government aggressively pursued criminal deportations. Consequently, removals of criminal aliens have occurred at record levels over the past decade.[92]

Deportation of criminal aliens raises serious moral and policy issues. The U.S. government deports criminal aliens after they have served their sentences. Some advocates have argued that the United States should not deport noncitizens whose criminal actions in this country led to imprisonment. Their incarceration punished them sufficiently, so the argument goes. Noncitizens convicted of a crime are punished through the criminal law and immigration law, which some claim is an unconstitutional form of double jeopardy.

Moreover, deportation of criminals may have adverse collateral consequences on foreign nations. There is a fear that, in deporting noncitizen criminals, the United States may actually be exporting American crime. For example, the deportation of Salvadoran gang members who mastered their criminal trade in the United States has damaged El Salvador by increasing crime rates in that country.[93] The political unpopularity of the criminal alien, however, makes it unlikely that there will be any narrowing of the criminal-removal provisions in the foreseeable future.

As with other costs associated with immigration, state and local governments might logically look to the federal government for financial assistance. The same considerations that militate in favor of revenue sharing with respect to public benefits also apply to the criminal costs of immigration and law enforcement.

Of course, any liberal admissions regime must ensure that criminals do not enter the United States. Nobody can or will support a law that allows the nation to become a haven for criminals. A nation-state's obligation to protect national security and public safety undisputedly justifies such restrictions. For that reason, an open-borders scheme would need a system for criminal background checks and narrowly tailored grounds for the exclusion of criminals. Nobody could defend allowing the migration of murderers and other hardened criminals who might see the United States as the place for a crime spree. At the same time, given the never-ending unpopularity of criminals and criminal aliens, over-broad exclusions based on public safety would always be a possibility.

Environmental Concerns

At various times, concerns have been raised about the environmental consequences of immigration. Restrictionists argue that the "flood" of immigrants coming to the United States will result in overpopulation. The argument effectively amounts to an economic concern with the allocation of a perceived scarce resource, in this case access to this country. To those who fear overpopulation of the United States, limits on immigration promise to keep a lid on population growth. Concerns with the world population, as well as the global environment, are secondary to those who adopt this type of "America-first" attitude.

Basically, the environmental argument is that the United States has met or exceeded its "carrying capacity" and cannot accommodate the current flow of immigrants coming to this country.[94] It is one of the most common restrictionist arguments. The Federation for Immigration Reform, a highly visible restrictionist advocacy group, regularly makes environmental arguments for limiting immigration.[95] After years of internal turmoil, a vocal faction of the Sierra Club unsuccessfully sought to make immigration control a central issue on the organization's agenda in 2005.[96]

Ultimately, anti-immigrant arguments based on environmental degradation and over-population are little more than a scare tactic. Environmental disaster is just one of the litany of negative consequences allegedly attributable to immigrants that anti-immigrant activists trot out to strike fear into the hearts of the general public. Environmental arguments often are thrown in as an afterthought to add fuel to the nativist fire. As exemplified by the internal dispute within the Sierra Club, these arguments, in certain circumstances, appeal at some level to environmentalists and their sympathizers.

According to the rationale for the environmental argument, the United States should be able to keep what it has in terms of the environment, and the rest of the world is simply out of luck. However, from an overall environmental perspective, the world as a whole may benefit from greater migration to the United States. This nation has environmental protections in place, a commitment to recycling, and a general awareness of, and sensitivity to, environmental issues, a combination that is rare in many countries. Many nations, particularly those in the developing world, lack the kind of environmental consciousness shown in the United States. Developing nations, for obvious reasons, often tend to focus more on economic development than on environmental protection.

Immigrants from the developing world come to the United States and live, work, and consume in a more environmentally conscious country than the one from which they came. As a result, immigrants use resources in a more environmentally sound way in this country. In addition, they do not contribute to the environmental degradation of their native country. Significant environmental problems found in much of the developing world, such as air and water pollution, thus might be reduced by the migration of people to the United States. Such environmental benefits militate in favor of more liberal immigration admissions to the United States. Consequently, an open-borders system might be a more "green" U.S. immigration policy than a closed-border regime.[97]

Moreover, despite persistent claims that the nation has reached its "carrying capacity," it is far from self-evident that the United States is overpopulated or that the country is even approaching its population limit. Although it is true that certain urban areas of the country have relatively high population densities, that density fails to approximate that found in certain cities and regions of the world. Moreover, many regions of the United States are not densely populated at all. In fact, some states, such as Iowa, have actively sought to attract immigrant workers in recent years. Today, many immigrants settle in the South and Midwest, where there is room to build and expand, a need for labor, and relatively inexpensive housing. Continued migration into less populous regions of the United States minimizes the risk of overpopulation in the major cities.

Even California, most closely associated with the metropolises of Los Angeles and the San Francisco Bay area, has thinly populated areas. In addition to its Mexican colonias, the Central Valley has seen the emergence of many diverse communities over the past twenty years. Today, Sikh Indians, Hmong, Vietnamese, Chinese, Russians, and many other groups make up a significant portion of the area's population. Besides adding much richness to the region, immigrants have contributed to a booming, robust economy that today includes manufacturing, technology, and other industries in addition to its world-renowned agricultural sector of state and local economies.

Put simply, the claim that immigration must, or could, be curtailed to save the environment in the United States has not been proved. Indeed, the current system, as well as proposed reforms, may damage the environment. Some observers, for example, even claim that the construction of massive fences along the U.S.-Mexico border may injure the natural habitat of desert animals.[98]

At a bare minimum, we as a nation must be careful to avoid having legitimate environmental concerns with pollution and overpopulation employed as scare tactics in the concerted efforts to build support for a nativist agenda. Similar issues often arise with respect to efforts at exclusionary zoning, in which local zoning laws may be used to exclude "undesirable" elements, often meaning the poor and racial minorities. Zoning, and planned growth, is a good thing; exclusionary zoning is not. Unfortunately, some restrictionists who seek to close the border to the people of the developing world want to do exactly the same thing as advocates of exclusionary zoning.

A Regional Migration Arrangement as the Second-Best Alternative

It goes without saying that, in the modern world, free trade is much more prevalent than free migration.[99] At the tail end of the twentieth century, regional common markets gained popularity. Most nations perceived the economic benefits of more integrated economies but were reluctant to move from a restricted to a fully open scheme immediately. However, in several important instances, labor migration agreements between nations evolved out of increased trade of goods and services.

At least initially, regional migration arrangements, such as the one that exists in much of Europe, represent a more politically acceptable alternative—at least in the first instance—to completely open borders.[100] Under such an arrangement, free trade of goods and services is accompanied by labor migration among nations within a designated region. Because regional arrangements develop only with the consent of sovereign nation-states, national sovereignty is respected. As a purely practical matter, it is far easier to obtain popular consent for regional arrangements because the people in the region are more likely to share important cultural and racial commonalities and have experience interacting with each other.

For similar reasons, regional arrangements have been advocated as a politically viable alternative to the current system for admitting *refugees* to the United States.[101] There has long been a concern with the numbers of refugees coming to this country. During the 1980s and 1990s, when many Central American and Haitian asylum seekers were entering the United States, public fear ran high. Many people feared a tidal wave of racially and culturally different foreigners coming to this country.

Under a regional arrangement, nations allow the resettlement of refugees facing persecution in nearby nations. Allowing for regional migration tends to ameliorate fears of opening the "floodgates" to immigrants. Because a regional arrangement provides entry only to "local" refugees, it offers the appearance of exercising control over the numbers of migrants coming into a nation. In addition, greater racial and cultural homogeneity among populations in a region tends to moderate opposition to a regional refugee resettlement plan.

The best-known example of a regional migration system exists in Europe, which shares some historical, cultural, political, and social commonalities with North America. After gaining experience with the free trade of goods and services, the member nations of the European Union (EU) concluded that the economic benefits of easy labor migration would, as a whole, also benefit the member states.[102] Today, labor migration is generally permitted within the EU nations. Although much feared, the elimination of border controls between the member nations proved to be relatively painfree. Indeed, the great success of the European Union has contributed to its potential expansion—other nations want in on a good thing. Consequently, in the future, the EU may be joined by as many as ten new members.[103]

The popularity of the EU demonstrates that there are clear economic benefits to regional arrangements. Labor, capital, and goods flow freely among nations. Labor migrates to the place of its most productive and efficient use. Labor, employers, consumers, and national economies stand to gain.

As a testament to its success, the European Union model is being imitated. Several regions of northern Europe, South America, and Africa have allowed, or are considering allowing, relatively easy migration among member states.[104] Muammar Gaddafi of Libya has called for a borderless Africa, which, if it ever became a reality, would make Africa the first continent to permit labor migration in modern times.[105] In certain regions, racial, ethnic, class, and cultural differences among citizens of different nations—even neighbors—may make such arrangements difficult. However, the fact that such arrangements are even being floated for consideration demonstrates that globalization is beginning to triumph over a world of insular nations and closed borders.

Despite their political advantages, regional regimes have serious costs. Regional blocs almost necessarily lead to border fortifications at the outer perimeter of the community of nations. The problems inherent in any system of border controls are therefore shifted from national to regional boundaries. With internal controls between the EU member nations eased, border controls were erected around the EU's outer perimeter to keep noncitizens from outside the Union from entering.[106] The result was the so-called Fortress Europe. The border controls were designed in no small part to thwart a mass migration from North Africa into France and Germany. As a condition of EU membership, Spain created its first comprehensive immigration law and sought to cut off migration from North Africa.[107]

Fortress Europe's external border controls have led to problems similar to those that have resulted from the United States's system of closed borders. Because of the borders at its external frontier, which are designed to bar the entry of migrants from the developing world, the EU has experienced problems with racial discrimination.[108] It has also seen increased undocumented immigration and greater diversification of the populations in certain nations.[109]

With aggressive enforcement of the borders at the perimeter of the common market, EU border enforcement has human costs that are strikingly similar to those seen in the United States. Migrants to Europe face perils like those that confront undocumented Mexican immigrants attempting to enter the United States do. Like Mexican migrants, undocumented migrants to Europe seek to evade border fortifications by making a hazardous journey across the Mediterranean Sea. Migrants from North Africa who successfully migrate encounter increased discrimination, at times even violence, in Spain, France, and other EU nations.[110] Muslims, including many born in France, face similar treatment, which resulted in mass unrest in that country in 2005.

The problems experienced with the emergence of Fortress Europe demonstrates why regional arrangements are a second-best alternative to liberal admissions systems. With a regional arrangement, the costs of closed borders do not completely disappear but are shifted to the outer boundaries of the regional arrangement. As a political matter, however, it is far easier to build popular support for smaller-scale migration plans than for an immediate move to a comprehensive system of liberal admissions.

Less controversial than open borders, a regional migration pact may be the most feasible solution to the United States's immigration woes for the time being. Even so, such an agreement would not come easily. The U.S. government adamantly opposed discussions among the United States, Canada, and Mexico on the issue of immigration while forming the North American Free Trade Agreement in the early 1990s. Although concern with Mexican migration continues to flourish in the United States, over the long haul, the tripartite trading relationship holds the potential for evolving into a European Union-like labor migration relationship.[111]

Indeed, there have already been signs that a North American Union could become a reality. Recent years saw the United States and Canada enter into an agreement involving refugees and cooperation on a variety of immigration measures designed to tighten security after September 11, 2001. This shows a willingness on the part of the two nations to work together on immigration issues.[112]

Similarly, over the course of the twentieth century, the United States and Mexico developed an increasingly close economic and political relationship. This is exemplified by the personal relationship between U.S. President George Bush, a former governor of the border state of Texas, and President Vicente Fox, of Mexico, a former Coca-Cola executive. In fact, the U.S. government has even enlisted Mexico to aid its border enforcement efforts. To this end, the Mexican government, at the behest of the U.S. government, has taken steps to keep Central Americans from traveling through Mexico en route to this country. The burgeoning relationship between the two neighboring nations creates the potential for future cooperation on migration issues well beyond simply fighting crime and drug trafficking.[113]

In recent years, the highest levels of the U.S. and Mexican governments have discussed migration between the two states. This represents a sharp turnaround from the early 1990s, when NAFTA's approval hinged on *not* addressing immigration. Only days before September 11,

2001, an agreement to regularize migration between the United States and Mexico appeared to be on the immediate horizon. Unfortunately, the migration pact under discussion never came to fruition. All discussion between the nations ceased on September 11, 2001. Since that fateful day, there has been a dramatic shift in the U.S. government's general stance on immigration. Border enforcement and national security and the "war on terror" put efforts to ease migration restrictions on hold indefinitely.[114] Since September 11, the U.S. government's priority has been tightening the border, not liberalizing migration controls. However, the fact that the U.S. and Mexican governments have extensively discussed migration between the nations in the past few years shows that, since the birth of NAFTA, times have changed.

Throughout his term in office, Mexico's President Vicente Fox continued to press for a bilateral migration arrangement.[115] In 2005, after a hiatus of several years following the events of September 11, the United States and Mexico again began to discuss migration between the two nations.[116] For Mexico, a migration accord has taken on increasing urgency because of the many deaths along the border. However, serious barriers remain. The antipathy toward immigrants—especially those from Mexico—in the United States and concern about opening the floodgates to mass migration remain major stumbling blocks. The diversity of peoples in North America and the economic disparities between the United States and Mexico militate against a regional migration pact. To make matters worse, Congress has increasingly demanded restrictionist measures and increased border enforcement along the United States's southern frontier.[117]

In the end, the signals are decidedly mixed as to whether there will be any kind of U.S.-Mexico migration agreement in the near future. Despite President Bush's discussion of a possible agreement, Congress has moved in the opposite direction. In 2005, Congress bolstered border enforcement with the REAL ID Act.[118] It then considered much more enforcement-oriented proposals. In 2005, the House of Representatives passed a stringent enforcement-oriented reform bill that provoked protests across the United States. Despite the protests, all of the serious immigration reform proposals that have followed include increased border enforcement. In 2006, Congress approved the extension of the fence along the U.S.-Mexico border. Congress, and the public, continues to fear opening the floodgates to Mexican migration and wants to do everything it can to shut the door. Terrorism added fuel to the fire, and the

U.S. government has used the "war on terror" to justify efforts to bolster border enforcement. Given the lack of any evidence that even a single terrorist has entered the United States from Mexico, these security fears lack credibility.

In the long run, some kind of migration accord will likely be reached between the United States and Mexico. Both Mexico and the United States have much at stake in continued labor migration between the two nations. The Mexican economy annually receives billions of dollars in remittances from Mexican nationals living and working in the United States.[119] It needs these resources to subsidize economic growth and dampen political discontent. Mexico thus has much to gain by ensuring that its citizens have access to jobs, that the risk of labor exploitation is reduced, and that migrants are able to secure a more durable immigration status than that held by undocumented immigrants.[120]

At the same time, the U.S. economy benefits handsomely from immigrant labor, particularly in the service industries, agriculture, and other low-skill, labor-intensive industries. Many U.S. employers rely heavily on undocumented labor. This deeply ingrained reliance has been built over generations and is unlikely to end with mere changes to the law. Absent a radical restructuring of the U.S. economy, immigration law and policy therefore must take the reliance on immigrant labor into account.

Ultimately, the key ingredient to significantly reducing migration from Mexico is economic growth in Mexico.[121] Policies that foster this growth are likely to diminish migration pressures. By benefiting the Mexican economy, free migration, for example, may serve to decrease the demand for future migration. However, economic growth is a painfully slow process. Consequently, the pressures fueling migration from Mexico to the United States are likely to remain for the foreseeable future.

Free migration among the NAFTA nations would be in keeping with certain existing political, economic, and social realities. Labor integration between the United States and Mexico is occurring. It has been fueled from the bottom up. Market forces have driven U.S. employers and Mexican workers in this direction for years. Governments and laws, however, have been left by the wayside. Law has been a minor hindrance to immigrants and employers but has not been an effective deterrent to unlawful conduct. Efforts to bar the employment of undocumented workers have been largely ineffective. Employer sanctions have not been vigorously enforced and in recent years have been enforced with even less enthusiasm than before. Certain industries in the United States, such as agriculture and construction and many service industries, rely on the type of low-wage labor provided by immigrants. Unlike other industries, which have increasingly moved operations overseas to exploit low-wage labor, jobs in these industries cannot be exported. Low-wage immigrant labor, therefore, remains essential to the U.S. economy.

Impediments to a regional arrangement do, of course, exist. The political unpopularity of immigration in the United States is one. Demographic differences are another. Racial, socioeconomic, and cultural differences among the populations of the NAFTA partners arguably exceed those of the original EU members. In addition, the staying power of anti-Mexican sentiment in the United States should not be underestimated. It has a lengthy history and is enduring. Fear of a mass migration of poor culturally and racially different people will likely generate considerable controversy for the foreseeable future and even greater fears about the national identity than currently exist.

Popular opposition, however, cannot forever prevent the United States from acting in its own national interest. Economic benefits make labor migration from Mexico desirable. Indeed, economic reality may make labor migration from Mexico inevitable. The United States can either deal with economic reality or continue the doomed policies of the past, spending billions of dollars, causing tragic human losses, and yet completely and utterly failing to achieve its goals.

Conclusion

Free labor migration is the next frontier for the global economy. As Economics 101 suggests, as long as the United States is a land of economic opportunity, labor migration for economic opportunity will occur whether we like it or not. People will continue to come to a nation where economic and political dreams can be realized.

Controversies will likely arise in the future because of the perceived wealth distribution consequences of immigration, just as they have in recent years. The consumption of public benefits by immigrants is a concern that must be addressed. However, the fact that there may be costs associated with public benefits is not dispositive on the issue of whether open borders make economic sense. Rather than maintaining limits on immigration to respond to this concern, policymakers should consider wealth redistribution policies to shift money from the beneficiaries of freer immigration to the losers and revenue sharing between the federal government and state and local governments. This would allow the United States to adopt economically sensible immigration policies while still ameliorating any negative impacts.

Economically, the United States has much to gain from freer labor migration. Economic analysis, which treats labor and capital as substitutable factors of production, teaches that both free trade and free labor movement benefit the United States. For that reason, the end of the twentieth century saw growing economic cooperation between nations. Some blocs of nations even allow for labor migration between and among all members.

Despite the potential economic benefits, the politics of liberal immigration in the United States and other nations are exceedingly difficult and complex. Domestic labor often fears an influx of cheap labor and its impact on the domestic wage scale. Cultural conservatives worry that immigration will change the racial, cultural, and national identity of the United States. These cultural concerns and bread-and-butter economic fears have historically held a powerful populist appeal and have been used to provoke restrictionist reactions. Care must be taken therefore to avoid a nativist backlash.

Any movement toward liberal admissions will likely encounter formidable bumps in the road. It is therefore likely that the United States might enjoy more success in first entering a regional migration pact similar to that which has emerged in Europe. Ultimately, globalization likely will transform labor markets just as it has changed markets for good and services. It is only a matter of time. The United States can either aggressively move now to be at the cutting edge of economic development or wait for the world to pass it by.

5

Why Open Borders Are Good for All Americans

Many commentators, policymakers, and citizens believe that the current immigration system requires immediate and fundamental reform.[1] For years, calls for reform have gripped the nation. In 2006, even the staid, middle-of-the-road American Bar Association joined the clamor for an overhaul of the U.S. immigration laws.[2] However, the public has made it clear that not just any reform will do. The harsh treatment of undocumented immigrants in some of the proposals under consideration in Congress in 2005–06 sparked outrage. In an unprecedented series of events in the spring of 2006, hundreds of thousands of American citizens joined arms with immigrants in protest in mass marches in cities across the United States.

For years, many types of immigration reforms have been tried and failed. There is no evidence that any of the current incremental reform proposals, almost all of which would bolster border enforcement, are likely to be any more successful. More far-reaching reform is needed. This chapter builds on the moral and economic arguments for more liberal immigration admissions outlined in Chapters 3 and 4 and offers additional policy reasons for dramatically opening the U.S. borders to labor migration.

U.S. immigration law must be changed to reflect the values that this nation trumpets as it seeks to export democracy to other parts of the world. To this end, this chapter analyzes how the U.S. government's commitment to racial equality and multiculturalism militates in favor of opening the borders. Open borders are more consistent than closed borders with the multicultural ideals that underlie modern civil rights sensibilities in the United States.

Moreover, allowing all residents of the United States, regardless of their immigration status, full membership in U.S. society is consistent with the democratic principles for which this nation proudly stands. Such a system would send a message that the United States values all people who live in our communities, light or dark, rich or poor, migrant or native-born citizen. It is much more consistent than current law with the "huddled masses" concept of immigration symbolized by the Statue of Liberty. Liberal admissions would also help to prevent the invidious discrimination, exploitation, abuse, and deaths that the current immigration laws allow, if not encourage.

We as a nation must recognize that, under current U.S. immigration law, undocumented immigration is a fact of modern social life. Many otherwise law-abiding citizens who hold positions of prestige and authority employ undocumented immigrants in their homes. They often have undocumented immigrants care for their children, clean the house, and work in their yards. In 2004, former New York City police commissioner Bernard Kerik withdrew as President Bush's nominee to be the first Secretary of the Department of Homeland Security, the federal agency now primarily entrusted with enforcing the immigration laws, because he had failed to pay taxes for a domestic-service worker who may have been undocumented. Kerik is not the first nominee to a high-level cabinet position to suffer that fate. Conservative pundit Linda Chavez withdrew as President Bush's first nominee for Secretary of Labor because she had previously employed an undocumented immigrant. Nor is this simply a problem for Republican Presidents. Kimba Wood and Zoe Baird, President Bill Clinton's first two nominees for the position of Attorney General, the highest law enforcement office in the United States, experienced the same fate.[3]

The presence of undocumented immigrants in the United States is a plain reality that needs to be addressed. Open borders would provide a pragmatic, long-term solution to this nation's undocumented-immigrant and related immigration problems. Freeing up migration through a liberal admissions policy would recognize that the enforcement of closed borders cannot stifle the strong, perhaps irresistible, economic, social, and political pressures that fuel today's international migration. Border controls, as currently configured in the United States, simply waste billions of dollars and result in thousands of deaths. They have not ended, and cannot end, unlawful immigration.

Like the United States's failed prohibition of the alcohol trade in the early twentieth century, effective enforcement of the immigration laws to halt undocumented immigration has proven virtually impossible. To make matters worse, border enforcement shares many of Prohibition's negative side effects: increased criminal activity, abusive law enforcement practices, and a caseload crisis in the courts. An inability to enforce the laws, whether they prohibit alcohol or dramatically restrict immigration, undermines and damages the legitimacy and moral force of the law. Elimination of border controls would help eliminate these costs by making the laws more realistic.

As summarized in Chapter 2, history shows that the cyclical fear of a flood of immigrants of different "races" destroying U.S. society often reaches fever pitch. These nativist outbursts have never been justified. The United States, however, has responded to the anti-immigrant impulse and has taken extreme action in the name of self-preservation. Time and time again, it has targeted vulnerable minorities, excluding, deporting, and otherwise punishing them for real and imagined offenses. History records these episodes with regret, embarrassment, and disbelief. But the errors are repeated and entirely predictable.

Even though it may seem ridiculous today, U.S. society once considered the German and the Irish unassimilable "races" that diluted and degraded Anglo-Saxon racial purity.[4] Although Chinese and Japanese immigrants were despised groups that generated a plethora of immigration restrictions in the late nineteenth and early twentieth centuries,[5] today people of Chinese and Japanese descent in the United States have higher average incomes than whites.[6] Southern and Eastern Europeans, whose immigration led to the creation of the national-origins quota system in 1924, are now generally viewed as part of the mainstream, rather than as people of different, inferior races.[7] The United States unfortunately has failed to learn from its mistakes. Since September 11, 2001, security concerns have distorted immigration law and policy in ways that, years from now, history almost assuredly will record with regret.[8]

Some observers, including the restrictionist Samuel Huntington, have complained that current levels of immigration have made the assimilation of immigrants difficult.[9] However, the United States has a long history of successfully integrating immigrants into U.S. society. The waves of immigration in the early twentieth century were, as a percentage of the U.S. population, larger than the current levels of immigration.[10] Over the course of the twentieth century, the nation slowly but surely adjusted. "Unassimilable aliens" are now part of mainstream America. This past success suggests that the United States could fully integrate immigrants into civil society in a legal regime without borders.

Moreover, given the influence of U.S. culture throughout the world in this high-tech information age, we might well expect immigrants today to be much more familiar with the United States, to be prepared for faster integration into society, and to be more capable of making informed judgments about immigration than were immigrants of previous generations. As time goes by, integration into U.S. society may be easier than it currently is. In any event, Latina/os currently are assimilating into U.S. social life.

Despite popular perceptions, most Latina/o immigrants, the largest component of the current immigration cohort, assimilate into the United States to a large degree. As a group, they learn English, participate in the workforce to a larger extent than native-born citizens, and embrace widely accepted American—often denominated "family"—values.[11] By economic and political measures, for example, Cuban Americans on average are better off than the average U.S. citizen.[12] Not all Latina/os are Cuban, or course, and many have not achieved similar levels of economic success. But the fact remains that immigrants assimilate to a far greater degree than is recognized by the restrictionists.

The assimilation of Latina/os can also be seen in their increasing political importance. Politicians across the political spectrum, including President Bush, increasingly and aggressively court the Latina/o vote. Mainstream politicians often take care to avoid taking positions on immigration and related issues that would tend to alienate this growing segment of the electorate.[13] The backlash against California governor Pete Wilson's support for Proposition 187 in 1994 taught Republican politicians the potential downside of taking strong anti-immigrant positions that anger Latina/os.[14] Since then, most mainstream Republican politicians have studiously avoided taking positions that could be characterized as anti-immigrant and anti-Latina/o. Not surprisingly, given the growing Latina/o population, Latina/os in recent years have greatly increased their representation in elected offices,[15] which demonstrates their increasing integration into U.S. social life.

A move away from closed borders is called for at this time in U.S. history. The law should be changed to create the legal presumption that a noncitizen can enter the country unless it can be demonstrated that he or she would pose a danger to the national security and public safety. This, of course, effectively would turn current U.S. immigration law on its head. Open, not closed, borders would be the norm. Easy, not difficult, entry would be the result.

A less dramatic change in the law would be to allow labor migration within the nations that are a party to the North American Free Trade Agreement. Over the past thirty years, a regional common market, which includes labor migration between and among the member states, has evolved in the European Union. A similar labor migration agreement among the NAFTA nations would recognize that migration from Mexico, perhaps Latin America generally, is inevitable,[16] and must be managed responsibly, efficiently, and safely.

Globalization, technological advances, and changing conceptions of the nation-state require serious study of new approaches to immigration and border controls.[17] Besides limiting the abuses and injuries that enforcement of the current immigration laws cause immigrants and U.S. citizens, a system of easy entry promises many benefits—economic and otherwise—to the United States. Importantly, allowing free labor migration would permit the U.S. government to effectively and efficiently focus enforcement efforts on protecting national security and public safety, a high priority after the terrorist acts of September 11, 2001.

The Impossibility of Enforcing Broad Immigration Restrictions

A move toward open borders would recognize the inherent difficulty, if not impossibility, of enforcing immigration restrictions in a manner that is consistent with liberal values. Open admission would recognize that the United States simply will not—and should not—adopt the types of policies represented by the Berlin Wall, complete with machine guns like those that once separated East and West Germany. Despite ever-increasing enforcement efforts, social, economic, and political pressures result in a continuous flow of migrants to the United States.

Draconian enforcement measures that result in the loss of human life but fail to significantly reduce undocumented immigration simply cannot be justified morally or as a matter of policy. Indeed, rather than deterring undocumented immigration or reducing the undocumented immigrant population, the aggressive border enforcement strategies adopted in the 1990s *increased* the permanent settlement of undocumented immigrants in the United States. Further escalation of border enforcement in the name of national security after September 11, 2001, failed to be any more effective. Millions of undocumented immigrants successfully evade strict immigration controls to live and work—many for years—in the United States.

The basic truth is that an ever-growing shadow population exists in this country. In 2005, the Pew Hispanic Center estimated that 10.3 million unauthorized migrants lived in the United States.[18] It increased the estimate in March 2006 to 11.5 to 12 million undocumented immigrants.[19] A comprehensive report on immigration by the Center recently found that "[f]rom 1992 to 2004, the unauthorized share of immigration inflows increased and the share that was legal decreased. *By the end of the period, more unauthorized migrants than authorized migrants were entering the United States.*"[20] More than 60 percent of the decline in immigration after 1999–2000, when immigration reached its recent peak primarily resulted from a drop in legal immigration.

An American Immigration Foundation Report prepared by respected immigration demographer Douglas S. Massey found that, among other things,

1. "Between 1986 and 2002 the number of Border Patrol officers tripled."
2. "The probability of apprehension along the U.S.-Mexico border fell . . . to an all-time low of 5 percent in 2002."
3. "The cost of making one arrest along the U.S.-Mexico border increased from $300 in 1992 to $1700 in 2002, an increase of 467 percent."
4. "From 1980 to 1992, the cost of hiring a *coyote* (smuggler) averaged around $400 per crossing, but rose to $1,200 in 1999 before leveling off."[21]

Throughout his administration, President George W. Bush pointed to the nation's ever-increasing shadow population of undocumented immigrants to support immigration reform. Despite the record levels of expenditures made to seal the U.S.-Mexican border, however, undocumented immigration continues largely unabated.[22] One much-publicized report concluded bluntly that "[t]here is no evidence that the border enforcement build-up . . . has substantially reduced unauthorized border crossings" and that "[d]espite large increases in spending and Border Patrol resources over the past nine years, the number of unauthorized immigrants increased to levels higher than those" before 1986.[23]

Nobody should be surprised that a large undocumented immigrant population lives in the United States. Undocumented immigrants live in most large urban areas, as well as in many suburban and rural communities. They are part of our communities. An annual "No Human Being Is Illegal" soccer tournament draws hundreds of participants, many of them undocumented themselves, to a field near the Rose Bowl in Pasadena, California.[24] In many localities, the parking lots at Home Depot stores serve as informal undocumented-immigrant day-laborer pickup points. Such points are well known among employers, including homeowners, workers who participate in this secondary labor market, and federal, state, and local law enforcement. Unfortunately, employers not infrequently abuse and exploit day laborers, who often toil for low pay in poor conditions.[25]

Immigrants literally are changing the face of the nation. In the past few decades, immigration flows moved away from states with high foreign-born populations, such as California and New York, to new settlement states, such as North Carolina and Iowa. Mexican immigrant communities are increasingly being established in areas outside the Southwest. Even Minnesota in the frigid far north of the United States, has seen the emergence of a Mexican migrant community.[26] The "browning" of America has become a widely known phenomenon.

Despite the public focus on undocumented immigration from Mexico, it is not only Mexican nationals who are migrating to the United States. Each year, U.S. immigration authorities apprehend thousands of immigrants from other nations who have entered or remained unlawfully in the United States. "Other than Mexican" apprehensions by U.S. immigration authorities increased sixfold from 1997 to 2005, from about 25,000 to nearly 120,000 each year. According to apprehension figures, the top five immigrant-sending nations other than Mexico in the twenty-first century are Honduras, Brazil, El Salvador, Guatemala, and Nicaragua. Interestingly, showing the role of media in global migration, the increase in migration from Brazil "may be due in part to the Brazilian soap opera 'America,' which follows a young woman's illegal journey through Mexico and has drawn a nightly viewing audience of over 40 million people since its inception" in March 2005.[27]

The fact that so much immigration, perhaps more than half of all migration, is outside formal legal channels stems from the restrictive nature of the current immigration laws. For Latin Americans of modest means, legal immigration to the United States is so difficult that unauthorized entry often is the only realistic possibility. Nationals from developing nations in other regions of the world also find it especially difficult to immigrate to the United States. Lack of available visas and aggressively enforced exclusion grounds bar their entry. In addition, discriminatory visa processing makes it even more unlikely that some prospective immigrants will be permitted the opportunity to migrate legally. For example, U.S. consular officers in Brazil have been accused in the past of relying on racial and class profiles in denying visa applications.[28]

Many immigrant visas are consistently oversubscribed by tens of thousands. Although the numerical limits are fixed, demand is not. Many more Mexicans, for example, apply for the same 25,600 visas than people from Iceland. Because demand far outstrips supply, potential immigrants from some nations, such as China, India, Mexico, and the Philippines, must wait for many years for admission. The per-country ceilings set by the U.S. immigration laws mean that similarly situated immigrants may wait in dramatically different time lines for one reason and one reason alone—because of their country of origin.

Noncitizens seeking to come to the United States on certain family-based visas wait many years longer if they are from China, India, Mexico, or the Philippines than they would if they were from most other nations.[29] As of May 2006, unmarried sons and daughters of U.S. citizens who sought to immigrate from Mexico and the Philippines faced a wait of fifteen years. If they were from just about any other country, the wait would be five years. A brother and a sister of an adult U.S. citizen from the Philippines had to wait almost twenty-three years to be admitted into the United States. If they had been from virtually any other nation, the wait would have been less than half that, ten years.[30] Disproportionately long lines encourage would-be immigrants to circumvent the law. Rather than keep immigrants hoping to enter the United States out, these unrealistic waits force many to enter through unauthorized means.

Some claim that undocumented immigrants fail to wait in line. But that claim fails to account for the harsh realities faced by many migrants who would prefer the opportunity to migrate legally. Many potential migrants, especially people of modest means from the developing world, have no avenue to migrate under the law. Others might face long lines so unrealistic that they provide no realistic avenue for migration. There is simply no line for them to wait in.

Closed borders and strict immigration enforcement have failed. One well-known comprehensive federal law enforcement effort met a similar fate and offers insights into the solution for the immigration problems faced by the United States.

The Parallels to Prohibition

In significant ways, migration controls in the modern United States resemble the United States's efforts to enforce the bar on the alcohol trade during Prohibition in the early twentieth century.[31] Not coincidentally, Prohibition emerged at a time like today when nativism had hit a fever pitch.[32] The enforcement of Prohibition fell most heavily on poor and working-class southern and eastern European immigrants—popularly considered at the time to be racially different—and on African American citizens.[33] Enforcement of the temperance laws thus fell disproportionately on minority peoples, much like the war on drugs and efforts to close the borders have in modern times.

Immigration enforcement, like Prohibition, tends to be selectively focused on vulnerable groups. Increasing at times of high levels of nativist sentiment, enforcement tends to focus almost myopically on poor and working-class noncitizens who attempt to evade border controls.[34] It does nothing about the large percentage of undocumented immigrants—many of whom are middle class or better off—who originally had the resources to enter the country legally on a temporary visa but later violated its terms by, for example, staying longer than authorized. This portion of the undocumented population constitutes roughly between 25 and 40 percent of all undocumented immigrants.[35] Like the enforcement of the alcohol laws, the racial impacts of immigration controls, as we have seen repeatedly, are unmistakable.

Like immigration, federal enforcement of Prohibition proved to be extremely difficult and, in the end, impossible. Alcohol remained available and in demand, and consumption continued. In essence, "the federal government was unable to enforce Prohibition in communities that had accepted—and even expected—hard drink."[36] Many otherwise law-abiding citizens did not consider alcohol trafficking and drinking to be truly criminal and knowingly violated the law.[37] People continued to buy, sell, and drink alcohol. With a ready and willing lucrative market available, organized crime moved in and flourished in the bootlegging industry.[38]

Unanticipated, but unquestionably negative, collateral consequences, resulted from the efforts to enforce the alcohol laws. Increased criminalization of alcohol trafficking offenses came with Prohibition. Law enforcement zealously—perhaps desperately—sought to suppress the alcohol trade.[39] However, law enforcement efforts were ineffective and often caused more problems than they solved. Excessive use of force by federal officials in enforcement efforts resulted in violence and fatalities. Aggressive law enforcement created a large backload of criminal cases in the courts.[40] In a form of jury nullification, juries occasionally refused to convict defendants for violation of alcohol-related laws.[41] This, of course, helped to undermine the very legitimacy of the law and its enforcement.

Ultimately, after years of experience made it clear that Prohibition had failed, the United States repealed the laws. In ending Prohibition, the U.S. government effectively admitted that enforcement of the ban on alcohol had been ineffective and counterproductive, with its costs outweighing any benefits. Later, the government found that more modest forms of regulation of the alcohol industry, such as licensing, were more realistic, enforceable, and effective.

As was the case for alcohol consumption during Prohibition, the ordinary law-abiding citizen does not consider the employment of undocumented workers to be truly criminal conduct. Many U.S. citizens, including several otherwise upstanding nominees for high-level cabinet positions, knowingly hired undocumented immigrants.[42] Large employers, such as Tyson Foods, the nation's largest meat and poultry producer and processor, hire large numbers of undocumented workers.[43] Indeed, some informed observers contend that the economic viability of the entire U.S. food and agriculture industry depends on undocumented labor.[44] In the end, economic imperatives result in mass violation of the immigration laws.

To the extent that violation of the immigration laws is viewed as criminal, unlawful immigration and the employment of undocumented immigrants are generally considered to be "victimless" crimes, like those punished under the drug and prostitution laws.[45] As Isabel Medina has observed:

> Congress criminalized the employment of undocumented aliens in 1986 to deter unauthorized entry in the hope of removing the aliens' goal—employment. Criminalization of the employment relationship, however, has not deterred illegal entry. Most examinations of this failure focus

on the inadequacy of enforcement efforts, and the complexity of the problem posed by unauthorized immigration. The principal reason that criminalization of employment of undocumented aliens has failed to deter unauthorized immigration, however, is that the criminalized behavior, employment, is highly valued by American society and does not possess the characteristics that modern American society relies upon to support the imposition of criminal sanctions. To the contrary, employing illegal aliens carries a forceful moral imperative: it is conduct which in certain contexts is required by an individual's values or morals. The moral tension surrounding the employment prohibition makes prosecutors reluctant to devote scarce financial resources to prosecute those who engage in such behaviors, judges reluctant to impose serious sanctions, and society reluctant to support strong enforcement efforts.[46]

Undocumented immigrants are generally not considered—except by ardent restrictionists—as equivalent to common criminals. Instead, they are treated as people who have come to the United States looking to work, make a living, and build a better life.[47] Employers voluntarily hire undocumented workers with enthusiasm. Many upstanding citizens are comfortable with employing undocumented workers to work in their homes and with their families. Often, people know of undocumented immigrants in their communities but, for the most part, do not report them to the authorities. For most people most of the time, undocumented immigrants simply fail to generate the palpable fear that common criminals do. This is true even in times when anti-immigrant sentiment is at its zenith and anti-immigrant activists are trying to vilify "illegal aliens" by vocally equating them with "criminal aliens."

At times, moral convictions may serve as the basis for assisting undocumented immigrants. Religious leaders occasionally join the immigration fray. In the 1980s, religious activists helped Central Americans enter the country and flee the violence of their homelands even though the conduct violated the law.[48] More recently, religious leaders have protested border enforcement measures put into place along the U.S. southern border with Mexico and provided humanitarian assistance to migrants in the desert.

Rather than reconsider efforts to seal the border, the U.S. government has been led by serious enforcement difficulties, and mounting political pressures, to further criminalize violations of the immigration laws.[49] Increasingly, Congress has transformed violations of the immigration laws into crimes, such as the newly minted crime of illegal re-entry into the country.[50] As it did during Prohibition, the criminalization has created a caseload crisis in the federal courts.

Criminal prosecutions for deported noncitizens' unlawful re-entry into the country have increased dramatically.[51] The great increase in such prosecutions has resulted in a spike in the workload of the federal courts. This has especially been the case in courts along the U.S.-Mexican border, which has led to the addition of federal judges in that region.[52] In fact, immigration prosecutions now dominate the dockets of some federal courts in the border region. For example, in fiscal year 2004, immigration cases recommended for prosecution increased by 65 percent in the federal courts. In one year, the Southern District in Texas saw a whopping 345 percent jump, from about 4,000 to more than 18,000 immigration cases.[53] It does not appear that the increase in prosecutions has substantially affected the level of undocumented migration to the United States.

The Caseload Crisis: The Immigration Bureaucracy and the Courts

At the turn of the century, a serious caseload crisis emerged in courts across the United States. It was largely created by aggressive deportation efforts and expedited review of removal orders by the immigration courts and the Board of Immigration Appeals.[54] The federal courts of appeals have seen nothing less than a flood of immigration appeals. In order to cope with the burden, some appellate courts adopted expedited procedures for quickly disposing of appeals. Despite the fact that immigrants have so much at stake in their appeals, which often decide whether they will be deported from the United States or enjoy a continued life here, the focus of the courts has been on efficiency.[55]

Appeals abound because immigrants often find it difficult to get a fair shake in administrative hearings and have little to lose by appealing. Immigration judges have been accused of being biased against immigrants.[56] In an extraordinary step, in 2006, Attorney General Alberto Gonzales, responding to intense public criticism, ordered an investigation into the quality of work of the nation's immigration courts. Among other things, he expressed deep concern with reports that the courts fail to show immigrants proper respect.[57] Gonzales's admonition to the immigration courts to change their ways came at a time when the media were beginning to report about the bias of the immigration courts.

Consider one flagrant example. In a case in which a noncitizen sought asylum on the basis of a claim of ethnic and religious persecution in Indonesia, an immigration judge stated:

> You have no right to be here. All of the applicants that are applying for asylum have no right to be here. You don't come to the United States to look for a job! That's not the purpose of asylum. You don't come here to look for a job, or look for a house, or look for a better car, and than as an afterthought say, well, the only way that I'm going to be able to stay here is if I can convince a Judge that I'm going to be persecuted. It's not the way the law works. . . . *You have to understand, the whole world does not revolve around you and the other Indonesians that just want to live here because they enjoy the United States better than they enjoy living in Indonesia. It is not a world that revolves around you and your ethnic group.*

Not surprisingly, in light of the immigration judge's unabashed bias in the case, the court of appeals set aside the denial of asylum.[58] The immigration judge was later removed indefinitely from the bench.[59]

Changes in the administrative adjudication of immigration appeals also contributed to the caseload crisis. Early in the Bush administration, the Board of Immigration Appeals (BIA), the administrative agency that hears appeals from rulings of the immigration courts, streamlined its procedures and reduced the number of Board members. The Attorney General removed from the BIA adjudicators viewed to be too pro-immigrant. Fewer board members, streamlined appeals, faster decisions, and more appeals all have adversely affected the decision-making quality of the Board. Even with the severe cutting of corners, the BIA continues to face a backlog of immigration appeals.[60] The result has been summary affirmances of removal orders, with little explanation. This, in turn, has led to a mass of appeals to the federal courts.[61] The number of immigration appeals has increased from fewer than 500 in 1981 to well over 10,000 in 2005.[62]

Even before the recent changes to its handling of appeals, BIA decision making had been long been criticized as lacking. The streamlining of the BIA process has further damaged the quality of its decisions. Federal judges frequently complain of the disturbing, low-quality decision making of the Board of Immigration Appeals. "Federal appellate judges in circuits around the country regularly express mounting concern that cases rushed through an administrative review process have not only flooded some circuits with appeals but have also caused lives to get lost in the shuffle of streamlining."[63]

A former University of Chicago law professor, Richard Posner, a law and economics conservative appointed to the federal bench by President Ronald Reagan, has emerged as a one of the most visible—and seemingly unlikely—critics of the BIA. In an asylum claim based on religious persecution, he criticized the BIA for (1) a lack of familiarity with foreign cultures; (2) an exaggerated notion of how much people know about their religion; (3) an unrealistic expectation about the availability of documentary evidence of religious membership; (4) insensitivity to the problems of translation of testimony and evaluating the demeanor of a witness from a different culture when that testimony is translated; and (5) reluctance to make clear determinations of the credibility of asylum applicants. More generally, Judge Posner questioned "[a]ffirmances by the Board of Immigration Appeals with no opinion or with a very short, unhelpful, boilerplate opinion, even when, as in this case, the immigration judge's opinion contains manifest errors of fact and logic."[64]

This case was not an outlier. In another case, Judge Posner was even more direct in his criticism of the administrative review system of removal decisions:

> In the year ending on the date of the argument, different panels of this court reversed the Board of Immigration Appeals in whole or part in a staggering 40 percent of the 136 petitions to review the Board that were resolved on the merits. The corresponding figure, for the 82 civil cases during this period in which the United States was the appellee, was 18 percent. Our criticisms of the Board and of the immigration judges have frequently been severe. *E.g.,* Dawoud v. Gonzales, 424 F.3d 608, 610 (7th Cir. 2005) ("the [immigration judge's] opinion is riddled with inappropriate and extraneous comments"); Ssali v. Gonzales, 424 F.3d 556, 563 (7th Cir. 2005) ("this very significant mistake suggests that the Board was not aware of the most basic facts of [immigration judge] employed in this case is an affront to [petitioner's] right to be heard"); Soumahoro v. Gonzales, 415 F.3d 732, 738 (7th Cir. 2005) (per curiam) (the immigration judge's factual conclusion is "totally unsupported by the record"); Grupee v. Gonzales, 400 F.3d 1026, 1028 (7th Cir. 2005)

(the immigration judge's unexplained conclusion is "hard to take seriously"); Kourski v. Ashcroft, 355 F.3d 1038, 1039 (7th Cir. 2004) ("there is a gaping hole in the reasoning of the board and the immigration judge"); Niam v. Ashcroft, 354 F.3d 652, 654 (7th Cir. 2003) ("the elementary principles of administrative law, the rule of logic, and common sense seem to have eluded the Board in this as in other cases"). Other circuits have been as critical. Wang v. Attorney General, 423 F.3d 260, 269 (3d Cir. 2005) ("the tone, the tenor, the disparagement, and the sarcasm of the [immigration judge] seem more appropriate to a court television show than a federal court proceeding"); Chen v. U.S. Dep't of Justice, 426 F.3d 104, 115 (2d Cir. 2005) (the immigration judge's finding is "grounded solely on speculation and conjecture"); Fiadjoe v. Attorney General, 411 F.3d 135, 154–55 (3d Cir. 2005) (the immigration judge's "hostile" and "extraordinarily abusive" conduct toward petitioner "by itself would require a rejection of his credibility finding"); Lopez-Umanzor v. Gonzales, 405 F.3d 1049, 1054 (9th Cir. 2005) ("the [immigration judge's] assessment of Petitioner's credibility was skewed by prejudgment, personal speculation, bias, and conjecture"); Korytnyuk v. Ashcroft, 396 F.3d 272, 292 (3rd Cir. 2005) ("it is the [immigration judge's] conclusion, not [the petitioner's] testimony, that 'strains credulity'").

This tension between judicial and administrative adjudicators is not due to judicial hostility to the nation's immigration policies or to a misconception of the proper standard of judicial review of administrative decisions. It is due to the fact that the adjudication of these cases at the administrative level has fallen below the minimum standards of legal justice. . . . Whether this is due to resource constraints or to other circumstances beyond the Board's and the Immigration Court's control, we do not know, though we note that the problem is not of recent origin. *. . . All that is clear is that it cannot be in the interest of the immigration authorities, the taxpayer, the federal judiciary, or citizens concerned with the effective enforcement of the nation's immigration laws for removal orders to be routinely nullified by the courts, and that the power of correction lies in the Department of Homeland Security, which prosecutes removal cases, and the Department of Justice, which adjudicates them in its Immigration Court and Board of Immigration Appeals.*[65]

Judge Posner's caustic criticism was so extraordinary that it made the front page of the *New York Times*.[66]

The Impossibility of Deporting All Undocumented Immigrants and Reducing the Undocumented Population

However popular the idea of removing all undocumented immigrants from the United States is, it is simply is not feasible. In 2004, Undersecretary of the Department of Homeland Security Asa Hutchinson candidly admitted that "it is 'not realistic' to think that law-enforcement authorities can arrest or deport the millions of illegal aliens now in the United States[. He further stated that he] did not think that the American public has the 'will . . . to uproot' those aliens."[67] In 2006, President Bush acknowledged that "[m]assive deportation of the people here is unrealistic. It's just not going to work."[68]

Consider the sheer costs of the massive deportation campaign needed to remove all undocumented immigrants from the United States. A 2005 study estimated that it would cost $41 billion a year for five years to fund any serious effort to remove all undocumented immigrants. It further concluded that

While the net benefits of adopting such a policy are largely speculative, we do know that spending $41 billion annually over five years ($206 billion in total) would:

1. Exceed the *entire* budget of the Department of Homeland Security for FY 2006 ($34.2 billion);
2. Approach the *total* amount of money required by the 33 federal agencies responsible for homeland security activities for FY 2006 ($49.9 billion);
3. More than double annual spending on border and transportation security ($19.3 billion);
4. Comprise half the annual cost of the Iraq War ($74 billion); and
5. More than double the annual cost of military operations in Afghanistan ($16.8 billion).[69]

In short, the costs of removal would be extremely high. In addition, because U.S. border enforcement has proven to be a miserable failure, there is no reason to believe that a new population of undocumented immigrants would not soon emerge to replace the old one. Border enforcement has failed in large part due to strong family, social, and economic pull factors that attract a steady flow of migrants to the United States. For well over a century, migration to the United States from

Mexico has established deep family connections and enduring social ties between Mexican citizens and persons in this country. A large population of persons of Mexican ancestry lives in the United States, a fact that both attracts more immigration from Mexico and influences the immigration debate.

Recent developments make enforcement of the immigration laws more difficult as a practical matter. About 10 percent of the families with children in the United States have mixed immigration-status families, that is, "famil[ies] in which one or more parents is a noncitizen and one or more children is a citizen."[70] Consequently, any effort to remove noncitizens unlawfully in the United States will adversely impact the families of U.S. citizens. Removals will break up families. This phenomenon will make more rigorous enforcement more controversial than it already is, reducing political support for strong enforcement measures. Politically, it is more difficult to deport immigrant parents when U.S. citizen children will also be effectively deported.[71]

Economic circumstances in Mexico also contribute to the continued migration. For many, perhaps most, Mexican citizens, economic opportunities are greater in the United States than in Mexico. It will likely take more than a generation for Mexico to experience the economic growth necessary to significantly reduce the pull of the U.S. economy on Mexican citizens. There is little evidence to suggest that, at least in the short run, the social and economic pressures fueling migration will change in any meaningful way.

Greater border enforcement has many regrettable collateral, but very real, effects. More undocumented migrants are dying in the trek to the United States, and more are staying in this country for longer periods than in the past. Large numbers of noncitizens are imprisoned for immigration crimes, and "the very profitable human smuggling industry" has expanded.[72] In an attempt to combat immigrant trafficking and compelled labor in the sex and other industries, Congress enacted the Trafficking Victims Protection Act of 2000,[73] which was reauthorized in 2003.[74] The Act provides a variety of immigration benefits and legal protections to the victims of human trafficking. Unfortunately, the law has failed to put an end to the trafficking of human beings to evade the immigration laws.

Over the past few years, the limited efficacy of border controls has been apparent. The massive security measures put in place after the tragedy of September 11, 2001, reportedly reduced undocumented immigration from Mexico for a short time. Government statistics, however, show that, a little more than a year after September 11, the rate of unlawful entry returned to its previous level.[75]

Few events could generate the political support and incentive for aggressive border enforcement created by the terrorist acts of September 11. Given that the aggressive border enforcement that followed has failed, it is difficult to envision any event that could prompt the sustained efforts to close the borders or provide the resources necessary to achieve that goal. Today, undocumented migration continues at the same levels as prior to September 11. If September 11 failed to result in the shutting of the borders, how can one expect the border ever to be truly sealed?

For generations, incremental reform strategies have failed to correct the U.S. immigration system. In 1981, a select Commission issued recommendations for immigration reform.[76] In the early 1990s, a blue-ribbon Commission on Immigration Reform, chaired by the respected Congresswoman Barbara Jordan, issued a series of reports containing many recommendations.[77] Commentators have suggested reforming the Border Patrol for years.[78] These reports and recommendations have fallen largely on deaf ears. Despite reform proposals and piecemeal reforms, there is no indication that the immigration controls or their enforcement can be reformed in an incremental manner that would reduce undocumented immigration.

Employer sanctions, passed by Congress in 1986, the so-called solution to illegal immigration, are for the most part not enforced today. Past efforts at workplace inspection have drawn protests from employers and immigrant rights activists. The Bush administration made workplace enforcement one of its lowest priorities. In 1999, only 240 full-time employees in the entire country were devoted to workplace enforcement of the immigration laws. In fiscal year 2003, the number dropped precipitously to a minuscule 90.[79] The result is little enforcement of the immigration laws in the workplace. Well-publicized immigration raids in 2007 have done little to meaningfully diminish the undocumented immigrant population.

In addition, despite the efforts to improve various systems tracking immigrants in the United States after September 11, 2001, the government's system for monitoring temporary visitors still has many weaknesses.[80] The system fails to keep track of all of the noncitizens in the country at any one time. Such a basic, and seemingly straightforward, safety measure must be implemented.

As Prohibition demonstrated, law cannot be effectively enforced when it faces overwhelming social, economic, and political resistance and the governed do not view as criminal, or immoral, what the law deems to be unlawful. Strict immigration controls that run counter to migration pressures simply cannot be enforced in the modern United States. Although removals are at all-time highs,[81] the undocumented population in the United States continues to grow. There is no end in sight. Rampant violation of the immigration laws undermines their very legitimacy. It shows how good and upstanding people in U.S. society today rely upon undocumented labor and how change in this regard is remote.

Reducing Racial Discrimination and the Exploitation of All Workers

As discussed in Chapter 3, U.S. immigration law and border enforcement are plagued by racial discrimination. The toleration of discrimination raises serious moral concerns and constitutes bad policy. It is inconsistent with efforts in other areas of U.S. law to eradicate racial discrimination in public schools, the workplace, housing, and American social life generally. The discrimination inherent in the immigration laws and their enforcement seriously undermines this greater struggle to eliminate discrimination.

Beyond its dubious morality, it is poor labor policy to allow the use of immigration law to be used to create a disposable, racially stratified labor force. The dual labor market, with immigrant labor of color concentrated in one low-wage market and citizens in a higher-wage one, injures U.S. citizen workers as well as immigrant workers. Failure to enforce labor standards for immigrant labor makes it difficult for domestic labor to maintain wages and working conditions. Rather than hire more expensive labor, employers will, if possible, look to the less expensive immigrant labor market to fulfill their needs. Closed borders have helped create this bifurcated labor force. Rather than waste money on border enforcement, the government would be well advised to devote its resources to enforcing labor protections for immigrant workers and decreasing employer incentive to go to the secondary market, a change that would benefit all workers, citizens and immigrants alike.

As discussed in Chapter 4, efforts to curtail immigration are not the answer to the claim that immigrants undercut the wage scale for domestic workers. Immigration enforcement that significantly restricts the supply of labor has proven to be largely impossible. Rather, efforts should be made to ensure that employers are in compliance with the laws and regulations that govern wages and conditions for all workers. So long as a dual labor market exists in the United States in which law fails to govern one market and in which low-wage labor is subject to easy exploitation, one can expect many employers to opt for immigrant labor over domestic workers.

Only by eliminating the dual labor market will it be possible to begin to take the necessary steps to enforce uniform wage and condition laws. With a new system of open admissions, resources could be shifted from border control, where expenditures have failed to accomplish the stated goals, to the enforcement of the labor laws. By helping to free up resources for efforts to end the exploitation of immigrant workers, a liberal admissions system would further national labor policy with minimal negative impact.

In calling for immigration reform, President Bush, in 2004, candidly acknowledged many of the realities of undocumented immigration, stating that

[Immigrants'] search for a better life is one of the most basic desires of human beings. Many undocumented workers have walked mile after mile, through the heat of the day and the cold of night. Some have risked their lives in dangerous desert border crossings, or entrusted their lives to the brutal rings of heartless human smugglers. Workers who seek only to earn a living end up in the shadows of American life—fearful, often abused and exploited. When they are victimized by crime, they are afraid to call the police, or seek recourse in the legal system. They are cut off from their families far away, fearing if they leave our country to visit relatives back home, they might never be able to return to their jobs.[82]

President Bush's views on undocumented immigrants are difficult to dispute. The immigration status quo cannot be justified morally or as a matter of policy. The laws must be changed.

Some commentators would no doubt contend that large-scale immigration would reduce social cohesion and possibly *increase* racism against immigrants of color.[83] The social cohesion argument further assumes that more permeable borders would be accompanied by a drastic increase in immigration. This is far from self-evident. The number of immigrants lawfully admitted into the United States annually ranged between 1 and 1.9 million during the 1990s.[84] In the early years of the twenty-first century, legal immigration rates have leveled off. In fiscal year 2003, the number of immigrants declined to about 706,000. In fiscal year 2004, the figure was 946,142.[85] Although these numbers may seem high to some observers, they hardly suggest that a "flood" of noncitizens will come to America under a liberal admissions system.

Of course, fears of a mass migration could result in opposition to open borders. As previously discussed, a slow phased-in approach to opening the borders might satisfy those with such concerns.

Just as fear of social unrest delayed—and could have ended—the dismantling of Jim Crow and the desegregation of American social life, fears of public opposition to immigrants could be used to justify strict immigration controls indefinitely. Fearing public opposition, the Supreme Court in 1955 ordered states to proceed with the desegregation of the public schools at "all deliberate speed,"[86] a decision that since that time has been roundly criticized.[87] Speculative assertions about public resistance should not be used to retard the nation's progress toward laws more in keeping with its values.

The national commitment to multiculturalism suggests that we should strive to welcome and accept people of different cultures and backgrounds and races. Although some segments of our society may indeed act in discriminatory ways, the answer is not to keep immigrants out of the country. There are more constructive, nondiscriminatory ways to counteract discrimination. Policies that foster integration, for example, appear more likely to lessen social tensions than futile attempts to close the borders.

Promoting the Integration of Immigrants into U.S. Society

Mexican immigrants have been accused of promoting social disintegration and exacerbating racial divisiveness by "refusing" to assimilate: living in separate ethnic enclaves, maintaining the Spanish language, and embracing rather than abandoning their culture.[88] The evidence, however, demonstrates that immigrants, including Latina/o immigrants, in fact assimilate to a certain extent by learning English and adopting American family and work values.[89] However, those who level such accusations refuse to acknowledge the evidence. They deeply fear the racial and cultural impacts of current levels of immigration and no doubt would have great reservations about open borders. Their point of view would unquestionably command the support of a vocal segment of the public.

The most extreme version of this perspective, at least in relatively polite discussion, is that the United States is a white nation and should remain that way. If one embraces this view, immigrants of color—and people of color generally—can never be fully integrated into American social life. As the journalist Peter Brimelow stated bluntly, "the American nation has always had a specific ethnic core. And that core has been white."[90]

Despite such assertions about this nation's racial center, the United States is undergoing an inevitable racial and cultural transformation. As Census 2000 demonstrated, the nation's racial demographics have changed dramatically over the past decade, despite the most extensive system of border controls in U.S. history.[91] Absent a return to the discredited national-origins quota scheme discussed in Chapter 2, reversal of this trend appears highly unlikely. The American public, moreover, would be unlikely to support draconian immigration enforcement measures that cannot be reconciled with liberal notions of individual rights that have taken deep root in American society. In light of modern developments, such as increased international intercourse, improved transportation, and the electronic age, reversal seems even more unlikely.

Nor can the perceived need to preserve "our culture" justify immigration controls. Due to both external pressures and internal fissures, cultures necessarily evolve over time.[92] The "culture" of the United States, to the extent it can be defined, has changed and will continue to change. To a large extent, cultural change is natural and inevitable. This is especially true given the demographic transformations being experienced by the United States. Circumstances beyond any one nation's controls, such as advancements in technology and travel, may well accelerate this transformation. Cultural changes simply cannot be forestalled by immigration controls.

Understandably, change is uncomfortable for a society and its members. Immigration has inevitably contributed to change and, at times, social tensions. However, fears of racial and cultural transformation cannot justify closed borders, just as they cannot justify the maintenance of racially segregated schools, workplaces, and neighborhoods. The sensible approach is to adopt laws and policies that help smooth the rough edges of ongoing social changes, rather than to engage in the futile task of seeking to prevent the inevitable change from coming.[93]

At various times in U.S. history, restrictionists have sounded the alarm that immigrants have not assimilated into the mainstream. Some commentators might claim that open borders could make this "assimilation" problem worse. However, a properly designed open-entry policy could promote the integration of immigrants into U.S. society. The U.S. government would, however, need to expend time and resources to ease the transition of immigrants into American social life.[94]

Commentators from different political persuasions disagree on the proper strategies to achieve the goal of integrating immigrants into the economic, political, and social fabric of the United States. They all, however, agree that integrating resident immigrants into the mainstream is a laudable goal worth pursuing.[95] Communitarians—who seek to ensure full community membership for immigrants—and liberals should support this view.[96]

As a historical matter, the integration of Mexican immigrants into American social life has proven difficult. This is due, in part, to the strained relationship between Mexican nationals and the U.S. government. As aptly summarized by Bernard Trujillo, Mexican immigrants have a bittersweet ambivalence about the United States:

> The patterns of Mexican migration we observe are partially attributable to the vibrant and ongoing relationships between Mexicans in Mexico and Mexicans (along with persons of Mexican descent) in the United States. *A Mexican national fixes her eyes on the U.S. with a mixture of hope and resentment: hope because she knows her labor will be welcomed by the economy and she will be welcomed by networks of Mexicans who have come weeks and generations before; resentment because she believes the border is fundamentally false.*[97]

Racial difference can make it difficult for the integration of immigrants and citizens of Mexican ancestry into mainstream U.S. society.[98] Discrimination against persons of Mexican ancestry is a central part of the history of the Mexican people in the United States.[99] This is particularly true in the Southwest, where border enforcement, with its focus on race, often contributes to racial tensions. U.S. citizens of Mexican ancestry also suffer from discrimination in jobs, education, and public accommodations.[100]

Open borders could help ameliorate some of the problems experienced by Mexican immigrants and Mexican-American citizens. Legal distinctions between immigrants and citizens, which are currently central to the immigration laws, serve to create in-groups and out-groups, promote interethnic tension, and breed discrimination against perceived outsiders. By tending to render such distinctions irrelevant, liberal admission policies would promote full community membership for all people living and working in U.S. society.

By minimizing, if not wholly, eliminating, the importance of immigration distinctions between people in the United States, a liberal admissions system would also tend to dampen the institutionalized stigmatization of domestic minorities, such as Mexican-Americans, who share ancestries with disfavored immigrants. In so doing, the law would help to promote the integration of noncitizens and certain groups of U.S. citizens into U.S. society.

In addition, reducing the significance of people's immigration status would be consistent with the U.S. government's policy of encouraging naturalization, the process that transforms immigrants into full-fledged U.S. citizens and signifies full legal integration into the United States. In the 1990s, the federal government, then under the leadership of President Clinton, facilitated the naturalization of immigrants through the Citizenship USA program.[101] Naturalization rates, particularly among Mexican immigrants, rose dramatically.[102] Although the program came under heated attack for allegedly being motivated by partisan political ends (namely to increase the number of Democratic voters),[103] federal policy, with the full support of reform proponents, continues to favor naturalization.[104]

The law also promotes immigrant assimilation—and avoids a potential caste system—by bestowing U.S. citizenship on children born in the United States to undocumented parents.[105] This rule is based on a well-settled interpretation of the Fourteenth Amendment, which provides that "[a]ll persons born or naturalized in the United States and subject to the jurisdiction thereof, are citizens of the United States and of the State wherein they reside." Until recently in U.S. history, birthright citizenship had gone unchallenged.[106] Over the past few decades, however, proposals have been made almost annually to end the long legal tradition of bestowing citizenship on these children.[107] In 2005, for example, a proposal to abolish birthright citizenship was introduced in Congress. To ensure the integration of immigrants into U.S. social life, birthright citizenship must be continued. Otherwise, the nation would likely see an expansion of the immigrant racial caste that currently exists in the United States.

Some might argue that an open-borders regime would "devalue" citizenship in the United States.[108] The use of the term "devaluation" in this context is misleading. All of a nation's residents should be treated fairly. The rights and privileges of citizens need not be diminished to increase the rights of immigrants. Any effort to maintain legal distinction to avoid "devaluation" of citizenship would require continued disparities in rights and maintenance of the status quo. Adopting a similar logic, whites could have argued that desegregation in the 1950s and 1960s "devalued" their whiteness.

Integration of immigrants into American social life figures as a policy-based rationale for the Supreme Court's decision in *Plyler v. Doe*,[109] which held that the states could not constitutionally bar undocumented immigrants from elementary- and secondary-education public schools. An education allows immigrant children a chance at full access to, and full membership in, U.S. society.[110] In guaranteeing access to an education, the Court recognized that denying undocumented children a public education was inherently unfair. It is unfair because in fact they live in this country and will in all likelihood be part of the nation's future labor force.[111] Fairness concerns and the hoped-for integration of immigrants into U.S. society have animated efforts in recent years to ensure that undocumented immigrants have access to higher education[112] and are eligible to obtain driver's licenses.[113]

If one is truly concerned with the integration of immigrants into American social life, policies that promote assimilation are the most direct answer. Although it is important to avoid the coerced assimilation endorsed by the U.S. government in the past,[114] policies that facilitate the integration of immigrants should be encouraged. Access to English-as-a-second-language courses, naturalization workshops, and community education programs would promote integration without raising the specter of the discredited coercive measures of the past. Such measures, if properly structured, would generally be welcomed by most of the immigrant community.

Efforts should be made to promote the economic and political integration of immigrants into U.S. society with or without the adoption of a more liberal admissions policy. A focus on integration would represent an improvement over the myopic focus on immigration restrictions that currently dominates immigration law and policy. Restrictions in some ways constitute the worst of both worlds—immigrants continue to enter the country, and no policies exist to facilitate their integration into U.S. society. Integration policies would benefit immigrants and benefit the nation by helping to ensure the political assimilation of immigrants.

Reducing Domestic Tension between State and Federal Governments

Immigration has been a source of tension between the state and the federal governments.[115] Historically, the federal government has had exclusive jurisdiction over immigration and has preempted state law in the area.[116] As explained in Chapter 4, state and local governments are frustrated by the fact that they bear costs for something over which they have no control. Because undocumented immigration has continued, and has imposed costs at the ground level, state and local governments often complain about the substantial costs of providing services to immigrants.

In the 1990s, California brought a lawsuit claiming that the federal government had failed to protect the state from a foreign "invasion" and sought damages.[117] In addition, California's Proposition 187, which would have barred undocumented children from the public schools and denied them public benefits, "sent a message" to the federal government that immigration was a problem that must be addressed.[118] That message was heard loudly and clearly. The Clinton administration responded by dramatically ramping up border enforcement and aggressively acting to crack down on illegal immigration.

The tension between state and federal governments on immigration stems in large part from the disproportionate allocation of immigration's costs and benefits between the two. The federal government collects the bulk of the taxes contributions from noncitizens, while state and local governments make substantial expenditures on services for undocumented and lawful immigrants. State and local governments specifically provide a public education, emergency health services, and certain other benefits and services to immigrants. The fiscal disconnect between revenues and costs provokes great tension, especially when state and local budgets are as tight as they have been in the United States over the past decade.

The out-of-pocket costs of immigration contribute significantly to anti-immigrant animus, even when dollars-and-cents concerns are not directly implicated. For example, states have sought to bar undocumented immigrants from securing driver's licenses, even though it is in the interest of public safety to license every driver on the roads.[119] At times, local governments have even sought to regulate immigration by using the trespass laws[120] or conducting immigration raids.[121] Fueled by economic fears, these policies are difficult to justify on moral, economic, or policy grounds. Nor are they successful immigration policies.

Absent the funding concerns, state and local governments might not be nearly as interested in immigration. Revenue sharing to help state and local governments pay the costs of immigration, especially if combined with a workable and enforceable immigration system, would do much to alleviate tensions between state and federal governments on the issue. It also would dampen the nativist impulse in the states.

Reducing International Tensions

Immigration has sporadically produced tensions between the United States and other nations. A move toward open entry would tend to reduce international tensions. It also could well improve this nation's relations with other countries and heighten the nation's stature in the eyes of the world.

Specifically, immigration has resulted in serious rifts between Mexico and the United States.[122] Border enforcement strategies and U.S. authorities' harsh treatment of Mexican nationals have contributed to the conflict. Nor has the Mexican government remained silent. For example, when, in the 1990s, the U.S. government named one of its new border enforcement operations in El Paso, Texas, "Operation Blockade," the Mexican government strongly protested. In response, the U.S. government changed the name to "Operation Hold-the-Line."[123] Similarly, Mexican officials vocally protested the anti-Mexican sentiment underlying the campaign in California for Proposition 187, a voter-approved initiative that would have barred undocumented immigrants from receiving public benefits.[124] In 2005 and 2006, Mexico reacted negatively to border enforcement bills pending in Congress. Eleven Latin American countries, including Mexico, lobbied against a strict border enforcement bill passed by the U.S. House of Representatives at the end of 2005.[125]

The Mexican government also protested the U.S. Congress's passage of a bill in 2006 authorizing the extension of the fence along the U.S.-Mexico border.

From 2001 to the present, the governments of Mexico and the United States have had ongoing discussions about migration, a major issue of interest to the two governments.[126] For the Mexican government, ending human rights abuses and ensuring the continued flows of remittances from migrants in the United States to Mexico[127] make U.S. immigration law relevant to its own national interests. Neither are served by border enforcement-only reforms. For well over a decade, however, U.S. lawmakers have failed to enact little more than laws that increase border enforcement.

A much-needed reconceptualization of the meaning and nature of the U.S.-Mexico border stands to benefit both nations.[128] An immigration scheme consistent with the economic, political, and social needs of the two nations, as has been outlined here, could be constructed. A more realistic legal regime would remedy the problems that plague immigration enforcement today and avoid repetitions of the mistakes of the past.

International tensions over migration are not limited to the United States and Mexico. Tighter border controls on the northern U.S. border after September 11 elicited protests from the Canadian government over the treatment of its citizens.[129] More generally, the proposed elimination of a visa waiver program for citizens of certain nations, designed to improve U.S. security, may have foreign-relations repercussions. According to the U.S. General Accounting Office, "[t]he decision to eliminate the program could negatively affect U.S. relations with participating countries, could discourage some business and tourism in the United States, and would increase the need for State Department resources."[130]

U.S. law generally seeks to limit the potential for negative foreign-relations consequences. For example, federal preemption of state regulation of immigration was premised in part on the potential for immigration law and its enforcement to have adverse foreign relations consequences. The foreign-policy implications of immigration decisions were also an important rationale for the plenary power doctrine, which shields the immigration laws from meaningful judicial review.[131] In addition, federal jurisdiction over disputes involving noncitizens and foreign states in the federal courts provides a degree of assurance that foreigners will receive fair treatment.[132]

Liberal admission would further U.S. foreign-policy interests.[133] A move toward open entry would tend to reduce international tensions. Migrants from any particular nation would not feel disfavored. Their governments would not see U.S. policy as discriminating against its nationals, as is the case today. Absent the elaborate mazes of exclusions, most migrants and potential migrants, as well as the governments of their homelands, would feel that they were welcomed, respected, and the equals of citizens of other nations.

The potential foreign-policy benefits are not limited to U.S-Mexican relations. Open borders could relieve tensions between the United States and other nations, as well. Multilateralism will be essential to fighting terrorism in the future,[134] as well as ensuring peace. Consequently, improving foreign relations through liberal admissions of immigrants is a benefit well worth considering.

Protecting the Nation from True Dangers to Public Safety and National Security

No political theory could justify endangering public safety. Even in a system of easy entry, a certain level of border enforcement and controls would be necessary to allow for the exclusion of noncitizens who truly endanger the national security and public safety.[135] Such limits on entry could be justified morally on grounds of self-defense. In terms of immigration restrictions, the United States should closely limit itself to those consistent with a liberal commitment to open borders. Terrorism, crime, and serious public-health risks are specific threats to the national security and public safety that the nation must consider. In the open-borders system proposed here, controls would be much narrower than the current restrictionist regime in place. As a moral matter, they should be based on individual assessments, rather than on group judgments based on statistical probabilities.

An anti-terror approach is consistent with the recommendations of the 9/11 Commission Report. The report suggests that the United States needs a better system to tracking noncitizens within the country and increased cooperation with other nations in exchanging information about terrorist activity. The Commission specifically recommends an entry/exit system that records who is in the United States. Such a system, however, cannot be effective if thousands, if not millions, of people are entering the country outside authorized channels.

Today, undocumented immigrants live under the government's radar. They are effectively invisible, unidentified, and unknown. It is essential that we keep better track of the millions of undocumented immigrants living in this country if we are serious about protecting the nation from terrorist acts. To this end, the United States also needs to work with other nations to secure accurate intelligence about persons who seek entry into the United States.[136]

Limited border controls designed to prevent specific threats would be fully justified.[137] Narrowly tailored controls would allow the nation to protect its national security and public safety in a manner consistent with both international law and individual rights.[138] To be true to the spirit of permeable borders, any national-security and public-safety exclusions, however, would need to be *narrow*. One possibility would be to limit the exclusion in a manner consistent with the test for regulating speech under the First Amendment, which allows speech to be abridged if it is directed at inciting or producing imminent lawless action and is likely to produce such conduct.[139] Noncitizens who pose an imminent threat to the nation's security could justifiably be denied entry into the United States.

In addition, the nation must be permitted to exclude convicted criminals, as well as terrorists, from entering the United States. Background checks into criminal histories of would-be immigrants are thus fully justified as a prerequisite to entry. Along similar lines, immigrants with certain communicable diseases, which would include many covered by current law, should be excludable.

Although border controls narrowly tailored to protect national security and public safety are necessary and appropriate, the risk is that Congress, in creating exceptions to the general rule of free entry, would allow the exceptions to overtake the rule by accretion, just as the list of exclusions in the U.S. immigration laws became longer and longer over time.

Historically, efforts to appear "tough on immigration" have offered short-run political benefits to politicians, whatever the harms to the immigrant community and whether or not the policy actually achieves its stated goals. Consequently, any liberal immigration admissions regime would likely be subject to minor incursions that, over time, would risk undermining the liberal admission principle.

Put simply, exceptions to a liberal admissions scheme could increase and ultimately swallow the general rule. As a result, any open migration system always would occupy a precarious place in U.S. law. It would remain a truly open and permeable border only if vigilance guaranteed its maintenance and forestalled the xenophobic pressures that periodically arise.

Particularized immigration controls based on individualized and specific threats might result in more effective enforcement of terrorism and related exclusions. This proved to be the case in the U.S. Customs Service inspections. In response to claims of racial profiling in customs searches at ports of entry, the agency promulgated standards and procedures governing intrusive searches. Implementation of the new rules *improved efficiency* in finding contraband while resulting in *fewer searches*.[140] Standards and fewer searches worked. Similarly, a number of state and local jurisdictions in the United States have implemented policies, procedures, and standards to govern traffic stops in order to eradicate racial profiling in law enforcement.[141] The hope is that standards will result in fewer, but more justified, traffic stops. These instances suggest that more narrowly tailored immigration enforcement might better protect public safety than the current across-the-board system of categorical exclusions.

Overbroad efforts to protect national security in the current U.S. immigration laws offer few concrete benefits and have resulted in widespread civil rights deprivations. Longstanding efforts to regulate the political ideology of immigrants through the immigration laws are a glaring example.[142] There is no evidence that the ideological restrictions, which are a stain on this nation's commitment to free expression, benefited the United States in any way. The overbroad definition of "terrorist" and "terrorist activity" in the U.S. immigration laws failed to stop the September 11 hijackers from lawfully entering the United States. The indiscriminate dragnet of Arabs and Muslims after September 11 produced little in the way of concrete information about those horrific events. To add insult to injury, the measures resulted in mass civil rights deprivations.

In addition to individualized security exclusions, other alternatives exist. For example, if the North American nations developed a European Union–style arrangement permitting labor migration among Canada, Mexico, and the United States, the partners could enhance security along their outer borders, akin to developing a "Fortress Europe," in the name of national security.[143] This strategy, of course, has both pros and cons. Still, it might calm concerns of the security-minded.

In sum, open borders, as outlined here, are entirely consistent with national security and public safety. Focusing border restrictions and immigration controls on true dangers to the national security and public safety would represent a stark improvement over the scattershot approach of restrictions that permeates current immigration law. Consequently, while making the nation's borders truer to the ideal of an open society, the United States would also be a safer place.

Conclusion

Strong policy arguments can be made for free migration between nations. Besides providing concrete benefits to the United States, open borders would eliminate both the civil rights deprivations that result from the current border enforcement efforts and the ripple effects of existing laws on U.S. citizens and lawful immigrants of particular national origin ancestries. Dismantling rigid border controls would reduce enforcement abuses, dampen racial discrimination, promote racial justice, and foster better treatment of all workers. Moreover, the United States stands to reap foreign-policy benefits and reduce tensions between itself and many other nations, particularly Mexico.

At the same time, national security and public safety can be better protected through an open-borders regime. The nation must ferret out true threats of terrorism and dangers to the public safety. A narrow focus on true risks to public safety is more likely to protect the nation than broad exclusions that are only loosely linked to true threats to U.S. society.

6

The Inevitability of
Permeable Borders

We unquestionably live in interesting times. In the spring of 2005, the Minutemen, whom President Bush has called "vigilantes," massed at the Mexican border in southern Arizona with the support of, among others, Congressman Tom Tancredo and the archrestrictionist Pat Buchanan. Governor Arnold Schwarzenegger of California entered the immigration imbroglio and endorsed the work of the Minutemen on Los Angeles talk show radio. A California legislator proposed an initiative that would create the California Border Police. Through the REAL ID Act, passed in 2005,[1] Congress imposed new requirements on state driver's licenses, made asylum claims tougher to prove, and fortified the border with Mexico. In late 2005, the House of Representatives passed a punitive immigration reform bill. In a response unprecedented in U.S. immigration history, hundreds of thousands of protesters took to the streets in cities across the United States.

Immigration unquestionably deserves the nation's attention. However, it warrants careful and thoughtful analysis, not sound bites that rile base instincts and insult and alienate members of the national community. Alarmists all too often play on public fears with immigration and immigrants. The demand ordinarily is for swift, immediate, and decisive action, often resulting in ill-considered border enforcement measures that fail to do the job.

Although immigration reform has been the topic of extensive public discussion, there has been no legislative proposal put on the table that would address the fact that the U.S. immigration laws are dramatically out of synch with the social, economic, and political realities of modern immigration in the global economy. Moreover, today's immigration laws are wholly inconsistent with the moral underpinnings of the United States of America. Put simply, the U.S. immigration laws are broken and must be fixed. Fixing them requires true comprehensive immigration reform, not mere tinkering at the margins.

Consider the incontrovertible facts. Immigrants make up about 10 percent of the U.S. population. As many as 12 million undocumented immigrants live in the United States. This large population exists even though, in the 1990s, the U.S. government dramatically bolstered border enforcement with Mexico and engaged in a number of high profile, military-style operations in border cities like El Paso, Texas, and San Diego, California. In an attempt to avoid the Border Patrol, undocumented immigrants today travel through isolated deserts and mountains, literally risking life and limb in hopes of making it to the land of the free and the home of the brave. As a result, over the past decade, thousands of migrants, almost all of them citizens of Mexico, have died attempting to cross the Southwest border.

Besides its deadly consequences, heightened immigration enforcement has spurred a booming industry in the trafficking of human beings. Criminal smugglers today charge undocumented immigrants thousands of dollars for passage to the United States. Smugglers show little respect for the safety of their human cargo and, at times, abandon migrants to die in the desert or on the high seas. Many migrants fortunate enough to survive the journey are forced to work as indentured servants to pay off the debts of passage to smugglers. Because trafficking arrangements are not in the least bit regulated, exploitation and abuse run rampant.

The obvious question is why immigrants are willing to pay thousands of dollars to risk their lives to come to the United States. In our heart of hearts, we all know the answer. Immigrants come in pursuit of the American Dream. They come for jobs. They come to join family members. Indeed, even for the undocumented, the United States is a land of great opportunity. Undocumented immigrants have little difficulty finding work. Because they work for relatively low wages, employers eagerly hire them.

Employer sanctions under U.S. immigration law have, for the most part, have failed. Employers resist enforcement at every turn, as do immigrant-rights advocates who fear the civil rights impacts of aggressive enforcement on immigrant communities. Nor have the amount of sanctions, usually a civil penalty of a few hundred dollars per violation, or the limited resources devoted to interior enforcement proven sufficient to deter the widespread employment of undocumented immigrants, who today are vital to the national economy.

The economic incentives for employers to exploit workers are great.

Many employers pay undocumented workers low—at least by U.S. standards—wages and provide few, if any, benefits. Employers gain. Lower wages have meant more profits, wealth, and economic growth. Consumers also benefit from undocumented labor. We pay less for fruit and vegetables, beef and poultry, restaurant meals, hotel rooms, domestic service work, yard work, and much more. The U.S. economy as a whole benefits from an infusion of cheap labor. In addition, many undocumented immigrants pay federal income taxes. The Social Security coffers gain billions of dollars from contributions made by undocumented immigrants. Because undocumented immigrants almost never access Social Security benefits, these contributions are all gain for the federal government and the baby boomers retiring in greater numbers every day.

The benefits of immigration, and undocumented immigration in particular, are often ignored in the public debate. Rather, groups such as the Minutemen and politicians like Congressmen Tom Tancredo myopically focus on the costs of immigration, decry illegal immigration and immigrants, and foment hatred. But they miss the big picture. Benefits accrue to each and every one of us, as well as to the federal government. As Chapter 4 demonstrates, the economic benefits, by many accounts, outweigh the costs associated with immigration.

There unquestionably are costs, however. State and local governments spend much money in providing services, including a public school education and emergency services, to immigrants within their jurisdictions. While state and local governments bear these substantial costs, they receive few of the revenues associated with immigrants. Instead, the federal government collects the bulk of tax monies. A fiscal disconnect contributes to the view at the state and local levels that immigration is out of control.

As contended in Chapter 5, immigration law today is not all that different from the anti-alcohol laws in place during the failed era of Prohibition. The laws fail to comport with social, political, and economic reality. Many Americans simply do not comply with the law. As was the case during Prohibition, widespread unlawful conduct has resulted. Indeed, two law-abiding Democratic nominees for Attorney General, as well as a prospective Republican Secretary of Homeland Security (known, ironically enough, for his tough law-and-order stance that helped clean up the streets of New York) and a prospective conservative Secretary of Labor withdrew their nominations because they had employed undocumented immigrants. The sustained demand for liquor doomed Prohibition. In order to avoid a similar fate, any serious immigration reform must recognize that there is a huge demand—and need—for immigrants in the U.S. economy.

The Need for Truly Comprehensive Immigration Reform

Unless the United States reforms its laws to address the fundamental reasons for immigration and undocumented immigrants, we can expect a flareup on this volatile issue every few years. This unfortunately has been the pattern for much of U.S. history. When a problem is identified with immigration, politicians scurry to act, often proposing half-baked reform efforts that do little to address the problem. In fact, many of the so-called solutions only make the problems worse. Those who suffer the most are the immigrants themselves, who in the name of reform are frequently punished with impunity.

Almost as constant as the changing of the seasons, the United States tinkers with its immigration laws nearly every year. Incremental immigration reforms like those of the past, however, are unlikely to address the fundamental problems with immigration regulation. Even much of the legislation supported by immigrant rights advocates, such as AgJobs in 2005, is unlikely to do anything but delay the need for immigration legislation that will address a new population of undocumented immigrants. In addition, the incremental reforms almost inevitably include "tough on immigrant" provisions, such as the employer sanctions provisions in the Immigration Reform and Control Act of 1986. By failing to address the fundamental issues of immigration, incremental reform has failed the United States time and time again.

To make matters worse, sporadic incremental reform measures have had devastating impacts on immigrant communities. In the past decade, for example, Congress greatly expanded the grounds for deportation, mandated detention—sometimes indefinite—for large numbers of immigrants facing deportation, and narrowed judicial review of many deportation and other immigration decisions. At the same time, Congress greatly increased the budget of the agencies in charge of immigration enforcement. The resulting rise of military-style border enforcement operations along the U.S.-Mexico border has transformed the region into nothing less than a war zone. Such punitive enforcement measures have resulted in record levels of immigrant deportations and deaths.

However, restrictionist measures have little long-term impact on immigration to the United States. The current immigration system does not work. It is violated on a daily basis by millions of employers and immigrants. As we have seen, the undocumented immigrant population has *increased* in the face of unprecedented enforcement efforts to close the borders, efforts that took on greater urgency after the events of September 11.

Efforts to exclude immigrants from our shores breed hate and intolerance of immigrants—of people who live and work in our communities. The government's tough immigration enforcement measures no less than stoke the fires of racism and nativism in the United States. Vigilantes like the Minutemen gain moral and political support by claiming to do nothing more than enforce the U.S. immigration laws because the federal government has failed to do so. Such activities contribute to the discrimination against immigrants. Unfortunately, vigilante activities and their side effects came in no small part from the fact that the current immigration laws simply cannot be enforced. The end result is the worst of all worlds—ineffective immigration laws that do nothing more than punish immigrants, waste money, and foment hatred.

What change is needed? The United States requires deep and enduring immigration reform. Generally, the United States would gain from more permeable, more open borders. The European Union, which allows labor migration among its member nations, provides one model. A North American Union would allow a more orderly system of migration between nations. This labor integration would be much more consistent with the economic interests of the United States and the economic reality on the street than is the current immigration system. It also would avoid the tension, hate, and deaths caused by current U.S. immigration law and policy.

The fundamental premise of the current U.S. immigration laws is that exclusion of immigrants is the norm and admission of noncitizens is the exception. This premise need not be the foundation of our laws and, if we ever want true reform, must be reexamined. This book hopes to shift the debate over immigration to consider the possibility of making the United States's borders more permeable to people, just as it generally is to goods, services, and capital. As a legal matter, the first step is to reverse the current presumptions in U.S. immigration laws and make the admission of migrants the norm and their exclusion the exception.

The Fundamental Problem with the Current Immigration Laws

The fundamental problem with current U.S. immigration law is that it is founded on the idea that it is permissible, desirable, and necessary to restrict immigration into the United States. A border is viewed as a barrier to entry, rather than as a port of entry. Unfortunately, policymakers and the public accept without question the idea that the United States can restrict immigration and assume that every nation-state must restrict immigration. Consistent with this underlying assumption, most recent immigration reform proposals move in the direction of closing the borders rather than attempting to make the migration of people into this country fairer, more efficient, and humane. To reform U.S. immigration laws, the nation must reconceptualize the importance and meaning of the international border.

More open migration policies deserve fuller analysis and public debate. Attempts to seal the border through augmented border enforcement have failed time and time again. The nation needs a dramatic new approach. With increasing frequency, observers have voiced support for the liberal admission of immigrants or at least a regime with narrower immigration restrictions. These arguments are well worth considering.

As outlined in Chapter 3, political theorists have found it extremely difficult to justify efforts to close national borders, especially in light of the nation's deep commitment to individual rights. In practice, closed borders implicate serious moral hazards. They result in rampant civil and human rights violations. Violence and death, racial discrimination, and the creation of an exploitable labor force all flow directly from the current system of immigration restrictions and enforcement in the modern United States.

Moreover, closed borders create a foundation for overzealous and publicly condemned enforcement measures, such as the United States's refusal to accept Jewish refugees during World War II and its failure to provide safe haven to Central Americans in the 1980s and to Haitians in the 1980s and 1990s. They have served as the foundation for the suppression of the rights of noncitizens. That has, in turn, led to harsh policies directed toward certain groups of U.S. citizens, as demonstrated by the internment of persons of Japanese ancestry, citizens and noncitizens alike, during World War II and by the indefinite detention of U.S.

citizens—Yaser Hamdi and Jose Padilla—without criminal charges or access to an attorney after the horrible events of September 11, 2001.

Chapter 4 summarized the strong economic arguments in favor of free migration. International trade principles suggest that labor migration is a net benefit to the national welfare. In an era of globalization, labor, as well as capital and goods, should be permitted and encouraged to cross national borders. The European Union allows labor migration between and within its member nations. The North American Free Trade Agreement, however, permits only free trade of goods and services. Labor faces closed borders in North America. The United States might learn from the European model about the benefits and practicality of freer labor migration.

Encouraging migration through an open-borders policy would recognize that border enforcement simply cannot stifle the strong economic, social, and political pressures that fuel international migration. As with the United States's failed prohibition of the alcohol trade in the early twentieth century, it has proven virtually impossible to enforce the immigration laws and to halt undocumented immigration. To make matters worse, border enforcement shares many of Prohibition's negative side effects. It promotes criminal activity, increases abusive law enforcement practices, contributes to a caseload crisis in the courts, and undermines the moral force and legitimacy of the law.

The restrictionist nightmare is that the elimination of border controls will open the "floodgates" and that millions upon millions of immigrants from around the world will overwhelm, if not destroy, the United States. This fear betrays the view that noncitizens the world over could not resist coming to the best of all countries if the opportunity existed. True, free migration might well result in initial population readjustments between nations. However, most people in foreign countries have no inclination to leave their native soil, no matter how onerous the conditions. They do not want to leave friends and family, and a familiar language and culture, to risk their lives for an uncertain future. For similar reasons, free movement among the fifty states has not generally led to mass migrations, even though significant economic, political, and social disparities exist among the states.

An offshoot of the floodgates argument is that, with large numbers of immigrants of color coming to the United States, racism and cultural conflict will increase. Samuel Huntington, whose views were discussed in Chapter 2, is the latest of the doomsayers who suggest that immigrants foment social conflict. The social-cohesion concern assumes that large numbers of migrants will come who are not already migrating. This is not necessarily the case. In any event, we will have change—cultural and otherwise—with or without permeable borders. Policies that promote the full integration of immigrants into U.S. society would do much to avoid any social tensions and strife that accompany that change. Developing constructive policies that integrate immigrants into U.S. society would be preferable to wasting money on doomed border enforcement measures.

Concerns about national security will also generate opposition to open borders. The events of September 11, 2001, have understandably raised legitimate concerns about national security and public safety. In the name of public safety, the highest levels of the federal government have engaged in massive efforts to restrict entry into the United States. Many noncitizens, from innocent researchers to students to poor and working people of color, have suffered. As a result of national security fears, constructive immigration reform efforts in recent years have fallen by the wayside. Specifically, serious discussions of a bilateral agreement regularizing migration between the United States and Mexico ended abruptly when the "war on terror" began.

However, open borders are fully consistent with efforts to prevent terrorism. More liberal migration would allow the government to devote its undivided attention to the true dangers to national security and public safety. Rather than trying to keep most noncitizens out of the country, the government could focus on terrorists, dangerous criminals, drugs, and other contraband in enforcing the borders. Valuable resources would no longer be wasted on fruitless efforts to shut the border, and these funds could go instead to identifying and eliminating these threats. Enforcement efforts could move beyond the morass of exclusion grounds, caps, ceilings, and many other complexities that have made enforcement of the Immigration and Nationality Act unwieldy, inefficient, and unfair.

Historically, U.S. immigration law has been overbroad in attacking the perceived evil of the day, whether it be terrorists, racial minorities, the poor, political dissidents, gays and lesbians, or the disabled. An effective "war on terror" should attempt to exclude from admission true dangers to national security and public safety, rather than simply trying to seal the borders, which has proven to be virtually impossible. As seen in other areas of law enforcement, more calculated immigration law enforcement has a greater likelihood of rooting out unlawful conduct than scattershot efforts that infringe on the civil rights of many people.

Overbroad enforcement efforts are not only ineffective. They are also counterproductive. The current laws have fueled the creation of criminal networks engaged in the trafficking of human beings that pose true risks to the national security and public safety. The current unrealistic laws promote undocumented immigration. We have no record of the identity or addresses of millions of undocumented immigrants who live in our communities. The current U.S. immigration system woefully fails to ensure the protection of national security.

By flipping the legal presumption and assuming that a migrant is admissible into the United States, the nation could focus scarce enforcement resources on the true dangers to U.S. society. Identity and security checks performed on all migrants seeking entry—and encouraging all to seek lawful entry—would permit better tracking of immigrants in the country, where they live, and what they are doing. Currently, the U.S. immigration system allows for millions to live under the radar, with no record of their identity or place of residence.

The Future

This book has analyzed the strong economic, social, and political forces that are fueling migration to the United States. It has described how the United States would benefit by opening its borders. It has shown that a long and porous border has existed and will continue to exist, whatever the barriers to entry erected by the U.S. government in the name of immigration reform. Finally, it has shown how the United States would benefit by opening its borders.

Time and time again, U.S. immigration law has been well behind global and domestic changes, resulting in numerous laws and incidents that we now regret as a nation. Sadly, the United States is still behind the times. In terms of immigration policy, the nation still lives in a world of kingdoms with moats, walls, and barriers, rather than a modern world of mass transportation, the Internet, and daily international intercourse.

It is a cliché to say that the globalizing economy and technological improvements in communication and transportation have made the world a smaller place. But it is true. Increased trade, movement, and interconnections between nations are much more common now than they have ever been. Many citizens of the modern world have ties to multiple nations. Migrants often have deep ties both to their native countries and to their countries of destination.[2]

To this point, the U.S. immigration laws have responded in rather limited ways to the phenomenon of globalization. Incremental reforms have done little to address the nation's true immigration needs. Similarly, the rights of immigrants have tended to expand over time but have done so in fits and starts.[3] After years of consideration, the U.S. government took the cautious step of recognizing dual nationality, which quickly grew in popularity among Mexican nationals living in the United States. However, the U.S. immigration laws have failed more generally to respond to the globalizing economy.

Open borders are consistent with the integrating world economy. This book has outlined the arguments for a far-reaching change in the U.S. immigration laws that would respond to the rapidly changing world in which we live. Open borders would mark a true revolution in current U.S. immigration law and would create an admissions system in which migration more closely approximates demand.

The elimination of exaggerated border controls would offer many benefits to the United States. As part of a globalizing economy, the nation stands to reap economic benefits from freer labor migration. As a matter of economic theory, international trade with Mexico and much of the world, which the United States has eagerly embraced, differs little from labor migration. A utilitarian approach would allow for labor migration and add the benefits of new labor to the national economy.

Importantly, the removal of controls would end the sheer brutality inherent in current immigration enforcement, which results in physical abuse, promotes racial discrimination, and relegates certain groups of U.S. citizens and lawful immigrants to second-class status both inside and outside the United States. Permeable borders would make allow for the admission of immigrants in numbers approximating the demand for immigration and make it unnecessary for many noncitizens seeking entry into the United States to circumvent the law. The immigration laws would not create the need for aggressive enforcement, with its discriminatory impacts and deadly results.

Last but not least, strong policy arguments exist for the abolition of border controls. Experience demonstrates that, at least within modern sensibilities, overzealous border controls simply cannot be enforced by the U.S. government. Undocumented immigration is not viewed as criminal by many law-abiding Americans. Nor is the employment of undocumented immigrants. Abolition of border controls would recognize the economic and social reality of immigration. Millions of undocumented immigrants make valuable contributions to the U.S. economy but are forced to live on the margins of society and, subject to exploitation because of their uncertain immigration status, work in poor conditions for substandard wages. Foreign-policy benefits would accrue from a system in which the nationals of other societies were welcomed rather than labeled a public menace, barred from entry, and treated as pariahs in our midst.

It may well be that "[d]espite the rapid globalization of the world economy, the countries of terra firma are unlikely to abandon the concept of individual, sovereign nations in favor of a world of free borders and unrestricted migration."[4] Times change, however. It is to be hoped that the time will come when the United States will realize that closed borders are far from inevitable and, in fact, do not serve the national interests. Closed borders result in immoral consequences that, in the annals of history, have shamed the United States and will continue to do so. The Berlin-Wall-lite that the government is in the process of erecting between the United States and Mexico is not consistent with American values and dreams. Rather, an "open Republic" is more consistent with the values for which this nation proudly stands.[5]

Because it is difficult to estimate the impacts of a move to open borders on migration, there are unquestionably risks in moving to a system of open entry. We cannot be certain how many people will take advantage of open entry into the United States, although the available evidence suggests that the nation would not experience a flood of migrants. A transitional program might ease the adjustment and minimize the risks of public disorder. However, the United States's past experience with virtually open borders suggests that a mass migration need not necessarily follow.

The successful European Union (EU) provides the model for a second-best alternative. Border controls among member states are minimal. Free migration within the member states has not resulted in mass migrations. Labor can now move to the location of highest demand and most efficient use. Growing pains, of course, resulted at the outset, but the system soon achieved stability and acceptance. Overall, the move to a common labor market was relatively uneventful.

However, the opening of internal borders in the EU was accompanied by a building of borders at the outer perimeters of the Union. Critics have claimed that a Fortress Europe has had negative effects on asylum seekers and created problems like those seen at the U.S. borders. North Africans seek to enter the EU through Spain by hazarding a dangerous crossing of the Mediterranean Sea. Migrants die. Hate crimes against immigrants have arisen with some frequency in the EU nations. In 2005, social strife resulted in France as Muslims protested their second-class status in French society. The problems experienced in Fortress Europe suggest that a North American Union is a second-best alternative to more generally permeable borders.

In the end, the politics for any true immigration reform effort will be challenging. Many reform proposals have been made by politicians and academics, but political support has not been forthcoming.[6] Nonetheless, the issue of immigration—and, more important, immigrants—is not going away. Indeed, as the United States remains the last true superpower and immigration has become a global phenomenon, it is increasing in importance. Economic globalization means that world migration is here to stay.[7] As a nation, we can no longer fool ourselves by pretending migrants will go away or listen if we tell them they are not welcome.

Ultimately, migration of people is inevitable. The United States must make an important choice. It can have laws that effectively and efficiently regulate admission into the country. Or, it can have laws, like those it currently has, that are inefficient, wasteful, and futile and that damage the nation.

Notes

1. Harold Meyerson, *A Deportation Tragedy*, WASH. POST, June 29, 2005, at A21. The Department of Homeland Security later decided to delay removal of Marie Gonzalez for a year while deporting her parents. *See* Elizabethe Holland, *Teen Stays, Parents Are Deported in a Tearful Goodbye at Airport*, ST. LOUIS POST-DISPATCH, July 6, 2005, at B1.

Immigrant success stories, combined with heartbreak resulting from the conduct of the U.S. government, are not uncommon. *See, e.g.*, Nicholas Riccardi, *Immigration Test Leaves Star Students in Free-Fall*, L.A. TIMES, July 19, 2005, at A1 (reporting on four high school honors students who were determined to be undocumented upon return from trip to Niagara Falls while participating in a national science competition in Buffalo, New York, and placed in removal proceedings by the federal government); Dan Frosch, *Four Arizona Students From Mexico Forestall Their Deportation*, N.Y. TIMES, July 22, 2005, at 13 (reporting that the immigration judge ruled that the students could not be deported because they had been racially profiled because of their Mexican appearance by immigration officers who stopped them and questioned their citizenship).

2. Tom Tancredo, *Minutemen's Weapons Are Cell Phones and Cameras*, TUCSON CITIZEN, Apr. 1, 2005, at 5B. Long before making this statement, Congressman Tancredo had been well known for his strong anti-immigrant views. For example, upon reading a newspaper story about a successful undocumented high school student, he contacted the immigration authorities in an attempt to have the young person deported. *See* Judith Graham, *Migrant's College Bid Turns Political; Lawmakers Seeks His Deportation*, CHI. TRIB., Sept. 27, 2002, at N8. In 2007 Tancredo announced that he would run for president on an anti-immigrant platform.

3. Moreover, migration is a global phenomenon. *See* UNITED NATIONS GEN. ASSEMBLY, REPORT OF THE SECRETARY GENERAL, INTERNATIONAL MIGRATION AND DEVELOPMENT (2006) (reporting that in 2005, there were 191 million international migrants in nations around the world).

4. *See, e.g.*, Teresa Watanabe & Hector Becerra, *500,000 Pack Streets to Protest Immigration Bills*, L.A. TIMES, Mar. 26, 2005, at A1 (Los Angeles);

Mark Johnson & Linda Spice, *Thousands March for Immigrants,* MILWAUKEE J. SENTINEL, Mar. 24, 2006, at A1 (Milwaukee); Nathaniel Hoffman, *Protest Supports Illegal Workers,* CONTRA COSTA TIMES, Mar. 22, 2006 (San Francisco); Oscar Avila & Antonio Olivo, *A Show of Strength: Thousands March to Loop for Immigrants' Rights,* CHI. TRIB., Mar. 11, 2006, at A1 (Chicago).

5. *See* Fox News/Opinion Dynamics Poll (May 3, 2005), available at www .foxnews.com/projects/pdf/050305_poll.pdf, last visited Nov. 27, 2006.

6. *See* League of United Latin American Citizens v. Wilson, 908 F. Supp. 755 (C.D. Cal. 1995) (holding that federal law preempted Proposition 187 because it sought to regulate immigration, an area exclusively within the jurisdiction of the federal government).

7. *See generally* PETER ANDREAS, BORDER GAMES: POLICING THE U.S.-MEXICO DIVIDE (2000); JOSEPH NEVINS, OPERATION GATEKEEPER: THE RISE OF THE "ILLEGAL ALIEN" AND THE MAKING OF THE U.S.-MEXICO BOUNDARY (2002).

8. *See* Kevin R. Johnson, *Driver's Licenses and Undocumented Immigrants: The Future of Civil Rights Law?,* 5 NEV. L.J. 213 (2004); María Pabón Lopez, *More Than A License to Drive: State Restrictions on the Use of Driver's Licenses by Noncitizens,* 29 S. ILL. U. L.J. 91 (2004/05); *see also* Sylvia R. Lazos Vargas, *Missouri, the "War on Terrorism," and Immigrants: Legal Challenges Post 9/11,* 67 MO. L. REV. 775, 798–807 (2002) (analyzing controversy in Missouri over driver's license eligibility for undocumented immigrants).

9. *See* REAL ID Act of 2005, Title B of the Emergency Supplemental Appropriations Act for Defense, the Global War on Terror, and Tsunami Relief, 2005, 109 Pub. L. No. 12, 119 Stat. 231 (2005).

10. *See* Emily Bazar, *Ariz., N.M., Declare Emergencies,* USA TODAY, Aug. 19, 2005, at 2A; Ralph Blumenthal, *Citing Border Violence, 2 States Declare a Crisis,* N.Y. TIMES, AUG. 17, 2005, at A14. The hope of the states was to secure financial assistance from the federal government for costs associated with immigration.

11. *See* Anand Vaishnav, *N.H. Judge Dismisses Immigrants' Trespass Charges,* BOSTON GLOBE, Aug. 13, 2005, at B3.

12. *See* CONGRESSIONAL RESEARCH SERVICE, ENFORCING IMMIGRATION LAW: THE ROLE OF STATE AND LOCAL LAW ENFORCEMENT (updated Oct. 13, 2005); Michael A. Olivas, *Immigration-Related State and Local Ordinances: Preemption, Prejudice, and the Proper Role for Enforcement,* 2007 U. CHI. LEG. FORUM (forthcoming 2007).

13. *See* Leo R. Chavez, *Spectacle in the Desert: The Minuteman Project on the U.S.-Mexico Border, in* GLOBAL VIGILANTES: ANTHROPOLOGICAL PERSPECTIVES ON JUSTICE AND VIOLENCE (David Pratten & Atreyee Sen eds., forthcoming 2007); *see also* CONG. RESEARCH SERV., CIVILIAN PATROLS ALONG THE BORDER: LEGAL AND POLICY ISSUES, at CRS6–12 (2006) (describing the Minuteman Project and other similar groups).

14. *See* Jean O. Pasco, *Campbell, 4 Others Face New Vote*, L.A. TIMES (Orange County ed.), Oct. 5, 2005, at B1.

15. *See* Peter Nicholas & Duke Helfand, *Threats Issued to Latino Leaders*, L.A. TIMES, Apr. 25, 2006, at B3.

16. *See, e.g.*, Lauren Gilbert, *Fields of Hope, Fields of Despair: Legisprudential and Historical Perspectives on the AgJobs Bill of 2003*, 42 HARV. J. LEGIS. 417 (2005) (analyzing failed efforts to pass bill that would have allowed for, among other things, opportunity for undocumented immigrants to regularize their immigration status).

17. *See* GLORIA ANZALDÚA, BORDERLANDS: LA FRONTERA: THE NEW MESTIZA (1987); RENATO ROSALDO, CULTURE & TRUTH: THE REMAKING OF SOCIAL ANALYSIS (1989); BORDER THEORY: THE LIMITS OF CULTURAL POLITICS (Scott Michaelsen & David E. Johnson eds., 1997).

18. Richard Thompson Ford, *Beyond Borders: A Partial Response to Richard Briffault*, 48 STAN. L. REV. 1173, 1194 (1996).

19. *See* Richard Briffault, *The Local Government Boundary Problem in Metropolitan Areas*, 48 STAN. L. REV. 1115 (1996); Richard Thompson Ford, *The Boundaries of Race: Political Geography in Legal Analysis*, 107 HARV. L. REV. 1843 (1994).

20. *See generally* JOSEPH STIGLITZ, GLOBALIZATION AND ITS DISCONTENTS (2002).

21. *See* Peter J. Spiro, *Dual Nationality and the Meaning of Citizenship*, 46 EMORY L.J. 1411 (1997). For expression of grave concern with the loyalties of dual citizens, see STANLEY A. RENSHON, THE 50 PERCENT AMERICAN: IMMIGRATION AND NATIONAL IDENTITY IN AN AGE OF TERROR (2005).

22. *See* Maria Puente, *These People Truly Span the Globe*, USA TODAY, June 30, 2005, at 7D.

23. *See generally* Kal Raustiala, *The Geography of Justice*, 73 FORDHAM L. REV. 2501 (2005). The fact that the enemy combatants are held outside the territory of the United States is the rationale for the limited rights given those persons were detained in Guantánamo Bay, Cuba. *See generally* Diane Marie Amann, *Guantánamo*, 42 COLUM. J. TRANSNAT'L L. 263 (2004).

24. *See* Mary Beth Sheridan, *Immigration Law as Anti-Terrorism Tool*, WASH. POST, June 13, 2005, at A1.

25. *See* Linda S. Bosniak, *Opposing Prop. 187: Undocumented Immigrants and the National Imagination*, 28 CONN. L. REV. 555, 571 (1996).

26. *See generally* Kevin R. Johnson, *Los Olvidados: Images of the Immigrant, Political Power of Noncitizens, and Immigration Law and Enforcement*, 1993 B.Y.U. L. REV. 1139.

27. ARISTIDE R. ZOLBERG, A NATION BY DESIGN: IMMIGRATION POLICY IN THE FASHIONING OF AMERICA 15 (2006).

28. Louis Henkin, *The Constitution as Compact and as Conscience: Individ-*

ual Rights Abroad and at Our Gates, 27 Wm. & Mary L. Rev. 11, 33 (1985) (emphasis added); *see also* R. George Wright, *Federal Immigration Law and the Case for Open Entry,* 27 Loy. L.A. L. Rev. 1265, 1266 n.11 (1994) (citing authorities that suggest that open borders are not a viable policy option).

29. Owen Fiss, *The Immigrant as Pariah, in* A Community of Equals: The Constitutional Protection of New Americans 3, 16 (Joshua Cohen & Joel Rogers eds., 1999) (emphasis added); *see* Michael Scaperlanda, *Polishing the Tarnished Golden Door,* 1993 Wis. L. Rev. 965, 1028 (arguing for more open membership criteria for immigrants while denying "advocat[ing] a constitutionally-based open border/open membership philosophy").

30. Frederick G. Whelan, *Citizenship and Freedom of Movement: An Open Admission Policy?, in* Open Borders? Closed Societies? The Ethical and Political Issues 3, 14 (Mark Gibney ed., 1988).

31. Frank H. Wu, *The Limits of Borders: A Moderate Proposal for Immigration Reform,* 7 Stan. L. & Pol'y Rev. 35, 39 (1996) (emphasis added) (footnote omitted).

32. *See* Kitty Calavita, *Immigration, Law, and Marginalization in a Global Economy: Notes from Spain,* 32 Law & Soc'y Rev. 529, 542–48 (1998).

33. *See* Gerald L. Neuman, *The Lost Century of American Immigration Law (1776–1875),* 93 Colum. L. Rev. 1833 (1993) (analyzing efforts of states to restrict immigration before first comprehensive federal immigration legislation).

34. *See* Laura Fernandez Feitl, *Caring for the Elderly Undocumented Workers in the United States: Discretionary Reality or Undeniable Duty?,* 13 Elder L.J. 227 (2005).

35. *See, e.g.,* Samuel P. Huntington, Who Are We? The Challenges to America's National Identity (2004); Peter Brimelow, Alien Nation: Common Sense About America's Immigration Disaster (1996); Arthur Schlesinger, The Disuniting of America: Reflections on a Multicultural Society (1992).

36. *See* Bill Ong Hing, *Beyond the Rhetoric of Assimilation and Cultural Pluralism: Addressing the Tension of Separatism and Conflict in an Immigration-Driven Society,* 81 Cal. L. Rev. 863 (1993).

37. *See* Kevin R. Johnson, *Race, The Immigration Laws, and Domestic Race Relations: A "Magic Mirror" Into the Heart of Darkness,* 73 Ind. L.J. 1111, 1148–58 (1998).

38. *See* Kevin R. Johnson, *The End of "Civil Rights" as We Know It? Immigration and Civil Rights in the New Millennium,* 49 UCLA L. Rev. 1481, 1505–08 (2002).

39. *See* Bill Ong Hing, *Vigilante Racism: The De-Americanization of Immigrant America,* 7 Mich. J. Race & L. 441 (2002).

40. *See* United States v. Brignoni-Ponce, 422 U.S. 873, 886–87 (1975).

41. *See* James F. Smith, *United States Immigration Law as We Know It:* El

Clandestino, *the American Gulag, Rounding Up the Usual Suspects,* 38 U.C. DAVIS L. REV. 747 (2005); Charles D. Weisselberg, *The Detention and Treatment of Aliens Three Years After September 11: A New World Views?,* 38 U.C. DAVIS L. REV. 815 (2005). *See generally* MARK DOW, AMERICAN GULAG: INSIDE U.S. IMMIGRATION PRISONS (2004); MICHAEL WELCH, DETAINED: IMMIGRATION LAWS AND THE EXPANDING I.N.S. JAIL COMPLEX (2002).

42. *See generally* DAVID G. GUTIÉRREZ, WALLS AND MIRRORS: MEXICAN AMERICANS, MEXICAN IMMIGRANTS, AND THE POLITICS OF ETHNICITY (1995).

43. *See* BILL ONG HING, MAKING AND REMAKING ASIAN AMERICA THROUGH IMMIGRATION POLICY 1850–1990, at 74 (1993).

44. For a thorough critique of U.S. immigration law and policy, combined with reform proposals, see BILL ONG HING, DEPORTING OUR SOULS: VALUES, MORALITY, AND IMMIGRATION POLICY (2006).

45. *See, e.g.,* Fiallo v. Bell, 430 U.S. 787, 792 (1977) (refusing to disturb gender preferences in immigration admission criteria and noting that "[t]his Court has repeatedly held that over no conceivable subject is the legislative power of Congress more complete than it is over the admission of immigrants") (citations and internal quotation marks omitted); Mathews v. Diaz, 426 U.S. 67, 80–81 (1976) (refusing to invalidate Congress's decision to deny federal benefits to noncitizens). For recent invocation of the doctrine by the Supreme Court in upholding the detention of criminal aliens pending removal, see Demore v. Kim, 538 U.S. 510, 521–22 (2003).

46. *Compare* Cornelia T.L. Pillard & T. Alexander Aleinikoff, *Skeptical Scrutiny of Plenary Power: Judicial and Executive Branch Decision Making in Miller v. Albright,* 1998 SUP. CT. REV. 1 (contending that the latest Supreme Court decision requires revisiting the plenary power doctrine), *and* Peter J. Spiro, *Explaining the End of Plenary Power,* 16 GEO. IMMIGR. L.J. 339 (2002) (pointing to signs of the plenary power doctrine's demise), *and* Gabriel J. Chin, *Is There a Plenary Power Doctrine? A Tentative Apology and Prediction for Our Strange but Unexceptional Constitutional Immigration Law,* 14 GEO. IMMIGR. L.J. 257 (2000) (questioning the current existence of the plenary power doctrine), *with* Kevin R. Johnson, *Race and Immigration Law and Enforcement: A Response to Is There a Plenary Power Doctrine?,* 14 GEO. IMMIGR. L.J. 289 (2000) (contending that the claim that the plenary power doctrine was dead was premature).

As is the case in immigration law, the U.S. Supreme Court has afforded the federal government "plenary power" over the rights of native people and U.S. territories, such as Puerto Rico. *See generally* T. ALEXANDER ALEINIKOFF, SEMBLANCES OF SOVEREIGNTY: THE CONSTITUTION, THE STATE AND AMERICAN CITIZENSHIP (2002); Sarah H. Cleveland, *Powers Inherent in Sovereignty: Indians, Aliens, Territories, and the Nineteenth Century Origins of Plenary Power Over Foreign Affairs,* 81 TEX. L. REV. 1 (2002) (same); Natsu Taylor Saito, *Asserting*

Plenary Power Over the "Other": Indians, Immigrants, Colonial Subjects, and Why U.S. Jurisprudence Needs to Incorporate International Law, 20 YALE L. & POL'Y REV. 427 (2002) (same).

47. *See* Chae Chin Ping v. United States (*The Chinese Exclusion Case*), 130 U.S. 581, 609 (1889).

48. *See* George A. Martínez, *Immigration and the "State of Nature"* (Mar. 2002) (unpublished manuscript, on file with author).

49. Harisiades v. Shaughnessy, 342 U.S. 580, 597 (1952) (Frankfurter, J., concurring).

50. *See, e.g.,* GERALD L. NEUMAN, STRANGERS TO THE CONSTITUTION: IMMI-GRANTS, BORDERS, AND FUNDAMENTAL LAW (1996); VICTOR ROMERO, ALIEN-ATED: IMMIGRANT RIGHTS, THE CONSTITUTION, AND EQUALITY IN AMERICA (2005); Stephen H. Legomsky, *Immigration Law and the Principle of Plenary Congressional Power*, 1984 SUP. CT. REV. 255; Michael Scaperlanda, *Partial Membership: Aliens and the Constitutional Community*, 81 IOWA L. REV. 707 (1996).

51. *See* Spiro, *Dual Nationality*, at 1475 & 1475 n.277 ("[O]ne would ex-pect liberals to support the principle of open borders . . . and yet they shy from the proposition.") (footnote citing, inter alia, JOHN RAWLS, POLITICAL LIBERAL-ISM 12 (1993)).

52. *See* Kevin R. Johnson, *Race Matters: Immigration Law and Policy Schol-arship, Law in the Ivory Tower, and the Legal Indifference of the Race Critique*, 2000 U. ILL. L. REV. 525, 528–35.

53. *See* NIGEL HARRIS, THINKING THE UNTHINKABLE: THE IMMIGRATION MYTH EXPOSED (2002); TERESA HAYTER, OPEN BORDERS: THE CASE AGAINST IMMIGRATION CONTROLS (2000); Gene Epstein, *New Melting Pot: How Immi-gration Helps Keep the U.S. Competitive and Financially Strong*, BARRON'S, Sept. 2, 2002, at 17; *Let the Huddled Masses In*, ECONOMIST, Mar. 31, 2001, at 15.

54. *See generally* KEVIN R. JOHNSON, THE "HUDDLED MASSES" MYTH: IM-MIGRATION AND CIVIL RIGHTS (2004).

55. STEPHEN H. LEGOMSKY, IMMIGRATION AND REFUGEE LAW AND POLICY 25 (4th ed. 2005).

56. *See generally* HENRY L. FEINGOLD, THE POLITICS OF RESCUE (1970); SAUL S. FRIEDMAN, NO HAVEN FOR THE OPPRESSED (1973); GORDON THOMAS & MAX MORGAN WITTS, VOYAGE OF THE DAMNED (1974).

57. *See* Korematsu v. United States, 323 U.S. 214 (1944). *See generally* ERIC K. YAMAMOTO ET AL., RACE, RIGHTS, AND REPARATION: LAW AND THE JAPANESE AMERICAN INTERNMENT (2001); Symposium, *The Long Shadow of* Korematsu, 40 B.C. L. REV. 1 (1998); Symposium, *Judgments Judged and Wrongs Remem-bered: Examining the Japanese American Civil Liberties Cases on Their Sixtieth Anniversary*, 68 LAW & CONTEMP. PROBS. 1 (2005).

58. *See* Hamdi v. United States, 542 U.S. 507 (2004) (holding that U.S. citizen labeled an "enemy combatant," detained indefinitely without charges and denied access to counsel, had the right to challenge his designation in a hearing with notice and an opportunity to be heard); Rumsfeld v. Padilla, 542 U.S. 426 (2004) (dismissing claims because habeas corpus petition of U.S. citizen held as "enemy combatant" was filed in district court lacking jurisdiction).

59. *See* Uniting and Strengthening America by Providing Appropriate Tools Required to Intercept and Obstruct Terrorism Act (USA PATRIOT Act), Pub. L. No. 107–56, 115 Stat. 272 (2001).

60. *See* Kevin R. Johnson, *Free Trade and Closed Borders: NAFTA and Mexican Immigration to the United States*, 27 U.C. DAVIS L. REV. 937 (1994); John A. Scanlan, *A View from the United States: Social, Economic, and Legal Change, the Persistence of the State, and Immigration Policy in the Coming Century*, 2 IND. J. GLOBAL LEG. STUD. 79, 123–25 (1994).

61. *See, e.g.*, GEORGE J. BORJAS, HEAVEN'S DOOR: IMMIGRATION POLICY AND THE AMERICAN ECONOMY (1999). For in-depth analysis of this issue, see Chapter 4.

62. *See* Lawrence H. Fuchs, *The Reactions of Black Americans to Immigration, in* IMMIGRATION RECONSIDERED: HISTORY, SOCIOLOGY, AND POLITICS 293 (Virginia Yans-McLaughlin ed., 1990); *see also* Jack Miles, *Blacks vs. Browns: The Struggle for the Bottom Rung*, ATL. MONTHLY, Oct. 2992, at 41 (contending that employers prefer hiring Latina/o immigrants to hiring African Americans).

63. *See* HECTOR DELGADO, NEW IMMIGRANTS, OLD UNIONS: ORGANIZING UNDOCUMENTED WORKERS IN LOS ANGELES (1994); Christopher David Ruiz Cameron, *The Labyrinth of Solidarity: Why the Future of the American Labor Movement Depends on Latino Workers*, 53 U. MIAMI L. REV. 1089 (1999).

64. *See, e.g.*, GARRET HARDIN, THE IMMIGRATION DILEMMA: AVOIDING THE TRAGEDY OF THE COMMONS (1995); LEON F. BOUVIER & LINDSAY GRANT, HOW MANY IMMIGRANTS? POPULATION, IMMIGRATION AND THE ENVIRONMENT (1994). For a response to the finite-resources argument employed by environmental restrictionists, see Peter L. Reich, *Environmental Metaphor in the Alien Benefits Debate*, 42 UCLA L. REV. 1577 (1995). Chapter 4 critically examines the environmental arguments in favor of greater immigration restrictions.

65. *See* Peter H. Schuck, *The Transformation of Immigration Law*, 84 CO-LUM. L. REV. 1, 89–90 (1984); Wright, *Federal Immigration Law*, at 1273–81.

66. ALAN DOWTY, CLOSED BORDERS: THE CONTEMPORARY ASSAULT ON FREEDOM OF MOVEMENT 223 (1987); *see* MICHAEL WALZER, SPHERES OF JUS-TICE 38 (1983); Joseph H. Carens, *Aliens and Citizens: The Case for Open Borders*, 49 REV. POL. 251, 270 (1987). Consider, for example, the deep reluctance of a refugee family to leave war-torn Ethiopia, as described in MAWI ASGEDOM, OF BEETLES AND ANGELS: A TRUE STORY OF THE AMERICAN DREAM (2001).

As Rubén G. Rumbaut stated,

It never ceases to surprise me that, in a world of 6.5 billion people, 98 percent are "stayers," living in the country of their birth; that the remaining two percent, international migrants of a bewildering variety of origins, migration motives, and modes of adaptation to their new environments, are at heart ambitious, determined, and intrepid souls, which is what makes migration the "selective" process that it is; and that, all things considered, so little focused attention is paid to either of those two facts.

Migration Policy Institute, Migration Information Source, http://www.migration information.org/USfocus/print.cfm?ID=361, last visited on Nov. 27, 2006.

67. *See* Roger Nett, *The Civil Right We Are Not Ready For: The Right of Free Movement of People on the Face of the Earth,* 81 ETHICS 212, 219–20 (1971).

68. *See* JULIAN L. SIMON, THE ECONOMIC CONSEQUENCES OF IMMIGRATION 373–74 (2d ed. 1999).

69. WORLD BANK EU8 QUARTERLY ECONOMIC REPORT, LABOR MIGRATION FROM THE EU MEMBER STATES (Sept. 2006).

70. *Id.* at 1.

71. *See* HUNTINGTON, WHO ARE WE?, at 221–56.

72. However, the Supreme Court cautioned the nation to proceed "with all deliberate speed" in desegregating the public schools to avoid social unrest, Brown v. Board of Education, 349 U.S. 294, 301 (1955), a ruling that has been roundly criticized.

73. NATHAN GLAZER, WE ARE ALL MULTICULTURALISTS NOW (1997).

74. *See The Aftermath of September 11: A Chronology,* 79 INTERPRETER RELEASES 1359 app. I (2002) (providing a chronology of the Bush administration's immediate legal responses to the events of September 11, 2001).

75. *See* Margaret Graham Tebo, *The Closing Door: U.S. Policies Leave Immigrants Separate and Unequal,* ABA J., Sept. 2002, at 43; *see also* Michele R. Pistone, A *Times Sensitive Response to Professor Aleinikoff's Detaining Plenary Power,* 16 GEO. IMMIGR. L.J. 391, 399–400 (2002) (observing that, after September 11, the nation moved from contemplating more open borders to considering policy options and controls that would enhance security).

76. For a sampling of criticism of the various measures, see TRAM NGUYEN, WE ARE ALL SUSPECTS NOW: UNTOLD STORIES FROM IMMIGRANT COMMUNITIES AFTER 9/11 (2005); Susan M. Akram & Kevin R. Johnson, *Race, Civil Rights, and Immigration Law After September 11, 2001: The Targeting of Arabs and Muslims,* 58 N.Y.U. ANN. SURVEY AM. L. 295 (2002); Raquel Aldana-Pindell, *The 9/11 "National Security" Cases: Three Principles Guiding Judges' Decision-Making,* 81 OR. L. REV. 985 (2002); Sameer M. Ashar, *Immigration Enforcement and Subordination: The Consequences of Racial Profiling After September 11,* 34 CONN. L. REV. 1185 (2002); David Cole, *Enemy Aliens,* 54

STAN. L. REV. 953 (2002); Bill Ong Hing, *Vigilante Racism: The De-Americanization of Immigrant America*, 7 Mich. J. Race & L. 441 (2002); Thomas W. Joo, *Presumed Disloyal: Executive Power, Judicial Deference, and the Construction of Race Before and After September 11*, 34 COLUM. HUM. RTS. L. REV. 1 (2002); Victor C. Romero, *Decoupling "Terrorist" From "Immigrant": An Enhanced Role for the Federal Courts Post 9/11*, 7 J. GENDER, RACE, & JUST. 201 (2003); Leti Volpp, *The Citizen and the Terrorist*, 49 UCLA L. REV. 1575 (2002). Many reports have documented the civil and human rights abuses in the Bush administration's counterterrorism measures. *See, e.g.*, MIGRATION POLICY INSTITUTE, AMERICA'S CHALLENGE: DOMESTIC SECURITY, CIVIL LIBERTIES, AND NATIONAL UNITY AFTER SEPTEMBER 11 (2003); U.S. DEP'T OF JUSTICE, SUPPLEMENTAL REPORT ON SEPTEMBER 11 DETAINEES: A REVIEW OF THE TREATMENT OF ALIENS HELD ON IMMIGRATION CHARGES IN CONNECTION WITH THE INVESTIGATION OF THE SEPTEMBER 11 ATTACKS (2003); U.S. OFFICE OF THE INSPECTOR GENERAL, THE SEPTEMBER 11 DETAINEES: A REVIEW OF THE TREATMENT OF ALIENS HELD ON IMMIGRATION CHARGES IN CONNECTION WITH THE INVESTIGATION OF THE SEPTEMBER 11 ATTACKS (2003); U.S. OFFICE OF THE INSPECTOR GENERAL, REPORT TO CONGRESS ON IMPLEMENTATION OF SECTION 1001 OF THE USA PATRIOT ACT (2003).

For a collection of incendiary arguments on the need to close the borders as part of the "war on terror," see MICHELLE MALKIN, INVASION: HOW AMERICA STILL WELCOMES TERRORISTS, CRIMINALS, AND OTHER FOREIGN MENACES TO OUR SHORES (2002); *see also* Jan C. Ting, *Unobjectionable but Insufficient—Federal Initiatives in Response to the September 11 Terrorist Attacks*, 34 CONN. L. REV. 1145 (2002) (questioning, in a more balanced manner, whether the United States had done enough in the "war on terrorism").

77. *See* Jonathan Peterson, *Noncitizens Must Report If They Move*, L.A. TIMES, July 23, 2002, at pt. 1, at 1.

78. *See* United States v. Cortez-Rocha, 394 F.3d 1115, 1123–24 (9th Cir. 2005).

79. *See* Kevin R. Johnson, *September 11 and Mexican Immigrants: Collateral Damage Comes Home*, 52 DEPAUL L. REV. 849, 852–65 (2003).

80. Peter Beinart, *The Wrong Place to Stop Terrorists*, WASH. POST, May 4, 2006, at A25 (discussing study making this finding); *see* ROBERT S. LEIKEN, THE QUANTITATIVE ANALYSIS OF TERRORISM AND IMMIGRATION: AN INITIAL EXPLORATION 2 (2006) ("Despite media alarms about terrorists concealed in the illegal traffic crossing the Mexican border, not a single [person charged or convicted of terrorist acts, or killed in such acts] entered from Mexico.") (footnote omitted).

81. *See* Barbara Hines, *So Near Yet So Far Away: The Effect of September 11th on Mexican Immigrants in the United States*, 8 TEX. HISP. J.L. & POL'Y 37 (2002); Johnson, *September 11 and Mexican Immigrants*.

82. To make matters worse, the Immigration and Naturalization Service

(INS), which until the spring of 2003 had primary responsibility for enforcing the immigration laws, has long been criticized as inefficient, if not downright incompetent. Criticism of the incompetence of the INS hit its zenith when the agency mailed visa renewals to two suspected September 11 hijackers months after their deaths. This misstep contributed to the push to reorganize the immigration bureaucracy and to the creation of the Department of Homeland Security. *See Sensenbrenner Leading the Charge for Immediate INS Overhaul: Belated Visa Approval Notification for Sept. 11 Terrorists Has Congress Clamoring for Control of the Immigration Agency,* 60 CONG. Q. WEEKLY, Mar. 16, 2002, at 705.

83. *See generally* JOHN HIGHAM, STRANGERS IN THE LAND: PATTERNS OF AMERICAN NATIVISM 1860–1925 (3d ed. 1994); JOHNSON, THE "HUDDLED MASSES" MYTH.

84. Wright, *Federal Immigration Law,* at 1298 (footnotes omitted).

85. *See, e.g.,* Gerald L. Neuman, *Justifying U.S. Naturalization Policies,* 35 VA. J. INT'L L. 237 (1994); Peter J. Spiro, *Questioning Barriers to Naturalization,* 31 GEO. IMMIGR. L.J. 479 (1999); *see also* Stephen H. Legomsky, *Why Citizenship?,* 35 VA. J. INT'L L. 279 (1994) (raising the question whether citizenship remains a necessary legal concept).

86. *See* RON HAYDUK, DEMOCRACY FOR ALL: RESTORING IMMIGRANT VOTING RIGHTS IN THE UNITED STATES (2006); Jamin B. Raskin, *Legal Aliens, Local Citizens: The Historical, Constitutional, and Theoretical Meanings of Alien Suffrage,* 141 U. PA. L. REV. 1391 (1993); Gerald M. Rosberg, *Aliens and Equal Protection: Why Not the Right to Vote?,* 75 MICH. L. REV. 1092 (1977); Tara Kini, Comment, *Sharing the Vote: Noncitizen Voting Rights in Local School Board Elections,* 93 CAL. L. REV. 271 (2005); *see also* JOAQUIN AVILA, POLITICAL APARTHEID IN CALIFORNIA: CONSEQUENCES OF EXCLUDING A GROWING NONCITIZEN POPULATION (UCLA Chicano Studies Research Center, Dec. 2003) (analyzing growing immigrant population in California disenfranchised from the political process).

NOTES TO CHAPTER 2

1. *See* MAE M. NGAI, IMPOSSIBLE SUBJECTS: ILLEGAL ALIENS AND THE MAKING OF MODERN AMERICA (2004). For analysis of the negative connotations of the term "alien," which is the centerpiece of the comprehensive federal immigration law, the Immigration and Nationality Act, see Kevin R. Johnson, *"Aliens" and the U.S. Immigration Laws: The Social and Legal Construction of Nonpersons,* 28 U. MIAMI INTER-AM. L. REV. 263 (1996–97).

2. For careful analysis of the positions of various interest groups in immigration and immigration reform, see CAROLYN WONG, LOBBYING FOR INCLUSION: RIGHTS POLITICS AND THE MAKING OF IMMIGRATION POLICY (2006).

3. Administration's Proposals on Immigration and Refugee Policy: Joint Hearing Before the Subcomm. on Immigration, Refugees, and International Law of the House Comm. on the Judiciary and Subcomm. on Immigration and Refugee Policy of the Senate Comm. on the Judiciary, 97th Cong., 1st Sess. 6 (1981).

4. *See* Illegal Immigration Reform and Immigrant Responsibility Act, Pub. L. No. 104–208, 110 Stat. 3009 (1996); Antiterrorism and Effective Death Penalty Act, Pub. L. No. 104–132, 110 Stat. 1214 (1996); Personal Responsibility and Work Opportunity Act, Pub. L. No. 104–193, 110 Stat. 2105 (1996).

5. For chilling accounts of the use and abuse of detention of noncitizens, see MARK DOW, AMERICAN GULAG (2004), and MICHAEL WELCH, DETAINED: IMMIGRATION LAWS AND THE EXPANDING I.N.S. JAIL COMPLEX (2002). *See also* ROBERT S. KAHN, OTHER PEOPLE'S BLOOD: U.S. IMMIGRATION PRISONS IN THE REAGAN DECADE (1996) (documenting mass detention of Central American asylum seekers in the 1980s).

6. *See, e.g.,* Daniel Kanstroom, *Deportation, Social Control, and Punishment: Some Thoughts About Why Hard Laws Make Bad Cases,* 113 HARV. L. REV. 1889 (2000); Teresa A. Miller, *Citizenship & Severity: Recent Immigration Reform and the New Penology,* 17 GEO. IMMIGR. L.J. 611 (2003); Nancy Morawetz, *Understanding the Impact of the 1996 Deportation Laws and the Limited Scope of Proposed Reforms,* 113 HARV. L. REV. 1936 (2000).

7. Uniting and Strengthening America by Providing Appropriate Tools Required to Intercept and Obstruct Terrorism (USA PATRIOT Act) Act, Pub. L. No. 107–56, 115 Stat. 272 (2001). In 2006, Congress extended, as modified, the Act. *See* Pub. L. No. 109–177, 120 Stat. 192 (2006).

8. *See* Bill Ong Hing, *Vigilante Racism: The De-Americanization of Immigrant America,* 7 MICH. J. RACE & L. 441 (2002); Thomas W. Joo, *Presumed Disloyal: Executive Power, Judicial Deference, and the Construction of Race Before and After September 11,* 34 COLUM. HUM. RTS. L. REV. 1 (2002).

9. *See, e.g.,* Steven W. Bender, *Sight, Sound, and Stereotype: The War on Terrorism and Its Consequences for Latinas/os,* 81 OR. L. REV. 1153 (2002); Kevin R. Johnson, *September 11 and Mexican Immigrants: Collateral Damage Comes Home,* 52 DEPAUL L. REV. 849 (2003); *see also* Michael A. Olivas, *The War on Terrorism Touches the Ivory Tower—Colleges and Universities After September 11: An Introduction,* 30 J. COLLEGE & UNIVERSITY L. 233 (2004) (analyzing impacts of new reporting requirements on foreign students and scholars).

10. *See* Shaughnessy v. United States *ex rel.* Mezei, 345 U.S. 206 (1953) (finding the U.S. government could indefinitely detain a long-term lawful permanent resident based on secret evidence that he was a danger to the national security); *see also* United States *ex rel.* Knauff v. Shaughnessy, 338 U.S. 537 (1950) (declining to disturb U.S. government's refusal to allow alien to come to United States to be with U.S. citizen spouse based on secret evidence that she was a danger to national security). *See generally* Charles D. Weisselberg, *The Exclusion*

and Detention of Aliens: Lessons From the Lives of Ellen Knauff and Ignatz Mezei, 143 U. PA. L. REV. 933 (1995).

11. *See generally* IAN HANEY LOPEZ, WHITE BY LAW: THE LEGAL CONSTRUCTION OF RACE (1996) (analyzing the requirement that an immigrant be white to naturalize).

12. Pub. L. No. 89–236, 79 Stat. 911 (1965).

13. *See* Gabriel J. Chin, *The Civil Rights Revolution Comes to Immigration Law: A New Look at the Immigration and Nationality Act of 1965,* 75 N.C. L. REV. 273 (1996).

14. *See, e.g.,* VERNON M. BRIGGS, JR., MASS IMMIGRATION AND THE NATIONAL INTEREST (1992). Chapter 4 discusses in detail the concern with the impact of immigration on U.S. workers.

15. *See* Gerald L. Neuman, *The Lost Century of American Immigration Law (1776–1875),* 93 COLUM. L. REV. 1833 (1993) (analyzing efforts of states to restrict immigration before congressional enactment of first comprehensive federal immigration legislation).

16. *See, e.g.,* League of United Latin American Citizens v. Wilson, 908 F. Supp. 755 (C.D. Cal. 1995) (holding that state law was preempted by federal law because it effectively sought to regulate immigration).

17. *See* Dillingham Commission Report, S. Doc. No. 758, 61st Cong. (3d sess. 1911). President Theodore Roosevelt appointed the Commission, which issued a 42-volume report. For commentary on the Dillingham Commission, see MALDWYN ALLEN JONES, AMERICAN IMMIGRATION 152–57 (2d ed. 1992).

18. Chae Chin Ping v. United States (*The Chinese Exclusion Case*), 130 U.S. 581, 606 (1889). For analysis of the Chinese exclusion laws from a gender perspective, see Kerry Abrams, *Polygamy, Prostitution, and the Federalization of Immigration Law,* 105 COLUM. L. REV. 641 (2005).

19. *See* Immigration & Nationality Act (INA), Pub. L. No. 414, 66 Stat. 163 (1952) (codified as amended in 8 U.S.C. §§ 1101–1524).

20. *See* Kevin R. Johnson, *Open Borders?,* 51 UCLA L. REV. 193, 214 & n.109 (2003).

21. *See* INA § 291, 8 U.S.C. § 1361.

22. *See* INA § 214(b), 8 U.S.C. § 1184(b).

23. *See* INA § 212(a), 8 U.S.C. § 1182(a).

24. *See* KEVIN R. JOHNSON, THE "HUDDLED MASSES" MYTH: IMMIGRATION AND CIVIL RIGHTS 91–108 (2004). For statistics for fiscal year 2002 showing that the public charge exclusion was by far the substantive ground (as opposed to procedural grounds, such as an incomplete application, for example) most frequently relied upon in denial of an immigrant visa by the State Department, see DEPARTMENT OF STATE, REPORT OF THE VISA OFFICE, at Table XX (2003), available at http://travel.state.gov/visa/about/report/report_1476.html, last visited Nov. 27, 2006.

25. INA § 212(a)(4), 8 U.S.C. § 1182(a)(4).

26. *See* Michael J. Sheridan, *The New Affidavit of Support and Other 1996 Amendments to Immigration Welfare Provisions Designed to Prevent Aliens From Becoming Public Charges*, 31 CREIGHTON L. REV. 741 (1998) (analyzing 1996 amendments).

27. INA § 213A(f)(1)(E), 8 U.S.C. § 1183a(f)(1)(E).

28. *See* INA § 213A, 8 U.S.C. § 1183a.

29. *See* James A.R. Nafziger, *Review of Visa Denials by Consular Officers*, 66 WASH. L. REV. 1 (1991); *see, e.g.*, Hermina Sague v. United States, 416 F. Supp. 217 (D.P.R. 1976).

30. *See* Bill Ong Hing, *Don't Give Me Your Tired, Your Poor: Conflicted Immigrant Stories and Welfare Reform*, 33 HARV. C.R.-C.L. L. REV. 159, 166–70 (1998).

31. *See* Kevin R. Johnson, *Judicial Acquiescence to the Executive Branch's Pursuit of Foreign Policy and Domestic Agendas in Immigration Matters: The Case of the Haitian Asylum-Seekers*, 7 GEO. IMMIGR. L.J. 1 (1993); Charles J. Ogletree, Jr., *America's Schizophrenic Immigration Policy: Race, Class, and Reason*, 41 B.C. L. REV. 755 (2000).

32. *See, e.g.*, ROGER DANIELS, GUARDING THE GOLDEN DOOR: AMERICAN IMMIGRATION AND IMMIGRANTS SINCE 1882 (2004); JOHN HIGHAM, STRANGERS TO THE LAND: PATTERNS OF AMERICAN NATIVISM 1860–1925 (3d 1994); BILL ONG HING, DEFINING AMERICA THROUGH IMMIGRATION POLICY (2004); DAVID M. REIMERS, OTHER IMMIGRANTS: THE GLOBAL ORIGINS OF THE AMERICAN PEOPLE (2005); LUCY E. SALYER, LAWS HARSH AS TIGERS: CHINESE IMMIGRANTS AND THE SHAPING OF MODERN IMMIGRATION LAW (1995); RONALD TAKAKI, STRANGERS FROM A DIFFERENT SHORE: A HISTORY OF ASIAN AMERICANS (1989).

33. MADISON GRANT, THE PASSING OF THE GREAT RACE, OR THE RACIAL BASIS OF EUROPEAN HISTORY (1916); LOTHROP STODDARD, THE RISING TIDE OF COLOR AGAINST WHITE WORLD-SUPREMACY (1920).

34. *See* MATTHEW FRYE JACOBSON, WHITENESS OF A DIFFERENT COLOR: EUROPEAN IMMIGRANTS AND THE ALCHEMY OF RACE (1998) (analyzing nativism directed at southern and eastern European immigrants that led to congressional passage of national origins quota system); *see also* DAVID R. ROEDIGER, WORKING TOWARD WHITENESS: HOW AMERICAN'S IMMIGRANTS BECOME WHITE, THE STRANGE JOURNEY FROM ELLIS ISLAND TO THE SUBURBS (2005) (analyzing how European immigrants eventually became treated as white).

35. VICTOR DAVIS HANSON, MEXIFORNIA: A STATE OF BECOMING (2003).

36. PATRICK J. BUCHANAN, STATE OF EMERGENCY: THE THIRD WORLD INVASION AND CONQUEST OF AMERICA (2006).

37. PATRICK J. BUCHANAN, DEATH OF THE WEST: HOW DYING POPULATIONS AND IMMIGRANT INVASIONS IMPERIL OUR COUNTRY AND CIVILIZATION (2002).

38. Michelle Malkin, Invasion: How America Still Welcomes Terrorists, Criminals, and Other Foreign Menaces to Our Shores (2002).

39. Peter Brimelow, Alien Nation: Common Sense About America's Immigration Disaster (1995).

40. Samuel P. Huntington, Who Are We? The Challenges to America's National Identity (2004).

41. Samuel P. Huntington, The Clash of Civilizations and the Remaking of the World (1998). For critical commentary on this book, including its racial and religious implications, see "The Clash of Civilizations?" Asian Responses (Salim Rashid ed., 1997).

42. Arthur Schlesinger, The Disuniting of America: Reflections on a Multicultural Society (1992).

43. See, e.g., George J. Borjas, Heaven's Door: Immigration and the American Economy (2001); George J. Borjas, Friends or Strangers? The Impact of Immigrants on the U.S. Economy (1990).

44. Todd Gitlin, The Twilight of Common Dreams: Why America Is Wracked by Culture Wars 161–65 (1995).

45. Michael Lind, Next American Nation: The New Nationalism and the Fourth American Revolution 129–37 (1996).

46. Roy Beck, The Case Against Immigration: The Moral, Economic, Social, and Environmental Reasons for Reducing U.S. Immigration Back to Traditional Levels (1996).

47. See Bill Ong Hing, *Beyond the Rhetoric of Assimilation and Cultural Pluralism: Addressing the Tension of Separatism and Conflict in an Immigration-Driven Society,* 81 Cal. L. Rev. 863 (1993).

48. See Karen Engle, *Constructing Good Aliens and Good Citizens: Legitimizing the War on Terror(ism),* 75 U. Colo. L. Rev. 59 (2004) (analyzing the "war on terrorism" within the history of immigration law and policy); *see also* Donald Kerwin, *Counterterrorism and Immigrant Rights Two Years Later,* 80 Interpreter Releases 1401, 1401 (Oct. 13, 2003) ("Immigration policy rapidly became the most visible domestic tool in the war on terror.").

49. See Pub. L. No. 109–177, 120 Stat. 192 (2006).

50. See http://www.americanpatrol.com/, last visited on Nov. 27, 2006.

51. The federal government estimated that, in January 2005, 10.5 million undocumented persons lived in the United States. *See* U.S. Dep't of Homeland Security, Estimates of the Unauthorized Population Residing in the United States, January 2005, at 214 (2006). Other estimates, discussed in Chapter 5, were considerably higher and have increased in recent years.

52. See Huntington, Who Are We?, at 11–12. For more positive analysis of the shift in national identity spurred by immigration, see Héctor Tobar, Translation Nation: Defining a New American Identity in the Spanish-Speaking United States (2005).

53. *See, e.g.*, BILL ONG HING, MAKING AND REMAKING ASIAN AMERICA THROUGH IMMIGRATION POLICY 1850–1990 (1993); JOHNSON, THE "HUDDLED MASSES" MYTH.

54. *See* Kevin R. Johnson, *The End of "Civil Rights" as We Know It? Immigration and Civil Rights in the New Millennium,* 49 UCLA L. REV. 1481 (2002).

55. *See, e.g.*, Nick Madigan, *Police Investigate Killings of Illegal Immigrants in Arizona Desert,* N.Y. TIMES, Oct. 23, 2003, at A1.

56. *See* Hoffman Plastic Compounds, Inc. v. NLRB, 535 U.S. 137 (2002).

57. *See, e.g.*, RICHARD ALBA & VICTOR NEE, REMAKING THE AMERICAN MAINSTREAM: ASSIMILATION AND CONTEMPORARY IMMIGRATION (2003); REINVENTING THE MELTING POT: THE NEW IMMIGRANTS AND WHAT IT MEANS TO BE AMERICAN (Tamar Jacoby ed., 2004); PETER D. SALINS, ASSIMILATION, AMERICAN STYLE (1997).

58. *See, e.g.*, GRANT; STODDARD.

59. Without discussing the details, Professor Huntington endorses in principle the reform proposals outlined in a series of reports issued by the U.S. Commission on Immigration Reform in the 1990s. *See* HUNTINGTON, WHO ARE WE?, at 200, 201, 243. The Commission's final report addressed policies designed to integrate immigrants into U.S. society, including a voluntary "Americanization" program that focused on promoting education and facilitating naturalization. *See* U.S. COMM'N ON IMMIGRATION REFORM, BECOMING AN AMERICAN: IMMIGRATION AND IMMIGRANT POLICY 25–58 (1997). The Commission emphasized that "[e]thnic and religious diversity based on personal freedom is compatible with national unity." *Id.* at 25.

60. *See* Samuel R. Gross & Debra Livingston, *Racial Profiling Under Attack,* 102 COLUM. L. REV. 1413 (2002).

61. *See* HUNTINGTON, WHO ARE WE?, at 221–56.

62. Like Peter Brimelow, *see* BRIMELOW, at 75, 215, 270, Professor Huntington does not express similar fears with immigration from Asia, *see* HUNTINGTON, WHO ARE WE?, at 187–88.

63. *See* Samuel P. Huntington, *The Hispanic Challenge,* FOREIGN POLICY, Mar./Apr. 2004, at 30.

64. *See Letters,* FOREIGN POLICY, May/June 2004, at 4.

65. *See* HANSON; BRIMELOW.

66. HUNTINGTON, WHO ARE WE?, at 221.

67. For critical legal analysis of the treaty that ended that war, see THE LEGACY OF THE MEXICAN & SPANISH AMERICAN WARS: LEGAL, LITERARY, AND HISTORICAL PERSPECTIVES (Gary D. Keller & Cordelia Candelaria eds., 2000); Symposium, *Understanding the Treaty of Guadalupe Hidalgo on Its 150th Anniversary,* 5 SW. J. L. TRADE IN THE AMERICAS 1 (1998).

68. *See* HUNTINGTON, WHO ARE WE?, at 230–43.

69. *See* Alejandro Portes & Min Zhou, *The New Second Generation: Seg-*

mented Assimilation and Its Variants, 64 ANNALS 74 (1993); Rubén G. Rumbaut, *The Crucible Within: Ethnic Identity, Self-Esteem, and Segmented Assimilation Among Children of Immigrants,* 28 INT'L MIGRATION REV. 748 (1994); *see also* Marcelo M. Suarez-Orozco, *Everything You Ever Wanted to Know About Assimilation But Were Afraid to Ask,* 129 DAEDALUS 1 (2000) (offering a sophisticated view of immigrant assimilation, including observation that immigrants of color face impediments to assimilation in the United States). *See generally* ALEJANDRO PORTES & RUBÉN RUMBAUT, LEGACIES: THE STUDY OF THE IMMIGRANT SECOND GENERATION (2001) (analyzing assimilation of second-generation immigrants).

70. *See* HUNTINGTON, WHO ARE WE?, at 232, 253. *But see* LINDA CHAVEZ, OUT OF THE BARRIO: TOWARD A NEW POLITICS OF HISPANIC ASSIMILATION (1992) (analyzing Hispanic assimilation).

71. *See Hispanic Pragmatism Seen In Survey,* N.Y. TIMES, Dec. 15, 1992, at A20.

72. *See* Linda Chavez, *Tequila Sunrise: The Slow But Steady Progress of Hispanic Immigrants,* POL'Y REV., Spring 1989, at 64.

73. *See* Frank Sharry, *Why Immigrants Are Good for America,* ORLANDO SENTINEL, Sept. 22, 1991, at G1.

74. *See generally* Anupam Chander, *Diaspora Bonds,* 76 N.Y.U L. REV. 1005 (2001).

75. *See* Pablo Ibarraran & Darren Lubotsky, Mexican Immigration and Self-Selection: New Evidence From the 2000 Mexican Census (National Bureau of Economic Research, June 2005), *available at* http://www.nber.org/papers/w11456, last visited Nov. 27, 2006.

76. *See* HUNTINGTON, WHO ARE WE?, at 238–39.

77. *See* Kevin R. Johnson, *Latina/os and the Political Process: The Need for Critical Inquiry,* 81 OR. L. REV. 917, 930–31 (2002).

78. For analysis of the growing Latina/o naturalization rate, see Louis DeSipio, *The Pressures of Perpetual Promise: Latinos and Politics, 1960–2003, in* THE COLUMBIA HISTORY OF LATINOS IN THE UNITED STATES SINCE 1960, at 421, 433–37 (David Gutiérrez ed., 2004).

79. *See* HUNTINGTON, WHO ARE WE?, at 218–19.

80. *See, e.g.,* NOAH PICKUS, TRUE FAITH AND ALLEGIANCE: IMMIGRATION AND AMERICAN CIVIC NATIONALISM (2005).

81. *See, e.g.,* JULIAN L. SIMON, THE ECONOMIC CONSEQUENCES OF IMMIGRATION (2d ed. 1999); Howard F. Chang, *Liberalized Immigration as Free Trade: Economic Welfare and the Optimal Immigration Policy,* 145 U. PA. L. REV. 1147 (1997); Alan O. Sykes, *The Welfare Economics of Immigration Law: A Theoretical Survey With an Analysis of U.S. Policy, in* JUSTICE IN IMMIGRATION 158 (Warren F. Schwartz ed., 1995).

82. *See* ANDREW SUM ET AL., IMMIGRANT WORKERS AND THE GREAT AMERI-

can Job Machine: The Contributions of New Foreign Immigration to National and Regional Labor Force Growth in the 1990s, at 38, 41–42 (National Business Roundtable, 2002); American Immigration Law Foundation, Mexican Immigrant Workers and the U.S. Economy: An Increasingly Vital Role (2002).

83. *See, e.g.*, Wayne A. Cornelius, *Death at the Border: Efficacy and Unintended Consequences of U.S. Immigration Control Policy, 1993–2000*, 27 Population & Dev. Rev. 661 (2001); Karl Eschbach et al., *Death at the Border*, 33 International Migration Rev. 430 (1999); Bill Ong Hing, *The Dark Side of Operation Gatekeeper*, 7 U.C. Davis J. Int'l L. & Pol'y 121 (2001).

84. *See, e.g.*, Ken Ellingwood, Hard Line: Life and Death on the U.S.-Mexico Border (2004); Sonia Nazario, Enrique's Journey: The Story of a Boy's Dangerous Odyssey to Reunite With His Mother (2006); Jorge Ramos, Dying to Cross: The Worst Immigrant Tragedy in American History (2005); Luis Alberto Urrea, The Devil's Highway: A True Story (2004).

85. Huntington, Who Are We?, at 196.

86. *See id.* at 199–204.

87. *See* Kevin R. Johnson, *The New Nativism: Something Old, Something New, Something Borrowed, Something Blue, in* Immigrants Out! The New Nativism and the Anti-Immigrant Impulse in the United States 165 (Juan F. Perea ed., 1997).

88. Huntington, Who Are We?, at 59–80.

89. *Id.* at 66–69. Professor Huntington credits the "American Creed" moniker to Gunnar Myrdal, The American Dilemma (1944).

90. *See* Huntington, Who Are We?, at 81–106. Peter Brimelow also has forcefully made the cultural argument for immigration restrictions, *see* Brimelow, at 178–90. For sustained criticism of Brimelow's analysis, see Peter H. Schuck, *Alien Rumination*, 105 Yale L.J. 1963, 1987–95 (1996) (book review).

91. Huntington, Who Are We?, at 129.

92. *See id.* at 204–13; *see also* Stanley A. Renshon, The 50 Percent American: Immigration and National Identity in an Age of Terror (2005). *But see* Peter J. Spiro, *Dual Nationality and the Meaning of Citizenship*, 46 Emory L.J. 1411 (1997) (offering contrary view).

93. *See* Huntington, Who Are We?, at 57–58.

94. *See id.* at 225.

95. *See generally* Linda S. Bosniak, *Exclusion and Membership: The Dual Identity of the Undocumented Worker Under United States Law*, 1988 Wis. L. Rev. 955.

96. *See* Immigration Reform and Control Act, Pub. L. No. 99–603 §§ 201–04, 100 Stat. 3359, 3394–3411 (1986) (codified at Immigration & Nationality Act § 245A, 8 U.S.C. § 1255a); *see also* Stephen H. Legomsky, Immigration

AND REFUGEE LAW AND POLICY 607–10 (4th ed. 2005) (discussing amnesty program). One immigration task force in 2006 recommended increased workplace enforcement of employer sanctions and more secure documents. *See* REPORT OF THE INDEPENDENT TASK FORCE ON IMMIGRATION AND AMERICA'S FUTURE: A NEW CHAPTER, at xviii (2006). However, employer sanctions to this point have failed to deter the employment of undocumented immigrants. *See* Michael I. Wishnie, *Prohibiting the Employment of Unauthorized Immigrants: The Experiment Fails*, 2007 U. CHI. LEG. FORUM (forthcoming 2007). There is little reason to believe that the U.S. government—and the public at large—would become truly committed to workplace enforcement of the immigration laws. In addition, given the economic incentives to violate the law, the employment of undocumented immigrants would likely continue, with ever more sophisticated fraudulent documents. More secure documents might be equated with national identification cards, which would rile civil libertarians. In any event, it is uncertain whether truly "secure" identification documents can be created given the economic incentives for markets in fraudulent documents.

97. *See, e.g.,* Harold Meyerson, *Bush's Retreat on Immigration Reform,* WASH. POST, July 21, 2004, at A19.

98. HUNTINGTON, WHO ARE WE?, at 225–26.

99. 457 U.S. 202 (1982).

100. 535 U.S. 137 (2002).

101. For analysis of the human costs, see Kevin R. Johnson, *"Melting Pot" or "Ring of Fire"? Assimilation and the Mexican-American Experience,* 85 CAL. L. REV. 1259, 1269–70 (1997).

102. HUNTINGTON, WHO ARE WE?, at 142.

103. George A. Martinez, *Latinos, Assimilation and the Law: A Philosophical Perspective,* 20 CHICANO-LATINO L. REV. 1, 6 (1999).

104. *See* Sylvia R. Lazos Vargas, *Deconstructing Homo[geneous] Americanus: The White Ethnic Immigrant Narrative and Its Exclusionary Effect,* 72 TUL. L. REV. 1493 (1998).

105. *See generally* BILL ONG HING, DEFINING AMERICA THROUGH IMMIGRATION POLICY (2004).

106. *See* HUNTINGTON, WHO ARE WE?, at 49.

107. *See* Margaret M. Russell, *Reopening the Emmett Till Case: Lessons and Challenges for Critical Race Practice,* 73 FORDHAM L. REV. 2101, 2112 (2005) ("Lynching were often public events, supported by prominent community members and advertised in newspapers. Sometimes people brought their children to observe. With the advent of cameras, many lynching 'parties' resulted in macabre photographs and postcards of people who posed with the corpses and body parts as 'souvenirs.'") (footnotes omitted). *See generally* JAMES ALLEN, WITHOUT SANCTUARY: LYNCHING PHOTOGRAPHY IN AMERICA (2000) (collecting photographs of lynchings in United States); 9 RACE, LAW, AND AMERICAN HISTORY

1700–1990: LYNCHING, RACIAL VIOLENCE, AND LAW (Paul Finkelmen ed., 1992) (analyzing history of lynching); David Garland, *Penal Excess and Surplus Meaning: Public Torture Lynchings in Twentieth-Century America,* 39 LAW & SOC'Y REV. 793 (2005) (analyzing history of public lynchings in communities across the United States).

108. 347 U.S. 483 (1954).

109. BRIMELOW, at 232.

110. *Id.* at 5.

111. HUNTINGTON, WHO ARE WE?, at 53.

112. *Id.* at 312.

113. *Id.* at 314.

114. *See e.g.,* CAROL M. SWAIN, THE NEW WHITE NATIONALISM IN AMERICA: ITS CHALLENGE TO INTEGRATION (2002).

115. Along similar lines, the state of Montana enacted a broad sedition law that allowed many German immigrants to be prosecuted for criticizing the U.S. government's role in World War I. *See* CLEMENS P. WORK, DARKEST BEFORE DAWN: SEDUCTION AND FREE SPEECH IN THE AMERICAN WEST (2005).

116. *See, e.g.,* Meyer v. Nebraska, 262 U.S. 390 (1923) (invalidating state law used to convict a teacher from teaching German to elementary school students); *see also* HIGHAM, at 196–200 (analyzing anti-German agitation in the United States before World War I).

117. *See* ALFREDO MIRANDÉ, GRINGO JUSTICE 107–45 (1987).

118. *See* GEORGE J. SANCHEZ, BECOMING MEXICAN AMERICAN 87–107 (1993); George F. Sanchez, *"Go After the Women": Americanization and the Mexican Immigrant Woman, 1915–1929, in* UNEQUAL SISTERS: A MULTICULTURAL READER IN U.S. WOMEN'S HISTORY 250 (Ellen C. DuBois & Vicki L. Ruiz eds., 1990).

119. *See generally* FRANCISCO E. BALDERRAMA & FRANCISCO RODRÍGUEZ, DECADE OF BETRAYAL: MEXICAN REPATRIATION IN THE 1930S (1995); CAMILLE GUERIN-GONZALES, MEXICAN WORKERS AND THE AMERICAN DREAM: IMMIGRATION, REPATRIATION, AND CALIFORNIA FARM LABOR, 1900–1939 (1994); ABRAHAM HOFFMAN, UNWANTED MEXICAN AMERICANS IN THE GREAT DEPRESSION: REPATRIATION PRESSURES, 1929–1939 (1974); Kevin R. Johnson, *The Forgotten "Repatriation" of Persons of Mexican Ancestry and Lessons for the "War on Terror,"* 26 PACE L. REV. 1 (2005)

120. *See generally* EDWIN J. ESCOBAR, RACE, POLICE, AND THE MAKING OF A POLITICAL IDENTITY: MEXICAN AMERICANS AND THE LOS ANGELES POLICE DEPARTMENT, 1900–1945, at 84–90 (1999); MAURICIO MAZÓN, THE ZOOT-SUIT RIOTS: THE PSYCHOLOGY OF SYMBOLIC ANNIHILATION (1984); EDUARDO OBREGÓN PAGÁN, MURDER AT THE SLEEPY LAGOON: ZOOT SUITS, RACE, & RIOT IN WARTIME L.A. (2003).

121. *See* KITTY CALAVITA, INSIDE THE STATE: THE BRACERO PROGRAM, IMMI-

GRATION AND THE I.N.S. (1992); ERNEST GALARZA, MERCHANTS OF LABOR: THE MEXICAN BRACERO STORY (1964).

122. *See generally* JUAN RAMON GARCÍA, OPERATION WETBACK: THE MASS DEPORTATION OF MEXICAN UNDOCUMENTED WORKERS IN 1954 (1980).

123. *See generally* Johnson, *The New Nativism*, at 165, 171–73 (analyzing treatment of Mexican immigrants by U.S. Supreme Court during this period).

124. *See* Kevin R. Johnson, *Public Benefits and Immigration: The Intersection of Immigration Status, Ethnicity, Gender, and Class*, 42 UCLA L. REV. 1509, 1519–41 (1995).

125. *See* Ruben J. García, *Critical Race Theory and Proposition 187: The Racial Politics of Immigration Law*, 17 CHICANO-LATINO L. REV. 138 (1995); Kevin R. Johnson, *An Essay on Immigration Politics, Popular Democracy, and California's Proposition 187: The Political Relevance and Legal Irrelevance of Race*, 70 WASH. L. REV. 629 (1995). Later, Governor Pete Wilson of California, who championed Proposition 187, fell from grace within the Republican Party for fanning nativist sympathies and disappeared from the political scene.

126. *See* Friendly House v. Napolitano, 419 F.3d 930 (9th Cir. 2005) (dismissing appeal of denial of injunction that would have barred implementation of Arizona initiative).

127. *See generally* RODOLFO ACUÑA, ANYTHING BUT MEXICAN: CHICANOS IN CONTEMPORARY LOS ANGELES (1995) (analyzing critically efforts by Mexican-Americans to embrace a Spanish as opposed to a Mexican identity in greater Los Angeles in the twentieth century).

128. *See generally* IGNACIO M. GARCIA, CHICANISMO: THE FORGING OF A MILITANT ETHOS AMONG MEXICAN AMERICANS (1997) (describing the emergence of the Chicana/o movement).

129. *See* T. Alexander Aleinikoff & Ruben G. Rumbaut, *Terms of Belonging: Are Models of Membership Self-Fulfilling Prophesies?*, 13 Geo. IMMIGR. L.J. 1, 14–21 (1998).

130. *See* Rachel F. Moran, *Bilingual Education as a Status Conflict*, 75 CAL. L. REV. 321 (1987).

131. *See* Johnson, *Race, The Immigration Laws, and Domestic Race Relations*, at 1119–47.

132. *See id.* at 46–49.

133. *See id.*

134. *See generally* JOHNSON (analyzing this history).

135. *See, e.g.*, Bill Ong Hing, *Answering Challenges of the New Immigrant-Driven Diversity: Considering Immigration Strategies*, 40 BRANDEIS L.J. 861 (2002) (outlining such strategies); Erin Kragh, *Forging a Common Culture: Integrating California's Illegal Immigrant Population*, 24 B.C. THIRD WORLD L.J. 373 (2004) (book review) (offering integration strategies as an alternative to heightened border enforcement).

136. *See* Kevin R. Johnson, *September 11 and Mexican Immigrants*, at 866–67.

137. *See* Commission for the Study of International Migration and Cooperative Economic Development, Unauthorized Migration: An Economic Development Response (1990).

138. *See* Kevin R. Johnson, *Latina/os and the Political Process*, at 930–31.

139. *See* Peter J. Spiro, *Questioning Barriers to Naturalization*, 13 Geo. Immigr. L.J. 479 (1999); Gerald L. Neuman, *Justifying U.S. Naturalization Policies*, 35 Va. J. Int'l L. 237 (1994).

140. *See* Ruben J. García, *Across the Borders: Immigrant Status and Identity in Law and LatCrit Theory*, 55 Fla. L. Rev. 511 (2003); Johnson, *Open Borders?*, at 226–30.

141. *See, e.g.,* Ruben J. García, *Ghost Workers in an Interconnected World: Going Beyond the Dichotomies of Domestic Immigration and Labor Laws*, 36 U. Mich. J.L. Ref. 737 (2003); Jennifer Gordon, *We Make the Road by Walking: Immigrant Workers, the Workplace Project, and the Struggle for Social Change*, 30 Harv. C.R.-C.L. L. Rev. 407 (1995); Lori A. Nessel, *Undocumented Immigrants in the Workplace: The Fallacy of Labor Protection and the Need for Reform*, 36 Harv. C.R.-C.L. L. Rev. 345 (2001).

142. *See* Executive Order 2005–16, Executive Order Creating New Americans Immigration Policy Council (Nov. 19, 2005).

NOTES TO CHAPTER 3

1. *See* Mary Ann Glendon, A World Made New: Eleanor Roosevelt and the Universal Declaration of Human Rights (2001); Diane Marie Amann, *Harmonic Convergence? Constitutional Criminal Procedure in an International Context*, 75 Ind. L.J. 809, 823–25 (2000).

2. *See, e.g.,* Phillip Cole, Philosophies of Exclusion: Liberal Political Theory and Immigration (2000); Matthew J. Gibney, The Ethics and Politics of Asylum: Liberal Democracy and the Response to Refugees 59–84 (2004); Stanley Hoffman, Duties Beyond Borders: On the Limits and Possibilities of Ethical International Politics (1981); David Miller, *The Ethical Significance of Nationality*, 98 Ethics 647 (1988); Timothy King, *Immigration From Developing Countries: Some Philosophical Issues*, 93 Ethics 525 (1983); Julian L. Simon, *The Case for Greatly Increased Immigration*, Pub. Int., Winter 1991, at 89; Ben J. Wattenberg & Karl Zingmeister, *The Case for More Immigration*, Commentary, Apr. 1990, at 19.

3. Peter H. Schuck, *The Transformation of Immigration Law*, 84 Colum. L. Rev. 1, 85 (1984).

4. Mark Tushnet, *Immigration Policy in Liberal Political Theory, in* Justice in Immigration 147, 155 (Warren F. Schwartz ed., 1995).

5. Mark Tushnet, *Open Borders, in* A COMMUNITY OF EQUALS: THE CONSTITUTIONAL PROTECTION OF NEW AMERICANS 69, 73 (Joshua Cohen & Joel Rogers eds., 1999). For moral and other arguments for the recongition of a right to migrate, see SATVINER SINGH JUSS, INTERNATIONAL MIGRATION AND GLOBAL JUSTICE (2006).

6. *See* Juan Castillo, *Church Leaps Into Migrant Fray; Austin Diocese Joins Catholic Bishops Push for Reforms,* AUSTIN AM. STATESMAN, Feb. 6, 2006, at A1.

7. *See* Father Brian Jordan, *My Ideal Immigration Policy, in* BLUEPRINTS FOR AN IDEAL LEGAL IMMIGRATION POLICY 43 (Richard D. Lamm & Alan Simpson eds., 2001); Terry Coonan, *There Are No Strangers Among Us: Catholic Social Teachings and U.S. Immigration Law,* 40 CATH. LAW. 105 (2000); Michael Scaperlanda, *Who Is My Neighbor? An Essay on Immigrants, Welfare Reform, and the Constitution,* 29 CONN. L. REV. 1587 (1997).

8. *See, e.g.,* ANN CRITTENDEN, SANCTUARY: A STORY OF AMERICAN CONSCIENCE AND THE LAW IN COLLISION (1988) (analyzing the sanctuary movement in the 1980s, in which religious workers and others sought to provide safe harbor to Central American refugees); IGNATIUS BAU, THIS GROUND IS HOLY: CHURCH SANCTUARY AND CENTRAL AMERICAN REFUGEES (1985) (offering a religious justification for the sanctuary movement).

9. Teresa Wanatabe, *Immigrants Gain the Pulpit,* L.A. TIMES, Mar. 1, 2006, at A1 (quoting Cardinal Mahony).

10. *See* Howard F. Chang, *Immigration Policy, Liberal Principles, and the Republican Tradition,* 85 GEO. L.J. 2105 (1997).

11. Immigration & Nationality Act § 212(a)(4), 8 U.S.C. § 1182(a)(4). *See generally* Kevin R. Johnson, *Public Benefits and Immigration: The Intersection of Immigration Status, Ethnicity, Gender, and Class,* 42 UCLA L. REV. 1509, 1519–28 (1995) (analyzing the history of the exclusion of the poor under the U.S. immigration laws). In 1996, Congress amended this ground to make it tougher for noncitizens to satisfy the income and other restrictions to avoid being classified as likely "public charges," thereby barring them from entry into the United States. *See* Michael J. Sheridan, *The New Affidavit of Support and Other 1996 Amendments to Immigration and Welfare Provisions Designed to Prevent Aliens From Becoming Public Charges,* 31 CREIGHTON L. REV. 741 (1998). These amendments complemented the denial of federal benefits to legal immigrants. *See* Personal Responsibility and Work Opportunity Reconciliation Act of 1996, Pub. L. No. 104–193, 110 Stat. 2260 (1996). For a critical analysis of the impact of welfare reform on immigrants, see Nora V. Demleitner, *The Fallacy of Social "Citizenship," or the Threat of Exclusion,* 12 GEO. IMMIGR. L.J. 35, 45–50 (1997); Berta Esperanza Hernández-Truyol & Kimberly A. Johns, *Global Rights, Local Wrongs, and Legal Fixes: An International Human Rights Critique of Immigration and Welfare "Reform,"* 71 SO. CAL. L. REV. 547

(1998); Connie Chang, Comment, *Immigrants Under the New Welfare Law: A Call for Uniformity, A Call for Justice,* 45 UCLA L. REV. 205 (1997).

12. *See* Cass R. Sunstein, *The Anticaste Principle,* 92 MICH. L. REV. 2410 (1994) (identifying the anticaste principle as a touchstone for equal protection analysis).

13. Saenz v. Roe, 526 U.S. 489, 500 (1999).

14. Pub. L. No. 101–336, 104 Stat. 327 (1990).

15. *See* Immigration & Nationality Act § 212(a)(1)(A)(I), 8 U.S.C. § 1182(a)(1)(A)(I).

16. *See* STEPHEN H. LEGOMSKY, IMMIGRATION AND REFUGEE LAW AND POLICY 442–43 (4th ed. 1995). Along these lines, the U.S. immigration laws historically have regulated sexuality by denying entry into the country of gays and lesbians. *See generally* EITHNE LUIBHÉID, ENTRY DENIED: CONTROLLING SEXUALITY AT THE BORDER (2002) (analyzing the history of U.S. immigration law's exclusion of "sexual deviants").

17. *See* Grutter v. Bollinger, 539 U.S. 306 (2003) (strictly scrutinizing race-conscious admissions program utilized by University of Michigan law school); Gratz v. Bollinger, 539 U.S. 244 (2003) (same for Michigan's undergraduate admissions); Adarand Constructors, Inc. v. Peña, 515 U.S. 200 (1995) (holding that all racial classifications, including those in a state program to increase government contracting with minority businesses, are subject to strict scrutiny); City of Richmond v. J.A. Croson Co., 488 U.S. 469 (1989) (to the same effect).

18. *See, e.g.,* Kevin R. Johnson, *Race, the Immigration Laws, and Domestic Race Relations: A "Magic Mirror" Into the Heart of Darkness,* 73 IND. L.J. 1111, 1119–47 (1998); Stephen H. Legomsky, *Immigration, Equality and Diversity,* 31 COLUM. J. TRANSNAT'L L. 319 (1993); Charles J. Ogletree, Jr., *America's Schizophrenic Immigration Policy: Race, Class, and Reason,* 41 B.C. L. REV. 755 (2000); Jan C. Ting, *"Other Than a Chinaman": How U.S. Immigration Law Resulted From and Still Reflects a Policy of Excluding and Restricting Asian Immigration,* 4 TEMP. POL. & CIV. RTS. L. REV. 301 (1995).

19. *See* Schuck, *The Transformation of Immigration Law,* at 85–90.

20. *See* Diane Marie Amann, *The International Criminal Court and the Sovereign State, in* GLOBAL GOVERNANCE AND INTERNATIONAL LEGAL THEORY 185 (Ige F. Dekker & Wouter G. Werner eds., 2004) (analyzing the social construction of national sovereignty).

21. Kitty Calavita, *U.S. Immigration Policy: Contradictions and Projections for the Future,* 2 IND. J. GLOBAL. LEG. STUDS. 143, 148–49 (1994) (emphasis added). *See generally* Kevin R. Johnson, *Los Olvidados: Images of the Immigrant, Political Power of Noncitizens, and Immigration Law and Enforcement,* 1993 BYU L. REV. 1139 (analyzing the weakness of immigrants in the political process).

22. *See* Satvinder S. Juss, *Free Movement and the World Order,* 16 INT'L J. REFUGEE L. 289 (2004).

23. *See* Roger Nett, *The Civil Right We Are Not Ready For: The Right of Free Movement of People on the Face of the Earth,* 81 ETHICS 212 (1971).

24. *See* Jacqueline Bhabha, *Reforming Immigration Policy,* BOSTON REVIEW, July 2005, available at http://www.bostonreview.net/BR30.3/bhabha.html; last visited Nov. 27, 2006.

25. *See* Seyla Benhabib, *The Law of Peoples, Distributive Justice, and Migrations,* 72 FORDHAM L. REV. 1761 (2004); Joseph H. Carens, *What We Owe People Who Stay,* BOSTON REVIEW, July 2005, available at http://www.boston review.net/BR30.3/carens.html; last visited Nov. 27, 2006.

26. *See* U.S. CONST., FOURTEENTH AMENDMENT ("All persons born or naturalized in the United States, and subject to the jurisdiction thereof, are citizens of the United States and the State wherein they reside."); Christopher L. Eisgruber, *Birthright Citizenship and the Constitution,* 72 N.Y.U. L. REV. 54 (1997). For a challenge to birthright citizenship, see PETER H. SCHUCK & ROGERS M. SMITH, CITIZENSHIP WITHOUT CONSENT: ILLEGAL ALIENS IN THE AMERICAN POLITY (1985).

27. *See* Joseph H. Carens, *Aliens and Citizens: The Case for Open Borders,* 49 REV. POL. 251 (1987).

28. *Id.* at 251 (emphasis in original).

29. *Id.* at 259. For this proposition, Carens relies on JOHN RAWLS, A THEORY OF JUSTICE 212–13 (1971); *see also* BRUCE A. ACKERMAN, SOCIAL JUSTICE IN THE LIBERAL STATE 95 (1980). ("The *only* reason for restricting immigration is to protect the ongoing process of liberal conversation itself.") (emphasis in original).

30. Carens, at 259 (emphasis added).

31. *See id.* at 264.

32. *See, e.g.,* United States v. Playboy Entertainment Group, Inc., 529 U.S. 803, 813–14 (2000); Sable Communications v. Federal Communications Comm'n, 492 U.S. 115, 126–27 (1989).

33. *See* MICHAEL WALZER, SPHERES OF JUSTICE 35–42, 61–63 (1983); *see also* WILL KYMLICKA, MULTICULTURAL CITIZENSHIP: A LIBERAL THEORY OF MINORITY RIGHTS 125 (1995); Linda S. Bosniak, *Membership, Equality, and the Difference That Alienage Makes,* 69 N.Y.U. L. REV. 1047, 1069–73 (1994). The Supreme Court has applied a communitarian rationale to uphold citizenship requirements for certain state jobs. *See, e.g.,* Cabell v. Chavez-Salido, 454 U.S. 432, 445–47 (1982) (probation officer); Foley v. Connelie, 435 U.S. 291, 296 (1978) (state police officer).

34. Bosniak, at 1072.

35. *See* Carens, at 266–67.

36. *See* Howard F. Chang, *Cultural Communities in a Global Labor Market:*

Immigration Restrictions as Residential Segregation, 2007 U. CHI. LEG. FORUM (forthcoming 2007).

37. *See* WALZER, at 40.

38. *See* Michael Scaperlanda, *Polishing the Tarnished Golden Door,* 1993 WIS. L. REV. 965, 972–1002; Ibrahim J. Wani, *Truth, Strangers, and Fiction: The Illegitimate Uses of Legal Fiction in Immigration Law,* 11 CARDOZO L. REV. 51, 63–83 (1989); Frank H. Wu, *The Limits of Borders: A Moderate Proposal for Immigration Reform,* 7 STAN. L. & POL'Y REV. 35, 39 (1996).

39. Chae Chan Ping v. United States (*The Chinese Exclusion Case*), 30 U.S. 581, 609 (1889); *see* Fong Yue Ting v. United States, 149 U.S. 698, 707 (1893) ("The right of a nation to expel or deport foreigners . . . is as absolute and unqualified as the right to prohibit and prevent their entrance into the country.").

40. *See* Chapter 1. For one novel approach of this type, see VICTOR C. ROMERO, ALIENATED: IMMIGRANT RIGHTS, THE CONSTITUTION, AND EQUALITY IN AMERICA (2005).

41. *See* R. George Wright, *Federal Immigration Law and the Case for Open Entry,* 27 LOY. L.A. L. REV. 1265, 1271–72 (1994).

42. *See, e.g.,* ALAN DOWTY, CLOSED BORDERS: THE CONTEMPORARY ASSAULT ON FREEDOM OF MOVEMENT (1987).

43. *See* Thomas Kleven, *Why International Law Favors Emigration Over Immigration,* 33 U. MIAMI INTER-AM. L. REV. 69 (2002).

44. *See* Joan Fitzpatrick & William McKay Bennett, *A Lion in the Path? The Influence of International Law on the Immigration Policy of the United States,* 70 WASH. L. REV. 589 (1995); Berta Esperanza Hernández-Truyol, *Natives, Newcomers and Nativism: A Human Rights Model for the Twenty-First Century,* 23 FORDHAM URB. L.J. 1075, 1113–29 (1996); *see also* Louis Henkin, *That "S" Word: Sovereignty, and Globalization, and Human Rights, et Cetera,* 68 FORDHAM L. REV. 1 (1999) (analyzing national sovereignty as an impediment to implementing international human rights norms). For skepticism about whether the U.S. immigration laws in fact conform to international law, see Kevin R. Johnson, *The Moral High Ground? The Relevance of International Law to Racial Discrimination in the U.S. Immigration Laws, in* MORAL IMPERIALISM: A CRITICAL ANTHOLOGY 285 (Berta Esperanza Hernández-Truyol ed., 2002).

45. *See* James A.R. Nafziger, *The General Admission of Aliens Under International Law,* 77 AM. J. INT'L L. 804 (1983).

46. *See* United Nations Convention Relating to the Status of Refugees, July 28, 1951, 189 U.N.T.S. 137 (1951); United Nations Protocol Relating to the Status of Refugees, Jan. 3, 1967, 606 U.N.T.S. 267 (1967); Convention Against Torture and Other Cruel, Inhuman or Degrading Treatment or Punishment, *opened for signature* Dec. 10, 1984, U.N. GAOR, 39th Sess., Supp. No. 51, at 197, U.N. Doc A/39/51 (1984).

47. *See* Antiterrorism and Effective Death Penalty Act of 1996, Pub. L. No. 104–132, 110 Stat. 1214 (1996); Illegal Immigration Reform and Immigrant Responsibility Act of 1996, Pub. L. No. 104–208, 110 Stat. 3009 (1996).

48. *See* Personal Responsibility and Work Opportunity Reconciliation Act of 1996, Pub. L. No. 104–193, 110 Stat. 2260 (1996).

49. PETER H. SCHUCK, CITIZENS, STRANGERS, AND IN-BETWEENS: ESSAYS ON IMMIGRATION AND CITIZENSHIP 143 (1998).

50. *See* Uniting and Strengthening America by Providing Appropriate Tools Required to Intercept and Obstruct Terrorism (USA PATRIOT Act) Act of 2001, Pub. L. No. 107–56, 115 Stat 272, 350–52; *see also* David Cole, *The New McCarthyism: Repeating History in the War on Terrorism*, 38 HARV. C.R.-C.L. L. REV. 1 (2003) (criticizing the USA PATRIOT Act and other measures that are part of the war on terror).

51. *See, e.g.,* Registration and Monitoring of Certain Nonimmigrants, 67 Fed. Reg. 52584, 52585 (Aug. 12, 2002) (justifying registration of noncitizens from select group of nations by relying on the plenary power doctrine).

52. *See* Saskia Sassen, *Regulating Immigration in a Global Age: A New Policy Landscape,* 570 ANNALS 65 (2000). For proposed regional alternatives to refugee admissions, see James C. Hathaway, *A Reconsideration of the Underlying Premise of Refugee Law,* 31 HARV. INT'L L.J. 129 (1997); James C. Hathaway & R. Alexander Neve, *Making International Refugee Law Relevant Again: A Proposal for Collectivized and Solution-Oriented Protection,* 10 HARV. HUM. RTS. J. 115 (1997); Peter H. Schuck, *Refugee Burden-Sharing: A Modest Proposal,* 22 YALE J. INT'L L. 243 (1997).

53. *See* Gerald L. Neuman, *The Lost Century of Immigration Law (1776–1875),* 93 COLUM. L. REV. 1833 (1993).

54. *See* ALFRED C. AMAN, JR., ADMINISTRATIVE LAW IN A GLOBAL ERA 1–2 (1992). The deregulation of industry in the United States has been criticized, however. *See generally* ALFRED E. KAHN, WHOM THE GODS WOULD DESTROY, OR HOW NOT TO DEREGULATE (2001); ROBERT KUTTNER, EVERYTHING FOR SALE: THE VIRTUES AND LIMITS OF MARKETS 225–80 (1997).

55. Wright, at 1294.

56. *See* WALZER, at 40; *see also* K. ANTHONY APPLAH & AMY GUTMANN, COLOR CONSCIOUS: THE POLITICAL MORALITY OF RACE (1996) (analyzing the morality of considering race in political dialogue); John Hasnas, *Equal Opportunity, Affirmative Action, and the Anti-Discrimination Principle: The Philosophical Basis for the Legal Prohibition of Discrimination,* 71 FORDHAM L. REV. 423 (2002) (studying the moral foundations for the antidiscrimination norm under U.S. law).

57. *See* United Nations International Convention on the Elimination of All Forms of Racial Discrimination, *opened for signature* Dec. 21, 1965, 660 U.N.T.S. 195 (entered into force on Jan. 4, 1969); *see also* Gabriel J. Chin, *Seg-*

regation's Last Stronghold: Race Discrimination and the Constitutional Law of Immigration, 46 UCLA L. Rev. 1, 60–61 (1998) (contending that various sources of international law, including the United Nations International Convention on the Elimination of All Forms of Racial Discrimination, prohibit racial discrimination in immigration laws); Berta Esperanza Hernández-Truyol, *Nativism, Terrorism, and Human Rights—The Global Wrongs of Reno v.* American-Arab Anti-Discrimination Committee, 31 COLUM. HUM. RTS. L. REV. 521, 555–56 (2000) (contending that the U.S. government's efforts to deport Muslim noncitizens violated the United Nations International Convention on the Elimination of All Forms of Racial Discrimination).

58. *See* THE MOVEMENT OF PERSONS ACROSS BORDERS 17–22 (American Society of International Law, Louis B. Sohn & Thomas Buergenthal eds., 1992).

59. *See* World Conference Against Racism, Racial Discrimination, Xenophobia and Related Intolerance, *available at* http://www.un.org/WCAR, last visited Nov. 30, 2007; Michelle E. Lyons, Note, *World Conference Against Racism: New Avenues for Slavery Reparations?*, 35 VAND. J. TRANSNAT'L L. 1235, 1236–37 (2002) (summarizing the themes of the conference).

60. *See generally* MARY L. DUDZIAK, COLD WAR CIVIL RIGHTS: RACE AND THE IMAGE OF AMERICAN DEMOCRACY (2002) (documenting history demonstrating that Cold War foreign policy pressures militated in favor of emerging recognition of civil rights in the United States).

61. 347 U.S. 483 (1954).

62. *See* Kevin R. Johnson, *The End of "Civil Rights" As We Know It? Immigration and Civil Rights in the New Millennium,* 49 UCLA L. REV. 1481, 1485, 1505 (2002).

63. *See* Howard F. Chang, *Immigration and the Workplace: Immigration Restrictions as Employment Discrimination,* 78 CHI.-KENT L. REV. 291 (2003).

64. *See, e.g.,* HUMAN RIGHTS WATCH, "WE ARE NOT THE ENEMY": HATE CRIMES AGAINST ARABS, MUSLIMS, AND THOSE PERCEIVED TO BE ARAB OR MUSLIM AFTER SEPTEMBER 11 (2002); Bill Ong Hing, *Vigilante Racism: The De-Americanization of Immigrant America,* 7 MICH. J. RACE & L. 441 (2002).

65. *See* Hiroshi Motomura, *Whose Alien Nation? Two Models of Constitutional Immigration Law,* 94 MICH. L. REV. 1927, 1947 (1996) (book review); Gerald M. Rosberg, *The Protection of Aliens From Discriminatory Treatment by the National Government,* 1977 SUP. CT. REV. 275, 327.

66. PUBLIC PAPERS OF THE PRESIDENTS OF THE UNITED STATES: HARRY S. TRUMAN 1952–1953, at 443 (1966). John F. Kennedy echoed this theme in calling for reform to the U.S. immigration laws in JOHN F. KENNEDY, A NATION OF IMMIGRANTS (rev. ed. 1964).

67. *See* Gabriel J. Chin, *The Civil Rights Revolution Comes to Immigration Law: A New Look at the Immigration and Nationality Act of 1965,* 75 N.C. L. REV. 273 (1996).

68. *See, e.g.,* Lolita K. Buckner Inniss, *Tricky Magic: Blacks as Immigrants and the Paradox of Foreignness,* 49 DePaul L. Rev. 85 (1999); Hope Lewis, *Global Intersections: Critical Race Feminist Human Rights and Inter/National Black Women,* 50 Me. L. Rev. 309 (1998); Camille A. Nelson, *Carriers of Globalization: Loss of Home and Self Within the African Diaspora,* 55 Fla. L. Rev. 539 (2003). Although often neglected in the study of U.S. immigration history, forced migrants from Africa constituted one of the earliest and largest immigrant groups to come to the United States. *See* Mary Sarah Bilder, *The Struggle Over Immigration: Indentured Servants, Slaves, and Articles of Commerce,* 61 Mo. L. Rev. 743 (1996).

69. *See* Johnson, *Race, the Immigration Laws, and Domestic Race Relations,* at 1148–54.

70. *See id.* at 1136–40.

71. *See* Kevin R. Johnson, *The Case Against Race Profiling in Immigration Enforcement,* 78 Wash. U. L.Q. 675, 711–16, 722–25 (2000). *See generally* Kenneth L. Karst, Belonging to America (1989) (analyzing efforts of various groups to secure full membership in U.S. society).

72. *See* Teresa Hayter, Open Borders: The Case Against Immigration Controls 21–36 (2d ed. 2004).

73. *See* Elizabeth S. Anderson & Richard H. Pildes, *Expressive Theories of Law: A General Restatement,* 148 U. Pa. L. Rev. 503 (2000); Dan M. Kahan, *The Secret Ambition of Deterrence,* 113 Harv. L. Rev. 413 (1999).

74. *See* Kevin R. Johnson, *"Aliens" and the U.S. Immigration Laws: The Social and Legal Construction of Nonpersons,* 28 U. Miami Inter-Am. L. Rev. 263 (1996–97).

75. *See generally* Lucy E. Salyer, Laws Harsh as Tigers: Chinese Immigrants and the Shaping of Modern Immigration Law (1995) (analyzing the Chinese exclusion laws and their legacy).

76. *See* Bill Ong Hing, Making and Remaking Asian America Through Immigration Policy 1850–1990, at 23–24 (1993). *See generally* Ronald T. Takaki, Strangers From a Different Shore: A History of Asian Americans (rev. ed. 1998) (analyzing the history of exclusion of Asian immigrants from the United States).

77. *See generally* Ian F. Haney López, White by Law: The Legal Construction of Race (1996).

78. *See, e.g.,* United States v. Thind, 261 U.S. 204 (1923); Ozawa v. United States, 260 U.S. 178 (1922).

79. *See, e.g.,* United States v. Brignoni-Ponce, 422 U.S. 873, 886–87 (1975) (holding that "Mexican appearance" was one relevant factor in, but alone not enough to justify, finding reasonable suspicion to conduct a stop to investigate whether the occupants of a car are illegal immigrants). *But see* United States v. Montero-Camargo, 208 F.3d 1122 (9th Cir. 2000) (en banc) (disregarding the

language in *Brignoni-Ponce* and holding that the Border Patrol cannot lawfully consider "Hispanic appearance" in deciding to make an immigration stop).

80. *See* Johnson, *Race, the Immigration Laws, and Domestic Race Relations,* at 1133; Stephen H. Legomsky, *Immigration, Equality and Diversity,* at 333; Bernard Trujillo, *Immigrant Visa Distribution: The Case of Mexico,* 2000 WIS. L. REV 713.

81. *See* U.S. DEP'T OF JUSTICE, 1999 STATISTICAL YEARBOOK OF THE IMMIGRATION AND NATURALIZATION SERVICE 44, 45 tbl.8 (2002) [hereinafter 1999 STATISTICAL YEARBOOK].

82. LEGOMSKY, at 343 (emphasis in original).

83. *See* Kevin R. Johnson, *September 11 and Mexican Immigrants: Collateral Damage Comes Home,* 52 DEPAUL L. REV. 849 (2003).

84. *See* 1999 INS STATISTICAL YEARBOOK, at 218–25 tbl.66.

85. *See id.* at 215–17 tbl.65.

86. *See* Press Release, U.S. Immigration & Naturalization Service, INS Sets New Removals Record; Fiscal Year 1999 Removals Reach 176,990 (Nov. 12, 1999); *see also* Bo Cooper, *A New Approach to Protection and Law Enforcement Under the Victims of Trafficking and Violence Protection Act,* 51 EMORY L.J. 1041, 1042 (2002) (stating that 1996 immigration reform legislation and increases in enforcement budget "resulted in a marked increase in the removal of criminal aliens from the country"); Margaret H. Taylor & Ronald F. Wright, *The Sentencing Judge as Immigration Judge,* 51 EMORY L.J 1131, 1134–38 (2002) (same).

87. *See* U.S. DEP'T OF JUSTICE, 1998 STATISTICAL YEARBOOK OF THE IMMIGRATION AND NATURALIZATION SERVICE 215–17 tbl.65 (2000) [hereinafter 1998 INS STATISTICAL YEARBOOK].

88. *See* U.S. DEP'T OF HOMELAND SECURITY, 2003 YEARBOOK OF IMMIGRATION STATISTICS 149–50 (2004).

89. *See* U.S. DEP'T OF HOMELAND SECURITY, 2004 YEARBOOK OF IMMIGRATION STATISTICS 159 (2006) (Table 40).

90. *See* OFFICE OF THE ATTORNEY GENERAL GRANT WOODS, STATE OF ARIZONA, RESULTS OF THE CHANDLER SURVEY (1997); Mary Romero & Marwah Serag, *Violation of Latino Civil Rights Resulting From INS and Local Police's Use of Race, Culture and Class Profiling: The Case of the Chandler Roundup in Arizona,* 52 CLEV. ST. L. REV. 75 (2005).

91. *See* LEGOMSKY, at 1209–23 (summarizing enforcement of employer sanctions).

92. Karl Eschbach et al., *Death at the Border,* 33 INT'L MIGRATION REV. 430 (1999) (analyzing the impacts of increased border enforcement strategies in the 1990s); Wayne A. Cornelius, *Death at the Border: Efficacy and Unintended Consequences of U.S. Immigration Control Policy,* 27 POPULATION & DEV. REV. 661 (2001) (same).

93. *See* Bill Ong Hing, *The Dark Side of Operation Gatekeeper*, 7 U.C. DAVIS J. INT'L L. & POL'Y 121, 123 (2001); *see, e.g.,* Simon Romero & David Barboza, *Trapped in Heat in Texas Truck, 18 People Die*, N.Y. TIMES, May 15, 2003, at A1.

94. John W. Fountain with Jim Yardley, *Skeletons Tell Tale of Gamble by Immigrants*, N.Y. TIMES, Oct. 16, 2002, at A1.

95. *See* KEN ELLINGWOOD, HARD LINE: LIFE AND DEATH ON THE U.S.-MEX-ICO BORDER (2004); SONIA NAZARIO, ENRIQUE'S JOURNEY: THE STORY OF A BOY'S DANGEROUS ODYSSEY TO REUNITE WITH HIS MOTHER (2006); JORGE RAMOS, DYING TO CROSS: THE WORST IMMIGRANT TRAGEDY IN AMERICAN HIS-TORY (2005); LUIS A. URREA, THE DEVIL'S HIGHWAY: A TRUE STORY (2004).

96. *See generally* TIMOTHY J. DUNN, THE MILITARIZATION OF THE U.S.-MEXICAN BORDER, 1978–1992: LOW INTENSITY CONFLICT DOCTRINE COMES HOME (1996); KARL ESCHBACH, JACQUELINE HAGAN, & NESTOR RODRIGUEZ, CAUSES AND TRENDS IN MIGRANT DEATHS ALONG THE U.S./MEXICO BORDER, 1985–1998 (2001); JOSEPH NEVINS, OPERATION GATEKEEPER (2002); Guillermo Alonso Meneses, *Human Rights and Undocumented Migration in the Mexican-U.S. Border*, 51 UCLA L. REV. 267 (2003).

97. *See* http://www.stopgatekeeper.org/English/index.html, last visited Nov. 27, 2006.

98. Hing, *The Dark Side of Operation Gatekeeper*, at 135 (emphasis added) (footnote omitted).

99. Jorge A. Vargas, *U.S. Border Patrol Abuses, Undocumented Mexican Workers, and International Human Rights*, 2 SAN DIEGO INT'L L.J. 1, 69 (2001) (emphasis added).

100. *See id.* at 42–64.

101. *See generally* JUAN RAMON GARCÍA, OPERATION WETBACK: THE MASS DEPORTATION OF MEXICAN UNDOCUMENTED WORKERS IN 1954 (1980) (analyzing the mass removal campaign that the Border Patrol referred to as "Operation Wetback"); ALFREDO MIRANDÈ, GRINGO JUSTICE (1987) (documenting history of human rights abuses by the Border Patrol and Immigration and Naturalization Service).

102. *See, e.g.,* AMNESTY INT'L, UNITED STATES OF AMERICA: HUMAN RIGHTS CONCERNS IN THE BORDER REGION WITH MEXICO (1998); AMERICAN FRIENDS SERVICE COMM., HUMAN AND CIVIL RIGHTS VIOLATIONS ON THE U.S. MEXICO BORDER 1995–97 (1998); HUMAN RIGHTS WATCH, CROSSING THE LINE: HU-MAN RIGHTS ABUSES ALONG THE U.S. BORDER WITH MEXICO PERSIST AMID CLIMATE OF IMPUNITY (1995).

103. *See* Hing, *The Dark Side of Operation Gatekeeper*, at 153–54; Cornelius, at 667–68; David Spener, *Smuggling Migrants Through South Texas: Challenges Posed by Operation Rio Grande, in* GLOBAL HUMAN SMUGGLING: COMPARATIVE PERSPECTIVES 129 (David Kyle & Rey Koslowski eds., 2001).

104. Elliot Spagat, *BC-Immigrants Killed,* INLAND VALLEY DAILY BULLETIN (Ontario, CA), July 9, 2005.

105. HUMAN RIGHTS CENTER (UNIVERSITY OF CALIFORNIA, BERKELEY), FREEDOM DENIED: FORCED LABOR IN CALIFORNIA 1 (2005).

106. *See* Lisa Sink, *Couple Convicted of Harboring Maid: They Face Up to 45 Years in Prison, Deportation,* MILWAUKEE JOURNAL SENTINEL, May 27, 2006, at A1 (reporting on verdict finding family had forced undocumented immigrant to work in their home); Michael Overall, *Pickle Verdict: Guilt: Judgment Exceeds $1 Million,* TULSA WORLD (Oklahoma), May 25, 2006, at A1 (reporting on verdict awarding $1.2 million to foreign workers held in "virtual slavery" by employer).

107. *See* Robert F. Castro, *Exorcising Tombstone's Evil Spirits: Eradicating Vigilante Ranch Enterprises Through Public Interest Litigation,* 20 LAW & INEQ. 203, 205–18 (2002); Nick Madigan, *Police Investigate Killings of Illegal Immigrants in Arizona Desert,* N.Y. TIMES, Oct. 23, 2002, at A13; Jerry Seper, *Arizona Militia Set to Patrol Border for Illegal Aliens,* WASH. TIMES, Dec. 9, 2002, at A5; *see also* Michael J. Nuñez, Note, *Violence at Our Border: Rights and Status of Immigrant Victims of Hate Crimes and Violence Along the Border Between the United States and Mexico,* 43 HASTINGS L.J. 1573 (1992) (analyzing hate crimes directed at undocumented immigrants along the southern border with Mexico).

108. *See* Cornelius, at 668–69.

109. *See, e.g.,* U.S. COMM'N ON IMMIGRATION REFORM, LEGAL IMMIGRATION SETTING PRIORITIES (1995); U.S. SELECT COMM'N ON IMMIGRATION & REFUGEE POLICY, U.S. IMMIGRATION POLICY AND THE NATIONAL INTEREST (1981).

110. *See* Zadvydas v. Davis, 533 U.S. 678 (2001).

111. *See* INS v. St. Cyr, 533 U.S. 289, 314 (2001). Judicial review is important to noncitizens, especially because the courts in the past have regularly reversed a relatively high percentage of the decisions of the immigration bureaucracy. *See* Peter H. Schuck & Theodore Hsien Wang, *Continuity and Change: Patterns of Immigration Litigation in the Courts, 1979–1990,* 45 STAN. L. REV. 115 (1992) (providing data from an empirical study of the judicial review of immigration decisions). As discussed in Chapter 5, courts reviewing immigration decisions often criticize the quality of the agency decision making.

112. *See St. Cyr,* 533 U.S. at 326; Daniel Kanstroom, *St. Cyr. or Insincere: The Strange Quality of Supreme Court Victory,* 16 GEO. IMMIGR. L.J. 413, 418–23 (2002); Nancy Morawetz, *Rethinking Retroactive Deportation Laws and the Due Process Clause,* 73 N.Y.U. L. REV. 97 (1998); *see also* Debra Lyn Bassett, *In the Wake of Schooner Peggy: Deconstructing Legislative Activity Analysis,* 69 U. CIN. L. REV. 453 (2001) (analyzing the Supreme Court's retroactivity analysis, specifically in the case of 1996 immigration reforms); Nancy Morawetz,

Understanding the Impact of the 1996 Deportation Laws and the Limited Scope of Proposed Reforms, 113 HARV. L. REV. 1936 (2000) (analyzing the harsh impacts of 1996 immigration reforms on criminal aliens that the U.S. government vigorously enforced).

113. *See* WALZER, at 48–50; Michael Walzer, *The Distribution of Membership, in* BOUNDARIES: NATIONAL AUTONOMY AND ITS LIMITS 1, 20 (Peter G. Brown & Henry Shue eds., 1981); Frederick G. Whelan, *Immigrants in American Law: Principles of U.S. Immigration Policy,* 44 U. PITT. L. REV. 447, 449 (1983).

114. Guy S. Goodwin-Gill, *Non-Refoulement and the New Asylum Seekers,* 26 VA. J. INT'L L. 897, 898 (1986).

115. *See generally* HENRY L. FEINGOLD, THE POLITICS OF RESCUE (1970); SAUL S. FRIEDMAN, NO HAVEN FOR THE OPPRESSED (1973); GORDON THOMAS & MAX MORGAN WITTS, VOYAGE OF THE DAMNED (1974).

116. 19 U.S.T. 629, 189 U.N.T.S. 137 (entered into force Apr. 22, 1954).

117. Pub. L. No. 96–212, 94 Stat. 102 (1980).

118. *See generally* Kevin R. Johnson, *A "Hard Look" at the Executive Branch's Asylum Decisions,* 1991 UTAH L. REV. 279.

119. Germany also has implemented increased measures to limit the number of asylum seekers from outside the European Union eligible for relief, *see* Maryellen Fullerton, *Failing the Test: Germany Leads Europe in Dismantling Refugee Protection,* 36 TEX. INT'L L.J. 231 (2001), which is consistent with the claim that a "Fortress Europe" accompanied the formation of the European Union.

120. *See* Orantes-Hernandez v. Thornburgh, 919 F.2d 549 (9th Cir. 1990); *see also* American Baptist Churches v. Thornburgh, 760 F. Supp. 796 (N.D. Cal. 1991) (settling class action in which the U.S. government was accused of bias against the asylum claims of Salvadorans).

121. *See* Sale v. Haitian Ctrs. Council Inc., 509 U.S. 155 (1993); *see also* Peter Margulies, *Difference and Distrust in Asylum Law: Haitian and Holocaust Refugee Narratives,* 6 ST. THOMAS L. REV. 135 (1993) (analyzing parallels between the treatment of Haitian and Holocaust refugees). At various times in the past decade, the U.S. government has treated Chinese, *see* Ting, at 310–11, and Cuban migrants in similar ways, *see* Richard A. Boswell, *Throwing Away the Key: Limits on Plenary Power?,* 18 MICH. J. INT'L L. 689, 705–08 (1997) (book review); Kevin R. Johnson, *Comparative Racialization: Culture and National Origin in the Latina/o Communities,* 78 DEN. U. L. REV. 633, 650–51 (2001). However, claims long have been, and continue to be, made that the U.S. government for racial and foreign policy reasons, has been more generous toward Cuban migrants than to Haitian migrants. *See* Kevin R. Johnson, *Judicial Acquiescence to the Executive Branch's Pursuit of Foreign Policy and Domestic Agendas in Immigration Matters: The Case of the Haitian Asylum-Seekers,* 7 GEO. IMMIGR. L.J. 1, 26–27 (1993).

122. *See* ANDREW SUM ET AL., IMMIGRANT WORKERS AND THE GREAT AMERICAN JOB MACHINE: THE CONTRIBUTIONS OF NEW FOREIGN IMMIGRATION TO NATIONAL AND REGIONAL LABOR FORCE GROWTH IN THE 1990S, at 38, 41–42 (National Business Roundtable, 2002); *see also* AMERICAN IMMIGRATION LAW FOUNDATION, MEXICAN IMMIGRANT WORKERS AND THE U.S. ECONOMY: AN INCREASINGLY VITAL ROLE (2002) (analyzing the importance of immigrant workers from Mexico to the U.S. economy).

123. *See* Fong Haw Tan v. Phelan, 333 U.S. 6, 10 (1948) ("[D]eportation is a drastic measure and at times the equivalent of banishment or exile."); Bridges v. Wixon, 326 U.S. 135, 147 (1945) ("[D]eportation may result in the loss 'of all that makes life worth living.' ") (citations omitted).

124. Despite their uncertain immigration status, undocumented immigrants have been involved in labor organizing activities. *See* HÈCTOR L. DELGADO, NEW IMMIGRANTS, OLD UNIONS: ORGANIZING UNDOCUMENTED WORKERS IN LOS ANGELES (1993); Christopher David Ruiz Cameron, *The Labyrinth of Solidarity: Why the Future of the American Labor Movement Depends on Latino Workers,* 53 U. MIAMI L. REV. 1089 (1999).

125. Hoffman Plastic Compounds, Inc. v. NLRB, 535 U.S. 137, 144 (2002). For sustained criticism of the *Hoffman Plastic* decision, see Christopher David Ruiz Cameron, *Borderline Decisions: Hoffman Plastic Compounds, the New Bracero Program, and the Supreme Court's Role in Making Federal Labor Policy,* 51 UCLA L. REV. 1 (2003); Robert Correales, *Does* Hoffman Plastic Compounds, Inc. *Produce Disposable Workers?,* 14 BERKELEY LA RAZA L.J. 103 (2003); Christopher Ho & Jennifer C. Chang, *Drawing the Line After* Hoffman Plastic Compounds, Inc. v. NLRB: *Strategies for Protecting Undocumented Workers in the Title VII Context and Beyond,* 22 HOFSTRA LAB. & EMP. L.J. 473 (2005).

126. *See* Robert I. Correales, *Workers' Compensation and Vocational Rehabilitation Benefits for Undocumented Workers: Reconciling the Purported Conflicts Between State Law, Federal Immigration Law, and Equal Protection to Prevent the Creation of a Disposable Workforce,* 81 DEN. U.L. REV. 347 (2003); Beth Lyons, *When More "Security" Equals Less Workplace Safety: Reconsidering U.S. Laws that Disadvantage Unauthorized Workers,* 6 U. PA. J. LAB. & EMPL. L. (2004); Jason Schumann, Note, *Working in the Shadows: Illegal Aliens' Entitlement to State Workers' Compensation,* 89 IOWA L. REV. 709 (2004).

127. *See* Espinoza v. Farah Mfg. Co., 414 U.S. 86 (1973); *see also* Ruben J. Garcia, *Across the Borders: Immigrant Status and Identity in Law and LatCrit Theory,* 55 FLA. L. REV. 511 (2003) (contending that Congress should amend Title VII of the Civil Rights Act of 1964 to bar discrimination against immigrants authorized for employment under the law).

128. *See* Immigration & Nationality Act § 274A, 8 U.S.C. § 1324a.

129. *See* U.S. COMM'N ON IMMIGRATION REFORM, U.S. IMMIGRATION POL-

ICY: RESTORING CREDIBILITY 52 (1994) (referring to "studies of discriminatory practices against foreign-sounding and foreign-looking applicants for employment" due to employer sanctions in 1986 immigration reform); *see, e.g.,* U.S. GEN. ACCOUNTING OFFICE, IMMIGRATION REFORM: EMPLOYER SANCTIONS AND THE QUESTION OF DISCRIMINATION 3–8 (1990); Cecelia M. Espenoza, *The Illusory Provisions of Sanctions: The Immigration Reform and Control Act of 1986,* 8 GEO. IMMIGR. L.J. 343, 347–48, 364–69, 381–83 (1994).

130. *Compare* Egbuna v. Time-Life Libraries Inc., 153 F.3d 184 (4th Cir. 1998) (finding that an undocumented immigrant was not qualified for employment and therefore could not pursue a discrimination claim under Title VII), *cert. denied,* 525 U.S. 1142 (1999) *with* Rivera v. NIBCO, Inc., 364 F.3d 1057 (9th Cir. 2004) (affirming lower court ruling that employer could not discover immigration status of plaintiffs in Title VII case).

131. *See Developments in the Law—Jobs and Borders,* 118 HARV. L. REV. 2175, 2234–47 (2005).

132. *See* Marion Crain & Ken Matheny, *"Labor's Divided Ranks": Privilege and the United Front Ideology,* 84 CORNELL L. REV. 1542, 1574–75 (1999); *see also* PETER B. DOERINGER & MICHAEL J. PIORE, INTERNAL LABOR MARKETS AND MANPOWER ANALYSIS 167- 69 (2d ed. 1985) (describing the economic theory of dual labor markets).

133. *See* Johnson, *The End of "Civil Rights" as We Know It?,* at 1496–99, 1505–06.

134. *See* Kelly E. Hyland, *Protecting Human Victims of Trafficking: An American Framework,* 16 BERKELEY WOMEN'S L.J. 29, 41 (2001); Julie A. Su, *Making the Invisible Visible: The Garment Industry's Dirty Laundry,* 1 J. GENDER, RACE, & JUST. 405 (1998).

135. *See* Hyland, at 40–41.

136. *See, e.g.,* Cleo J. Kung, Comment, *Supporting the Snakeheads: Human Smuggling From China and the 1996 Amendment to the U.S. Statutory Definition of "Refugee,"* 90 J. CRIM. L. & CRIMINOLOGY 1271 (2000). *See generally* PETER KWONG, FORBIDDEN WORKERS: ILLEGAL CHINESE IMMIGRANTS AND AMERICAN LABOR (1997) (documenting the history of undocumented migration from China, including modern smuggling operations that exploit Chinese laborers).

137. *See* Free the Slaves & Human Rights Center of the University of California, *Hidden Slaves: Forced Labor in the United States,* 23 BERKELEY J. INT'L L. 47 (2005).

138. *See* JENNIFER GORDON, SUBURBAN SWEATSHOP: THE FIGHT FOR IMMIGRANT RIGHTS (2005).

139. *Developments in the Law—Jobs and Borders,* at 2186–87 (emphasis added); *see* Rosy Kandiathil, *Global Sex Trafficking Victims Protection Act of 2000: Legislative Responses to the Problem of Modern Slavery,* 12 MICH. J.

GENDER & L. 87 (2005); Symposium, *Trafficking in Human Beings: A Global Concern*, 1 INTERCULTURAL HUM. RTS. L. REV. 1 (2005–06); Susan W. Tiefenbrun, *Sex Slavery in the United States and Its Law to Stop It Here and Abroad*, 11 WM. & MARY J. WOMEN & L. 317 (2005); Susan W. Tiefenbrun, *The Domestic and International Impact of the U.S. Victims of Trafficking Protection Act of 2000: Does Law Deter Crime?* 2 LOY. U. CHI INT'L L. REV. 193 (2005).

140. *See* Maria L. Ontiveros, *To Help Those Most in Need: Undocumented Workers' Rights and Remedies Under Title VII*, 20 N.Y.U. REV. L. & SOC. CHANGE 607 (1993–1994); Donna E. Young, *Working Across Borders: Global Restructuring and Women's Work*, 2001 UTAH L. REV. 1.

141. *See* Hyland, at 41–42; Suzanne H. Jackson, *To Honor and Obey: Trafficking in "Mail-Order Brides,"* 70 GEO. WASH. L. REV. 475 (2002); Susan W. Tiefenbrun, *Sex Sells But Drugs Don't Talk: Trafficking of Women Sex Workers and an Economic Solution*, 24 T. JEFFERSON L. REV. 161 (2002); *Symposium on Sexual Slavery: The Trafficking of Women and Girls Into the United States for Sexual Exploitation*, 13 HASTINGS WOMEN'S L.J. 1 (2002).

142. *See* Jennifer M. Chacón, *Misery and Myopia: Understanding the Failures of U.S. Efforts to Stop Human Trafficking*, 74 FORDHAM L. REV. 2977 (2006); Debbie Nathan, *Oversexed*, NATION, Aug. 29, 2005, *available at* http://www.thenation.com/doc/20050829/nathan, last visited Nov. 30, 2006. For a case study of the trafficking and abuse of highly skilled workers, see Michael A. Scaperlanda, *Human Trafficking in the Heartland: Greed, Visa Fraud, and the Saga of Indian Nationals "Enslaved" by a Tulsa Company*, 2 LOY. U. CHI. INT'L L. REV. 219 (2005).

143. *See* William R. Tamayo, *The Role of the EEOC in Protecting Civil Rights of Farm Workers*, 33 U.C. DAVIS L. REV. 1075 (2000) (discussing enforcement of sexual harassment claim involving immigrant farmworker).

144. *See* Nina Bernstein, *Invisible to Most, Immigrant Women Line Up for Day Labor*, N.Y. TIMES, Aug. 15, 2005, at A1.

145. *See* Mary Romero, *Nanny Diaries and Other Stories: Imagining Immigrant Women's Labor in the Social Reproduction of American Families*, 52 DEPAUL L. REV. 809 (2003); Margaret L. Satterthwaite, *Crossing Borders, Claiming Rights: Using Human Rights Law to Empower Women Migrant Workers*, 8 YALE HUM. RTS. & DEV. L.J. 1 (2005).

146. *See* Mary Romero, *Immigration, the Servant Problem, and the Legacy of the Domestic Labor Debate: "Where Can You Find Good Help These Days!,"* 53 U. MIAMI L. REV. 1045 (1999). *See generally* MARY ROMERO, MAID IN THE U.S.A. (10th anniversary ed., 2002); RHACEL SALAZAR PARREÑAS, SERVANTS OF GLOBALIZATION: WOMEN, MIGRATION AND DOMESTIC WORK (2001).

147. Pub. L. No. 106–386, 114 Stat. 1466 (2000); Pub. L. No. 108–193, 117 Stat. 2875 (2003).

148. *See* U.S. GEN. ACCOUNTABILITY OFFICE, HUMAN TRAFFICKING: BETTER

DATA, STRATEGY, AND REPORTING NEEDED TO ENHANCE U.S. ANTITRAFFICKING EFFORTS ABROAD (GAO-06-825) (2006); U.S. GEN. ACCOUNTABILITY OFFICE, COMBATING ALIEN SMUGGLING: THE FEDERAL RESPONSE CAN BE IMPROVED (GAO-05-892T) (2005).

149. *See* Linda Bosniak, *Human Rights, State Sovereignty and the Protection of Undocumented Migrants Under the International Migrant Workers Convention*, 25 INT'L MIGRATION REV. 737 (1991); Beth Lyon, *New International Human Rights Standards on Unauthorized Worker Rights: Seizing an Opportunity to Pull Governments Out of the Shadows*, 10 REFUGEES & HUM. RTS. 551 (2005); *see also* Lori A. Nessel, *Undocumented Immigrants in the Workplace: The Fallacy of Labor Protection and the Need for Reform*, 36 HARV. C.R.-C.L. L. REV. 345, 395–404 (2001) (questioning the morality of punishing undocumented workers for their unlawful status).

150. G.A. Res. 217A(III), U.N. GAOR, 3d Sess., at 71, U.N. Doc. A/810 (1948).

151. 30 I.L.M. 1517 (1991).

152. 999 U.N.T.S. 171, *entered into force* Mar. 23, 1976.

153. *See* William R. Tamayo, *When the "Coloreds" Are Neither Black nor Citizens: The United States Civil Rights Movement and Global Migration*, 2 ASIAN L.J. 1, 26–29 (1995) (outlining how these international instruments might be used by civil rights activists); *see also* RICHARD B. LILLICH, THE HUMAN RIGHTS OF ALIENS IN CONTEMPORARY INTERNATIONAL LAW 41–48 (1984) (discussing the rights of noncitizens under international law). For an analysis of the protections of migrants under the United Nations International Convention for the Protection of Migrants, see CARMEN TIBURCIO, THE HUMAN RIGHTS OF ALIENS UNDER INTERNATIONAL AND COMPARATIVE LAW 150–51, 268 (2001).

154. *Developments in the Law—Jobs and Borders*, at 2247–70.

155. *See* Guadalupe T. Luna, *Immigrants, Cops and Slumlords in the Midwest*, 29 S. ILL. U. L.J. 61 (2005).

156. *See* Jane E. Larson, *Free Markets Deep in the Heart of Texas*, 84 GEO. L. J. 179 (1995).

157. *See* Lora Jo Foo, *The Vulnerable and Exploitable Immigrant Workforce and the Need for Strengthening Worker Protective Legislation*, 103 YALE L.J. 2179 (1994); Nessel; Ontiveros.

158. *See* Maria Elena Bickerton, Note, *Prospects for a Bilateral Immigration Agreement With Mexico: Lessons From the Bracero Program*, 79 TEX. L. REV. 895 (2001).

159. *See* KITTY CALAVITA, INSIDE THE STATE: THE BRACERO PROGRAM, IMMIGRATION, AND THE I.N.S. 29, 45–46, 64–66, 70–71 (1992).

160. *See* Howard F. Chang, *Liberal Ideals and Political Feasibility: Guest-Worker Programs as Second-Best Policies*, 27 N.C. J. INT'L L. & COM. REG. 465 (2002).

161. *See* Gerald P. Lopez, *Undocumented Mexican Migration: In Search of a Just Immigration Law and Policy,* 28 UCLA L. REV. 615 (1981). *See generally* JOHN A. ADAMS, BORDERING THE FUTURE: THE IMPACT OF MEXICO ON THE UNITED STATES (2006) (analyzing relationship between United States and Mexico on a variety of issues, including, but not limited to, immigration).

162. For an argument along these lines, see PETER LAUFER, WETBACK NATION: THE CASE FOR OPENING THE MEXICAN-AMERICAN BORDER (2004).

163. *See* Néstor P. Rodriguez, *The Social Construction of the U.S.-Mexico Border, in* IMMIGRANTS OUT! THE NEW NATIVISM AND THE ANTI-IMMIGRANT IMPULSE IN THE UNITED STATES 223, 233–34 (Juan F. Perea ed., 1997).

164. *See generally* DOUGLAS S. MASSEY ET AL., BEYOND SMOKE AND MIRRORS: MEXICAN IMMIGRATION IN AN ERA OF ECONOMIC INTEGRATION (2002) (summarizing the history of Mexican immigration to the United States and U.S. immigration controls).

165. *See, e.g.,* CALAVITA.

166. *See id.* (analyzing the Bracero Program and its impacts).

167. *See* ALEJANDRO PORTES & RUBÉN G. RUMBAUT, IMMIGRANT AMERICA: A PORTRAIT 230–34 (1990); WAYNE A. CORNELIUS, MEXICAN MIGRATION TO THE UNITED STATES: THE LIMITS OF GOVERNMENT INTERVENTION 2–4 (Working Papers in U.S. Mexican Studies No. 5, 1981); Douglas S. Massey, *The Social and Economic Origins of Immigration,* 510 ANNALS 60, 68–70 (1990).

168. *See* GARCÍA (discussing the 1954 mass removal campaign of Mexican immigrants); FRANCISCO E. BALDERRAMA & RAYMOND RODRÍGUEZ, DECADE OF BETRAYAL: MEXICAN REPATRIATION IN THE 1930S (1995) (analyzing the history of the "repatriation" of persons of Mexican ancestry during the Great Depression); CAMILLE GUERIN-GONZALES, MEXICAN WORKERS AND AMERICAN DREAMS: IMMIGRATION: REPATRIATION, AND CALIFORNIA FARM LABOR, 1900–1939 (1994) (same).

169. *See* 1999 INS STATISTICAL YEARBOOK, at 27 tbl. 3.

170. *See* 1999 INS STATISTICAL YEARBOOK, at 240 tbl. 1.

171. *See* U.S. DEP'T OF HOMELAND SECURITY, ESTIMATES OF THE UNAUTHORIZED POPULATION RESIDING IN THE UNITED STATES: JANUARY 2005, at 214 (2006).

172. *See* JEFFREY S. PASSEL UNAUTHORIZED MIGRANTS: NUMBERS AND CHARACTERISTICS 3–4 (Pew Hispanic Center 2005).

173. *See id.* at 11.

174. *See* Sylvia R. Lazos Vargas, *"Latina/o-ization" of the Midwest: Cambio de Colores (Change of Colores) as Agromaquilas Expand into the Heartland,* 13 LA RAZA L.J. 343 (2002).

175. *See* JEFFREY S. PASSEL, THE SIZE AND CHARACTERISTICS OF THE UNAUTHORIZED MIGRANT POPULATION IN THE U.S. (Pew Hispanic Center, Mar. 7, 2006).

176. *See* Robert Suro, Survey of Mexican Migrants: Attitudes About Immigration and Major Demographic Characteristics 2 (Pew Hispanic Center, 2005).

177. *See* Rachel F. Moran, *Demography and Distrust: The Latino Challenge to Civil Rights and Immigration Policy in the 1990s and Beyond,* 8 La Raza L.J. 1, 13–24 (1995); Maria L. Ontiveros, *Forging Our Identity: Transformative Resistance in the Areas of Work, Class, and the Law,* 33 U.C. Davis L. Rev. 1057, 1062–70 (2000); Roger Rouse, *Mexican Migration and the Social Space of Postmodernism,* 1 Diaspora 8 (1991); Enid Trucios-Haynes, *The Role of Transnational Identity and Migration,* 28 U. Miami Inter-Am. L. Rev. 293 (1996–97).

178. *See* T. Alexander Aleinikoff, Between Principles and Politics: The Direction of U.S. Citizenship Policy 30–36 (1998); Jorge A. Vargas, *Dual Nationality for Mexicans,* 35 San Diego L. Rev. 823 (1998). *See generally* Peter J. Spiro, *Dual Nationality and the Meaning of Citizenship,* 46 Emory L.J. 1411 (1997) (analyzing the impacts of dual nationality in modern times).

179. *See Developments in the Law—Immigration Policy and the Rights of Aliens,* 96 Harv. L. Rev. 1286, 1465 n.13 (1983); *see also* Lucy A. Williams, *Property, Wealth and Inequality Through the Lens of Globalization: Lessons From the United States and Mexico,* 34 Ind. L. Rev. 1243 (2001) (analyzing the economic impacts of globalization on the United States, Mexico, and workers in both countries).

180. *See* Frank del Olmo, *Keeping People Out Also Keeps Them In,* L.A. Times, July 8, 2001, at M5; Ginger Thompson, *Mexico Leader Presses U.S. to Resolve Migrants' Issues,* N.Y. Times, Nov. 27, 2002, at A12.

NOTES TO CHAPTER 4

1. Tito Bruecker & Richard Portes, *It Makes Economic Sense to Open Borders,* Financial Times, June 10, 2005, at 19.

2. *In Praise of Huddled Masses,* Wall St. J., July 3, 1984, at 24.

3. For a discussion of the role of immigrants in the U.S. labor market, see Congressional Budget Office, The Role of Immigrants in the U.S. Labor Market (Nov. 2005).

4. *See* Larry J. Obhof, *The Irrationality of Enforcement? An Economic Analysis of U.S. Immigration Law,* 12 Kan. J.L. & Pub. Pol'y 163 (2002).

5. *See* Chris Nuttall, *Intel Chief Calls for Easing of Visa Curbs,* Fin. Times, Feb. 8, 2006, at 6; S. Mitra Kalita, *For Green Card Applicants, Waiting Is the Hardest Part,* Wash. Post, July 23, 2005, at D.

6. Walter A. Ewing, *From Denial to Acceptance: Effectively Regulating Immigration to the United States,* 16 Stan. L. & Pol'y Rev. 445, 445–46 (2005) (emphasis added). Immigrants also have contributed to the creation of many

new businesses, especially in the high-tech field. *See* STUART ANDERSON AND MICHAELA PLATZER, AMERICAN MADE: THE IMPACT OF IMMIGRANT ENTREPRE-NEURS AND PROFESSIONALS ON U.S. COMPETITIVENESS (2006).

7. IMMIGRATION POLICY CENTER, ECONOMIC GROWTH AND IMMIGRATION: BRIDGING THE DEMOGRAPHIC DIVIDE (Nov. 2005).

8. *See* AMERICAN IMMIGRATION LAW FOUNDATION, MEXICAN IMMIGRANT WORKERS AND THE U.S. ECONOMY: AN INCREASINGLY VITAL ROLE (2002); AN-DREW SUM ET AL., IMMIGRANT WORKERS AND THE GREAT AMERICAN JOB MA-CHINE: THE CONTRIBUTIONS OF NEW FOREIGN IMMIGRATION TO NATIONAL AND REGIONAL LABOR FORCE GROWTH IN THE 1990S (National Business Roundtable, 2002).

9. *See* Richard W. Stevenson, *Greenspan Holds Forth Before a Friendly Panel*, N.Y. TIMES, Jan. 27, 2000, at C1; *Alan Greenspan Is Embraced as a Champion of the Huddled Masses*, WALL ST. J., Mar. 14, 2000.

10. *See* RAKESH KOCHHAR, LATINO LABOR REPORT, 2004: MORE JOBS FOR NEW IMMIGRANTS BUT AT LOWER WAGES 1–2 (Pew Hispanic Center, May 2005), at http://pewhispanic.org/files/reports/45.pdf, last visited Nov. 27, 2006.

11. *See* Sherri Day, *Jury Clears Tyson Foods in Use of Illegal Immigrants*, N.Y. TIMES, Mar. 27, 2003, at A14; David Barboza, *Tyson Foods Indicted in Plan to Smuggle Illegal Workers*, N.Y. TIMES, Dec. 20, 2001, at A1.

12. *See, e.g.,* Douglas B. Brill, *100 Workers Arrested at Wal-Mart Site*, MORNING CALL (Allentown, Pennsylvania), Nov. 18, 2005, at B4; Charles Toutant, *Wal-Mart Class-Action Plaintiffs Wield "Smoking Gun,"* N.J. L.J., Nov. 14, 2005.

13. *See* David Bacon, *And the Winner Is . . .* , AM. PROSPECT, Nov. 2005, at A12.

14. AMERICAN FARM BUREAU FEDERATION, IMPACT OF MIGRANT LABOR RE-STRICTIONS ON THE AGRICULTURAL SECTOR 1 (Feb. 2006) (emphasis added).

15. JOHN KENNETH GALBRAITH, THE NATURE OF MASS POVERTY 134 (1979).

16. *See* KENICHI OHMAE, THE BORDERLESS WORLD: POWER AND STRATEGY IN THE INTERLINKED ECONOMY (rev. ed. 1999).

17. KITTY CALAVITA, U.S. IMMIGRATION LAW AND THE CONTROL OF LABOR, 1820–1924, at 152 (1984) (analyzing business efforts to loosen immigration re-strictions in the 1920s).

18. Max Frisch, *Uberfremdung I, in* SCHWEIZ ALS HEIMAT? 219 (1990).

19. ECONOMIC REPORT OF THE PRESIDENT 93 (2005) (emphasis added).

20. *See* R. George Wright, *Federal Immigration Law and the Case for Open Entry*, 27 LOY. L.A. L. REV. 1265, 1281–89 (1994).

21. *In Praise of Huddled Masses*, WALL ST. J., July 3, 1984, at 24; *see The Simpson Curtain*, WALL ST. J., Feb. 1, 1990, at A8 ("Our view is, borders should be open.").

22. *See* CALAVITA, at 151–57; JULIAN SAMORA, LOS MOJADOS: THE WET-BACK STORY 33–57 (1971) (contending that the Border Patrol's enforcement efforts were closely related to the needs of growers); John A. Scanlan, *Immigration Law and the Illusion of Numerical Control*, 36 U. MIAMI L. REV. 819, 836 (1982) (recognizing efforts of business to ease restrictive immigration policies).

23. Pub. L. No 99–603, 100 Stat. 3359 (1986).

24. *See* Brian Grow, *Embracing Illegals*, BUS. WEEK, July 18, 2005, at 56.

25. Alan O. Sykes, *The Welfare Economics of Immigration Law: A Theoretical Survey With an Analysis of U.S. Policy, in* JUSTICE IN IMMIGRATION 158, 159 (Warren A. Schwartz, ed., 1995).

26. *See* Howard F. Chang, *Liberalized Immigration as Free Trade: Economic Welfare and the Optimal Immigration Policy*, 145 U. PA. L. REV. 1147 (1997); Howard F. Chang, *Migration as International Trade: The Economic Gains From the Liberalized Movement of Labor*, 3 UCLA J. INT'L L. & FOREIGN AFF. 371 (1999) [hereinafter Chang, *Migration as International Trade*]; *see also* Obhof (analyzing the adverse economic impact of current U.S. immigration law). *But see* JULIAN L. SIMON, THE ECONOMIC CONSEQUENCES OF IMMIGRATION at 365–66 (2d ed. 1999) (disputing that international trade and immigration are equivalent economically).

27. Bob Hamilton & John Whalley, *Efficiency and Distributional Implications of Global Restrictions on Labor Mobility*, 14 J. DEV. ECON. 61, 74 (1984).

28. GALBRAITH, at 136 (emphasis added).

29. *See, e.g.,* ROY BECK, THE CASE AGAINST IMMIGRATION: THE MORAL, ECONOMIC, SOCIAL, AND ENVIRONMENTAL REASONS FOR REDUCING U.S. IMMIGRATION BACK TO TRADITIONAL LEVELS (1996); GEORGE J. BORJAS, HEAVEN'S DOOR: IMMIGRATION POLICY AND THE AMERICAN ECONOMY (1999); PETER BRIMELOW, ALIEN NATION: COMMON SENSE ABOUT AMERICA'S IMMIGRATION DISASTER 137–77 (2d ed. 1996).

30. *See, e.g.,* SIMON; *see also* Michael A. Olivas, *Immigration Law Teaching and Scholarship in the Ivory Tower: A Response to Race Matters*, 2000 U. ILL. L. REV. 613, 632–35 (reviewing studies on the economic costs and benefits of immigration).

31. *See* NATIONAL RESEARCH COUNCIL, THE IMMIGRATION DEBATE: STUDIES ON THE ECONOMIC, DEMOGRAPHIC, AND FISCAL EFFECTS OF IMMIGRATION (1998); *see also* BILL ONG HING, TO BE AN AMERICAN 76–106 (1997) (summarizing various studies on the economic consequences of immigration); STEVEN H. LEGOMSKY, IMMIGRATION AND REFUGEE LAW AND POLICY 61–75 (4th ed. 2005) (same); Peter H. Schuck, *Alien Rumination*, 105 YALE L.J. 1963, 1981–87 (1996) (book review) (analyzing various economic studies on immigration, and concluding that any adverse economic impacts were small compared to the overall size the U.S. economy).

32. *See* LEGOMSKY, at 250 ("Since [1952], one central value that United States immigration laws have long promoted, albeit to varying degrees, is family unity.") (footnote omitted).

33. *See, e.g.,* BORJAS; SIMON; Gary S. Becker, *Give Us Your Skilled Masses,* Nov. 30, 2005, at A18; Sykes.

34. For analysis of the brain drain problem, INTERNATIONAL MIGRATION, REMITTANCES, AND THE BRAIN DRAIN (World Bank, Caglar Ozden & Maurice Schiff eds., 2005) and DEVESH KAPUR & JOHN McHALE, GIVE US YOUR BEST AND BRIGHTEST (2005).

35. Enid Trucios-Haynes, *Temporary Workers and Future Immigration Policy Conflicts: Protecting U.S. Workers and Satisfying the Demand for Global Human Capital,* 40 BRANDEIS L.J. 967, 986 (2002) (footnote omitted).

36. *See, e.g.,* Fran Ansley, *Inclusive Boundaries and Other (Im)possible Paths Toward Community Development in a Global World,* 150 U. PA. L. REV. 353 (2001); Gil Gott, *Critical Race Globalism? Global Political Economy, and the Intersections of Race, Nation, and Class,* 33 U.C. DAVIS L. REV. 1503 (2000); Chantal Thomas, *Globalization and the Reproduction of Hierarchy,* 33 U.C. DAVIS L. REV. 1451 (2000); Sylvia R. Lazos Vargas, *Globalization or Global Subordination? How LatCrit Links the Local to Global and the Global to the Local,* 33 U.C. DAVIS L. REV. 1429, 1436–50 (2000).

37. *See* Clyde Summers, *The Battle in Seattle: Free Trade, Labor Rights, and Societal Values,* 22 U. PA. J. INT'L ECON. L. 61 (2001); Susan Tiefenbrun, *Free Trade and Protectionism: The Semiotics of Seattle,* 17 ARIZ. J. INT'L & COMP. L. 257 (2000).

38. *See* CONTEMPORARY DEBATES IN APPLIED ETHICS 211–14 (Andrew I. Cohen & Christopher Heath Wellman eds., 2005).

39. *See, e.g.,* PHILIP L. MARTIN & DAVID A. MARTIN, THE ENDLESS QUEST: HELPING AMERICA'S FARM WORKERS (1994).

40. *See, e.g.,* VERNON M. BRIGGS, JR., MASS IMMIGRATION AND THE NATIONAL INTEREST 211–15 (1992); MICHAEL LIND, THE NEXT AMERICAN NATION: THE NEW NATIONALISM AND THE FOURTH AMERICAN REVOLUTION 181–216 (1996).

41. *See, e.g.,* BRIGGS, at 213–15; Steven Schulman & Robert C. Smith, *Immigration and African Americans, in* AFRICAN AMERICANS IN THE U.S. ECONOMY 199 (Cecilia A. Conrad, John Whitehead, Patrick Mason, & James Stewart eds., 2005); LIND, 139–216; HELP OR HINDRANCE? THE ECONOMIC IMPLICATIONS OF IMMIGRATION FOR AFRICAN AMERICANS (Daniel S. Hamermesh & Frank D. Bean, eds., 1998); STRANGERS AT THE GATES: NEW IMMIGRANTS IN URBAN AMERICA (Roger Waldinger ed., 2001); ROGER WALDINGER, STILL THE PROMISED CITY? AFRICAN-AMERICANS AND NEW IMMIGRANTS IN POSTINDUSTRIAL NEW YORK (1996); *see also* Lawrence H. Fuchs, *The Reactions of Black*

Americans to Immigration, in IMMIGRATION RECONSIDERED: HISTORY, SOCIOLOGY, AND POLITICS 293 (Virginia Yans-McLaughlin ed., 1990) (analyzing public opinion polls showing that African Americans historically have supported immigration restrictions); Marion Crain & Ken Matheny, *Labor's Identity Crisis,* 89 CAL. L. REV. 1767, 1826–27 (2001) (noting the conflict between African American and Latina/o immigrant workers).

42. *See* GEORGE J. BORJAS & LAWRENCE F. KATZ, THE EVOLUTION OF THE MEXICAN BORN WORKFORCE IN THE UNITED STATES (Apr. 2005).

43. *See* Chang, *Migration as International Trade,* at 408–09 (citing and summarizing studies).

44. *See* Eduardo Porter, *Cost of Illegal Immigration May Be Less Than Meets the Eye,* N.Y. TIMES, Apr. 16, 2006, at § 3, p. 3. One study concludes that immigration generally increases the wage level and constitutes only a small fraction of the increase in the wage gap between the college educated and high school dropouts from 1990 to 2004. *See* GIANMARCO I.P. OTTAVIANO & GIOVANNI PERI, RETHINKING THE EFFECTS OF IMMIGRATION ON WAGES (July 2006).

45. *See* ROGER WALDINGER & MICHAEL I. LICHTER, HOW THE OTHER HALF WORKS: IMMIGRATION AND THE SOCIAL ORGANIZATION OF LABOR (2003); ETHNIC LOS ANGELES (Roger Waldinger & Mehdi Bozorgmehr eds., 1996); WALDINGER, STILL THE PROMISED CITY?

46. *See* Leticia Saucedo, *The Browning of the American Workplace: Protecting Workers in Increasingly Latino-ized Occupations,* 80 NOTRE DAME L. REV. 303 (2004).

47. *See* Roger Waldinger, *Black/Immigrant Competition Re-Assessed: New Evidence From Los Angeles,* 40 SOC. PERSPECTIVES 365 (1997).

48. *See* RONALD G. EHRENBERG & ROBERT S. SMITH, MODERN LABOR ECONOMICS: THEORY AND PUBLIC POLICY 353 (5th ed. 1994).

49. *See* Lawrence F. Katz & Kevin M. Murphy, *Changes in Relative Wages, 1963–1987: Supply and Demand Factors,* 107 Q. J. OF ECON. 35 (1992).

50. GIOVANNI PERRI, IMMIGRANTS, SKILLS, AND WAGES: REASSESSING THE ECONOMIC GAINS FROM IMMIGRATION (Immigration Policy Center, 2006) (emphasis added).

51. *See* Chang, *Migration as International Trade,* at 409–10.

52. *See generally* MICHAEL B. KATZ, THE UNDESERVING POOR: FROM THE WAR ON POVERTY TO THE WAR ON WELFARE (1990) (analyzing the politics of welfare).

53. *See* DAVID CARD, IS THE NEW IMMIGRATION REALLY SO BAD? (National Bureau of Economic Research Working Paper, Aug. 2005).

54. *See* GIANMARCO I.P. OTTAVIANO, RETHINKING GAINS FROM IMMIGRATION: THEORY AND EVIDENCE FROM THE U.S. (Nat'l Bureau of Economic Research Working Paper, Sept. 2005).

55. *See* 3 PHILIP S. FONER, HISTORY OF THE LABOR MOVEMENT IN THE

UNITED STATES 256–81 (1964) (describing the traditionally restrictionist positions of the American Federation of Labor).

56. *See* SUSAN FERRISS & RICARDO SANDOVAL, THE FIGHT IN THE FIELDS 242–44 (1997).

57. *See* Crain & Matheny, at 1828–30.

58. *See* Frederick M. Abbott, *Foundation-Building for Western Hemispheric Integration*, 17 NW. J. INT'L L. & BUS. 900, 922 (1996–97). *See generally* DALE HATHAWAY, ALLIES ACROSS THE BORDER: MEXICO'S "AUTHENTIC LABOR FRONT" AND GLOBAL SOLIDARITY (2000) (analyzing efforts by Mexican labor unions to organize workers across borders).

59. *See* AFL-CIO, Immigration, Feb. 16, 2000. For a report on the success of the AFL-CIO's new emphasis, see Rosanna M. Kreychman & Heather H. Volik, *The Immigrant Workers Project of the AFL-CIO*, 50 N.Y.L. SCH. L. REV. 561 (2005/06).

60. *See* Linda Bosniak, *Citizenship and Work*, 27 N.C. J. INT'L L. & COM. REG. 497, 503–05 (2002).

61. *See* EHRENBERG & SMITH, at 351.

62. *See* Hoffman Plastic Compounds, Inc. v. NLRB, 535 U.S. 137 (2002).

63. *See generally* Kevin R. Johnson, *Public Benefits and Immigration: The Intersection of Immigration Status, Ethnicity, Gender, and Class*, 42 UCLA L. REV. 1509 (1995).

64. *See* Howard F. Chang, *The Immigration Paradox: Poverty, Distributive Justice, and Liberal Egalitarianism*, 52 DEPAUL L. REV. 759 (2003) (analyzing complexities caused by the fact that many citizens are unwilling to bear fiscal costs associated with immigration).

65. *See generally* Johnson, *Public Benefits and Immigration* (analyzing the impacts of Proposition 187 in light of the history of concern with immigrant public benefit consumption); Kevin R. Johnson, *An Essay on Immigration Politics, Popular Democracy, and California's Proposition 187: The Political Relevance and Legal Irrelevance of Race*, 70 WASH. L. REV. 629 (1995) (analyzing the anti-Mexican sentiment at the core of the initiative campaign); Ruben J. Garcia, Comment, *Critical Race Theory and Proposition 187: The Racial Politics of Immigration Law*, 17 CHICANO-LATINO L. REV. 118 (1995) (same). A federal court invalidated the bulk of Proposition 187 as an unconstitutional encroachment on federal power over immigration. *See* League of United Latin Am. Citizens v. Wilson, 908 F. Supp. 755 (C.D. Cal. 1995).

66. *See* EHRENBERG & SMITH, at 355.

67. *See* B. LINDSAY LOWELL & ROBERTO SURO, THE IMPROVING EDUCATIONAL PROFILE OF LATINO IMMIGRANTS (Pew Hispanic Center Report, 2002).

68. *See* Mark Fineman, *Mexico Redraws Faces of Migrants*, L.A. TIMES, July 11, 2001, at A3 (reporting the findings of a report of the Mexican National Population Council).

69. Congress later restored certain benefits to legal immigrants. *See* Noncitizen Benefit Clarification and Other Technical Amendments of 1998, Pub. L. No. 105–306, 112 Stat. 2926 (1998).

70. Francine J. Lipman, *Taxing Undocumented Immigrants: Separate, Unequal and Without Representation*, 9 HARV. LATINO L. REV. 1, 5 (2006) (footnotes omitted); *see* Derrick Z. Jackson, *Undocumented Workers Contribute Plenty*, BOSTON GLOBE, Apr. 12, 2006, at 13; *see also* Kathleen Pender, *Losing Out on a Huge Cash Stash*, S.F. CHRON., Apr. 11, 2006, at C1 (reporting on Standard & Poor's analysis concluding that the cost of providing services to undocumented immigrants are largely offset by economic benefits).

71. *See* Laura Fernandez Feitl, *Caring for the Elderly Undocumented Workers in the United States: Discretionary Reality or Undeniable Duty?*, 13 ELDER L.J. 227 (2005); Eduardo Porter, *Illegal Immigrants Are Bolstering Social Security With Billions*, N.Y. TIMES, Apr. 5, 2005, at 1.

72. *See* Johnson, *Public Benefits and Immigration*, at 1523 n.50.

73. *See* GORDON H. HANSON, IMMIGRATION POLICY (Nat'l Bureau of Economic Research (July 2004); GORDON H. HANSON, WHY DOES IMMIGRATION DIVIDE AMERICA? PUBLIC FINANCE AND POLITICAL OPPOSITION TO OPEN BORDERS (Nat'l Bureau of Economic Research (March 2005).

74. *See* Nathanael J. Scheer, Note and Comment, *Keeping the Promise: Financing EMTALA's Guarantee of Emergency Medical Care for Undocumented Aliens in Arizona*, 35 ARIZ. ST. L.J. 1413, 1413–14 (2003).

75. *See, e.g.,* CENTER FOR CONTINUING STUDY OF THE CALIFORNIA ECONOMY, THE IMPACT OF IMMIGRATION ON THE CALIFORNIA ECONOMY: 2005 CALIFORNIA REGIONAL ECONOMIES PROJECT (2005); MISSISSIPPI OFFICE OF THE STATE AUDITOR, THE IMPACT OF ILLEGAL IMMIGRATION ON MISSISSIPPI: COSTS AND POPULATION TRENDS (2006).

76. *See* Johnson, *Public Benefits and Immigration*, at 1539–41; Stephen H. Legomsky, *Immigration, Federalism, and the Welfare State*, 42 UCLA L. REV. 1453, 1470–74 (1995).

77. *See* Legomsky, *Immigration, Federalism, and the Welfare State*, at 1470–74 (analyzing why federal government should provide funds to states for costs associated with immigration).

78. *See, e.g.,* Graham v. Richardson, 403 U.S. 365 (1971); League of United Latin American Citizens v. Wilson, 997 F. Supp. 1244 (C.D. Cal. 1997).

79. *See* Arizona v. United States, 104 F.3d 1095 (9th Cir.), *cert. denied*, 522 U.S. 806 (1997); California v. United States, 104 F.3d 1086 (9th Cir. 1997); Chiles v. United States, 69 F.3d 1084 (11th Cir. 1995), *cert. denied*, 517 U.S. 1188 (1996); New Jersey v. United States, 91 F.3d 463 (3d Cir. 1996); Padavan v. United States, 82 F.3d 23 (2d Cir. 1996); Texas v. United States, 106 F.3d 661 (5th Cir. 1997).

80. *See* Hiroshi Motomura, *Federalism, International Human Rights, and*

Immigration Exceptionalism, 70 U. COLO. L. REV. 1361, 1366–68 (1999); Jay T. Jorgensen, Comment, *The Practical Power of State and Local Governments to Enforce Federal Immigration Laws,* 1997 BYU L. REV. 899, 937–39.

81. 457 U.S. 202, 218–19 (footnote omitted).

82. *See* Michael A. Olivas, *IIRIRA, the DREAM Act, and Undocumented College Student Residency,* 30 J. C. & UNIV. L. 435 (2004); Victor C. Romero, *Postsecondary School Education Benefits for Undocumented Immigrants: Promises and Pitfalls,* 27 N.C. J. INT'L L. & COM. REG. 393 (2002); Kathleen A. Connolly, Comment, *In Search of the American Dream: An Examination of Undocumented Students, In-State Tuition, and the DREAM Act,* 55 CATH. U. L. REV. 193 (2005).

83. *See* Josh Burek, *California Clash: Tuition for Illegal Immigrants,* CHR. SCI. MON., Dec. 19, 2005, at 2; Stuart Silverstein, *Out of State Students Sue Over Tuition,* L.A. TIMES, Dec. 15, 2005, at B3.

84. *See* Richard Sybert, *Population, Immigration and Growth in California,* 31 SAN DIEGO L. REV. 945, 982–84 (1994).

85. Schuck, at 1988–89 (emphasis added).

86. KRISTIN F. BUTCHER & A. M. PIEHL, WHY ARE IMMIGRANTS' INCARCERATION RATES SO LOW? EVIDENCE OF SELECTIVE IMMIGRATION, DETERRENCE, AND PUNISHMENT 2 (Federal Reserve Bank of Chicago, Nov. 2005) (emphasis added).

87. *See* Robert J. Sampson, *Open Doors Don't Invite Criminals,* WALL STREET J., March 11, 2006, at A27.

88. *See* Robert A. Mikos, *Enforcing State Law in Congress's Shadow,* 90 CORNELL L. REV. 1411, 1444–56 (2005).

89. *See* Peter H. Schuck & John Williams, *Removing Criminal Aliens: The Pitfalls and Promises of Federalism,* 22 HARV. J.L. & PUB. POL'Y 367 (1999); U.S. Senator Jeff Sessions & Cynthia Hayden, *Immigration in the Twenty-First Century: The Growing Role for State & Local Law Enforcement in the Realm of Immigration Law,* 16 STAN. L. & POL'Y REV. 323 (2005).

90. *See* Huyen Pham, *The Inherent Flaws in the Inherent Authority Position: Why Inviting Local Enforcement of Immigration Laws Violates the Constitution,* 31 FLA. ST. U. L. REV. 965 (2004); Michael J. Wishnie, *Civil Liberties in a New America: State and Local Police Enforcement of Immigration Laws,* 6 U. PA. J. CONST. L. 1084 (2004).

91. *See* Bill Ong Hing, *Deported for Shoplifting?,* WASH. POST, Dec. 29, 2002, at B7.

92. *See* Kevin R. Johnson, *September 11 and Mexican Immigrants: Collateral Damage Comes Home,* 52 DEPAUL L. REV. 849, 853–55 (2003).

93. *See* Robert J. Lopez, Rich Connell & Chris Kraul, *Gang Uses Deportation to Its Advantage to Flourish in U.S.,* L.A. TIMES, Oct. 30, 2005, at A1.

94. *See, e.g.,* OTIS L. GRAHAM, UNGUARDED GATES: A HISTORY OF AMERICA'S IMMIGRATION CRISIS 135–49 (2004).

95. *See* Peter L. Reich, *Environmental Metaphor in the Alien Benefits Debate*, 42 UCLA L. REV. 1577, 1579–81 (1995) (describing roots of Federation of American Immigration Reform in environmental movement).

96. *See* Kenneth R. Weiss, *Sierra Club Members Vote to Stay Neutral in Immigration Debate*, L.A. TIMES, Apr. 26, 2005, at B3.

97. *See* Lee Hall, *Aliens on Spaceship Earth: The Sierra Club Elections*, 10 BENDER'S IMMIGRATION BULLETIN, July 1, 2005, at 1091.

98. *See* Anne Minard, *U.S. Immigration Law Could Harm Desert Animals, Critics Say,"* NAT'L GEOGRAPHIC NEWS, Mar. 31, 2006, at http://news.national geographic.com/news/2006/03/0331_060331_desert_fence.html, last visited Aug. 21, 2006.

99. *See* PAUL R. KRUGMAN & MAURICE OBSTFELD, INTERNATIONAL ECONOMICS: THEORY AND POLICY 177–78 (3d ed. 1994).

100. *See* Roger Nett, *The Civil Right We Are Not Ready For: The Right of Free Movement of People on the Face of the Earth*, 81 ETHICS 212, 227 (1971).

101. *See* James C. Hathaway, *A Reconsideration of the Underlying Premise of Refugee Law*, 31 HARV. INT'L L.J. 129 (1990).

102. *See generally* Randall Hansen, *Migration to Europe Since 1945: Its History and Its Lessons*, POL. Q., 2005, at 25.

103. *See* Keith B. Richburg, *The EU and the Power of the People*, WASH. POST, Nov. 8, 2002, at A27.

104. *See* Larry Rohter, *South American Trading Bloc Frees Movement of Its People*, N.Y. TIMES, Nov. 24, 2002, at § 1, p. 6.

105. *See* Paul de Bendern, *Maverick Gaddafi Calls for Borderless Africa*, REUTERS, July 4, 2005.

106. *See* Kevin R. Johnson, *Regional Integration in North America and Europe: Lessons About Civil Rights and Equal Citizenship*, 9 U. MIAMI INT'L & COMP. L. REV. 33, 40–43 (2000–2001).

107. *See* Kitty Calavita, *Immigration, Law, and Marginalization in a Global Economy: Notes From Spain*, 32 LAW & SOC'Y REV. 529, 542–48 (1998).

108. *See* Bob Hepple, *Race and Law in Fortress Europe*, 67 MOD. L. REV. 1 (2004); Lydia Esteve Gonzalez & Richard MacBride, *Fortress Europe: Fear of Immigration? Present and Future of Immigration Law and Policy in Spain*, 6 U.C. DAVIS J. INT'L L. & POL'Y 153 (2000). *See generally* CHRISTIAN JOPPKE, SELECTING BY ORIGIN: ETHNIC MIGRATION IN THE LIBERAL STATE (2005).

109. *See* Michael A. Becker, Note, *Managing Diversity in the European Union: Inclusive European Citizenship and Third-Country Nationals*, 7 YALE HUM. RTS. & DEV. L.J. 132 (2004); Aristides Diaz-Pedrosa, Note, *A Tale of Competing Policies: The Creation of Havens for Illegal Immigrants and the Black Market Economy*, 37 CORNELL INT'L L.J. 431 (2004).

110. *See* Johnson, *Regional Integration in North America and Europe*, at 42–43.

111. *See* JASON ACKLESON, ACHIEVING "SECURITY AND PROSPERITY": MIGRATION AND NORTH AMERICAN ECONOMIC INTEGRATION (Feb. 2006) (Immigration Policy Center); T. Alexander Aleinikoff, *Legal Immigration Reform: Toward Rationality and Equity, in* BLUEPRINTS FOR AN IDEAL LEGAL IMMIGRATION POLICY 5, 5–6 (Richard D. Lamm & Alan Simpson eds., 2001); Kevin R. Johnson, *Free Trade and Closed Borders: NAFTA and Mexican Immigration to the United States*, 27 U.C. DAVIS L. REV. 937 (1994); John A. Scanlan, *A View From the United States-Social, Economic, and Legal Change, the Persistence of the State, and Immigration Policy in the Coming Century*, 2 IND. J. GLOBAL LEG. STUDS. 79, 123–25 (1994); Gabriela A. Gallegos, Comment, *Border Matters: Redefining the National Interest in U.S.-Mexico Immigration and Trade Policy*, 92 CAL. L. REV. 1729 (2004); Elizabeth L. Gunn, Note, *Regionalizing Labor Policy Through NAFTA: Beyond President Bush's Temporary Worker Proposal*, 28 B.C. INT'L & COMP. L. REV. 353 (2005).

112. *See* Agreement for Cooperation in the Examination of Refugee Status Claims from Nationals of Third Countries, Aug. 30, 2002, U.S.-Canada at http://www.cic.gc.ca/english/policy/safe-third.html, last visited Nov. 27, 2006; Audrey Macklin, *Disappointing Refugees: Reflections on the Canada-U.S. Safe Third Country Agreement*, 36 COLUM. HUM. RTS. L. REV. 365 (2005); *Special ABA Committee Report on the Canada-U.S. Border: Balancing Trade, Security, and Migrant Rights in the Post-9/11 Era: ABA Immigration and Nationality Committee, International Law Section*, 19 GEO. IMMIGR. L.J. 199 (2004).

113. *See* Alan D. Bersin, *El Tercer Pais: Reinventing the U.S./Mexico Border*, 48 STAN. L. REV. 1413 (1996).

114. *See* Johnson, *September 11 and Mexican Immigrants*, at 866–67.

115. *See* Richard Boudreaux, *Frustration Marks Fox, Bush Talks*, L.A. TIMES, Oct. 27, 2002, at 3. Frustration over the inability to secure a migration accord with the United States ultimately contributed to the resignation of Mexico's prominent foreign minister, Jorge Castañeda. *See* Tim Weiner, *Foreign Minister in Mexico Will Quit, Frustrated by the U.S.*, N.Y. TIMES, Jan. 9, 2003, at A5.

116. *See* David Stout, *Bush and Neighbors Promise to Cooperate*, INT'L HERALD TRIB., Mar. 24, 2005, at 5.

117. *See* CONGRESSIONAL RESEARCH SERV., MEXICO-U.S. RELATIONS: ISSUES FOR THE 109TH CONGRESS 8–13 (updated June 2, 2005).

118. *See* REAL ID Act of 2005, Title B of the Emergency Supplemental Appropriations Act for Defense, the Global War on Terror, and Tsunami Relief, 2005, 109 Pub. L. No. 12, 119 Stat. 231 (2005).

119. *See* Jorge A. Vargas, *U.S. Border Patrol Abuses, Undocumented Mexican Workers, and International Human Rights*, 2 SAN DIEGO INT'L L. J. 1, 80 (2001); Alexander C. O'Neill, Note, *Emigrant Remittances: Policies to Increase Inflows and Maximize Benefits*, 9 IND. J. GLOBAL LEGAL STUD. 345 (2001).

120. The Mexican government's interest in protecting migrant labor in the United States thus is not solely humanitarian; increasing wages and benefits for Mexican migrants also increases remittances to Mexico. *See* Richard Griswold del Castillo, *Mexican Intellectuals' Perception of Mexican Americans and Chicanos, 1920-Present*, 27 AZTLÁN 33, 49 (2002).

121. *See* U.S. COMM'N FOR THE STUDY OF INT'L MIGRATION AND COOPERATIVE ECON. DEV., UNAUTHORIZED MIGRATION: AN ECONOMIC DEVELOPMENT RESPONSE (1990); Philip L. Martin, *Economic Integration and Migration: The Case of NAFTA*, 3 UCLA J. INT'L L. & FOREIGN AFF. 419 (1998).

NOTES TO CHAPTER 5

1. *See* DOUGLAS S. MASSEY, BACKFIRE AT THE BORDER: WHY ENFORCEMENT WITHOUT LEGALIZATION CANNOT STOP ILLEGAL IMMIGRATION 1 (Cato Inst. 2005).

2. *See* Patricia Manson, *ABA Calls for Overhaul of Immigration*, CHI. DAILY LAW BULL., Feb. 14, 2006, at 1.

3. *See* Mike Allen & Jim VanderHei, *Homeland Security Nominee Kerik Pulls Out*, WASH. POST, Dec. 11, 2004, at A1; Eric Lipton & William K. Rashbaum, *Kerik Withdraws as Bush's Nominee for Security Post*, N.Y. TIMES, Dec. 11, 2004, at A1.

4. *See* JOHN HIGHAM, STRANGERS IN THE LAND: PATTERNS OF AMERICAN NATIVISM 1860–1925, at 29, 196–200 (3d ed. 1994). For analysis of the integration of German immigrants into U.S. society in the early twentieth century, see Allan C. Carlson, *The Peculiar Legacy of German-Americans*, SOCIETY, Jan.-Feb. 2003, at 77.

5. *See* Kevin R. Johnson, *Race, The Immigration Laws, and Domestic Race Relations: A "Magic Mirror" Into the Heart of Darkness*, 73 IND. L. J. 1111, 1120–27 (1998).

6. *See* Daniel A. Farber & Suzanna Sherry, *Is the Radical Critique of Merit Anti-Semitic?*, 83 CAL. L. REV. 853, 869–71 (1995) (reviewing economic data). Because this statistical information can be taken out of context, it must be used carefully. *See* Robert S. Chang, *Toward an Asian American Legal Scholarship: Critical Race Theory, Post-Structuralism, and Narrative Space*, 81 CAL. L. REV. 1243, 1258–65 (1993). Racism against Asian Americans, including persons of Chinese and Japanese ancestry, remains a serious social problem in the modern United States. *See generally* ROBERT S. CHANG, DISORIENTED: ASIAN AMERICANS, LAW, AND THE NATION-STATE (1999); FRANK H. WU, YELLOW: RACE IN AMERICA BEYOND BLACK AND WHITE (2002).

7. *See* Johnson, *Race, The Immigration Laws, and Domestic Race Relations*, at 1127–31.

8. *See* Karen C. Tumlin, Comment, *Suspect First: How Terrorism Policy Is Reshaping Immigration Policy,* 92 CAL. L. REV. 1173 (2004).

9. *See, e.g.,* PETER BRIMELOW, ALIEN NATION: COMMON SENSE ABOUT AMERICA'S IMMIGRATION DISASTER (1996) (advocating a moratorium on immigration because of, among other things, difficulties in the assimilation of immigrants).

10. *See* Peter H. Schuck, *Immigration at the Turn of the New Century,* 33 CASE W. RES. J. INT'L L. 1, 3 (2001) (providing data).

11. *See* Kevin R. Johnson, *"Melting Pot" or "Ring of Fire"? Assimilation and the Mexican-American Experience,* 85 CAL. L. REV. 1259, 1281 (1997). *See generally* LINDA CHÁVEZ, OUT OF THE BARRIO: TOWARD A NEW POLITICS OF HISPANIC ASSIMILATION (1991) (analyzing assimilation of Latina/os in U.S. society); PETER D. SALINS, ASSIMILATION, AMERICAN STYLE (1997) (offering a positive view of immigrant assimilation in U.S. history).

12. *See* Berta Esperanza Hernández-Truyol, *Building Bridges-Latinas and Latinos at the Crossroads: Realities, Rhetoric and Replacement,* 25 COLUM. HUM. RTS. L. REV. 369, 383–93 (1994); *see also* Alice G. Abreu, *Lessons From LatCrit: Insiders and Outsiders, All at the Same Time,* 53 U. MIAMI L. REV. 787 (1999) (reflecting on the identity of Cuban Americans and how it relates to the identities of other Latina/os).

13. *See* Ricardo Alonso-Zaldivar, *Latinos Give Bush High Job Approval Rating, Poll Shows,* L.A. TIMES, Aug. 21, 2002, at A10; Matea Gold, *Rivals Go After Davis' Latino Support,* L.A. TIMES, July 13, 2002, at B12.

14. *See* Matea Gold, *Simon Takes Chance With Pete Wilson Endorsement,* L.A. TIMES, Oct. 24, 2002, at B1; James Sterngold, *Hoping to Run California, and Recast the Republicans,* N.Y. TIMES, Jan. 28, 2002, at A8.

15. *See* Steve Scott, *Competing for the New Majority Vote,* 31 CAL. J. 16, 18 (2000) (discussing the rapid increase in Latina/o elected officials in California).

16. *See* Ryan D. Frei, Comment, *Reforming U.S. Immigration Policy in an Era of Latin American Immigration: The Logic Inherent in Accommodating the Inevitable,* 39 U. RICH. L. REV. 1355 (2005).

17. *See* Saskia Sassen, *Regulating Immigration in a Global Age: A New Policy Landscape,* 570 ANNALS AM. ACAD. POL. & SOC. SCI. 65 (2000).

18. *See* JEFFREY S. PASSEL, UNAUTHORIZED MIGRANTS: NUMBERS AND CHARACTERISTICS 3–4 (Pew Hispanic Center 2005).

19. *See* JEFFREY S. PASSEL, THE SIZE AND CHARACTERISTICS OF THE UNAUTHORIZED MIGRANT POPULATION IN THE U.S. (Pew Hispanic Center, Mar. 7, 2006).

20. JEFFERY S. PASSEL & ROBERTO SURO, RISE, PEAK, AND DECLINE: TRENDS IN U.S. IMMIGRATION 1992–2004, at iii (Pew Hispanic Center, Sept. 2005) (emphasis added).

21. DOUGLAS S. MASSEY, BEYOND THE BORDER BUILDUP: TOWARDS A NEW APPROACH TO MEXICO-U.S. MIGRATION 1 (American Immigration Law Foundation, Sept. 2005).

22. *See generally* PETER ANDREAS, BORDER GAMES: POLICING THE U.S.-MEXICO DIVIDE (2000) (analyzing the lack of effectiveness of border enforcement); DOUGLAS S. MASSEY ET AL., BEYOND SMOKE AND MIRRORS: MEXICAN IMMIGRATION IN AN ERA OF ECONOMIC INTEGRATION 163 (2002); (characterizing current U.S. border enforcement as "smoke and mirrors").

23. BELINDA I. REYES ET AL., HOLDING THE LINE? THE EFFECT OF THE RECENT BORDER BUILD-UP ON UNAUTHORIZED IMMIGRATION, at viii, xii (Public Policy Institute of California, 2002); *see* Manuela Angelucci, U.S. Border Enforcement and the Net Flow of Mexican Illegal Migration (IZA, June 2005). For a study showing that even some Border Patrol officers believe that the current border enforcement strategy is misguided, see ROBERT LEE MARIL, PATROLLING CHAOS: THE U.S. BORDER PATROL IN DEEP SOUTH TEXAS (2004).

24. *See* Anna Gorman, *A Day's Labor of Love,* L.A. TIMES, Aug 22, 2005, at B3.

25. *See* generally ABEL VALENZUELA JR. ET AL., ON THE CORNER: DAY LABOR IN THE UNITED STATES (2006) (studying day laborers in United States).

26. *See* Eduardo Porter & Elisabeth Malkin, *Way North of the Border: In Minnesota, a Community of Mexican Immigrants Takes Root,* N.Y. TIMES, Sept. 30, 2005, at C1.

27. CONGRESSIONAL RESEARCH SERV., BORDER SECURITY: APPREHENSION OF "OTHER THAN MEXICAN" ALIENS, at CRS-11, 17, 18 (Sept. 2005).

28. *See* Olsen v. Albright, 990 F. Supp. 31 (D.D.C. 1997) (granting summary judgment in favor of former State Department consular officer who claimed he was unlawfully terminated for failing to follow agency practice of discriminating on basis of visa applicant's race, ethnicity, national origin, economic class, and physical appearance).

29. *See* CONGRESSIONAL RESEARCH SERVICE, U.S. IMMIGRATION POLICY ON PERMANENT ADMISSIONS (Sept. 2005).

30. *See* U.S. Dep't of State, Visa Bulletin for May 2006 (Apr. 2006), http://www.travel.state.gov/visa/frvi/bulletin/bulletin_2868.html (last visited Nov. 27, 2006).

31. *See* Charles H. Whitebread, *Freeing Ourselves From the Prohibition Idea in the Twenty-First Century,* 33 SUFFOLK U.L. REV. 235, 237–40 (2000). *See generally* HERBERT ASBURY, THE GREAT ILLUSION: AN INFORMAL HISTORY OF PROHIBITION (1950) (describing the emergence of Prohibition in the United States). A similar analogy has been made between Prohibition and the modern war on drugs. *See, e.g.,* David D. Cole, *Formalism, Realism, and the War on Drugs,* 35 SUFFOLK U.L. REV. 241 (2001); Erik Grant Luna, *Our Vietnam: The Prohibition Apocalypse,* 46 DEPAUL L. REV. 483 (1997); Charles H. White-

bread, *"Us" and "Them" and the Nature of Moral Regulation,* 74 S. CAL. L. REV. 361 (2000) [hereinafter Whitebread, *Moral Regulation*].

32. *See* HIGHAM, at 267–68; Kenneth L. Karst, *Paths to Belonging: The Constitution and Cultural Identity,* 64 N.C. L. REV. 303, 314–15 (1986).

33. *See* William J. Stuntz, *The Pathological Politics of Criminal Law,* 100 MICH. L. REV. 505, 574–75 (2001); William J. Stuntz, *The Legal Construction of Norms: Self-Defeating Crimes,* 86 VA. L. REV. 1871, 1877–78 (2000).

34. *See generally* Kevin R. Johnson, *Public Benefits and Immigration: The Intersection of Immigration Status, Ethnicity, Gender, and Class,* 42 UCLA L. REV. 1509 (1995) (analyzing history of discrimination against the poor in the U.S. immigration laws).

35. *See* PASSEL, at 19.

36. Sidney J. Spaeth, Comment, *The Twenty-First Amendment and State Control Over Intoxicating Liquor: Accommodating the Federal Interest,* 79 CAL. L. REV. 161, 162 (1991).

37. *See* Whitebread, *Moral Regulation,* at 364–65.

38. *See* Nora V. Demleitner, *Organized Crime and Prohibition: What Difference Does Legalization Make?,* 15 WHITTIER L. REV. 613 (1994); Benito Gaguine, *The Federal Alcohol Administration,* 7 GEO. WASH. L. REV. 844, 845 (1939).

39. *See* LAURENCE F. SCHMECKEBIER, THE BUREAU OF PROHIBITION: ITS HISTORY, ACTIVITIES AND ORGANIZATION 53 (1929) ("A too free use of firearms has been one of the criticisms directed against prohibition agents, and alleged cases of unjustifiable use of weapons have been reported.").

40. *See* Rory K. Little, *Myths and Principles of Federalization,* 46 HASTINGS L.J. 1029, 1068 (1995); Thomas J. Maroney, *Fifty Years of Federalization of Criminal Law: Sounding the Alarm or "Crying Wolf"?,* 50 SYRACUSE L. REV. 1317, 1324–25 (2000).

41. *See* Edwin R. Keedy, *Administration of the Criminal Law,* 31 YALE L.J. 240, 240 (1922). Juries today at times have been willing to act in a similar way by refusing to convict in certain instances despite strong evidence that a drug crime had been committed. *See* Paul Butler, *Racially Based Jury Nullification: Black Power in the Criminal Justice System,* 105 YALE L.J. 677 (1995).

42. *See* Linda Kelly, *The Fantastic Adventure of Supermom and the Alien: Educating Immigration Policy on the Facts of Life,* 31 CONN. L. REV. 1045, 1069 (1999) (discussing the cases of Zoe Baird and Kimba Wood, both of whom withdrew from consideration for Attorney General after their nominations because of controversies involving their employment of undocumented domestic service workers); Mary Romero, *Immigration, the Servant Problem, and the Legacy of the Domestic Labor Debate: "Where Can You Find Good Help These Days!,"* 53 U. MIAMI L. REV. 1045, 1057–62 (1999) (same).

43. *See* David Barboza, *Tyson Foods Indicted in Plan to Smuggle Illegal*

Workers, N.Y. TIMES, Dec. 20, 2001, at A1. Tyson Foods was indicted by the federal government, and later acquitted, for allegedly trafficking in immigrant workers. *See* Sherri Day, *Jury Clears Tyson Foods in Use of Illegal Immigrants,* N.Y. TIMES, Mar. 27, 2003, at A14.

44. *See* David Barboza, *Meatpackers' Profits Hinge on Pool of Immigrant Labor,* N.Y. TIMES, Dec. 21, 2001, at A26.

45. *See* Maria Isabel Medina, *The Criminalization of Immigration Law: Employer Sanctions and Marriage Fraud,* 5 GEO. MASON L. REV. 669, 717–29 (1997); *see also* United States v. Hibbler, 159 F.3d 233, 237 (6th Cir. 1998) (referring to immigration violations as " 'victimless' crimes") (quoting United States v. Boos, 127 F.3d 1207, 1210 (9th Cir. 1997)); Robert W. McGee, *Some Thoughts on the Relationship Between Property Rights and Immigration Policy,* 42 CLEV. ST. L. REV. 495, 504 (1994) (same).

46. Medina, at 671–72 (footnotes omitted).

47. *See, e.g.,* BILL ONG HING, TO BE AN AMERICAN: CULTURAL PLURALISM AND THE RHETORIC OF ASSIMILATION 32–43 (2000) (relating the story of Rodolfo Martinez Padilla, an immigrant from Mexico); Gerald P. López, *The Work We Know So Little About,* 42 STAN. L. REV. 1 (1989) (recounting the story of undocumented immigrant woman working on the economic fringes of U.S. society).

48. *See* ANN CRITTENDEN, SANCTUARY: A STORY OF AMERICAN CONSCIENCE AND THE LAW IN COLLISION (1988) (analyzing the sanctuary movement in the 1980s in which religious workers and others sought to provide sanctuary to Central American refugees); IGNATIUS BAU, THIS GROUND IS HOLY: CHURCH SANCTUARY AND CENTRAL AMERICAN REFUGEES (1985) (offering a religious justification for the sanctuary movement).

49. *See generally* Bill Ong Hing, *The Immigrant as Criminal: Punishing Dreamers,* 9 HASTINGS WOMEN'S L.J. 79 (1998); Medina.

50. *See* 8 U.S.C. § 1326(a) (1998).

51. *See, e.g.,* Almendarez-Torres v. United States, 523 U.S. 224 (1998); *see also* Pamela A. MacLean, *Study Suggests Hispanic Men Face Excessive Prosecution,* DAILY RECORDER (Sacramento), Oct. 11, 2001, at 1 (reporting that Latina/os were subject to high rates of criminal prosecution under the illegal entry law).

52. *See* Sen. Dianne Feinstein, *Senate Approves Five New Urgently Needed Federal Judgeships for San Diego,* CONG. PRESS RELEASES, Dec. 21, 2001; Pamela Manson, *Congress OKs Two New Federal Judgeships for Texas,* 16 TEX. LAW. 8 (2001); Diane Jennings, *Border Court Overwhelms Judges: Officials Say Drug, Immigration Hearings Strain System,* DALLAS MORNING NEWS, June 17, 2001, at 41A.

53. *See* Prosecution of Immigration Cases Surge in U.S., *Transactional*

Records Access Clearinghouse, http://trac.syr.edu/tracins/latest/131/, last visited Jan. 31, 2006.

54. *See* John R.B. Palmer, Stephen W. Yale-Loehr, & Elizabeth Croning, *Why Are So Many People Challenging Immigration Appeals Decisions in Federal Court? An Empirical Analysis of the Recent Surge in Petitions for Review,* 20 GEO. IMMIGR. L.J. 1 (2005).

55. *See* Libby Sander, *7th Circuit Grapples With Difficulty of Asylum Cases,* CHI. LAW., Dec. 2005, at 17 (discussing court of appeal criticism of immigration decisions and how the U.S. Court of Appeals for the Second Circuit became so overwhelmed by immigration appeals that it eliminated oral argument in all asylum cases).

56. *See* Pamela A. MacLean, *Immigration Judges Come Under Fire,* NAT'L L.J., Jan. 30, 2006, at 1; Christina B. LaBrie, *Third Circuit Describes "Disturbing Pattern of IJ Misconduct" in Asylum Cases,* IMMIGRATION DAILY, Oct. 22, 2005, at http://www.ilw.com/articles/2005,1027-labrie.shtm, last visited Nov. 27, 2006; *see, e.g.,* Cham v. Attorney General, 445 F.3d 683 (3d Cir. 2006) (granting petition for review because of bias of immigration judge); Shah v. Attorney General, 446 F.3d 429 (3d Cir. 2006) (reaching same conclusion in case involving same immigration judge); Wang v. Attorney General, 423 F.3d 260 (3d Cir. 2005) (finding that, based on conduct at hearing, immigration judge was not neutral and impartial in denying asylum claim); Nuru v. Gonzales, 404 F.3d 1207, 1229 (9th Cir. 2005) (to same effect).

57. *See* Justin Scheck, *Gonzales Tells IJs to Do Better and Be Polite,* RECORDER (San Francisco), Jan. 11, 2006, at 1.

58. Sukwanputra v. Gonzales, 434 F.3d 627, 638 (3d Cir. 2006) (emphasis added).

59. *See* Gaiutra Bahadur, *"Bullying" Immigration Judge Absent, Replaced,* PHIL. INQUIRER, June 2, 2006, at A1.

60. *See* U.S. GEN. ACCOUNTABILITY OFFICE, IMMIGRATION BENEFITS: IMPROVEMENTS NEEDED TO ADDRESS BACKLOGS AND ENSURE QUALITY OF ADJUDICATIONS (Nov. 2005).

61. *See* Evelyn H. Cruz, *Double the Injustice, Twice the Harm: The Impact of the Board of Immigration Appeals's Summary Affirmance Procedures,* 16 STAN. L. & POL'Y REV. 481 (2005).

62. *See* Recent Cases, *Immigration Law—Administrative Adjudication—Third and Seventh Circuits Condemn Pattern of Error in Immigration Courts,* 119 HARV. L. REV. 2596, 2596 (2006) (Figure 1).

63. Pamela A. MacLean, *Judges Blast Immigration Rulings,* NAT'L L.J., Oct. 24, 2005, at S1.

64. Iao v. Gonzales, 400 F.3d 530, 534–35 (7th Cir. 2005).

65. Benslimane v. Gonzales, 430 F.3d 828, 829–30 (7th Cir. 2005) (emphasis

added); *see* Pasha v. Gonzales, 433 F.3d 530, 531 (7th Cir. 2005) (Posner, J.) ("At the risk of sounding like a broken record, we reiterate our oft-expressed concern with adjudication of asylum claims by the Immigration Court and the Board of Immigration Appeals and with the defense of the BIA's asylum decisions in this court. . . .") (citation omitted).

66. *See* Adam Liptak, *Courts Criticize Judges' Handling of Asylum Cases,* N.Y. TIMES, Dec. 26, 2005, at A1.

67. Jerry Seper, *Rounding Up All Illegals "Not Realistic,"* WASH. TIMES, Sept. 10, 2004, at A1 (quoting Undersecretary Hutchinson).

68. Elisabeth Bumiller, *In Immigration Remarks, Bush Hints He Favors Senate Plan,* N.Y. TIMES, Apr. 25, 2006, at A22 (quoting President Bush).

69. RAJEEV GOYLE & DAVID A. JAEGER, DEPORTING THE UNDOCUMENTED: A COST ASSESSMENT (Center for American Progress, July 2005) (emphasis in original) (some emphasis added).

70. Michael E. Fix & Wendy Zimmerman, *All Under One Roof: Mixed-Status Families in an Era of Reform* 1 (Oct. 1999), http://www.urban.org/publications/409100.html, last visited on Nov. 27, 2006.

71. *See* Edith Z. Friedler, *From Extreme Hardship to Extreme Deference: United States Deportation of Its Own Children,* 22 HAST. CONST. L.Q. 491 (1995); Bill Piatt, *Born as Second Class Citizens in the U.S.A.: Children of Undocumented Parents,* 63 NOTRE DAME L. REV. 35 (1988).

72. REYES ET AL., at xiii.

73. Pub. L. No. 106–386, 114 Stat. 1464 (2000).

74. *See* Trafficking Victims Protection Reauthorization Act of 2003, Pub. L. No. 108–93, 117 Stat. 2875 (2003).

75. *See* Jim Yardley, *Mexicans' Bids to Enter U.S. Rebound to Pre-9/11 Levels,* N.Y. TIMES, Nov. 24, 2002, at 24 (analyzing U.S. government data); *see also* Hugh Dellios, *Visiting Home Is Gift Enough,* CHI. TRIB., Dec. 26, 2002, at 1 (reporting that Mexican immigrants were once again returning to Mexico for the Christmas holidays to visit family and friends).

76. *See* SELECT COMM'N ON IMMIGRATION AND REFUGEE POLICY, U.S. IMMIGRATION POLICY AND THE NATIONAL INTEREST, STAFF REPORT (1981).

77. *See, e.g.,* U.S. COMM'N ON IMMIGRATION REFORM, U.S. IMMIGRATION POLICY: RESTORING CREDIBILITY (1994).

78. *See, e.g.,* Bill Ong Hing, *Border Patrol Abuse: Evaluating Complaint Procedures Available to Victims,* 9 GEO. IMMIGR. L.J. 757 (1995).

79. *See* U.S. GEN. ACCOUNTABILITY OFFICE, IMMIGRATION ENFORCEMENT: PRELIMINARY OBSERVATIONS ON EMPLOYMENT VERIFICATION AND WORKSITE ENFORCEMENT EFFORTS 3 (2005).

80. *See* U.S. DEP'T OF HOMELAND SECURITY, OFFICE OF INSPECTOR GENERAL, REVIEW OF THE IMMIGRATION AND CUSTOMS ENFORCEMENT'S COMPLIANCE ENFORCEMENT UNIT (Sept. 2005) (identifying deficiencies in systems that

allow for identification of noncitizens who have violated the terms of their visas and concluding that systems are "incomplete").

81. *See* Rachel Osband, *Current Developments in the Executive Branch: ICE Announces Record Levels of Removals for FY 2004*, 19 GEO. IMMIGR. L.J. 193 (2004).

82. *President Bush Proposes New Temporary Worker Program* (Jan. 7, 2004).

83. *See, e.g.*, OTIS L. GRAHAM, UNGUARDED GATES: A HISTORY OF AMERICA'S IMMIGRATION CRISIS 117–33 (2004).

84. *See* U.S. DEP'T OF JUSTICE, 2000 STATISTICAL YEARBOOK OF THE IMMIGRATION AND NATURALIZATION SERVICE 237 tbl.58 (2002).

85. *See* U.S. OFFICE OF IMMIGRATION STATISTICS, 2004 YEARBOOK OF IMMIGRATION STATISTICS 5 (2006).

86. Brown v. Board of Education, 349 U.S. 294, 301 (1955).

87. *See* Paul D. Carrington, *Restoring Vitality to State and Local Politics by Correcting the Excessive Independence of the Supreme Court*, 50 ALA. L. REV. 397, 436–44 (1999); Cheryl I. Harris, *Whiteness as Property*, 106 HARV. L. REV. 1707, 1750–57 (1993).

88. *See, e.g.*, BRIMELOW; PATRICK J. BUCHANAN, THE DEATH OF THE WEST: HOW DYING POPULATIONS AND IMMIGRANT INVASIONS IMPERIL OUR COUNTRY AND CIVILIZATION 97–149 (2002); SAMUEL P. HUNTINGTON, WHO ARE WE? THE CHALLENGES TO AMERICAN NATIONAL IDENTITY (2004); JOHN J. MILLER, THE UNMAKING OF AMERICANS: HOW MULTICULTURALISM HAS UNDERMINED THE ASSIMILATION ETHIC (1998); ARTHUR M. SCHLESINGER, JR., THE DISUNITING OF AMERICA: REFLECTIONS ON A MULTICULTURAL SOCIETY (rev. ed. 1998).

89. *See generally* PEW HISPANIC CENTER/KAISER FAMILY FOUNDATION, 2002 NATIONAL SURVEY OF LATINOS (2002) (summarizing a comprehensive survey of Latina/os in the United States and showing that they tend to assimilate).

90. BRIMELOW, at 10; *see* BUCHANAN, at 97–149 (embracing similar views); CAROL M. SWAIN, THE NEW WHITE NATIONALISM IN AMERICA: ITS CHALLENGE TO INTEGRATION 84–108 (2002) (summarizing white nationalist objections to current levels of immigration and fear of demographic changes to U.S. society).

91. *See* Kevin R. Johnson, *The End of "Civil Rights" as We Know It? Immigration and Civil Rights in the New Millennium*, 49 UCLA L. REV. 1481, 1482 & n.1 (2002).

92. *See* Leti Volpp, *Talking "Culture": Gender, Race, Nation, and the Politics of Multiculturalism*, 96 COLUM. L. REV. 1573, 1589 (1996) ("Culture is not some monolithic, fixed, and static essence.") (footnote omitted). *See generally* Madhavi Sunder, *Cultural Dissent*, 54 STAN. L. REV. 495 (2001) (analyzing the legal implications of the dynamic nature of culture).

93. *See* ERIC K. YAMAMOTO, INTERRACIAL JUSTICE: CONFLICT AND RECONCILIATION IN POST–CIVIL RIGHTS AMERICA (1999); Bill Ong Hing, *Beyond the*

Rhetoric of Assimilation and Cultural Pluralism: Addressing the Tension of Separatism and Conflict in an Immigration-Driven Multiracial Society, 81 CAL. L. REV. 863 (1993); Deborah Ramirez, *Multicultural Empowerment: It's Not Just Black and White Anymore,* 47 STAN. L. REV. 957 (1995); Alexandra Natapoff, Note, *Trouble in Paradise: Equal Protection and the Dilemma of Interminority Group Conflict,* 47 STAN. L. REV. 1059 (1995).

94. *See* Jagdish Bhagwati, *Borders Beyond Control,* FOREIGN AFF., Jan.-Feb. 2003, at 98, 103–04.

95. *See* U.S. COMM'N ON IMMIGRATION REFORM, BECOMING AN AMERICAN: IMMIGRATION & IMMIGRANT POLICY 25–58 (1997) (offering policy initiatives to facilitate the integration of immigrants into U.S. society). *Compare* BRIMELOW, at 211–16 (contending that immigrants are failing to assimilate into U.S. society), *with* Bill Ong Hing, *Answering Challenges of the New Immigrant-Driven Diversity: Considering Integration Strategies,* 40 BRANDEIS L.J. 861, 888–98 (2002) (offering proposals that would promote the integration of immigrants into U.S. society).

96. *See* MICHAEL WALZER, SPHERES OF JUSTICE (1983); Linda S. Bosniak, *Membership, Equality, and the Difference That Alienage Makes,* 69 N.Y.U. L. REV. 1047, 1068–87 (1994).

97. Bernard Trujillo, *Immigrant Visa Distribution: The Case of Mexico,* 2000 WIS. L. REV. 713, 721 (emphasis added).

98. *See* Sylvia R. Lazos Vargas, *Deconstructing Homo[geneous] Americanus: The White Ethnic Immigrant Narrative and Its Exclusionary Effect,* 72 TUL. L. REV. 1493 (1998); George A. Martínez, *Latinos, Assimilation and the Law: A Philosophical Perspective,* 20 CHICANO-LATINO L. REV. 1 (2000).

99. *See generally* RODOLFO ACUÑA, OCCUPIED AMERICA: A HISTORY OF CHICANOS (3d ed. 1988); TOMÁS ALMAGUER, RACIAL FAULT LINES: THE HISTORICAL ORIGINS OF WHITE SUPREMACY IN CALIFORNIA (1994); CAREY MCWILLIAMS, NORTH FROM MEXICO: THE SPANISH-SPEAKING PEOPLE OF THE UNITED STATES (1949).

100. *See* Ian F. Haney López, *Institutional Racism: Judicial Conduct and a New Theory of Racial Discrimination,* 109 YALE L.J. 1717 (2000); George A. Martínez, *Legal Indeterminacy, Judicial Discretion and the Mexican-American Litigation Experience: 1930–1980,* 27 U.C. DAVIS L. REV. 555 (1994); *see, e.g.,* Castaneda v. Partida, 430 U.S. 482 (1977); Hernandez v. Texas, 347 U.S. 475 (1954).

101. *See* Doris Meissner, *Putting the "N" Back Into INS: Comments on the Immigration and Naturalization Service,* 35 VA. J. INT'L L. 1 (1994).

102. *See* U.S. DEP'T OF JUSTICE, 1998 STATISTICAL YEARBOOK OF THE IMMIGRATION AND NATURALIZATION SERVICE 170 (2000). Changes in Mexican law permitting dual nationality, as well as the growth of anti-immigrant sentiment, contributed to the increase in the naturalization rate of Mexican immigrants.

103. *See, e.g.,* Bob Barr, *High Crimes and Misdemeanors: The Clinton-Gore Scandals and the Question of Impeachment,* 2 TEX. REV. L. & POL. 1, 44–50 (1997) (contending that the abuse of the naturalization process was one of many grounds justifying the impeachment of President Clinton). The Justice Department's Office of the Inspector General found that the Clinton administration had not acted for political ends in its Citizenship USA program, although some naturalization petitions were erroneously approved because of hasty processing. *See IG Report Finds INS's "Citizenship USA" Program Was Flawed, but Not for Political Reasons,* 77 INTERPRETER RELEASES 1198 (2000).

104. *See* U.S. COMM'N ON IMMIGRATION REFORM, BECOMING AN AMERICAN, at 46–58.

105. *See* United States v. Wong Kim Ark, 169 U.S. 649 (1898).

106. *See* PETER H. SCHUCK & ROGERS M. SMITH, CITIZENS WITHOUT CONSENT: ILLEGAL ALIENS IN THE AMERICAN POLITY (1985). *But see* Gerald L. Neuman, *Back to Dred Scott?,* 24 SAN DIEGO L. REV. 485 (1987) (book review) (critically reviewing *Citizens Without Consent*); David S. Schwartz, *The Amorality of Consent,* 74 CAL. L. REV. 2143 (1986) (book review) (questioning the morality of Schuck and Smith's suggestion that the Fourteenth Amendment need not bestow citizenship on children of undocumented immigrants born in the United States).

107. *See* Christopher L. Eisgruber, *Birthright Citizenship and the Constitution,* 72 N.Y.U. L. REV. 54 (1997) (defending the birthright citizenship rule in the face of challenges to the rule); Note, *The Birthright Citizenship Amendment: A Threat to Equality,* 107 HARV. L. REV. 1026 (1994) (contending that changing birthright citizenship in the United States would threaten equality).

108. *See* Peter H. Schuck, *Membership in the Liberal Polity: The Devaluation of American Citizenship,* 3 GEO. IMMIGR. L.J. 1 (1989).

109. 457 U.S. 202 (1982).

110. This was one of the justifications for Brown v. Board of Education, 347 U.S. 483, 493 (1954) ("In these days, it is doubtful that any child may reasonably be expected to succeed in life if he is denied the opportunity of an education.").

111. *See Plyler v. Doe,* 457 U.S. at 237–38, 241 (Powell, J., concurring); *id.* at 242 (Burger, C.J., dissenting).

112. *See* Victor C. Romero, *Postsecondary School Education Benefits for Undocumented Immigrants: Promises and Pitfalls,* 27 N.C. J. INT'L L. & COM. REG. 393 (2002); Michael A. Olivas, *Storytelling Out of School: Undocumented College Residency, Race, and Reaction,* 22 HASTINGS CONST. L.Q. 1019 (1995).

113. *See* Kevin R. Johnson, *Driver's Licenses and Undocumented Immigrants: The Future of Civil Rights Law?,* 5 NEV. L.J. 213 (2004)

114. *See* HING, at 19–20.

115. *See* Donald F. Kettl, *Border Wars,* CONG. Q., June 2005, at 20.

116. *See* DeCanas v. Bica, 424 U.S. 351, 354 (1976) ("Power to regulate immigration is unquestionably exclusively a federal power.") (citations omitted).

117. *See* Wilson v. United States, 104 F.3d 1086 (9th Cir. 1997) (rejecting claim by state that federal government failed to guarantee a republican form of government under Invasion and Guarantee Clause of Article IV of the U.S. Constitution for failing to limit immigration into state); *see also* Chiles v. United States, 69 F.3d 1094 (11th Cir. 1995), *cert. denied*, 517 U.S. 1188 (1996) (same).

118. *See generally* Kevin R. Johnson, *An Essay on Immigration Politics, Popular Democracy, and California's Proposition 187: The Political Relevance and Legal Irrelevance of Race*, 70 WASH. L. REV. 629 (1995) (analyzing the anti-Mexican sentiment at the core of the initiative campaign); Ruben J. Garcia, Comment, *Critical Race Theory and Proposition 187: The Racial Politics of Immigration Law*, 17 CHICANO-LATINO L. REV. 118 (1995) (same).

119. *See* Johnson, *Driver's Licenses and Undocumented Immigrants*.

120. *See* Pam Belluck, *Novel Tack on Illegal Immigration: Trespass Charge*, N.Y. TIMES, July 13, 2005, at A14.

121. *See* Mary Romero & Marwah Serag, *Violation of Latino Civil Rights Resulting from INS and Local Police's Use of Race, Culture and Class Profiling: The Case of the Chandler Roundup in Arizona*, 52 CLEV. ST. L. REV. 75 (2005).

122. *See* Mary Beth Sheridan, *U.S. Sting Angers Mexican Officials*, CHI. SUN TIMES, May 31, 1998, at 27; Mark Fineman, *New U.S. Law on Migrants Has Mexico Up in Arms*, L.A. TIMES, Apr. 3, 1997, at A17; Eric Malnic et al., *U.S. Will Review Case of Clubbed Immigrants*, RECORD (Hackensack), Apr. 3, 1996, at A17. For an analysis of several measures necessary to improve U.S.-Mexico relations, see Hale E. Sheppard, *Salvaging Trade, Economic and Political Relations With Mexico in the Aftermath of the Terrorist Attacks: A Call for a Reevaluation of U.S. Law and Policy*, 20 B.U. INT'L L.J. 33 (2002).

123. *See* Tim Golden, *U.S. Blockade of Workers Enrages Mexican Town*, N.Y. TIMES, Oct. 1, 1993, at A3.

124. *See* Peter J. Spiro, *The States and Immigration in an Era of Demi-Sovereignties*, 35 VA. J. INT'L L. 121, 158, 165–66 (1994).

125. *See* Jerry Seper, *Pro-Immigration Forces to March on Washington*, WASH. TIMES, Feb. 20, 2006, at A3.

126. *See* CONGRESSIONAL RESEARCH SERVICE, MEXICO-UNITED STATES DIALOGUE ON MIGRATION AND BORDER ISSUES, 2001–2006 (Jan. 2006).

127. *See* Michael J. Trebilcock & Matthew Sudak, *The Political Economy of Emigration and Immigration*, 81 N.Y.U. L. REV. 234, 256 (2006) (stating that, in 2000, remittances to Mexico from migrants in United States exceeded $6.5 billion).

128. *See* Gabriela A. Gallegos, Comment, *Border Matters: Redefining the National Interest in U.S.-Mexico Immigration and Trade Policy*, 92 CAL. L. REV. 1729 (2004).

129. *See* Glenn Kessler, *Powell Aims to Reassure Canadians,* Wash. Post, Nov. 15, 2002, at A30; Tonda MacCharles, *We're Both at Risk, Powell Tells Canada,* Toronto Star, Nov. 15, 2002, at A7; *see also* Jim Rankin, *Canadian in Passport Fiasco,* Toronto Star, Feb. 14, 2003, at A1 (reporting that the Immigration and Naturalization Service accused a Canadian citizen of using a forged Canadian passport and subjected her to expedited removal to India).

130. U.S. Gen. Accounting Office, Border Security: Implications of Eliminating the Visa Waiver Program 3–4 (2002).

131. *See* INS v. Abudu, 485 U.S. 94, 110 (1988); Mathews v. Diaz, 426 U.S. 67, 81 n.17 (1976).

132. *See* Kevin R. Johnson, *Why Alienage Jurisdiction? Historical Foundations and Modern Justifications for Federal Jurisdiction Over Disputes Involving Noncitizens,* 21 Yale J. Int'l L. 1, 10–16 (1996); *see, e.g.,* 28 U.S.C. § 1332; Alien Tort Claims Act, 28 U.S.C. § 1350 (2003) (codified as amended); Torture Victim Protection Act, Pub. L. No. 102–256, 106 Stat. 97 (1992) (codified as amended); Foreign Sovereign Immunities Act, Pub. L. No. 94–583, 90 Stat. 2892 (1976) (codified as amended).

133. At times, individual U.S. immigration decisions appear to have been improperly influenced by foreign policy concerns, particularly with respect to noncitizens seeking asylum in this country because they fear persecution in their homelands. *See* Kevin R. Johnson, *A "Hard Look" at the Executive Branch's Asylum Decisions,* 1991 Utah L. Rev. 279; *see also* Peter Margulies, *Democratic Transitions and the Future of Asylum Law,* 71 U. Colo. L. Rev. 3 (2000) (contending that the State Department makes hasty judgments based on foreign policy in asylum and refugee cases).

134. *See* John W. Head, *What Has Not Changed Since September 11—The Benefits of Multilateralism,* 12 Kan. J.L. & Pub. Pol'y 1 (2002).

135. None of this discussion should be read as endorsing the overbroad definition of "terrorist activity" and "terrorist" in the current U.S. immigration laws, which have been cogently criticized. *See* Gerald L. Neuman, *Terrorism, Selective Deportation and the First Amendment After* Reno v. AADC, 14 Geo. Immigr. L.J. 313, 322–27 (2000); Nadine Strossen, *Criticisms of Federal Counter-Terrorism Laws,* 20 Harv. J.L. & Pub. Pol'y 531 (1997); Michael J. Whidden, Note, *Unequal Justice: Arabs in America and United States Antiterrorism Legislation,* 69 Fordham L. Rev. 2825, 2871–74 (2001).

136. *See* Nat'l Comm'n on Terrorist Acts upon the United States, The 9/11 Commission Report 389–90 (2004).

137. *See* Joseph H. Carens, *Aliens and Citizens: The Case for Open Borders,* 49 Rev. Pol. 251, 260 (1987).

138. *See* Thomas M. Franck, *Terrorism and the Right of Self-Defense,* 95 Am. J. Int'l L. 839 (2001) (discussing the right of self-defense against terrorism); Michael J. Glennon, *The Fog of Law: Self-Defense, Inherence, and Inco-*

herence in Article 51 of the United Nations Charter, 25 Harv. J.L. & Pub. Pol'y 539 (2002) (same).

139. *See* Brandenburg v. Ohio, 395 U.S. 444, 447 (1969) (finding that the First Amendment barred the regulation of speech "except where . . . advocacy is directed to inciting or producing imminent lawless action and is likely to incite or produce such action") (footnote omitted).

140. *See* Kevin R. Johnson, *U.S. Border Enforcement: Drugs, Migrants, and the Rule of Law,* 47 Vill. L. Rev. 897, 912–15 (2002) (reviewing studies showing that Custom Service searches at the border became more effective after the imposition of limits on officer discretion).

141. *See id.* at 918–19.

142. *See generally* Kevin R. Johnson, *The Antiterrorism Act, The Immigration Reform Act, and Ideological Regulation in the Immigration Laws: Important Lessons for Citizens and Noncitizens,* 28 St. Mary's L.J. 833, 841–69 (1997) (analyzing the history of political restrictions in U.S. immigration laws); John A. Scanlan, *Aliens in the Marketplace of Ideas: The Government, the Academy, and the McCarran-Walter Act,* 66 Tex. L. Rev. 1481 (1988) (criticizing ideological regulation in immigration laws).

143. *See* James H. Johnson, Jr., *U.S. Immigration Reform, Homeland Security, and Global Economic Competitiveness in the Aftermath of the September 11, 2001 Terrorist Attacks,* 27 N.C. J. Int'l L. & Com. Reg. 419, 457–59 (2002) (advocating this sort of "perimeter security strategy" with the cooperation of Canada, Mexico, and the United States).

NOTES TO CHAPTER 6

1. *See* REAL ID Act of 2005, Title B of the Emergency Supplemental Appropriations Act for Defense, the Global War on Terror, and Tsunami Relief, 2005, 109 Pub. L. No. 12, 119 Stat. 231 (2005).

2. *See* Kim Barry, *Home and Away: The Construction of Citizenship in an Emigration Context,* 81 N.Y.U. L. Rev. 11 (2006); Anupam Chander, *Diaspora Bonds,* 76 N.Y.U. L. Rev. 1005, 1006 (2001); Peter J. Spiro, *The Citizenship Dilemma,* 51 Stan. L. Rev. 597, 621–25 (1999).

3. *See generally* Peter H. Schuck, *The Transformation of Immigration Law,* 84 Colum. L. Rev. 1 (1984) (documenting pressures for a change to classical immigration law).

4. Victor C. Romero, *Expanding the Circle of Membership by Reconstruction of the "Alien": Lessons From Social Psychology and the "Promise Enforcement" Cases,* 32 U. Mich. J.L. Ref. 1, 5 (1998) (footnote omitted).

5. *See* Jost Delbrück, *Global Migration-Immigration-Multiethnicity: Challenges to the Concept of the Nation-State,* 2 Ind. J. Global Leg. Studs. 45, 48

(1994) (offering the idea of an "Open Republic" as an alternative to the conventional wisdom of nation-states with closed borders).

6. *See, e.g.*, DOUGLAS S. MASSEY, JORGE DURAND, & NOLAN J. MALONE, BEYOND SMOKE AND MIRRORS: MEXICAN IMMIGRATION IN AN ERA OF ECONOMIC INTEGRATION 142–64 (2002).

7. *See id.* at 3–6.

Index

9/11 Commission, report of, 196. *See also* September 11, 2001; National security; Public safety and national security; "War on Terror"

AFL-CIO and immigration, 24, 148. *See also* Organized labor and immigration; United Farm Workers and immigration; Wage impacts of immigration

Affirmative action, concern with, 75. *See also* Multiculturalism; Huntington, Samuel

Africa, immigration from, 105, 240n68; immigration in, 162

African Americans, 13, 23, 76, 130, 143–147, 176; impact of immigration on, 23, 143–147; lynching of, 76, 230–231n107. *See also* Jim Crow; Economic benefits of liberal migration; Undocumented immigrants; Wage impacts of immigration; Wealth distribution concerns with immigration

Alien and Sedition Acts, 50; similar Montana law, 231n115. *See also* Anti-immigrant sentiment; Immigration law, U.S.; Nativism

Alien Nation (book). *See* Brimelow, Peter; Nativism

"Aliens," dehumanizing impact of terminology, 107. *See also* Anti-immigrant sentiment, "Criminal aliens"; "Illegal aliens"; Nativism

American Bar Association, on immigration reform, 168. *See also* Immigration reform

American Farm Bureau, study on economic benefits of immigrants to agriculture, 234. *See also* Economic benefits of liberal migration

American Friends Service Committee, report on border enforcement by, 112. *See also* Border enforcement; "Death on the border"; Morality of immigration restrictions

American Immigration Foundation, report on border enforcement by, 173. *See also* Border enforcement; "Death on the border"; Morality of immigration restrictions

American Patrol, anti-immigrant group, 61. *See also* Anti-immigrant sentiment; Minutemen; Nativism

Americans with Disabilities Act, 90. *See also* Exclusions of immigrants under U.S. immigration law

Amnesty, 73. *See also* Immigration Reform and Control Act of 1986; Immigration reform

Amnesty International, report on border enforcement by, 112. *See also* Border enforcement; "Death on the border"

Angel Island, 107. *See also* Chinese exclusion laws; Chinese immigrants; Detention

Anti-immigrant sentiment, 4–5, 13–14, 58–61, 150, 164, 167, 178. *See also* American Patrol; Huntington, Samuel; Minutemen; Nativism; Proposition 187

Arab and Muslim noncitizens, 9, 13, 14, 21, 32, 33, 49, 57, 58, 61, 69, 99, 104–105, 106. *See also* September 11, 2001; USA PATRIOT Act; "War on Terror"

Arizona, initiative similar to Proposition 187, 150. *See also* Anti-immigrant sentiment; Nativism; Proposition 187

Ashcroft, John, U.S. Attorney General, 32–33. *See also* September 11, 2001; "War on Terror"

Asian immigration, 51, 53, 79, 105, 170. *See also* Chinese exclusion laws; Chinese immigrants

Assimilation of immigrants, 47, 62–85, 170–171; coerced assimilation, 79–82; failure to assimilate, 47–48, 62–85, 170–171; history of in United States, 68; human costs of, 74–75, 230n101; immigrants of color, 68–69; Latina/os, 171; policies that promote assimilation of immigrants, 188–193; segmented assimilation, 66–67. *See also* English language; Huntington, Samuel; Integration of immigrants in U.S. society; Multiculturalism

Asylum, 57; bias in U.S. decisions, 271n133. *See also* Board of Immigration Appeals; Haitian Refugees; Immigration courts; Refugee admissions

Aztlán, feared reconquest of Southwestern United States as part of Mexico, 66. *See also* Buchanan, Patrick; Huntington, Samuel; Mexican immigrants; Undocumented immigrants

Baird, Zoe, nominee for U.S. Attorney General, 169

Beck, Roy, on restricting immigration, 60

Berlin Wall, 172, 210

Bilingual education. *See* Education; English language

Blagojevich, Rod, Illinois Governor, on integration of immigrants, 85. *See also* Assimilation of immigrants; Integration of immigrants in U.S. society

Blue Shield, of California, of Georgia, marketing to undocumented immigrants, 139

Board of Immigration Appeals, criticism of, 179–182. *See also* Immigration courts; Posner, Judge Richard

Border. *See* Border enforcement; Border fence; U.S.-Mexico border

Border enforcement, vii, 33, 36, 98–99; border fence, 164; deaths, 3, 111–116; ineffectiveness of increased enforcement, 86, 114–115, 133, 135, 164–165, 171–

176, 262n23. *See also* Border fence; Border Patrol; "Death on the border"; Employer sanctions; Immigration law, U.S.; U.S.-Mexico border; Workplace enforcement

Border fence, 16, 164. *See also* U.S.-Mexico border

Border Patrol, 5, 80, 112, 125, 173, 185, 201; abuse of immigrants, 80; increase in officers, 173. *See also* Border enforcement; "Death on the border"

Borders, meaning of, 7–10; as social constructs, 7–8; loss of control of, 48. *See also* Floodgates concern with immigration; Psychological resistance to open borders

Borjas, George, Harvard economist, 60, 145. *See also* Economic benefits of liberal migration

"Bracero" (guestworker) program, 80–81, 124–125, 126. *See also* Guestworker program; Immigration reform

"Brain drain," 143, 253n34

Brazil, migration from, 174

Brimelow, Peter, author of *Alien Nation* (book), 59, 65, 77, 114, 189, 229n90

Brown v. Board of Education (1954), 76, 103. *See also* African Americans; Jim Crow; U.S. Supreme Court

Buchanan, Patrick, restrictionist advocate, 5, 59, 114, 138, 200

Bush, George W., U.S. President, 16, 18, 32, 33, 99, 124, 138, 169, 171, 173, 180, 185, 187; questioning efficacy of massive deportation campaign, 183; referring to Minutemen as "vigilantes," 200

Bustamante, Cruz, former California Lieutenant Governor, death threat on, 6

Calavita, Kitty, 136

California and immigration, 52, 193, 194. *See also* Davis, Gray; Driver's licenses; Proposition 187; Schwarzenegger, Arnold; Wilson, Pete

California Rural Legal Assistance Foundation, on border deaths, 112. *See also* Border enforcement; "Death on the border"; Morality of immigration restrictions

Canada and U.S. immigration policy, 163, 195; limited enforcement of the U.S.-Canada border, 109. *See also* European Union and immigration; North American Free Trade Agreement; North American Union; Open borders; U.S.-Mexico border

Carens, Joseph, 92–94, 95. *See also* Liberal theory; Morality of immigration restrictions

Castañeda, Jorge, Foreign Minister, Mexico, 259n115. *See also* Mexican government

Catholic Church, 88. *See also* Mahony, Cardinal Roger; Morality of immigration restrictions; Religious views on immigration

Census 2000, changing racial demographics of United States, 189

Chandler (Arizona) "Round-up," 110. *See also* Border enforcement

Chang, Howard, 141. *See also* Economic benefits of liberal migration

Chávez, César, and immigration, 147–148. *See also* United Farm Workers and immigration

Chavez, Linda, nominee for U.S. Secretary of Labor, 169

Chinese Exclusion Case, The (*Chae Chan Ping v. United States*) (1889), 96. *See also* Chinese exclusion laws; Chinese immigrants

Chinese exclusion laws, 23, 48, 50, 52–53, 95–96, 107–08, 115, 116, 144, 147; gender perspective on, 224n18. *See also* The Chinese Exclusion Case; Chinese immigrants

Chinese immigrants, 10, 15, 20, 23, 52–53, 107–108, 170, 244n121. *See also* Asian immigration; Chinese exclusion laws; The Chinese Exclusion Case

Citizenship, birthright, 92, 191–192, 236n26. *See also* Dual citizenship and nationality; Naturalization

Civil Rights Act of 1964, lack of protections for undocumented workers, 121–122

Civil rights consequences of immigration laws and their enforcement, 20. *See also* Border enforcement; "Death on the border"; Morality of immigration restrictions; Race of immigrants; Racial discrimination in immigration laws; Racial profiling in immigration enforcement

Civil rights movement and amendment of U.S. immigration laws, 51

Clinton, Bill, U.S. President, 4, 49, 85, 169, 193

Closed borders. *See* Immigration law, U.S.; Liberal theory; Plenary power doctrine

CNN, 58

Communitarian theory, 92–85, 190; justifying immigration restrictions through, 93–94; liberal theory, conflict with, 92–95; rationale for citizenship requirements, 236n33. *See also* Liberal theory; Morality of immigration restrictions; Walzer, Michael

Complementarity of skills, 146. *See also* Economic benefits of liberal migration

Crime, costs of immigrant crime, 155–158

"Criminal aliens," 4, 156; deportation of, 109–110, 156–157, 177–178; impact of 1996 immigration reforms on, 156; lack of empirical support that immigrants have higher crime rate than general population, 156. *See also* "Aliens"; Crime; Criminal immigration prosecutions; Criminalization of the immigration laws; "Illegal aliens"

Criminal immigration prosecutions, dramatic increase in, 179

Criminalization of the immigration laws, 177–179; illegal re-entry, 179

Cultural concerns with immigration, 65, 67, 82. *See also* Brimelow, Peter; Huntington, Samuel

Davis, Gray, California Governor, 4. *See also* California and immigration; Driver's licenses

"A Day Without a Mexican" (film), 135. *See also* Mexican immigration; Undocumented immigrants

"Death on the border," 3, 13, 71, 111–116, 164; crimes and violence on border, 111–116, 201 *See also* Border enforcement; Border fence; Border Patrol; Morality of immigration restrictions; Racial profiling in immigration

"Death on the border" (*continued*)
enforcement; Undocumented immigrants; U.S.-Mexico border

Democratic Party, views on immigration, 10, 138–139

Deportation, costs of removal of all undocumented immigrants, 183–186; fear of, 46, open-admissions system in, 39–40; record levels of, 57. *See also* "Criminal aliens"; Detention; Undocumented immigrants

Detention, 14, 49, 107, 116, 118–119, 157, 203, 217n45, 223n5; indefinite detention, 50, 205–206. *See also* "Criminal aliens"

Development, Relief and Education for Alien Minors (DREAM) Act, 155. *See also* Education; Higher Education

Dillingham Commission, 53, 156, 224n17. *See also* National origins quota system

Diversity visas, 108–109. *See also* Immigration law, U.S.

Dobbs, Lou, 58. *See also* Anti-immigrant sentiment; Nativism

Driver's licenses, eligibility of undocumented immigrants for, 4–5, 73, 151, 192, 194. *See also* Public benefits and immigrants; Public safety and national security; National security; September 11, 2001; "War on Terror"

Drywallers' strike, 149. *See also* Janitors for Justice movement; Organized labor and immigration

Dual citizenship and nationality, 8, 72, 128, 209, 268n102; concerns with loyalties of, 215n21. *See also* Citizenship; Naturalization

Dual labor market, 42, 63, 92, 119–125, 149, 186–187. *See also* Economic benefits of liberal migration; Morality of immigration restrictions; Undocumented immigrants

East Germany, 84. *See also* Berlin Wall

Economic benefits of liberal migration, 22, 54, 119, 131–167; economic growth in 1990s due to immigrant labor, 133; economic justifications for liberal immigration policies, 137–141; impact on African American workers, 143–147; labor market benefits, 132–133; international trade analogy, 141–143

Economic Report of the President (2005), 136–137

Education, undocumented immigrant access to, 154. *See also* Development, Relief and Education for Alien Minors (DREAM) Act; Higher education; *Plyler v. Doe*

El Salvador, deportation of gang members to, 157; refugees from, 93, 118. *See also* Refugee Admissions

Employer benefits from immigrant labor, 137–141. *See also* Economic benefits of liberal migration; *Wall Street Journal*

Employer sanctions, 137–138; failure of, 185, 201, 203, 229–230n96. *See also* Immigration Reform and Control Act of 1986; Immigration law, U.S.; Undocumented immigrants; Workplace enforcement

English language, 65, 66, 67, 68–69, 81–82, 171, 188, language regulation, 81–82; English-as-second-language (ESL) classes, 31, 84; language as proxy for race, 65. *See also* Assimilation of immigrants; Huntington, Samuel; Integration of immigrants in U.S. society

Environmental concerns with immigration, 24, 158–160, 219n64; claim that United States has met its "carrying capacity," 159. *See also* Sierra Club

Ethnic enclaves, 6, 124, 188. *See also* Assimilation of immigrants; Integration of immigrants in U.S. society

European Union and immigration, 9, 12, 19, 22–23, 28–30, 99, 106, 129, 141, 160, 162–163, 166, 172, 198, 204, 206, 211; Fortress Europe, 162–163, 198, 211, 244n119; model for United States, 43–44, 160–166, 198, 210–211. *See also* North American Free Trade Agreement; North American Union

Exclusion of dangers to public safety and national security, 31–35, 38–39. *See also* Immigration Law, U.S.; Public safety and national security; National security; September 11, 2001; "War on terror"

Exclusion of immigrants under U.S. immigration law, 52–58; Chinese exclusion laws, 53; Criminals, 5; gays and lesbians, 50, 54, 55, 235n16; HIV exclusion, 90–91, 106; modern exclusion grounds, 55. *See also* Chinese exclusion laws; Immigration law, U.S.; Exclusion of dangers to public safety and national security

Fear, of change, 136, 189–190; of permeable borders, 26–35. *See also* Floodgates concern with immigration

Federal courts, increase in immigration appeals, 179–181. *See also* Board of Immigration Appeals; Immigration courts; Judicial review

Federal preemption of state immigration laws, reasons for, 52. *See also* Proposition 187

Federal/state tensions on allocation of costs and benefits of immigration, 43, 152–154, 193–194, 214n10

Federation for American Immigration Reform, restrictionist group, 158

Financial Times, 131, 132. *See also* Economic benefits of liberal migration

First Amendment, 93, 197

Fiss, Owen, on open borders, 11. *See also* Open borders

Floodgates concern with immigration, 26–35, 107, 138, 161, 164, 166, 170, 187–188, 206–207, 210; phased implementation of open-borders system to avoid mass migration, 30. *See also* Fear; Psychological resistance to open borders

Food Stamps, 151. *See also* Public benefits and immigrants; Temporary Assistance to Needy Families

Forced prostitution, 123. *See also* Human trafficking; Sex trafficking; Slavery

Foreign policy consequences of liberal migration policies, 194–196, 270n122. *See also* International tensions resulting from immigration laws and policies

Fortress Europe, 162–163, 198, 211, 244n119. *See also* European Union and immigration

Fox News, 58

Fox, Vicente, President of Mexico, 129, 163, 164. *See also* Mexican government

Frankfurter, Associate Justice Felix, on plenary power doctrine, 17. *See also* Plenary power doctrine; U.S. Supreme Court

Free movement, likely impacts of, 26–35; psychological resistance to, 36; public safety and national security risks, 31–35; social cohesion impacts, 30–31; "war on terror," consistency with, 31–35, 38–39. *See also* Floodgates concern with immigration; Open-admissions system; Open borders; Psychological resistance to open borders

Frisch, Max, on guest workers, 136. *See also* "Bracero" (guestworker) program; Guestworker program

Gaddafi, Muammar, Libya, on immigration in Africa, 162. *See also* Africa

Galbraith, John Kenneth, economist, 134–135, 141–142. *See also* Economic benefits of liberal migration

Gates, Bill, Microsoft, on immigration, 132. *See also* Economic benefits of liberal migration

German immigration, integration of German immigrants in United States, 260n4; nativist response to, 79. *See also* Anti-immigrant sentiment; Assimilation of immigrants; English language; Integration of immigrants in U.S. society; Nativism

Gitlin, Todd, on restricting immigration, 60

Glazer, Nathan, on multiculturalism, 31. *See also* Multiculturalism

Globalization, 17–18, 22, 25–26, 69–70, 99, 132–133, 135–136, 143–144, 162, 167, 171–172, 208–209, 211; necessitating re-conceptionalization of citizenship, 69–70; necessitating reform of U.S. immigration laws, 12, 208–209. *See also* Economic benefits of liberal migration; European Union and immigration; North America Free Trade Agreement; North American Union

Gonzales, Alberto, U.S. Attorney General, criticism of immigration judges 179–180. *See also* Immigration courts; Board of Immigration Appeals; Posner, Judge Richard

Grant, Madison, on restricting immigration, 59

Greenspan, Alan, former chair, Federal Reserve Board, on economic benefits of immigrant labor, 133. *See also* Economic benefits of liberal migration

Guantánamo Bay, Cuba, 99, 215n23. *See also* September 11, 2001; "War on Terror"

Guatemala, refugees from, 93, 118. *See also* Refugee admissions

Guestworker program, 124. *See also* "Bracero" (guestworker) program

Haitian refugees, 3, 12, 57, 93, 118, 119, 161, 205, 244n121. *See also* Refugee admissions

Hamdi, Yaser, 21, 206. *See also* September 11, 2001; "War on Terror"

Hanson, Victor Davis, on restricting immigration, 59, 65. *See also* Mexican immigrants, Undocumented immigrants

Henkin, Louis, on open borders, 11. *See also* Open borders

Hernandez, Esequiel, killing of by U.S. military along border, 112. *See also* Border enforcement; "Death on the border"; Morality of immigration restrictions

Higher education, undocumented immigrant access to, 73, 154–155. *See also* Development, Relief and Education for Alien Minors (DREAM) Act; Education

HIV exclusion, 90–91, 106. *See also* Exclusion of immigrants under U.S. immigration law

Hoffman Plastic Compounds, Inc. v. NLRB (2002), 74, 120, 149; criticism of, 245n125. *See also* U.S. Supreme Court

Human inertia as counter to mass migration, 26–35, 219–220n66. *See also* Floodgates concern with immigration

Human Rights Watch, report on border enforcement by, 112. *See also* Border enforcement; "Death on the border"

Human trafficking, 35, 86, 123–124, 208, 247n142. *See also* Forced prostitution; Sex trafficking; Slavery; Trafficking Victims Protection Act of 2000; Trafficking

Victims Protection Reauthorization Act of 2003

Humanitarian treatment of immigrants, call for, 88–89. *See also* Morality of immigration restrictions; Religious views on immigration

Huntington, Samuel, 30, 59, 60, 94, 170, 206–207, 227n59; *Who Are We? The Challenges to America's National Identity* 62–85, 86–87, 206–207, fear of immigration from Mexico 64–71 *See also* Assimilation of immigrants; Brimelow, Peter; Cultural concerns with immigration; Integration of immigrants in U.S. society; Mexican immigrants; Undocumented immigrants

Hurricane Katrina (August 2005), 12

Hutchinson, Asa, Undersecretary of the Department of Homeland Security, questioning efficacy of massive deportation campaign, 183. *See also* Deportation

Identification. *See* Driver's licenses; Matricular consular (Mexican identification card)

"Illegal aliens," 106; negative connotations of terminology, 46–47, 106, 222n1. *See also* "Aliens"; "Criminal aliens"; Mexican immigrants; Undocumented immigrants

Immigrant businesses, 250–251n6. *See also* Economic benefits of liberal migration

Immigrant rights movement, 3–4; spring 2006 marches, 4, 63, 168, 200

Immigrants, limited political power of, 47

Immigration Act of 1965, 51,103

Immigration and Nationality Act of 1952, 33, 46, 54, 105, 207, 222n1; exclusion grounds, 55; presumption of exclusion, 54. *See also* Border enforcement; Exclusion of immigrants under U.S. immigration law; Immigration law, U.S.

Immigration and Naturalization Service (INS). *See* U.S. Immigration and Naturalization Service(INS)

Immigration courts, mistreatment of immigrants, 179–182. *See also* Board of Immigration Appeals

Immigration impacts on African American workers, 23, 143–147. *See also* African Americans

Immigration law, U.S., assumptions underlying, 6–7, 8–9, 205–208; complex requirements of, 34–35; criminalization of, 178–179; deregulation of, 101; discriminatory impacts of modern immigration laws, 51–52; diversity visas, 108–109; early history of, 52–53, 100–101; employer sanctions, 185, 201, 229–230n96; exclusion grounds, 52–58; federal preemption of state immigration laws, reasons for, 52; futility of immigration enforcement, 171–176; history of, 45–86; increased border enforcement in 1990s, 48–49; impacts on Mexican immigrants (including deaths), 109–115; per country ceilings, impact of, 175; racial discrimination resulting from enforcement of, 25; racism in, 50–51; widespread violation of, 25. *See also* Border enforcement; Chinese exclusion laws; "Death on the border"; Immigration Act of 1965; Immigration and Nationality Act of 1952; Immigration reform; Immigration Reform and Control Act of 1986; Mexican immigrants; National origins quota system; Plenary power doctrine; REAL ID Act; Undocumented immigrants; USA PATRIOT Act

Immigration Policy Center, on economic benefits of immigration, 133. *See also* Economic benefits of liberal migration

Immigration reform, 1–44; failure to enact in recent years, 6; proposals for, 18–26, 36–44; need for, 168–199, 203–204

Immigration Reform and Control Act of 1986, 137–138, 203. *See also* Employer sanctions; Undocumented immigrants

Integration of immigrants in U.S. society, 73, 69–70, 188–193. *See also* Assimilation of immigrants; English language; Huntington, Samuel

International law, protections from immigrant labor exploitation, 124; emigration, rights to, 97; migrants, rights of, 248n153; refugees, rights of, 87–88, 99, 117–118; skepticism about whether U.S.

immigration laws comply with, 237n44; sovereign power to restrict immigration on, 17, 97–100

International tensions resulting from immigration laws and policies, 194–196, 270n122. *See also* Foreign policy consequences of liberal migration policies

Internment of persons of Japanese ancestry, 21, 115, 205

Janitors for Justice movement, 149. *See also* Drywallers' strike; Organized labor and immigration

Jewish refugees and the Holocaust, 21, 117–118, 205. *See also* Anti-immigrant sentiment, Nativism

Jim Crow, 31, 51, 72, 76, 104, 115, 122, 129, 188. *See also* African Americans

Jordan, Barbara, member, Congress, 185. *See also* Immigration reform; U.S. Commission on Immigration Reform

Judicial review, 53–54, 116, 243n111. *See also* The Chinese Exclusion Case; Federal courts; Plenary power doctrine

Katz, Lawrence, Harvard economist, 145

Kennedy, John F., U.S. President, on immigration, 239n66

Kerik, Bernard, nominee for Secretary of U.S. Department of Homeland Security (New York City Police Chief), 169

Labor laws, need for increased enforcement of, 186–187. See also *Hoffman Plastic Compounds, Inc. v. NLRB*; Organized labor and immigration

Legalization. *See* Amnesty; Immigration reform

Legomsky, Stephen H., on diversity visas, 109

Liberal theory, commitment to rights, 87–88, 91–92, 92–95; open borders, consistency with, 98–99; plenary power doctrine, inconsistent with, 95–100. *See also* Carens, Joseph; Communitarian theory; Morality of immigration restrictions; Open-admission system; Open borders

Lind, Michael, on restricting immigration; 60

Mahony, Cardinal Roger, 89. *See also* Catholic Church; Religious views on immigration

Malkin, Michelle, 59

Massey, Douglas S., 173

Matricular consular (Mexican identification card), acceptance by businesses, 139

McCarthy era, 50

Medina, Isabel, 177–178

"Melting pot" metaphor for immigration, 72. *See also* Assimilation of immigrants; Integration of immigrants in U.S. society

Mexican government, interest in protecting migrants, 260n120; protests of U.S. immigration policies, 194–195. *See also* Fox, Vicente; Mexican immigrants; Mexican migration; Mexico; Remittances; U.S.-Mexico border

Mexican immigrants, 10, 14, 21, 115, 190–191; anti-Mexican sentiment, 150, 164, 166; settlement in South and Midwest, 174; special moral obligation by United States to, 125–129, 184. *See also* Anti-immigrant sentiment; "Death on the border"; Huntington, Samuel; Nativism; Proposition 187; Undocumented immigrants

Mexican migration, as a problem, 48, 62–85, 64–71, 80; experience with, 54–55, 190–191. *See also* Huntington, Samuel; Mexican immigrants; Undocumented immigrants

Mexico, 26, 30, 33; economic development in, 165

Minutemen, 1, 5, 41, 61, 106, 114, 200, 204; "vigilantes," as referred to by President George W. Bush, 5, 200. *See also* Anti-immigrant sentiment; Nativism

Mixed immigration status families, 184

Morality of immigration restrictions, 20–21, 87–130; ending discriminatory enforcement of border controls, 107–111; exploitable labor force, creation of, 119–125; immoral treatment of immigrants and refugees, 116–119; moral case for open borders, 100–129; reducing racial discrimination, 103–107; special obligations to Mexican immigrants, 125–129. *See also* Communitarian theory; "Death on the border"; Dual

labor market; Liberal theory; Religious views on immigration; Undocumented immigrants

Mormon Church, 88. *See also* Religious views on immigration

Multiculturalism, 31, 47, 60–61, 63, 76–77, 77–78, 83, 105, 106, 168, 188; as threat to United States, 75. *See also* Assimilation of immigrants; Glazer, Nathan; Huntington, Samuel; Integration of immigrants in U.S. society

Muslim noncitizens. *See* Arab and Muslim noncitizens; September 11, 2001; USA PATRIOT Act; "War on Terror"

Nafziger, James, on international law limits on migration restrictions, 97

National Association for the Advancement of Colored People, 78. *See also* African Americans

National identity and immigration, 13, 51, 62–85, 226n52. *See also* Huntington, Samuel

National origins quota system. 48, 50, 51, 53, 59, 72, 105, 170, 189; repeal of, 105. *See also* Dillingham Commission; Exclusions of immigrants under U.S. immigration law; Immigration law, U.S.

National security, 31–35, 38–39, 196–199, 271n135. *See also* Public safety and national security; September 11, 2001; USA PATRIOT Act; "War on Terror"

National sovereignty and immigration, 40, 91, 95–98. *See also* Plenary power doctrine

Nativism, 2, 14, 17, 45–86, 107, 136, 167, 170, 204, 207–208; civil rights concerns, 75–76; Prohibition era in, 176; responses to, 82–85. *See also* American Patrol; Anti-immigrant sentiment; Huntington, Samuel; Minutemen; Proposition 187

Naturalization, 31, 39, 84–85, 227n59; Citizenship USA Program, criticisms of, 191, 269n103; rates, increasing, 69, 191, 268n102; of Mexicans, 66, 69, 228n78; whiteness requirement for, 50–51, 107–108. *See also* Citizenship; Dual citizenship and nationality

Neuman, Gerald, 100

New York Times, on border deaths, 111; on Judge Richard Posner's criticism of Board of Immigration Appeals, 182. *See also* "Death on the border"; Posner, Judge Richard

Noncitizens, limited political power of, 16–17

North American Free Trade Agreement, 22, 44, 141, 163–164, 165, 166, 172, 206. *See also* European Union and immigration; North American Union

North American Union, as a possible reform, 22, 129, 160–166, 198, 204. *See also* European Union and immigration; North American Free Trade Agreement

Open-admissions system, 37–38; limits, 38–39; possible phased implementation, 30; protecting public safety and national security, 196–199. *See also* Floodgates concern with immigration; Free movement; Liberal theory; Morality of immigration restrictions; Open borders

Open borders, 6–7, 9, 100–130; benefits of, 40–41; deportation in, 39–40; economic benefits of, 131–167; fears of permeable borders, 26–35; immigration scholars on, 11, 15, 18–26; moral arguments for, 101–120, 234n5; not a solution to all immigration problems, 42–43; reduction of international tensions, 194–196; reduction of racial discrimination, 188–193; reduction of tension between state and federal governments, 193–194; taboo of open borders, 10–16. *See also* Floodgates concern with immigration; Free movement; Liberal theory; Morality of immigration restrictions, Open-admissions system

Operation Blockade, 123. *See also* Border enforcement; Border Patrol; "Death on the border"; Operation Hold-the-Line

Operation Gatekeeper, 112. *See also* Border enforcement; Border Patrol; "Death on the border"

Operation Hold-the-Line, 194. *See also* Border enforcement; Border Patrol; "Death on the border"; Operation Blockade

"Operation Wetback" (1954), 20, 57, 81, 126. *See also* Border enforcement; Border Patrol

Organized labor and immigration, 23, 144, 147–150, 245n124. *See also* AFL-CIO; United Farm Workers and immigration; Wage impacts of immigration

Padilla, Jose, 21, 206. *See also* September 11, 2001; "War on Terror"

Permeability of borders as inevitable, 200–211. *See also* Open-admissions system; Open borders

Pew Hispanic Center, estimates of undocumented immigrant population, 173. *See also* Undocumented immigrants

Plenary power doctrine, 16–18, 52–53, 116, 119, 195; liberal theory and, 95–100; other areas of law, 217–218n46. *See also* The Chinese Exclusion Case; Chinese exclusion laws; Chinese immigrants

Plyler v. Doe (1982), 74, 154, 155, 192. *See also* Education; Higher education; U.S. Supreme Court

Policy arguments for more liberal immigration, 24–25, 168–199. *See also* Open-admissions system; Open borders; Economic benefits of liberal migration; Liberal theory; Morality of immigration restrictions

Population adjustments with permeable borders, 30. *See also* Floodgates concern with immigration; Psychological resistance to open borders

Posner, Judge Richard; criticism of immigration decisions, 181–182. *See also* Board of Immigration Appeals; Immigration courts

Prohibition, 25, 113, 133, 169–170, 185–186, 202–203, 206; parallels to current immigration enforcement, 176–179; parallels to "war on drugs," 262–263n31; racially disparate enforcement of, 176

Proposition 187 (California), 4, 150, 171, 193, 194, 232n125, 255n65. *See also* California and immigration

Psychological resistance to open borders, 36; fear of change, 189–190; fear of

Psychological resistance (*continued*)
permeable borders, 26–35. *See also*
Floodgates concern with immigration
Public benefits and immigrants, 4, 12, 56,
124, 150–155, 193–194; driver's license
as public benefit, 151; public benefits as
magnets to immigrants, 12. *See also*
Driver's licenses; Proposition 187; Public
charge exclusion
Public-charge exclusion, 55–57, 89–90,
224n24, 234–235n11; disparate impacts
of, 56–57; to exclude immigrants from
Mexico, 83. *See also* Exclusion of immigrants under U.S. immigration law;
Immigration law, U.S.; Public benefits
and immigrants
Public health, restrictions on immigrant
admissions, 197. *See also* Public safety
and national security; HIV exclusion
Public opinion polls on immigration, 4
Public safety and national security, 31–35,
38–39, 196–199, 271n135. *See also*
Public health
Puerto Rico, migration experience, 28–29;
plenary power doctrine over rights of
people in, 217–218n46. *See also* Floodgates concern with immigration

Quebec, 62

Race of immigrants, 13, 31, 59, 68, 77–
78, 115, 166, 170, 191–192. *See also*
Anti-immigrant sentiment; Arab and
Muslim noncitizens; Asian immigration;
Chinese exclusion laws; Chinese immigrants; Civil rights consequences of immigration laws and their enforcement;
Huntington, Samuel; Mexican immigrants; Nativism; Undocumented
immigrants
Racial discrimination in immigration laws,
13–15, 103–111; discriminatory
impacts of immigration laws, 51–52,
90, 176; reducing racial discrimination,
186–188. *See also* Anti-immigrant sentiment; Nativism; Racial profiling in
immigration enforcement
Racial profiling in immigration enforcement, 14, 108, 110, 175, 198, 213n1.
See also Border enforcement; Border

Patrol; Racial discrimination in immi-
gration laws; Workplace enforcement
Racism, against Asian Americans, 260n6.
See also Anti-immigrant sentiment; Ra-
cial discrimination in immigration laws
Reagan, Ronald, U.S. President, 181
REAL ID Act, 5, 16, 164, 200. *See also*
Immigration and Nationality Act of
1952; Immigration law, U.S.
Red Scare, 50
Refugee Act of 1980, 118. *See also*
Refugee admissions
Refugee admissions, 57, 161; immorality
of U.S. treatment of refugees, 87–88,
116–119; regional alternatives, 238n52.
See also Haitian refugees; Morality of
immigration restrictions
Regional migration arrangement in North
America, 160–166. *See also* European
Union and immigration; North Ameri-
can Free Trade Agreement; North
American Union
Rehnquist, Chief Justice William, 117.
See also U.S. Supreme Court
Religious views on immigration, 88–89,
178. *See also* Catholic Church; Mahony,
Cardinal Roger; Morality of immigra-
tion restrictions; Liberal theory;
Mormon Church
Remittances, from Mexican migrants in
the United States, 128, 165, 195,
260n120. *See also* Mexican government;
Mexican immigrants; Undocumented
immigrants
Repatriation of persons of Mexican ances-
try during Great Depression, 10, 57, 80,
126. *See also* Anti-immigrant sentiment;
Mexican immigrants; Nativism; Public
benefits and immigration; Public charge
exclusion
Republican Party, views on immigration,
9–10, 138–139, 171
Right to travel, 90. See also *Saenz v. Roe*
(1999)
Ryder, Winona, criminal problems of, 157

Saenz v. Roe (1999), on right to travel
between states, 90
Sanctuary cities, San Francisco, 89. *See
also* Morality of immigration restric-

tions; Religious views on immigration;
Undocumented immigrants
Sanctuary movement, in 1980s, 88–89.
See also Morality of immigration restrictions; Religious views on immigration;
Undocumented immigrants
Schlesinger, Arthur, Harvard historian, 60
Schuck, Peter, 98, 156
Schwarzenegger, Arnold, California Governor, 4, 5, 200. *See also* California and
immigration; Driver's licenses
September 11, 2001, vii, 2, 9, 14, 18, 21,
32, 33, 35, 36, 49–50, 57, 58, 61, 65,
69, 82, 84, 98–99, 104, 105, 109, 115,
116, 163, 164, 170, 172, 184–185, 195,
198, 204, 206, 207; U.S. government's
response to and criticism of, 32–33,
104–105, 220–221n76. *See also* Arab
and Muslim noncitizens; Public safety
and national security; National security;
USA PATRIOT Act; "War on Terror"
Sex trafficking, 123. *See also* Forced prostitution; Human trafficking; Slavery
Sexual orientation, exclusion based on, 50,
235n16. *See also* Exclusion of immigrants under U.S. immigration law
Sierra Club, 158. *See also* Environmental
concerns with immigration
Slavery, 113–114, 122–123. *See also*
Forced prostitution; Human trafficking;
Sex trafficking
Smith, William French, former U.S. Attorney General, on loss of control of U.S.
borders, 48. *See also* Undocumented
immigrants, U.S.-Mexico border
Smugglers, 113–114; increasing costs
charged by, 173. *See also* Forced prostitution; Human Trafficking; Sex trafficking; Slavery
Social Security contributions of undocumented immigrants, 151–152. *See also*
Taxes paid by undocumented immigrants
Soviet Union, former, 97
State efforts to regulate immigration, 52;
in early U.S history 100–101. *See also*
California and immigration, Proposition
187
State lawsuits against federal government
over "foreign invasion," 193

States, fiscal impacts of immigration on,
153–154, 167, 193–194, 214n10. *See
also* Public benefits and immigration;
Proposition 187
Statue of Liberty, 1–2, 169
Stoddard, Lothrop, on restricting immigration, 59

Tancredo, Tom, U.S. House of Representatives, candidate for President, 213n2; on
restricting immigration, 1, 5, 114, 138,
200, 202, 213n2
Taxes paid by undocumented immigrants,
151–152. *See also* Economic benefits of
liberal migration; Social Security contributions of undocumented immigrants
Temporary Assistance to Needy Families,
151. *See also* Food Stamps; Public
benefits and immigrants
Terrorism. *See* National security; Public
safety and national security; September
11, 2001; USA PATRIOT Act; "War on
Terror"
Texas Rangers, 80. *See also* Border Patrol
Trafficking Victims Protection Act of 2000,
123, 184. *See also* Forced prostitution;
Human trafficking; Sex trafficking;
Slavery
Trafficking Victims Protection Reautho-
rization Act of 2003, 123, 184. *See also*
Forced prostitution; Human trafficking;
Sex trafficking; Slavery
Transfer policies, to redistribute economic
benefits of immigration, 146. *See also*
Wealth distribution concerns with
immigration
Travel, right to in United States, 89–90.
See also *Saenz v. Roe* (1999)
Trujillo, Bernard, on Mexican immigrants,
190. *See also* Mexican immigrants;
Undocumented immigrants
Truman, Harry, U.S. President, veto of
Immigration and Nationality Act of
1952, 105. *See also* Immigration and
National Act of 1952; Immigration law,
U.S.; National origins quota system
Tushnet, Mark, on liberal theory and
immigration, 88
Tyson Foods, hiring of undocumented
immigrant workers, 134, 177,

Tyson Foods (*continued*)
263–264n43. *See also* Employer sanctions; Undocumented immigrants; Workplace enforcement

Undocumented immigrants, 23, 34, 35, 41–42, 63, 72–73, 80–81, 111, 119–125, 139–140, 169, 176, 177–178, 196–197; as consumers, 139–140; as criminals, 178; estimated population, 61, 72, 104, 127, 169, 172–173, 201; federal government estimate of, 127, 226n51; lack of legal protections for, 121–125; racial caste of labor, as, 104, 122, 129–130; shadows of U.S. social life, 187; success stories, 213n1; women, mistreatment of, 123–124. *See also* "Aliens"; "Death on the border"; "Illegal aliens"; Jim Crow; Mexican immigrants; Mexican migration; Remittances
United Farm Workers and immigration, 147–148. *See also* Chávez, César; Organized labor and immigration
United Nations Convention on the Status of Refugees, 118
Unskilled workers, impacts of immigration on. *See* African American workers; Wage impacts of immigration; Wealth distribution concerns with immigration
U.S. Commission on Immigration Reform, 115, 185, 227n59
U.S. Constitution, 31, 38, 94; commitment to liberal theory, 87. *See also* Plenary power doctrine
U.S. Customs Service, searches by, 198
U.S. Department of Homeland Security, 117, 169, 183, 184, 213n1, 222n82. *See also* Border enforcement; Border Patrol; Public safety and national security; National security; September 11, 2001; "War on Terror"
U.S. Department of Justice, 183
U.S. General Accountability Office, on human smuggling, 124. *See also* Forced prostitution; Human trafficking; Sex trafficking; Slavery
U.S. General Accounting Office, report on proposed elimination of visa waiver program, 195. *See also* Foreign policy consequences of liberal migration policies;

International tensions resulting from immigration laws and policies
U.S. Immigration and Naturalization Service (INS), 4, 116, 221–222n82. *See also* Border enforcement; Border Patrol; U.S. Department of Homeland Security
U.S.-Mexican War, 66; treaty that ended, 227n67. *See also* Aztlán
U.S.-Mexico border, vii, 33, 58, 61, 70, 86, 111–116, 160, 164, 173, 195, 203; as war zone, 203. *See also* Border enforcement; Border Patrol; "Death on the border"; Undocumented immigrants
U.S. Select Commission on Immigration and Refugee Policy, 115
U.S. Supreme Court, German language schools, 79; immigration stops, 14; plenary power doctrine, 53–54, 95–96; protections for undocumented workers, 120; right to travel, 89–90. *See also* The Chinese Exclusion Case; Plenary power doctrine
USA PATRIOT Act (Uniting and Strengthening America by Providing Appropriate Tools Required to Intercept and Obstruct Terrorism Act), 21, 49, 61, 99. *See also* Arab and Muslim noncitizens; Immigration law, U.S.; Public safety and national security; National security; September 11, 2001; "War on Terror"

Vigilantes, on border, 114, 115. *See also* American Patrol; Anti-immigrant sentiment; Minutemen; Nativism; U.S.-Mexico border
Villaraigosa, Antonio, Mayor of Los Angeles, death threat on, 6

Wage impacts of immigration, 23, 42, 48, 60, 143–150, 167, 254n44. *See also* African Americans; Economic benefits of liberal migration; Organized labor and immigration; United Farm Workers and immigration; Wealth distribution concerns with immigration
Wall Street Journal, views on immigration, 131, 132, 137, 156. *See also* Economic benefits of liberal migration
Wallace, George (former Governor of Alabama), 5

Wal-Mart, hiring of undocumented immigrant workers, 134. *See also* Employer sanctions; Undocumented immigrants; Workplace enforcement

Walzer, Michael, 93–95. *See also* Communitarian theory; Morality of immigration restrictions

"War on Terror," vii, 18, 21, 31–35, 49–50, 99, 115, 117, 165, 207, 220–221n76. *See also* Arab and Muslim noncitizens; Public safety and national security; National security; September 11, 2001; USA PATRIOT Act

Wealth distribution concerns with immigration, 23–24, 42, 143–147, 167. *See also* African Americans; Economic benefits of liberal migration; Organized labor and immigration; United Farm Workers and immigration; Wage impacts of immigration

Welfare reform (1996), 12, 24, 151, 234–235n11; influence of Black "welfare queen" stereotype on welfare reform, 150–151. *See also* Public benefits and immigration; Public charge exclusion

Wells Fargo Bank, marketing to undocumented immigrants, 139

Whelan, Frederick, on open borders, 11

Who Are We? The Challenges to America's National Identity (book) 62–85, 86–87, 206–207. *See also* Huntington, Samuel

Wilson, Pete, California Governor, 171, 232n125. *See also* Anti-immigrant sentiment; California and immigration; Nativism; Proposition 187; Republican Party

Wood, Kimba, nominee for U.S. Attorney General, 169

Workplace enforcement, 110–111, 229–230n96; Nebraska operation 134. *See also* Border enforcement; Employer sanctions; Immigration law, U.S

World Conference Against Racism, Racial Discrimination, Xenophobia, and Related Intolerance, 103. *See also* International law; Race of immigrants; Racial discrimination in immigration laws; Racial profiling in immigration enforcement

World Trade Organization, 141, 143

Workplace enforcement, 110–111, 229–230n96; Nebraska operation 134. *See also* Border enforcement; Employer sanctions; Immigration laws, U.S

Wright, R. George, on open borders, 96–97

Wu, Frank, on open borders, 11

Yugoslavia, 62, 77

"Zoot Suit" riots, 80. *See also* Anti-immigrant sentiment; Assimilation of immigrants; Integration of immigrants in U.S. society; Mexican immigrants; Nativism; Race of immigrants; Repatriation of persons of Mexican ancestry during Great Depression

About the Author

Kevin R. Johnson is Associate Dean for Academic Affairs, School of Law, and Mabie-Apallas Professor of Public Interest Law and Chicana/o Studies at the University of California, Davis. He is author or editor of several books, including *How Did You Get to Be Mexican? A White/Brown Man's Search for Identity; A Reader on Race, Civil Rights, and American Law: A Multiracial Approach; Mixed Race America and the Law: A Reader* (also published by NYU Press in the Critical America series); and *The "Huddled Masses" Myth: Immigration and Civil Rights.*